iOS Cloud Development FOR DUMMIES®

by Neal Goldstein

WILEY

John Wiley & Sons, Inc.

iOS Cloud Development For Dummies®

Published by
John Wiley & Sons, Inc.
111 River Street
Hoboken, NJ 07030-5774

www.wiley.com

Published by John Wiley & Sons, Inc., Hoboken, New Jersey

Published simultaneously in Canada

For general information on our other products and services, please contact our Customer Care Department within the U.S. at 877-762-2974, outside the U.S. at 317-572-3993, or fax 317-572-4002.

For technical support, please visit www.wiley.com/techsupport.

Wiley publishes in a variety of print and electronic formats and by print-on-demand. Some material included with standard print versions of this book may not be included in e-books or in print-on-demand. If this book refers to media such as a CD or DVD that is not included in the version you purchased, you may download this material at http://booksupport.wiley.com. For more information about Wiley products, visit www.wiley.com.

Library of Congress Control Number: 2012944693

ISBN 978-1-118-02623-6 (pbk); ISBN 978-1-118-22226-3 (ebk); ISBN 978-1-118-23582-9 (ebk); ISBN 978-1-118-26073-9 (ebk)

Manufactured in the United States of America

10 9 8 7 6 5 4 3 2 1

About the Author

Neal Goldstein is a recognized leader in making state-of-the-art and cutting-edge technologies practical for commercial and enterprise development. He was one of the first technologists to work with commercial developers at firms such as Apple Computer, Lucasfilm, and Microsoft to develop commercial applications using object-based programming technologies. He was a pioneer in moving that approach into the corporate world for developers at Liberty Mutual Insurance, USWest (now Verizon), National Car Rental, EDS, and Continental Airlines, showing them how object-oriented programming could solve enterprise-wide problems. His book (with Jeff Alger) on object-oriented development, *Developing Object-Oriented Software for the Macintosh* (Addison Wesley, 1992), introduced the idea of scenarios and patterns to developers. He was an early advocate of the Microsoft .NET framework, and he successfully introduced it into many enterprises, including Charles Schwab. He was one of the earliest developers of Service Oriented Architecture (SOA), and as Senior Vice President of Advanced Technology and the Chief Architect at Charles Schwab, he built an integrated SOA solution that spanned the enterprise, from desktop PCs to servers to complex network mainframes. (He holds four patents as a result.) As one of IBM's largest customers, he introduced the folks at IBM to SOA at the enterprise level and encouraged them to head in that direction.

Since the release of the iPhone SDK in March 2008, he has been focusing on mobile applications. He has had eight applications in the App Store. These include a series of Travel Photo Guides (developed with his partners at mobilefortytwo), and a Digital Field Guides series (`http://lp.wileypub.com/DestinationDFGiPhoneApp`), developed in partnership with John Wiley & Sons, Inc. He also has a free app called Expense Diary that allows you to keep track of things like expenses, mileage, and time by adding them to your calendar.

He has developed mobile strategies for a number of businesses, ranging from National Cinemedia to the American Automobile Association (AAA). His strategies focus on Mobile 2.0 — integrating mobile across the enterprise, creating a consistent user experience across devices and applications in an application ecosystem, and developing a user experience architecture that both leverages — and is constrained by — the device. He has spent the last three years working with mobile device users and developers to determine what makes mobile devices so appealing, what users want from an application on a phone or tablet, and what makes an app compelling. These efforts have resulted in the Application Ecosystem model for mobile applications and an underlying Model Application Controller Architecture based on web services that has become a key element in his client work and his books.

In his copious spare time, he also teaches introductory and advanced classes on iPhone and iPad development (for clients as well as some public classes) and does expert witness work.

Along with those apps and his consulting, he has written several books on iPhone programming: *iPhone Application Development For Dummies* (multiple editions) (Wiley), *Objective-C For Dummies* (Wiley), and he co-authored (with Tony Bove) *iPad Application Development For Dummies* (including multiple editions) (Wiley) and *iPhone Application Development All-in-One For Dummies* (Wiley). He's also the primary author (with Jon Manning and Paris Buttfield-Addison) of *iPhone & iPad Game Development For Dummies*.

Dedication

To my friends and family — especially to my children, Sarah and Evan, and to my wife, Linda. She deserves special recognition for her support and patience and for maintaining her (and my) sense of humor. Without her support, I never would have been able to write 12 books in 3.5 years. Thank you so much.

This is for you

As day follows night

The tunnel ends in the light

Finally time to play

Author's Acknowledgments

Acquisitions Editor Katie Feltman has done a superb job of maintaining the vision of this book and keeping this project on track. The editing team on this book was the A+ team and I would give anything to work with them on every book I do. Project editor Paul Levesque is the project editor's project editor, and the best in the known and unknown universe. If there were one, he would deserve an entry in the Hitchhiker's Guide to the Galaxy. Copy editor Virginia Sanders did an amazing job, helping to both clarify things and pointing out inconsistencies in places I had long forgotten about. Tech editor Jesse Feiler kept me on my toes and his comments made this a better book. Great job, team, and I deeply appreciate all of your work.

Thanks again to my agent Carole Jelen for her continued work and support in putting and keeping these projects together.

Publisher's Acknowledgments

We're proud of this book; please send us your comments at http://dummies.custhelp.com. For other comments, please contact our Customer Care Department within the U.S. at 877-762-2974, outside the U.S. at 317-572-3993, or fax 317-572-4002.

Some of the people who helped bring this book to market include the following:

Acquisitions, Editorial

Senior Project Editor: Paul Levesque

Acquisitions Editor: Katie Feltman

Copy Editor: Virginia Sanders

Technical Editor: Jesse Feiler

Editorial Manager: Leah Michael

Editorial Assistant: Leslie Saxman

Sr. Editorial Assistant: Cherie Case

Cover Photo: ©iStockphoto.com / Marcin Krygier; ©iStockphoto.com / ranplett

Cartoons: Rich Tennant (www.the5thwave.com)

Composition Services

Project Coordinator: Sheree Montgomery

Layout and Graphics: Lavonne Roberts

Proofreaders: Lindsay Amones, John Greenough

Indexer: Potomac Indexing, LLC

Publishing and Editorial for Technology Dummies

Richard Swadley, Vice President and Executive Group Publisher

Andy Cummings, Vice President and Publisher

Mary Bednarek, Executive Acquisitions Director

Mary C. Corder, Editorial Director

Publishing for Consumer Dummies

Kathleen Nebenhaus, Vice President and Executive Publisher

Composition Services

Debbie Stailey, Director of Composition Services

Contents at a Glance

Table of Contents

Part II: Adding iCloud 47

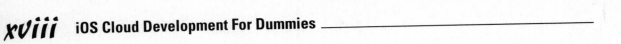

Introduction

When you talk about iOS cloud programming, you're talking about two distinct things. The one is iCloud, which is implemented for you by Apple and allows you to synch data between devices. The other is web services, which enable you to have some of your app's processing done by a remote computer somewhere in the middle of who-knows-where. iCloud is relatively new; web services have been around for a long time.

In fact, web services and I go way back.

Although I had used them for quite a while, the value of web services was driven home when I was consulting for a large mainframe-based organization. (Yes, that was a long time ago.) The organization had acquired a company and needed to interface the two computer systems. The systems were very different, and time-to-market and (especially) cost considerations made wholesale rewriting of the acquired company's systems impractical, not to mention foolish.

So, instead I took the functionality of the acquiring company's computer systems and made that functionality accessible (*wrapping them* as the terminology goes) as web services. Then all I had to do was go in and make some small changes to the acquired company's system to call those web services and, *voilà,* I was done.

Okay, the solution required a bit more work than that, but a lot less than rewriting all those COBOL programs. (I told you this was a long time ago.)

Worked great.

Later on, I did the same thing for a company whose architecture had stood them well for years but was becoming brittle with the new demands of customer access on the web — it was getting harder and harder to add the functionality needed in an Internet-based, real-time world. In addition, the company's current architecture was synchronous, so the slightest hiccup could cause the whole system to grind to a halt.

In that situation, I wrapped existing functionality in an asynchronous service-oriented architecture that made it easy to add new functionality as well as replace the old technology as necessary without breaking anything.

Worked great there, too.

Given this successful background in service-oriented architecture — an architecture that serves as the foundation for all web services — you can imagine that I jumped at the chance when the folks at Wiley asked me to write a book on cloud computing.

Even though all this talk about wrapping and service-oriented architecture may not sound like the web services you've heard about, it actually is the same thing. Web services, like objects, allow you to hide the implementation behind a defined interface, allowing you to evolve the implementation without breaking the clients. And, as described in Chapter 6, this is one of the things that make web services so powerful.

Hiding the implementation is exactly what you'll be doing in this book — having a server in the cloud do some processing for you. Although this time, instead of wrapping existing functionality, you'll write the service as well (with lots of help from me).

I'll let you in on a little secret. I also jumped at the chance to write this book because it is my firm belief that web services (and here I include iCloud) provide a game changer within a game changer. When the iPhone SDK was first released, I saw a game changer that could rank right up there with the introduction of the Macintosh personal computer. When web services get added to the mix, they elevate a mobile device to a full-fledged computing device as well as extend the value that technology can provide to the everyday user.

What makes this even easier is iOS 5 and, more importantly, Xcode 4.3, where the nuts and bolts of application development — especially the ability to take advantage of web services — have changed dramatically. Even though Xcode 4.3 has added much more functionality to the Integrated Development Environment (IDE) with which you develop iOS applications, especially when it comes to writing syntactically correct (and bug-free) code that's better able to manage memory, it's the whole storyboard concept that is the real headline.

Storyboards, one of my all-time favorite new features, allow you to develop applications in a new way, with much less code and a better idea of what the flow of the application (and subsequent user experience) will be.

But what's more, storyboards all of a sudden make it easier to develop universal applications — applications that run with equal aplomb on the iPad or iPhone — using the same code base! And when you do that, using iCloud and web services becomes a whole lot easier.

This is great stuff!

About This Book

iOS Cloud Development For Dummies is a guide to using iCloud, using web services on iOS devices, and developing your own web services. This book distills the hundreds (or even thousands) of pages of documentation (not to mention my own development experience) into only what's necessary to start you developing and using web services. But this is no recipe book that leaves it up to you to put it all together; rather, it starts with an existing universal application and shows you how to extend its functionality. You'll be able to share data between an iPad and iPhone running the app, and you'll be able to keep the application data current by using web services.

I assume that you're in this for the long haul and you want to master the use of web services. I use a real-world application to show the concepts and give you the background on how things actually work. So be prepared! There may be some places where you might want to say, "Get on with it," but — based on my experience, including eight apps in the App Store, 12 books (and counting), and untold hours spent on in-person classes and technical talks — I'm giving you what you need to move from following recipes in a cookbook by rote to modifying and even creating your own recipes.

Conventions Used in This Book

Code examples in this book appear in a monospaced font so that they stand out. That means the code you see will look like this:

```
#import <UIKit/ UIKit.h>
```

Objective-C is based on C, which (I want to remind you) *is* case-sensitive, so please enter the code that appears in this book *exactly* as it appears in the text. I also use the standard Objective-C naming conventions — for example, class names always start with a capital letter, and the names of methods and instance variables always start with a lowercase letter.

The width of a page may force me to show you a single line of code on two lines. This can be a problem with *string literals* — text with quotes around it — so when you see a string on two lines, you'll need to keep it on a single line in your code.

All those details are also true for the Python programming language (which I explain to you as you need it). In addition, Python is based on indentation, so I make sure to point out where you need to be careful.

Let me also mention that all URLs in this book look like this:

`www.nealgoldstein.com`

Sometimes I ask you to delete some of the code you have in place for your project in order to make room for new stuff. When that happens, I refer to code I want you to delete as bolded-underlined-italicized code, because said code will show up as bold, underlined, and italic. Simple enough. For example,

```
Delete this
```

If you're ever uncertain about anything in the code, you can always look at the source code on my website at `www.nealgoldstein.com`. From time to time, I provide updates for the code there and post other things you may find useful. (You can grab the same material from the *For Dummies* website at `www.dummies.com/go/iosclouddev`.)

To make things easier for you, I also have you download two Xcode projects — RoadTrip and Road Trip Editor. You can find these two projects at my website at `www.nealgoldstein.com` and of course from the handy *For Dummies* website at `www.dummies.com/go/iosclouddev`.

Foolish Assumptions

To begin developing apps that use web services — as well as the services themselves — you're going to need an Intel-based Macintosh computer with the latest possible version of the OS X on it. You also need to download the iOS Software Development Kit (SDK), which is free. And, oh yeah, you need an iPad or an iPhone. You'll also use the Simulator that Apple provides with the iPad SDK during the initial stages of development, but at some point, you'll want to test your application on a real, live device. Note as well that, when you're working with iCloud, you'll need access to two devices if you want to be able to test your work.

This book is not an introductory book. It assumes that you have some knowledge of iOS development, object-oriented programming, and Objective-C. On the other hand, it assumes you know nothing about networking, the cloud, or web services.

How This Book Is Organized

iOS Cloud Development For Dummies has five main parts.

Part I: Mobile Apps Need to Be Mobile

In Part I, I explain why users find their mobile devices so compelling and also explore how applications can take advantage of the similar and unique characteristics of the iPhone and the iPad. I explain the Application Ecosystem, where users can choose the right device for the right job with their application data shared between the devices.

I also show you how web services can help you create more compelling applications that increase the mobility of the user while still keeping them firmly plugged in to their person ecosystems.

You also embark on a brief tour of the RoadTrip app — a universal app that runs on both the iPhone and iPad. This is the app you'll be extending and enhancing to make it far more appealing to a user by evolving it to a true Application Ecosystem app by adding iCloud support and web services.

Part II: Adding iCloud

In this part of the book, you discover how you can use iCloud to synchronize data between two devices running the same application. I explain Core Data, which is a way to store persistent objects, and I show you how to use Core Data to manage the points of interest you have in your itinerary — all parts of the RoadTrip app that you'll get to know in detail.

I start with the Core Data stack and then show you how to use Core Data within an application. Then I show you how to use Core Data to add iCloud support, enabling you to manage that trick of sharing data between multiple devices running RoadTrip.

Part III: Web Services

Part III starts you on the process of having your application actually use web services. I start by explaining about networks, the Internet, and the World Wide Web and the technology behind web services.

You then begin your real work by stepping through what actually happens when you make use of a web service — in this case, the Google Geocoder web service. I take you through how to use the URL loading system to make asynchronous web service requests, and I show you how to parse both XML and JSON response to use the web service data in your application.

In the process, you'll create two classes that you will continue to use in the book and can easily use in your own applications.

The first is the `WSManager` — it handles the actual construction of your web service request. The second is the `WSLoader`, which uses the URL loading system to asynchronously make the request and download the response from a web service.

Part IV: Building Your Own Web Service

Part IV is where you actually get to build your own web services.

You use Google App Engine to host your web service as well as GoogleAppEngineLauncher to develop your web services on your local machine.

I take you through the criteria for good web services and the specification of the web services that you'll use in RoadTrip and in the Road Trip Editor, which will enable you to add and delete points of interest from your web services database. (The actual Adding and Deleting business gets covered in an extra special Bonus Chapter, available for download from this book's website.)

I explain how Google App Engine works and give you a tutorial (in context) on how to code your web services in Python.

I close by talking a bit about security, and then you finally get to upload your app to App Engine, and off you go.

Part V: The Part of Tens

Part V consists of some tips to help you avoid having to discover everything the hard way. This part talks about approaching application development in an adult way right from the beginning (without taking the fun out of it, I assure you). I also revisit the RoadTrip app and explain what else you would need to do to make this app a commercial and critical success.

Icons Used in This Book

This icon indicates a useful pointer that you shouldn't skip.

This icon represents a friendly reminder. It describes a vital point that you should keep in mind while proceeding through a particular section of the chapter.

This icon signifies that the accompanying explanation may be informative (dare I say "interesting"?), but it isn't essential to understanding iPad application development. Feel free to skip past these tidbits if you like (though skipping while learning may be tricky).

This icon alerts you to potential problems that you may encounter along the way. Read and obey these blurbs to avoid trouble.

Where to Go from Here

It's time to explore the cloud!

Also, be sure to visit my website, `www.nealgoldstein.com`, and the companion website for this book, `www.dummies.com/go/iosclouddev`, for source code, a handy Bonus Chapter, and other information. For updates to this edition, check out `www.dummies.com/go/iosclouddevupdates`. Now, go out there and have some fun!

Part I

Mobile Apps Need to Be Mobile

"Are you sure this is how we're supposed to access the cloud?"

In this part . . .

You've decided that it's time to be in the cloud. In this part, I explain why that's a smart decision and then go on to tell you how you can really take advantage of cloud computing. I also go ahead and explain RoadTrip, the sample app you'll work with throughout this book. RoadTrip is an almost commercially viable app (but please don't go selling it in the store) that just needs a few more features to make it take off. After I explain RoadTrip's nuts and bolts, you'll be set to take the next step and elevate it to the cloud.

Chapter 1

Compelling Mobile Applications

In This Chapter

- Discovering what makes mobile devices so appealing
- Acknowledging the strengths and weaknesses of mobile devices
- Working with Application Ecosystems
- Tweaking your Model Application Controller

Let me be honest with you. The dirty little secret is that cloud computing is nothing new. It's really just a variation (yet another one) on client-server computing.

The *client-server* model of computing distributes the tasks of an application between the providers of a resource or service (called *servers*) and service requesters (called *clients*). It's been around for quite a while — since the 1980s, in fact, when it was used in the context of personal computers on a network (usually a LAN). It has evolved over time and is also one of the central ideas of network computing. As I explain in Chapter 2, the Internet's main application protocols, HTTP, SMTP, Telnet, and DNS use client-server computing, and web browsers and web servers have a client server relationship.

I talk a lot about client-server in this book, but in this chapter I concentrate on your application design. And, although this book focuses on the client-server design and implementation in an application, I spend at least a little time talking about your application functionality as well. I'd hate to have you spend all that time implementing iCloud and web services in an application that no one finds particularly useful.

So start at the beginning with a simple question: What is it about the iPhone and the iPad that makes them so appealing?

What Makes Mobile Devices So Compelling

Although I had been somewhat involved with the mobile platform for a number of years, it became my number one passion when the iPhone SDK was released in March of 2008.

It became obvious at that point that the SDK was a real game changer, up there with the release of the Macintosh.

I realized that the iPhone wasn't simply a smaller personal computer. It was, in fact, an entirely new way of using technology, one that could create an entirely new user experience

"Why?" you ask? Let me count the ways.

First of all, because your iPhone is *always on,* it gives you *immediate access* to everything that's important to you — your personal contacts, calendar, music, videos, and even games. And if what you want isn't right there on the iPhone, you can immediately access it through the Internet using its "always there" connection. It also gives you immediate access to everyone that's important to you through the phone itself, text messaging, and (recently) notifications and Voice over IP.

But to be honest, that access is already possible on your personal computer. The new wrinkle comes from the fact that *the phone can come with you* — you don't have to go to it. Moreover, you're always connected through the cellular network, rather than tethered to an Ethernet cable or relying on the limited reach of Wi-Fi. What's more, not only does it come with you, but *it knows where it is,* letting you know where you are. It even knows its orientation, heading, and movement as you take it from place to place.

And not only does it come with you, but it also works as you move. Certain applications are able to run in background and update you with information you might be interested in as you travel from place to place.

Well, to continue being honest, that's also possible on your personal computer using a cellular modem.

What really makes an iPhone different from a small, portable personal computer is the way you interact with it. The Multi-Touch experience makes you more naturally connected to the device. You can cup it in your hand and interact with the iPhone directly, with no mouse or keyboard acting as an intermediary. You can even use gestures whenever possible rather than controls. This interaction creates a degree of *intimacy,* making the technology disappear, as it becomes a personal extension of the user. An app may have an infrastructure the size of Texas behind it, but to the user, it always appears to be just him and his app.

Of course, it's not just another small mobile personal computer for another reason. Although its features make it possible to be something beyond a personal computer and do things that either can't be done — or done easily — on a personal computer, this is a two-edged sword. A laptop does some things far better than an iPhone, and it's critical to understand that an iPhone *is not a replacement* for a laptop computer either.

And then along came the iPad, and things changed yet again, albeit not so dramatically.

Creating zero degrees of separation

The iPhone and iPad create what I call *zero degrees of separation* between the user and his or her Personal Ecosystem, an ecosystem I define as being made up of

- Themselves and their personal stuff
- Other people
- Things such as events, information, data, institutions, tools, and entertainment
- The device

Having that zero degrees of separation produces a sense of freedom. The user isn't tethered to her desktop and has everything she needs with her, or if not, she can get it and can instantaneously communicate to anyone anywhere.

Benefiting from the mobility, not the mobile devices

Achieving zero degrees of separation may be the equivalent of technological Nirvana, but it still sounds a bit abstract. Back in the world of brass tacks, the beauty of the iPad and iPhone comes from the fact that there are applications and features on both devices that dramatically enhance the mobility of the user.

I must admit than when I first started working with the iPhone (and later the iPad), I focused mainly on the mobile device and its features. But after thinking about it for several years (okay, I guess I'm not really the world's fastest thinker), I realized that the real value lies not in the mobility of the device, but rather in the mobility of the user. In fact, a large part of the appeal of the device is that it makes being mobile much easier.

- The iPhone is small and unobtrusive enough to have it with you wherever you go. More importantly, it allows you to carry all your personal stuff with you — things such as contacts and calendars, music and videos, and even games. Add in the camera (the iPhone is the second-most-popular camera on Flickr), and you have everything you need.

  And even though the iPad may not be as mobile if you don't have 3G and you may not be able to fit it in your pocket, it's still small enough to feel like you can take it with you. With iPad in hand, you can lounge on your couch or bed and feel connected to everything.

- The device is easily connected. This fact leads to an interesting corollary: You don't need to have everything stored on the device. All you really need to know is how to jump on the Internet and grab what you need from there (or have an application that does it for you). That functionality lets you perform tasks and access information from anywhere.
- The device knows where it is, its orientation, and can even show you on a map.
- Thanks to the phone, Voice over IP, e-mail, and SMS, you can instantaneously communicate with anyone anywhere.

Increasing the quality of life

At the end of the day, mobile devices and applications enable the kind of Personal Ecosystem you see illustrated in Figure 1-1. More importantly, the iPhone and iPad show how people can successfully use mobile devices to improve the quality of their everyday (non-technical) life.

Although engineers think in terms of applications, it really is all about the role a device can play as part of a user experience linked to what flesh and blood people actually do in the real world.

I talk more about creating applications that achieve that goal, but before I do, I want to explore something that developers often tend to ignore, and that is how the device itself engages the user.

Making the technology disappear

Hats off to mobility and all that, but enhancing mobility (on its own) is not enough. As I said before, I can be mobile using a laptop and a cellular modem. But what you can't take away from the iPhone and iPad is how easy being mobile can be with their help.

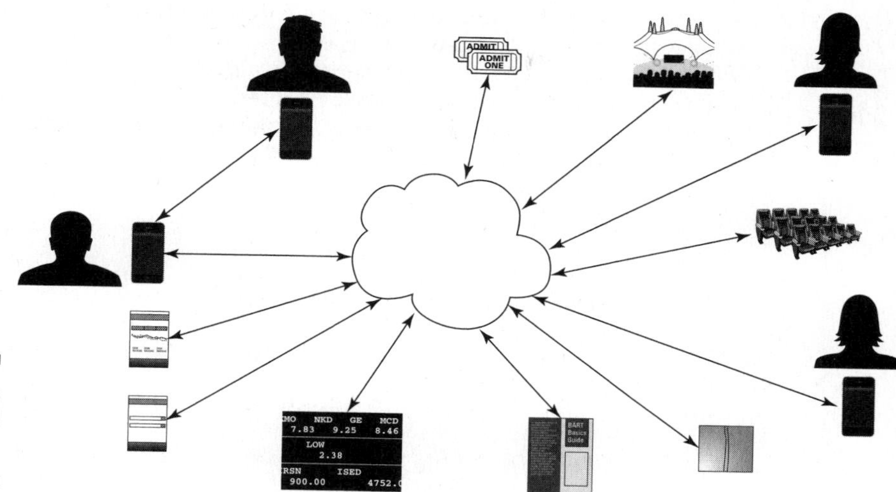

Figure 1-1: A Personal Ecosystem.

So while people normally speak about user experience *in using applications*, I'm here to tell you that *the device itself* also creates a unique user experience. When an application is done right on an iPad or iPhone, a couple of things happen:

- **Direct manipulation makes people feel more in control.** On the desktop, that meant a keyboard and mouse; on the iPhone and iPad, the Multi-Touch interface serves the same purpose. People use their fingers, rather than a mouse, to select and manipulate objects onscreen. In fact, using fingers gives a user a more immediate sense of control; there's no longer anything between the user and the object onscreen.

  The moves that do the work, called *gestures,* give the user a heightened sense of control and intimacy with the device. There's a set of standard gestures — tap, pinch-close, pinch-open, flick, and drag — that are used in the applications supplied with the iPhone.

- **There's a consistency within the device.** One other thing that makes the device so appealing in this regard is the consistency of the use of gestures across applications as well as standard user interface components.

- **Immediate feedback keeps the users engaged.** Great applications respond to every user action with some visible feedback, such as highlighting list items briefly when users tap them. Users have come to expect onscreen objects to be visible while they manipulate those objects.

  In addition, the iPhone and iPad use animation to provide feedback. (I especially like the flipping transitions in the Weather application when I touch the Info button.)

The iPhone allows an immediacy and intimacy as it blends mobility and the power of the desktop to create a new kind of freedom. I like to use the term *user experience* because it implies more than a pretty user interface and nice graphics. A *compelling* user experience enables users to do what they need to do with a minimum of fuss and bother. But more than that, it forces you to think past a clean interface and even beyond basic convenience (such as not having to scroll through menus to do something simple).

Reveling in the aesthetics

Smart design, elegant controls, and quality, quality, quality are all elements that the iPhone and iPad are known for. Speaking of quality, although you're probably pretty much used to it by now, it doesn't hurt to remind yourself how extraordinary the quality of the screen — and thus media playback — can be. Although it is tempting to think of the iPad here, the iPhone delivers that experience as well, albeit in a smaller format.

Never underestimate the importance of style and panache — and the cool factor. There were, after all, MP3 players before the iPod, smart phones before the iPhone, and tablets before the iPad.

All praise aside, though, I want to make one thing absolutely clear: This is not about being an Apple fan. It's about recognizing how these characteristics of the Apple devices appeal to ordinary (not technical) people and make such devices special in their eyes.

An Application Ecosystem

In one corner, you have a light, small mobile device that you can take with you — one that almost disappears as it become part of your daily life. In the other corner, you have a device that shines at presentation and can immerse you in content — a device you can think of as something between an iPhone and a Mac.

But oftentimes it's not one or the other. I would, for example, want to use an iPad to research and plan a road trip, but while I'm travelling I'd like to be able to access all that information on my iPhone — it's a lot easier to take along as I explore. What I don't want is one app for planning and a different app for traveling. What I want is a seamless integration between the two, and although I may prefer to do one task on one device versus the other, I also want to be able to do either on both. It's a function of user interface design and (how I access) primary versus secondary functionality based on what the device does best.

What's more, go ahead and add the laptop/desktop back into the mix. (Yes, personal computers have a place in this new world.) A word to the wise: Don't ignore the laptop, or even the desktop. If I have to do a lot of manipulation or data entry, the laptop is far better at that than the iPad.

What you end up with is an Application Ecosystem, kind of like what you see in Figure 1-2. The idea here is to distribute functionality to the device that does it best. And to do that, it would help to understand what application functionality is best suited for which device.

For example, imagine an application aimed at photographers. Its claim to fame would be that it could show you the best sites to photograph, pinpoint those sites on a map, tell you the best time of day to take the photographs, and list the setting to use on your camera. On an iPad, you could take advantage of the large display to go through the proposed photographs and decide which ones you wanted to take. You could select those photographs to create a shot list that you could then order by time of day and location. Then, when you were done, you could access that shot list from your iPhone. That means you could then carry just the iPhone with you; as you took the photographs, you could update the ones you had taken with the actual settings and time of day and then be able to access that information from your iPad.

Or imagine a road trip. You would plan it on your iPad and then access directions, maps, hotel reservations, and places to eat from your iPhone. You could even take notes on your phone about your experience and add your photographs from your phone to document your trip. You could then use your iPad to create a trip album.

The possibilities are endless.

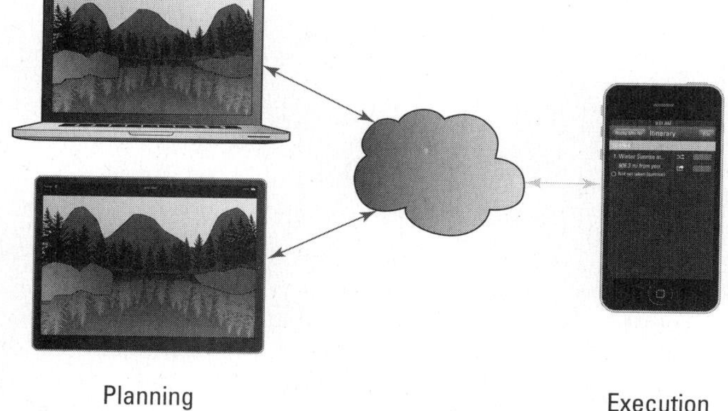

Figure 1-2: The Application Ecosystem.

If you want the right device for the right function and you want seamlessness and consistency across all platforms, does that mean one universal app, or two or three apps with lots of duplicate functionality? In the past, that would have been a difficult question to answer. Now, fortunately, the answer's pretty simple: You don't need lots of apps — that's where iCloud and Xcode come in.

iCloud and universal apps

My ideas about the Application Ecosystem predated iCloud. Way back when, I talked about creating web services to allow a user to share data between two devices using the same application. And even though creating web services can be pretty easy (as you'll see in Part IV of the book), it's always better and a heck of a lot easier to *use* than to *build* — and iCloud does indeed make things much easier. You'll find that out for yourself in Part II.

One of the requirements for running the same application on both the iPhone and iPad is that the user interface and user experience be optimized for the device. Before Xcode 4.2 and Storyboards, creating universal apps wasn't that easy, but creating an app for each device turned into a development and maintenance nightmare.

Storyboards have completely turned that around. I now have no qualms recommending that you use a universal app to implement iCloud and web services, and that's the approach this book takes.

While iCloud does let you share data between the same application running on different devices, and universal apps do allow you to have the same business logic on all your devices, neither allows you to implement that zero degrees of separation I mention at the beginning of this chapter, where the user has everything she needs with her, or if not, can get it and can instantaneously communicate to anyone anywhere. For that to work, you need data that's continually being updated. What's more, iCloud doesn't allow multiple users to access shared data — something you would definitely want in a social networking or calendar application for example.

For that last piece of the puzzle, we turn to web services.

Web services

Web services really are a way to take full advantage of the benefits of client-server computing. I've highlighted a number of them in the discussion so far, but I summarize them here:

- **Offload processing and data** to a larger, more powerful computer, allowing you to create applications that would normally tax the device's capability.
- Deliver the most **up-to-date information.**
- Allow multiple applications — even multiple instances of the same application — to **share data.**
- Have a greater control over data and business rules, enabling a way to make them **authoritative.**
- Deliver a **seamless and consistent user experience** across not only multiple types of devices (tablet, phones, the web), but also across multiple applications that share data and business rules.

That's all fine and dandy, but if you're going to go down the path of an Application Ecosystem (as you will in this book), you also need an implementable architecture within which to design your applications. Fortunately, all you have to do is evolve an architecture you should already be familiar with: the Model View Controller, *the* design pattern you (or almost anyone, for that matter) would use to develop applications for the iPhone or iPad. But before I explain how to extend the Model View Controller pattern to designing applications in an Application Ecosystem using web services, I'm thinking a little review wouldn't hurt.

The Model View Controller (MVC) Architecture

The Model View Controller (MVC) Architecture (often referred to as a design pattern) is a well-established way to group application functions into objects. Variations of it have been around at least since the early days of Smalltalk, one of the very first object-oriented languages. The MVC is a *high-level* pattern, which means it addresses the architecture of an application and classifies objects according to the (very) general roles they play in an application.

The MVC pattern creates, in effect, a miniature universe for the application, populated with three kinds of objects. It also specifies roles and responsibilities for all three objects as well as spelling out the way they're supposed to interact with each other. To make things more concrete (that is, to keep your head from exploding), imagine a big, beautiful, 60-inch flat-screen TV. Here's the gist:

- **Model objects:** These objects together make up the content engine of your application. They contain the application's data and logic — making your application more than just a pretty face. In a road trip application, for example, the model knows all the details of the trip and — if such details are not resident on the device — where to find them.

  You can think of the *model* (which may be one object or several that interact) as a particular television program. The TV program, quite frankly, doesn't care about what TV set it's being shown on.

  In fact, the model shouldn't care. Even though it owns its data, it should have no connection at all to the user interface and should be blissfully ignorant about what's being done with its data.

- **View objects:** These objects display things on the screen and respond to user actions. Pretty much anything you can see is a kind of view object — the window and all the controls, for example. Your view knows how to display information that it has gotten from the model object, and how to get any input from the user the model may need. But the view itself should know nothing about the model. It may handle a request to tell the user a little more about the giant ball of twine owned by Ripley's Believe It or Not in Brooks, Missouri, although it doesn't care about the content options it displays for you.

  You can think of the *view* as a television screen that doesn't care about what program it's showing or what channel you just selected.

  If the view knows nothing about the model, and the model knows nothing about the view, how do you get data and other notifications to pass from one to the other? To get that conversation started (for example, the model says, "I've just updated my data," and the view says, "Hey, give me something to display!"), you need the third element in the MVC triumvirate — the controller.

- **Controller objects:** These objects connect the application's view objects to its model objects. They supply the view objects with what they need to display (getting it from the model) and also provide the model with user input from the view.

  You can think of the *controller* as the circuitry that pulls the show off of the cable and sends it to the screen, or it can request a particular pay-per-view show.

Figure 1-3 shows what an MVC pattern would look like for an iPhone. (You'll also notice a greyed-out iPad and a laptop as well. That's because the same architecture is used on those devices.)

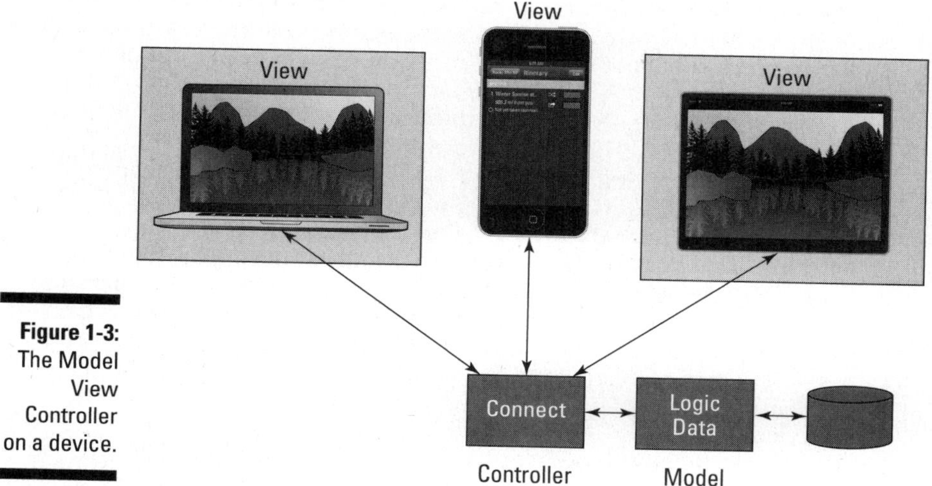

Figure 1-3: The Model View Controller on a device.

Evolving the Model View Controller

Here's your takeaway of the day: The Model View Controller is not limited to working just within an application. You can evolve it to implement the Application Ecosystem powered by web services. If you end up doing that, you replace the *View* with an *Application* that delivers a user experience tailored to the device — a Model *Application* Controller — supported by web services in the cloud. This setup enables you to tailor the user experience to the device while maintaining a seamless and consistent user experience. Figure 1-4 gives you an idea of what that would look like.

What exactly does a seamless and consistent user experience really mean?

To start with, what it does *not* mean is the identical user interface or look and feel across devices.

What it *does* mean is a user experience based on what the device does best, with the same underlying data, business rules, and logic underlying the various user interfaces. It also means that the user experiences the same application functionality where applicable — doing the same things in the same way — although the functionality is based on the device characteristics. It also means the user has access to whatever tasks he has done on any other device — changing his profile information, for example, or adding information on a trip he may be creating.

The Model Application Controller Architecture is based on a synthesis of client-server, service-oriented, and object-oriented architectures that I explain in more detail in Chapter 6.

Using this architecture, the views in the Model View Controller become the applications you see in Figure 1-4. These applications become primarily responsible for delivering a user experience best tailored to the capabilities and limitations of the device. These applications have the "normal" MVC Architecture. They have the views that you would expect, and these views do what views do best, such as display data and receive input from the user — all the stuff I explain in "The Model View Controller (MVC) pattern" section, earlier in the chapter. Similarly, the applications have controllers that do controller-like things — connect the model and the view, in other words — although instead of the model being (completely) co-located on the device, some part of it lives in the cloud, and the device controllers send web service requests to another set of controllers (or service routers), which connect to the effective model for the application. These controllers provide the services for all the applications in an Application Ecosystem, enabling a seamless experience when the user moves from device to device. The user gets a consistency of business rules and logic as well as a consistent experience. The key is to design the applications running on each device to take advantage of the strengths and limitations of each device in a way that is as consistent as possible across devices.

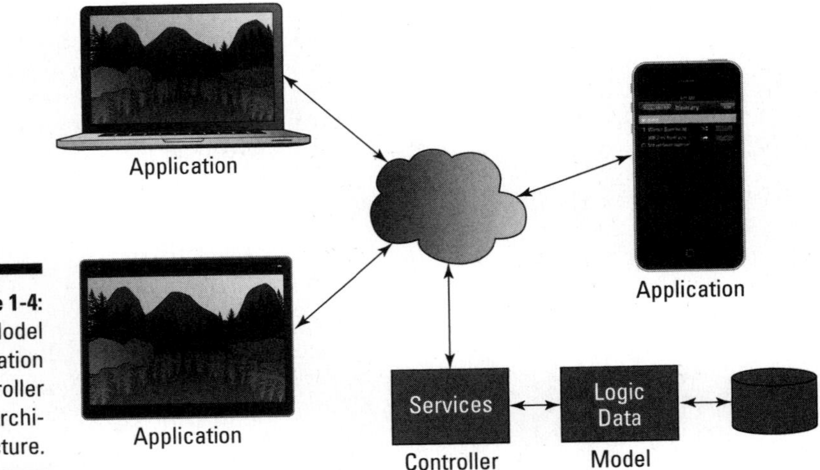

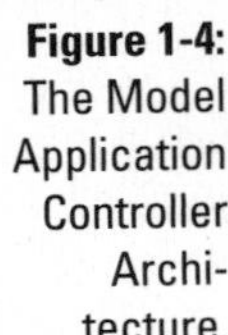
Figure 1-4: The Model Application Controller Architecture.

This even works for a Multi-Application Ecosystem, where you can create consistency across multiple applications, as shown in Figure 1-5.

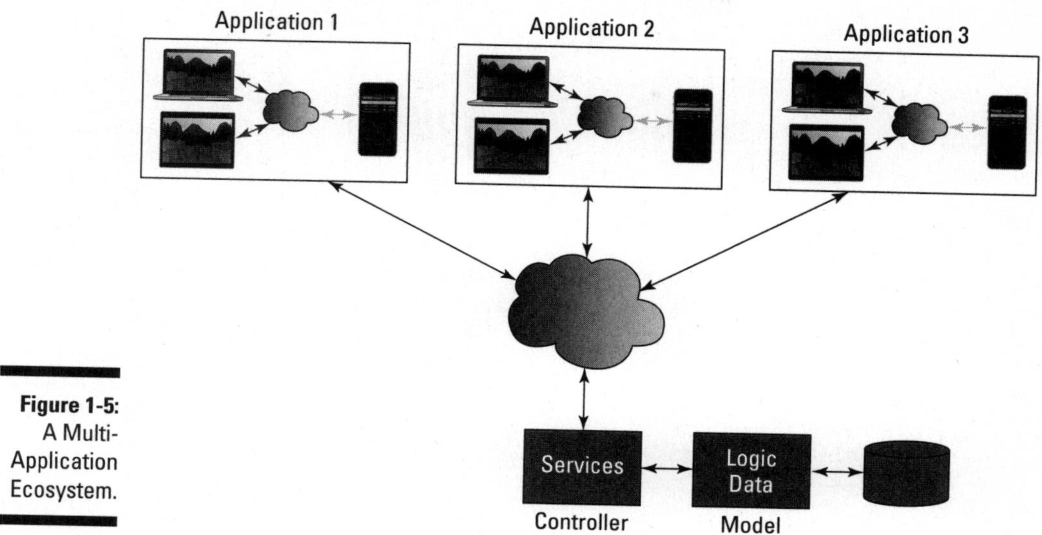

Figure 1-5: A Multi-Application Ecosystem.

In this case, you can maintain a seamless and consistent user experience across related applications — for example, a single user sign in or allowing a user to maintain the same profile or preferences across applications.

Pretty impressive, right? Welcome to Mobile 2.0.

Chapter 2

The Lonely RoadTrip App

In This Chapter

- Discovering the RoadTrip app
- Exploring RoadTrip's features and functions
- Seeing how RoadTrip's Itinerary feature works
- Adding points of interest
- Working through how RTModel manages points of interest and the itinerary

As you dive into this book, you'll discover that there are at least four critically important skills you'll need to take away from the work you do on the RoadTrip app. They are as follows:

1. How to implement the application ecosystem in such a way that you can share user data between a user's various devices so that the app you create will work well on the right device for the right job.
2. How to share application data and logic across all devices running the same application so you can keep them all up to date and consistent without having to publish new versions of your app.
3. How to deal with the *asynchronous* nature of cloud computing, especially its direct impact on both the current view and hidden views that may be impacted by the completion of a task. This task is made more complex on the iPad because you may have multiple views visible at the same time.
4. How to deal with the connections in an application's architecture and the indirect impact a change in one view may have on other visible and hidden views. (See the comment in Step 2 about the iPad.)

Starting at Square 7

Now, I could have taken the easy way out to show you the mechanics of using iCloud and web services by having you develop a simple application on the iPhone. By doing that, however, I would not have been able to really accomplish the goal I had set for myself, which centered around you, dear reader, walking away from this book secure in your knowledge of the four preceding skills.

So, instead of taking the easy way out, I decided to build upon an existing application — known affectionately as RoadTrip, which I had helped readers develop in both *iPhone Application Development For Dummies,* 4th Edition and *iPad Application Development For Dummies,* 3rd Edition. By building upon RoadTrip, I show you how a complex, real-world application can make use of the unique opportunities provided by iCloud and web services.

The iPhone version of RoadTrip and the iPad version of RoadTrip are very similar, but not identical. And don't worry if you haven't read those particular books — I explain the app in detail in this chapter.

The RoadTrip application had the reader implement the basic functionality of:

1. Choosing a destination
2. Presenting events happening at that destination
3. Displaying on a map the default points of interest included with the application
4. Displaying on a map a customized point of interest or an address the user enters

For this book, I took RoadTrip and extended it a bit so I could meet the four goals I list earlier. Here are the extensions I added:

- I added the logic to allow the user to create her own itinerary by choosing from the points of interest included in the application. The user can then add or delete points of interest from the itinerary at any point.

  This is a great example of the right device for the right job. The user might want to create the itinerary on the iPad because its display is bigger and can display two views at the same time. When it comes time to actually hit the road, though, the user may want to access (or even update) the itinerary on the iPhone because it's a lot more mobile and easier to carry around. (As you'll soon see, this accessing and updating business is a job for iCloud.)

- Instead of displaying all the points of interest on the map, I have the map display only those listed in the itinerary.

- I added the iPhone user interface in the storyboard. In *iPad Application Development For Dummies,* 3rd Edition, I had the reader create a universal app, although I left it up to the reader to create the iPhone user interface on his own.

In this chapter, I take you on a tour of the RoadTrip app. In the chapters to come, you extend RoadTrip so that it can take advantage of A) iCloud support to share a user's itinerary amongst all her devices, and B) web services so that you, as the developer, can add more points of interest and the user can have immediate access to them without you having to add them as defaults to the app and send out a new version.

Before I get you started on your tour of the RoadTrip app, I want to make a couple of additional points:

- Starting with a fully functioning app makes the task of mastering the whole iCloud/web services ball of wax a lot easier. If something doesn't work, you can be sure it's in your implementation of the iCloud or web services functionality and not in the app functionality itself. Starting from Square Seven rather than Square One also parallels the incremental development process, where you add functionality in a methodical step-by-step basis.
- I've set up the system architecture for the application in such a way that the changes you have to make are either implemented in new classes or limited to a small number of existing classes. (Hey, I'm a big fan of making a task as easy as possible.) In fact, adding the iCloud functionality is mostly isolated to the `RTModel` class, with minor changes to the `ItineraryController` class. Adding web services requires mostly changes to the `RTModel` class, with minor changes to the `PointsOfInterestController` class.

So to start things off, go ahead and download the RoadTrip Project from `www.nealgoldstein.com/support/downloads/%20`(you can check out my website while you are there), or the *For Dummies* website associated with this book. While you're at it, you should also download the RoadTrip Editor Project at this time, although you won't be using that until you make your way to the Bonus Chapter, "Adding and Deleting Points of Interest," available for download from this book's website. That app will enable you to add and delete points of interest from your web service.

Ready for the tour? In the rest of the chapter, I explain how RoadTrip works, concentrating mostly on the functionality you'll be working with as part of your iCloud and web services boot camp — more specifically, adding and deleting points of interest to an itinerary. I strongly suggest that you build and run the RoadTrip app and explore its functionality as I go through this chapter, as well as do some exploring of the app on your own.

The RoadTrip App

Necessity is the mother of invention, and the original RoadTrip idea was inspired by a necessity of a sort. My daughter was about to leave on a 7,000-mile road trip around the United States and I walked in one day and found her on her living room floor, with maps and tour books spread out every which way. Although I never did develop the app for her, or my evil twin Skippy who was also planning a road trip, it did start me thinking about how much better it would be if she didn't have to spread out these maps and paper all over her car.

I eventually decided that the road-trip planning scenario really called for two apps: one that was optimized for the planning that could take advantage of the larger screen size on an iPad (as well as the ability to see two views), and the other that was optimized for travel with the smaller and more mobile iPhone being the better solution. Of course, I wanted to be able to do everything on either device, but the user interface would be targeted to take advantage of a device's specific features. Not wanting to write the same app twice led me down the universal app route using storyboards — much easier these days, by the way, with the arrival of Xcode 4 and iOS 5. Using a storyboard enables me to have single code base while still employing a user interface tailored for the device. What's more, all the work to determine which user interface to present is done for you at runtime without any effort on your part.

In Figures 2-1 through 2-3, you can see how the iPad user interface takes advantage of the larger display and the ability to see two views at once. In Figure 2-1, the pane on the left displays the application functionality in what Xcode calls the *Master view*. The pane on the right displays the appropriately named Detail view — with the weather being displayed as the default view when you launch the app and have selected a destination). (For more on Master and Detail views, check out *iPad Application Development For Dummies,* 3rd edition.)

This division into Master view and Detail view is an elegant way of allowing the user to pick a task from the navigation tree on the left and see the content associated with that task on the right. This elegance becomes even more apparent when you want to add a point of interest to your itinerary and display it in a List view, as shown in Figure 2-2, or when you want to add a point of interest to your itinerary by selecting the point of interest from the list on the left and display it on the map, as you can see in Figure 2-3.

While I'm on the topic of points of interest, you can even add your own customized point of interest, as shown in Figure 2-4.

You can see the same kind of functionality that you see on the iPad on the iPhone (although you'll can only see one view at a time) in Figure 2-5.

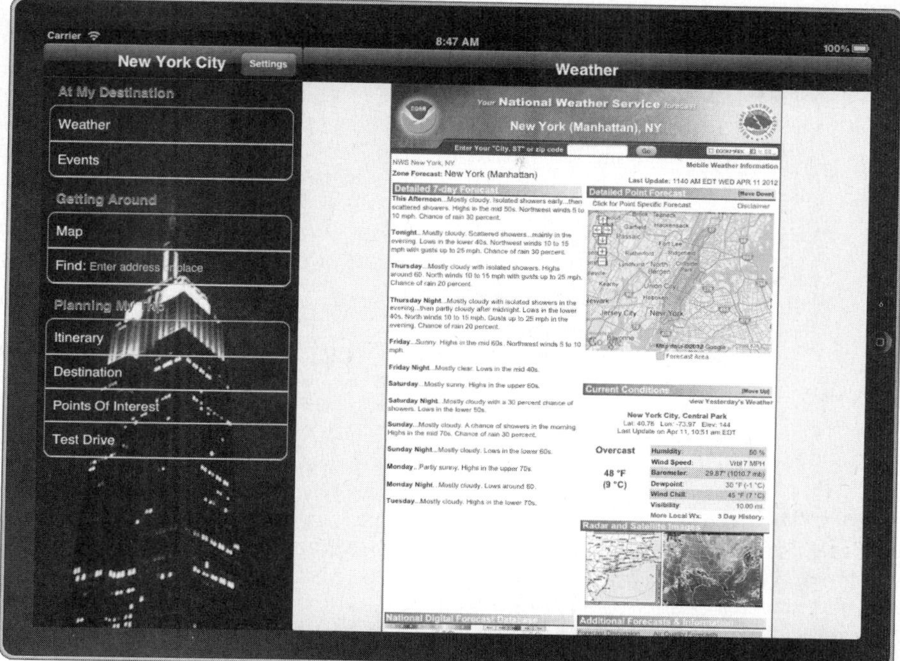

Figure 2-1: A real-life example of the Master view and Detail view combination.

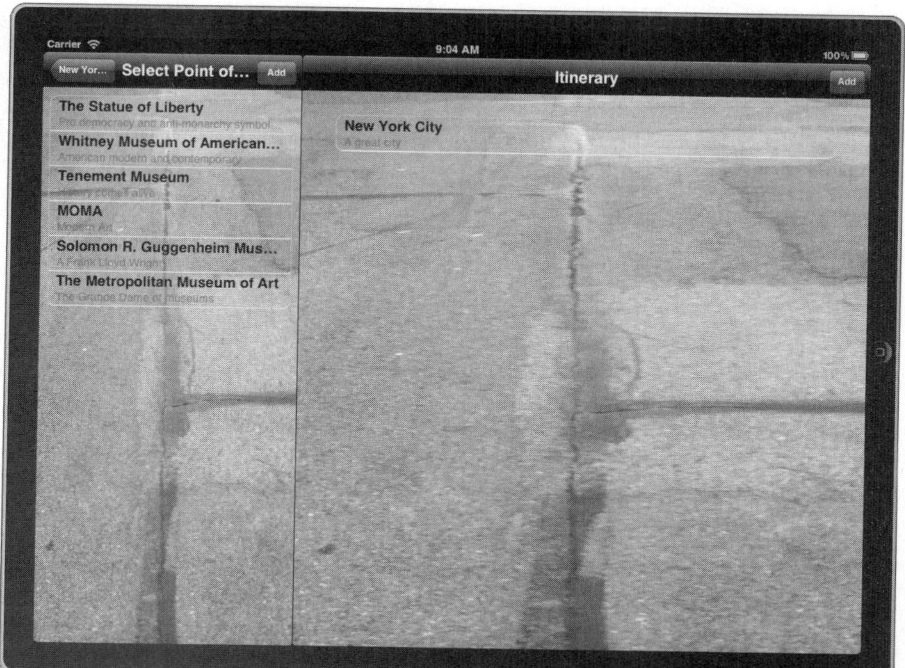

Figure 2-2: Add a point of interest to your itinerary.

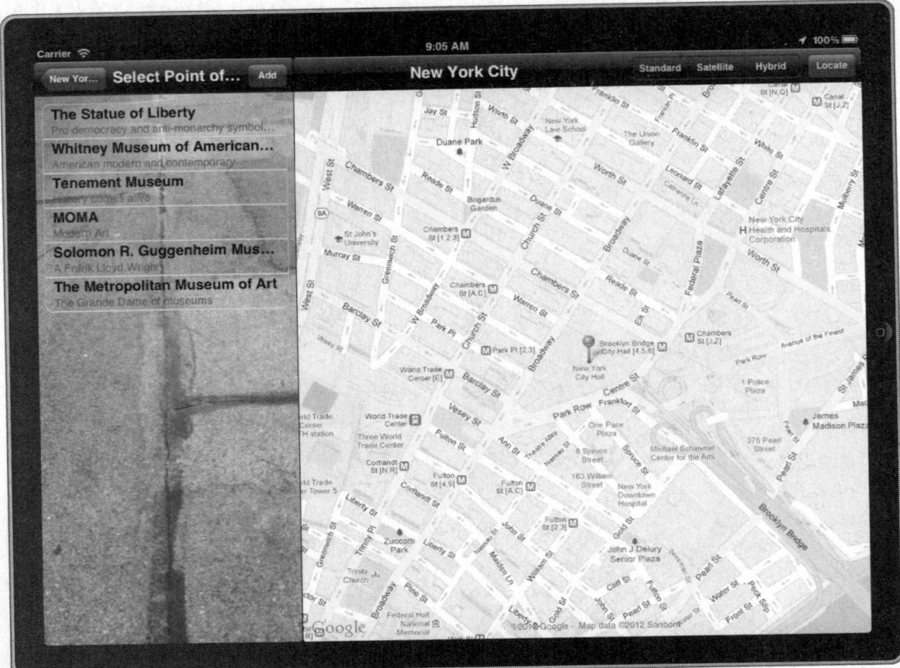

Figure 2-3: Add a point of interest to your map.

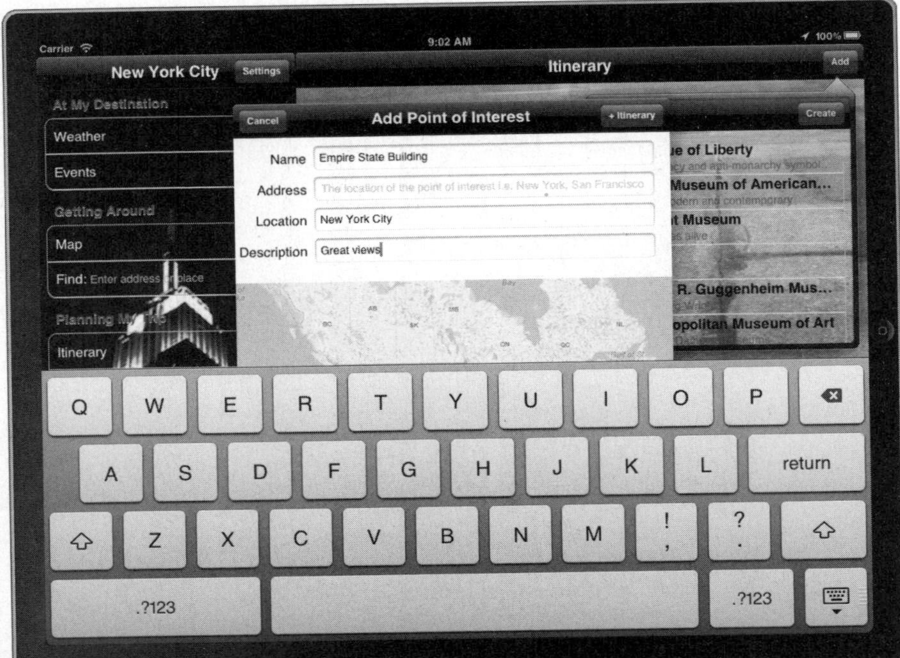

Figure 2-4: I've always wanted to see New Jersey's fabulous skyline.

On the iPhone version of RoadTrip, the main tasks you'd want to do on the road — things like checking the weather, going over maps and checking for events — are on the main screen (Figure 2-5, left). Tasks associated with the pre-trip planning, however, are all on a supplemental screen (Figure 2-5, right).

Major caveat here! The user interface I've described and the user experience I'm about to explain aren't necessarily the "best" in terms of design and usability. That's because I'm first and foremost concerned with being able to use RoadTrip as a vehicle to get you up and running on the Cloud Computing Technology side, and not on the Design and User Interface and Experience for a Travel App side. So I end up doing some things — and not doing some things — in the name of optimizing your learning experience. The long and short of it is that the RoadTrip application could use some tweaks to make it production ready (and I indicate some of those tweaks throughout the book) and I describe the broader, application-wide issues in Chapter 16.

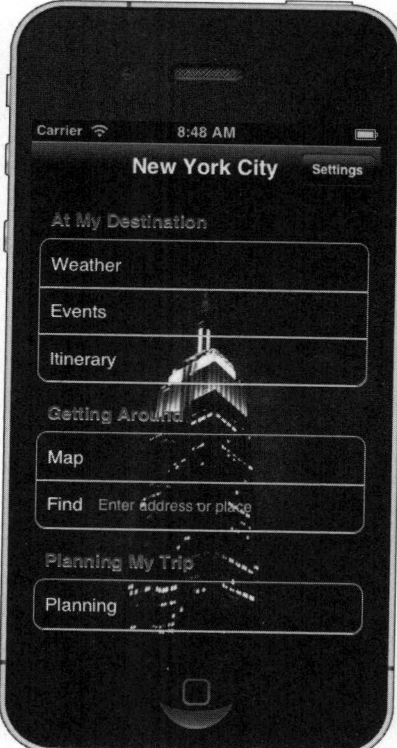

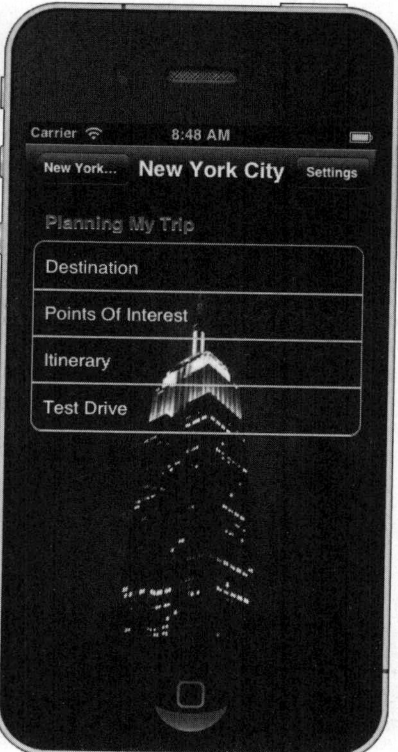

Figure 2-5: Using RoadTrip on the iPhone.

Before I start in with the explanations about the points of interest and the itinerary implementation — stuff you'll use (and modify) when you implement iCloud and web services — let me run through the rest of RoadTrip's functionality. Although it's possible to do everything on both devices, I use the iPad version for the screenshots because the split screen makes it easier to get a handle on the RoadTrip application as whole.

The tasks I came up with for my RoadTrip app are as follows:

- **Get real-time weather access.** Snow in New York in August? Not likely, but these days you never can tell. You can see real-time weather access at work in Figure 2-6.
- **Find out what's going on wherever you are.** Figure 2-7 shows an event that a user might be interested in, with fancy page turning no less.
- **Bring up a map based on the destination.** The map shows the destination, offers points of interest, and even allows the user to zero in on his current location, as shown in Figure 2-8.

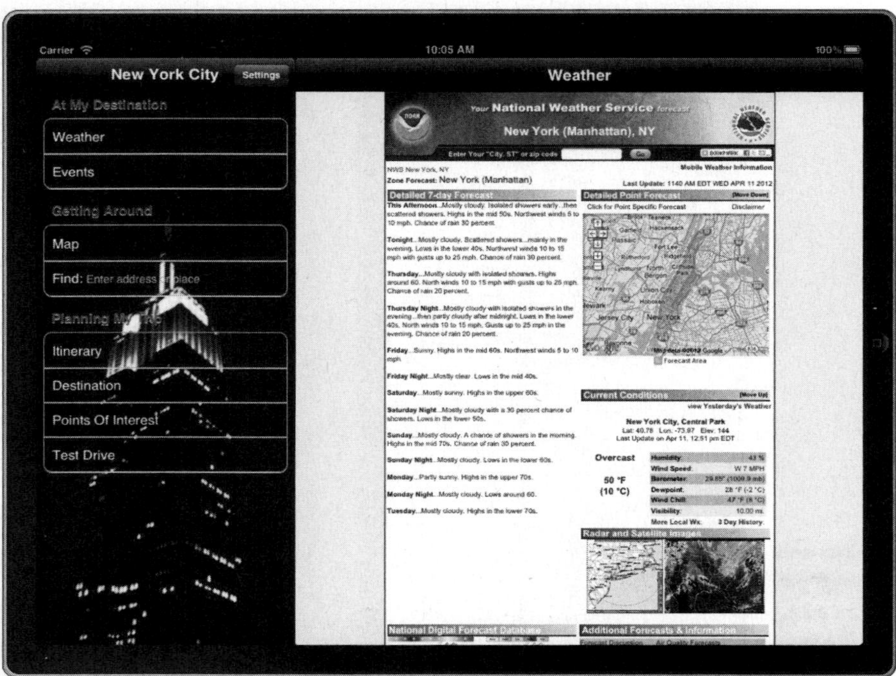

Figure 2-6: The weather in New York.

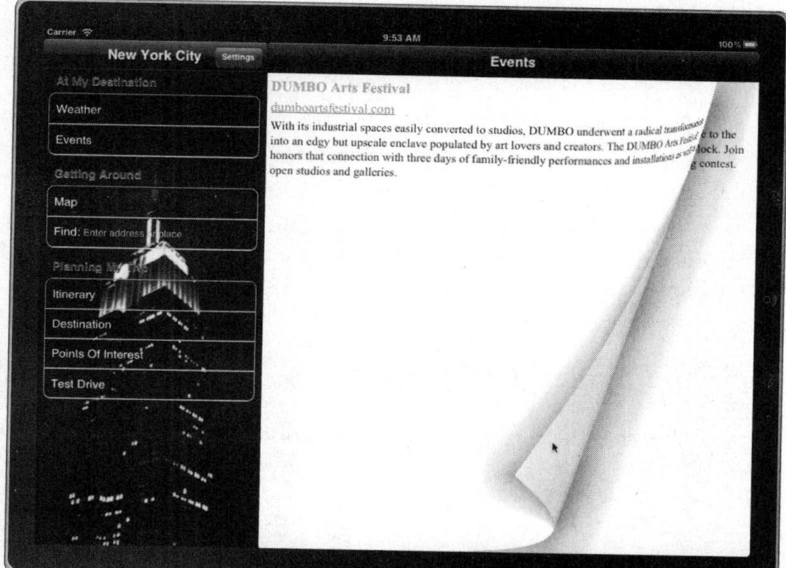

Figure 2-7: RoadTrip describes some things for you to do while in a city.

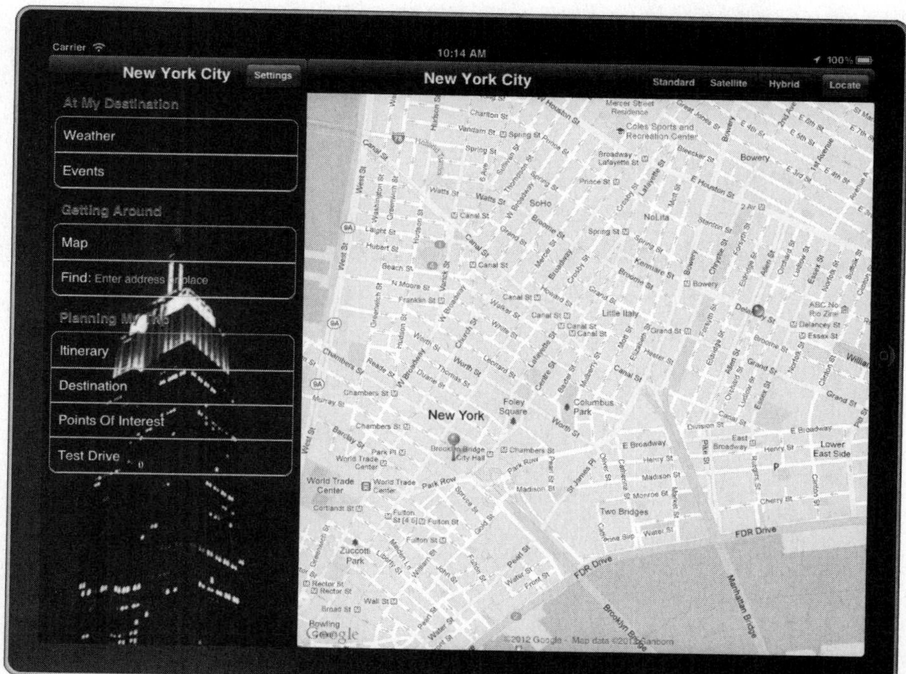

Figure 2-8: Finding your way with pinpoint accuracy.

- **Find a place on a map.** If the user has an address that she wants to find on the map, she should be able to do that *and* get its GPS coordinates. Figure 2-9 gives an example of finding a point of interest on a map.
- **Choose your destination, as shown in Figure 2-10.**
- **Turn off those annoying notifications about how far you are from your destination. (See Figure 2-11.)**
- **If you choose a location from the Find selection (refer to Figure 2-8) and shake the device, it will tell you how far away you are from that location, as shown in Figure 2-12.**

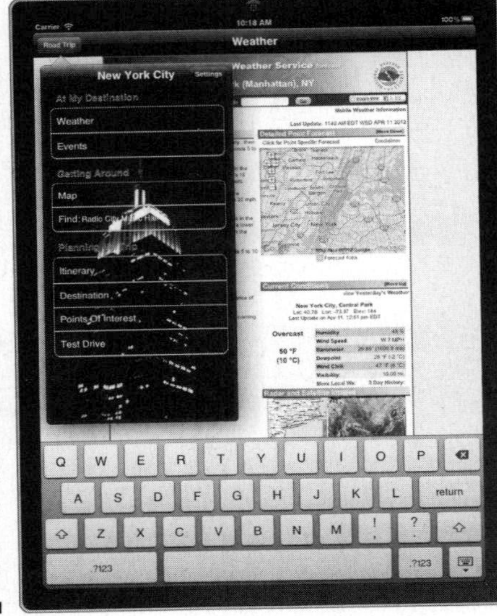

Figure 2-9: Where is Radio City Music Hall, anyway?

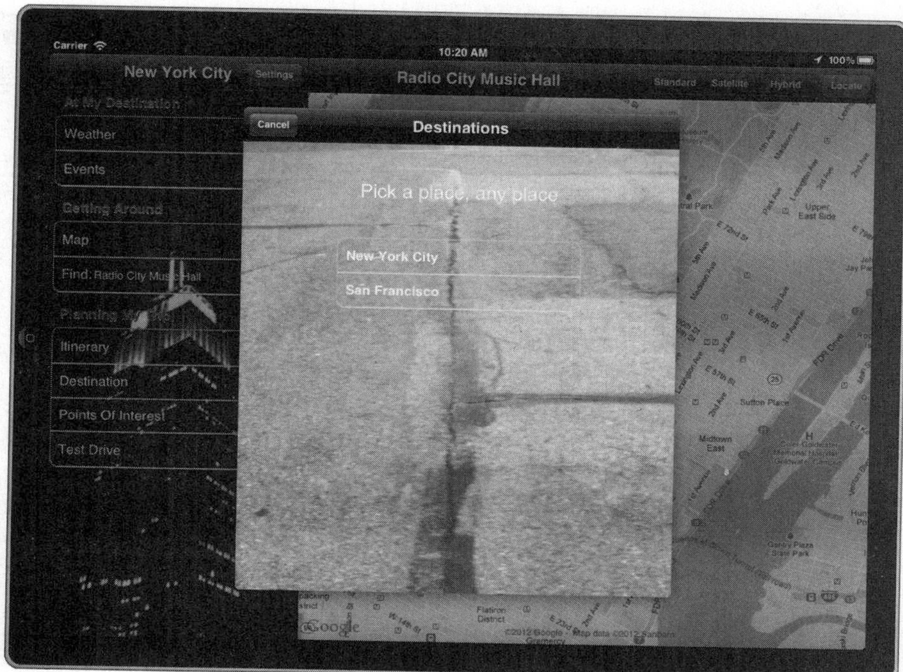

Figure 2-10: Where would I like to go today?

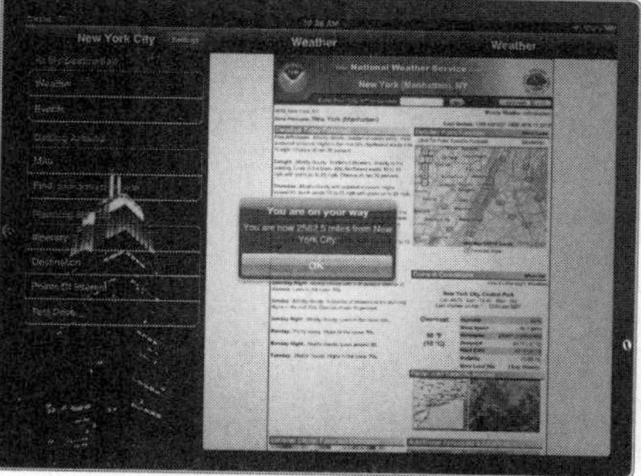

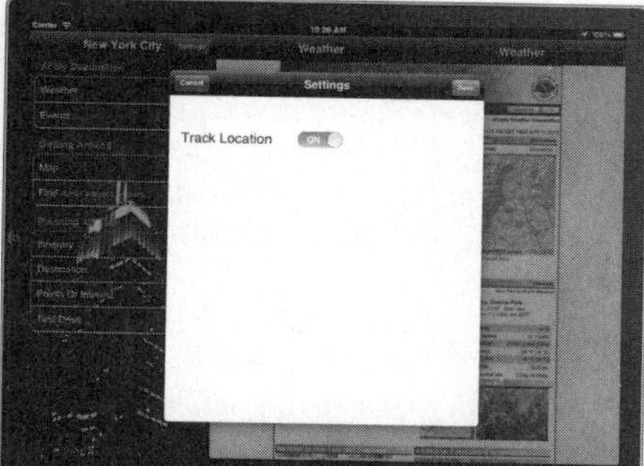

Figure 2-11: Enough already.

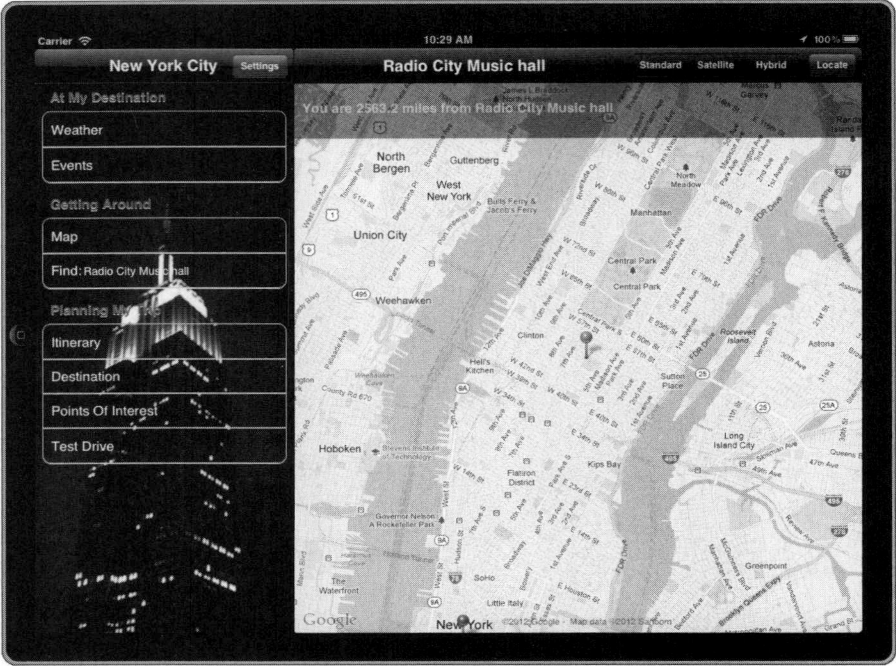

Figure 2-12: A long way to drive for a movie

Points of Interest and the Itinerary

All this talk about the wonders of RoadTrip is fine and dandy, but the point here is to take the current version of the RoadTrip application and upgrade it so that it can take advantage of iCloud and web services.

The first thing you'll do in Part II of this book is add iCloud support. That means that if you add a point of interest from the Points of Interest list to your Itinerary list on the iPad (refer to Figure 2-2), it will also automatically show up on the iPhone, and vice versa.

You'll be using Core Data to implement iCloud support — more on that in Part II as well.

You'll also be changing how you actually get the points of interest that you display. (Again, refer to Figure 2-2.) The points of interest that get displayed by default are currently bundled in the app in the `Destinations.plist` file shown in Figure 2-13. In the upgraded version of the app, you'll be getting the points of interest from a web service. (I'll also be showing you how to use another application — RoadTrip Editor — to add and delete points of interest, but I explain that application in the Bonus Chapter, "Adding and Deleting Points of Interest.")

RoadTrip.xcodeproj — Destinations.plist

RoadTrip › RoadTrip Resources › Destinations.plist › No Selection

Key	Type	Value
PointsOfInterest	Array	(6 items)
▼Item 0	Diction...	(6 items)
Name	String	The Statue of Liberty
Description	String	Pro democracy and anti-monarchy symbol of freedon
Latitude	Number	40.689244
Longitude	Number	-74.04451400000001
Location	String	New York City
Address	String	
▼Item 1	Diction...	(6 items)
Name	String	Whitney Museum of American Art
Description	String	American modern and contemporary
Latitude	Number	40.773508
Longitude	Number	-73.964454
Location	String	New York City
Address	String	
▼Item 2	Diction...	(6 items)
Name	String	Tenement Museum
Description	String	History comes alive
Latitude	Number	40.719114
Longitude	Number	-73.98998899999999
Location	String	New York City
Address	String	
▼Item 3	Diction...	(6 items)
Name	String	MOMA
Description	String	Modern Art
Latitude	Number	40.760669
Longitude	Number	-73.976269
Location	String	New York City
Address	String	
▼Item 4	Diction...	(6 items)
Name	String	Solomon R. Guggenheim Museum
Description	String	A Frank Lloyd Wright
Latitude	Number	40.782946
Longitude	Number	-73.95891
Location	String	New York City
Address	String	
▼Item 5	Diction...	(6 items)
Name	String	The Metropolitan Museum of Art
Description	String	The Grande Dame of museums
Latitude	Number	40.779012
Longitude	Number	-73.962383
Location	String	New York City
Address	String	

Figure 2-13: Not many places to go.

The Itinerary view you see back in Figure 2-2 is managed by the `Itinerary Controller`, and like all other good little controllers, it manages the connection between the model (in this case, the `RTModel`) and the view (in this case, a Table view). The `ItineraryController` is a subclass of the `RTDetailViewController` (a `UIViewController`) which has all the logic for managing the popover and the button that displays in Portrait orientation on the iPad. (The `RTDetailViewController` is not germane to adding iCloud and web services support, but I do cover it in great detail in my *iPad Software Development For Dummies,* 3rd Edition, if you're interested.)

What gets displayed in the `ItineraryController`'s Table view is in the data encapsulated in a `PointOfInterest` object. The code for its interface looks like the following:

```
@interface PointOfInterest : NSObject <MKAnnotation>

@property (nonatomic, readwrite)
                    CLLocationCoordinate2D coordinate;
@property (nonatomic, readwrite, copy) NSString *title;
@property (nonatomic, readwrite, copy) NSString *subtitle;
@property (nonatomic, readwrite, copy) NSString *address;
@property (nonatomic, readwrite, copy) NSString *location;
@property (nonatomic, readwrite, copy) NSString *comment;
- (id)initWithData:(NSDictionary *)data;
- (NSDictionary *)returnPointOfInterestData;
@end
```

A `PointOfInterest` object supplies the data the `ItineraryController` sends to the Table view to display in its `tableView:cellForRowAtIndexPath:` method, as shown in the bolded parts of Listing 2-1.

Listing 2-1: Displaying PointOfInterest data in the Table View

```
- (UITableViewCell *)tableView:(UITableView *)tableView
          cellForRowAtIndexPath:(NSIndexPath *)indexPath
{
  UITableViewCell *cell = [tableView
       dequeueReusableCellWithIdentifier:kItineraryCell];
  PointOfInterest *pointOfInterest =
       [itineraryPointsOfInterest
                           objectAtIndex:indexPath.row];
  cell.textLabel.text = pointOfInterest.title;
  cell.detailTextLabel.text = pointOfInterest.subtitle;
  return cell;
}
```

The `ItineraryController` has a reference to an array of `PointOfInterest` objects that make up the itinerary — `itineraryPointsOfInterest`. This array is managed by the `RTModel`, and I'll get to that shortly.

The `PointOfInterestController` works in the exact same way as the `ItineraryController`, and `pointsOfInterest` is its reference to the `PointOfInterest` objects that are not part of the itinerary.

The `PointOfInterest` objects you see displayed in the itinerary and the Point of Interest Table views together make up the complete set of points of interest available to the user. Every point of interest is always in either one list or the other, but never in both. When the user chooses a point of interest to add to his itinerary (by selecting a row in its Table view) the `PointsOfInterestController`, in its `tableView:didSelectRowAtInd` exPath: method, sends the addToItinerary:objectAtIndex: message to the RTModel, as shown in Listing 2-2.

Listing 2-2: Selecting a Point of Interest to Add to the Itinerar

```
- (void)tableView:(UITableView *)tableView
           didSelectRowAtIndexPath:(NSIndexPath *)indexPath
{
  [tableView deselectRowAtIndexPath:
                                  indexPath animated:YES];

  [[RTModel model] addToItinerary:
           [pointsOfInterest objectAtIndex:indexPath.row]];
}
```

As shown in Listing 2-3, the RTModel simply removes the point of interest from the PointsOfInterestController array, adds it to the Itinerary Controller array, and then notifies the controllers of the change by posting a notification. (I explain the ins and outs of notifications in Chapters 3 and 4.) The controllers respond by reloading their respective views.

Listing 2-3: Adding a PointOfInterest to the Itinerary

```
- (void)addToItinerary:
                      (PointOfInterest *)pointOfInterest {

  [itinerary addObject:pointOfInterest];
  [pointsOfInterest removeObject:pointOfInterest];

  [itineraryData addObject:
           [pointOfInterest returnPointOfInterestData]];
  RTAppDelegate *appDelegate =
           [[UIApplication sharedApplication] delegate];
  NSString *fileComponent =
    [NSString stringWithFormat:@"%@%@%@", @"Itinerary",
           appDelegate.destinationPreference, @".poi"];
  NSString *filePath = [RTModel filePath:fileComponent];
  NSURL *itineraryDataURL =
                        [NSURL fileURLWithPath:filePath];
  [itineraryData writeToURL:itineraryDataURL
                                       atomically:YES];
  [[NSNotificationCenter defaultCenter] postNotific
         ationName:@"ItineraryChanged" object:self
         userInfo:nil];
  [[NSNotificationCenter defaultCenter] postNotificatio
         nName:@"PointsOfInterestChanged" object:self
         userInfo:nil];
```

(continued)

Listing 2-3 ***(continued)***

```
  UIAlertView *alert = [[UIAlertView alloc]
       initWithTitle:pointOfInterest.title
       message:@"Was added to your itinerary"
       delegate:self cancelButtonTitle:@"Thanks"
       otherButtonTitles:nil];
  [alert show];
}
```

Similarly, when the user removes a point of interest from his itinerary by tapping the Deletion control and then the Delete button when the Table view is in editing mode, the `ItineraryController`, in its `tableView:commitEditingStyle:forRowAtIndexPath:` method, sends the `removeFromItinerary:` message to the `RTModel`, as shown in Listing 2-4.

Listing 2-4: Deleting a Point of Interest Using tableView: commitEditingStyle:forRowAtIndexPath:

```
- (void)tableView:(UITableView *)tableView
    commitEditingStyle:
      (UITableViewCellEditingStyle)editingStyle
             forRowAtIndexPath:(NSIndexPath *)indexPath {

  PointOfInterest *pointOfInterest =
     [itineraryPointsOfInterest
                         objectAtIndex:indexPath.row];
  [[RTModel model] removeFromItinerary:pointOfInterest];
}
```

And, as you might have guessed, this time the `RTModel` simply removes the `PointOfInterest` from the `ItineraryController` array (`itinerary`) and adds it to the `PointsOfInterestController` array (`pointsOfInterest`) and then notifies the controllers of what's happened by posting a notification. The controllers respond by reloading their respective views. (I go into this in a bit more detail in Chapter 4.)

Actually, there's a bit more going on in `RTModel` than simply the removal of a `PointOfInterest` object from one array and the adding of it to another. `RTModel` also removes the point of interest data from an itinerary file (and then saves the file) which it then uses to restore the itinerary's array. It also maintains a file of points of interest which contains all the points of interest, including those currently in the itinerary, but filters what is in the `PointsOfInterestController` array by not including those points of interest in the itinerary when it creates the `pointsOfInterest` array from the data file. (I show you how that works in the next section when I present Listing 2-6.)

Both controllers have no idea — nor do they care — where those PointOfInterest objects come from; they are supplied by the RTModel (as they should be). So, except for changing a few RTModel method names and types in the ItineraryController, the modifications to support iCloud (and subsequently web services) are all encapsulated in the RTModel.

How RTModel Manages the Data

This section gives you an overview of how RTModel manages the itinerary and points of interest; for more detail, check out Chapter 4, where I walk you through all the modifications you need to make in order to use Core Data. (As for web services, you have to wait until Chapter 11 to get the scoop on the modifications you need to make in order to use them.)

The RTModel creates and manages the two arrays — itinerary and pointsOfInterest. The itineraryPointsOfInterest instance variable in the ItineraryController refers to itinerary, and the pointsOfInterest instance variable in the PointsOfInterestController refers to pointsOfInterest.

When the RTModel is created, it uses two methods — one to load the itinerary (loadItinerary) and another to load its points of interest (loadPointsOfInterest).

When RoadTrip is launched for the first time, the RTModel creates an empty itinerary file and an empty itinerary array in its loadItinerary method, as you can see in Listing 2-5.

Listing 2-5: loadItinerary

```
- (void)loadItinerary {

  RTAppDelegate *appDelegate =
            [[UIApplication sharedApplication] delegate];
  NSString *fileComponent = [NSString
          stringWithFormat:@"%@%@%@", @"Itinerary",
          appDelegate.destinationPreference, @".poi"];
  NSString *filePath = [RTModel filePath:fileComponent];
  NSURL *itineraryDataURL =
                      [NSURL fileURLWithPath:filePath];
  itineraryData = [NSMutableArray
               arrayWithContentsOfURL:itineraryDataURL];

  if (itineraryData) {
```

(continued)

Listing 2-5 ***(continued)***

```
    itinerary = [NSMutableArray
                    arrayWithCapacity:[itineraryData count]];
    for (NSDictionary *pointOfInterestData in
                                          itineraryData) {
      PointOfInterest *pointOfInterest =
           [[PointOfInterest alloc]
                      initWithData:pointOfInterestData];
      [itinerary addObject:pointOfInterest];
    }
  }
  else {
    NSDictionary *destinationPointOfInterestData =
      [destinationData objectForKey:
                                 @"DestinationLocation"];
    itineraryData = [NSMutableArray
          arrayWithObject:destinationPointOfInterestData];
    [itineraryData writeToURL:itineraryDataURL
                                          atomically:YES];
    PointOfInterest *destinationPointOfInterest =
      [[PointOfInterest alloc]
            initWithData:destinationPointOfInterestData];
    itinerary = [NSMutableArray
               arrayWithObject:destinationPointOfInterest];
  }
}
```

Then, in the `loadPointsOfInterest` method, it takes the points of interest data from the `Destinations.plist` (refer to Figure 2-13; it's an `NSDictionary` object) and adds it to `pointOfInterestData`. The method stores that data in a file (see Listing 2-6) and also creates the `PointsOfInterest` array.

Listing 2-6: Loading the Points of Interest for the First Time

```
- (void) loadPointsOfInterest {

  RTAppDelegate *appDelegate =
            [[UIApplication sharedApplication] delegate];
  NSString *fileComponent =
     [NSString stringWithFormat:@"%@%@%@", @"POI",
               appDelegate.destinationPreference, @".poi"];
  NSString *filePath = [RTModel filePath:fileComponent];
  NSURL *pointsOfInterestDataURL =
                        [NSURL fileURLWithPath:filePath];
  pointsOfInterestData = [NSMutableArray
         arrayWithContentsOfURL:pointsOfInterestDataURL];

  if (!pointsOfInterestData) {
    pointsOfInterestData = [NSMutableArray arrayWithArray:
```

```
      [destinationData objectForKey:@"PointsOfInterest"]];
    [pointsOfInterestData writeToURL:
                  pointsOfInterestDataURL atomically:YES];
  }
  pointsOfInterest =
           [NSMutableArray arrayWithCapacity:
                        [pointsOfInterestData count]];

  BOOL isInItinerary = NO;

  for (NSDictionary *aPointOfInterest in
                               pointsOfInterestData) {
    for (PointOfInterest *pointOfInterest in itinerary) {
      if ([pointOfInterest.title isEqualToString:
           [aPointOfInterest objectForKey:@"Name"]])
                                  isInItinerary = YES;
    }
    if (!isInItinerary) {
      [pointsOfInterest addObject:[[PointOfInterest alloc]
                        initWithData:aPointOfInterest]];
    }
    else {
      isInItinerary = NO;
    }
  }
}
```

Notice that, before the `loadPointsOfInterest` method adds a point of interest to the `pointsOfInterest` array, it checks to see whether that point of interest is in the `itinerary` array. Of course, there won't be any points of interest in the `itinerary` the first time the application is launched, but on subsequent launches, it won't add any `PointOfInterest` that is already in the `itinerary` to the `pointsOfInterest` array.

```
  BOOL isInItinerary = NO;

  for (NSDictionary *aPointOfInterest in
                               pointsOfInterestData) {
    for (PointOfInterest *pointOfInterest in itinerary) {
      if ([pointOfInterest.title isEqualToString:
           [aPointOfInterest objectForKey:@"Name"]])
                                  isInItinerary = YES;
    }
    if (!isInItinerary) {
      [pointsOfInterest addObject:[[PointOfInterest alloc]
                        initWithData:aPointOfInterest]];
    }
    else {
      isInItinerary = NO;
    }
  }
}
```

When the user selects a `PointOfInterest` to add to his itinerary, the `RTModel` method `addPointOfInterest:` removes the `PointOfInterest` from the `pointsOfInterest` array and adds it to the `itinerary` array, as you can see in Listing 2-7. It also takes the `PointsOfInterest` data, adds it to the `itineraryData` array, and saves the `itineraryData` array to the file system. (Note that the `PointsOfInterest` method `returnPointOfInterestData` returns its data in a dictionary.) All this converting back and forth from `NSDictionary` to the `PointsOfInterest` object and then back to the dictionary is necessary because you can't simply store the `PointsOfInterest` object as an object . . . yet — but that's what you have Code Data do for you in Chapter 4.

Listing 2-7: Adding a PointOfInterest to the Itinerary

```
- (void)addPointOfInterest:(NSMutableDictionary *)
                                    pointOfInterestData {

  void (^clGeocodeCompletionHandler)(NSArray *, NSError *)
         = ^(NSArray *placemarks, NSError *error){
    CLPlacemark *placemark = [placemarks objectAtIndex:0];
    if (error!= nil || placemark == nil) {
      NSLog(@"Geocoder Failure! Error code: %u,
           description: %@, and reason: %@", error.
           code, [error localizedDescription], [error
           localizedFailureReason]);
      UIAlertView *alert = [[UIAlertView alloc]
          initWithTitle:@"Couldn't add"
          message:[pointOfInterestData
          objectForKey:@"location"] delegate:self
          cancelButtonTitle:@"Thanks"
          otherButtonTitles:nil];
      [alert show];
    }
    else {

      [pointOfInterestData setObject:[NSNumber
         numberWithDouble:placemark.location.coordinate.
                             latitude] forKey:@"Latitude"];
      [pointOfInterestData setObject:[NSNumber
         numberWithDouble:placemark.location.coordinate.
                           longitude] forKey:@"Longitude"];

      RTAppDelegate *appDelegate = [[UIApplication
          sharedApplication] delegate];
      NSString *fileComponent =
        [NSString stringWithFormat:@"%@%@%@", @"POI",
              appDelegate.destinationPreference, @".poi"];
      NSString *filePath =
                         [RTModel filePath:fileComponent];
```

```
      NSURL *pointsOfInterestDataURL =
                         [NSURL fileURLWithPath:filePath];
      [pointsOfInterestData
                            addObject:pointOfInterestData];
      [pointsOfInterestData
         writeToURL:pointsOfInterestDataURL
                                      atomically:YES];

      PointOfInterest *addedPointOfInterest =
        [[PointOfInterest alloc]
                      initWithData:pointOfInterestData];
      [self addToItinerary:addedPointOfInterest];
    }
  };

  CLGeocoder* geocoder = [[CLGeocoder alloc] init];
  NSString* findLocation = [[pointOfInterestData
    objectForKey:@"Address"] isEqualToString:@""] ?
    [pointOfInterestData objectForKey:@"Name"]:
           [pointOfInterestData objectForKey:@"Address"];
  [geocoder geocodeAddressString:findLocation completionHa
         ndler:clGeocodeCompletionHandler];
}
```

When the user creates a new point of interest (refer to Figure 2-4), the `AddPointOfInterestController` sends the data in an `NSDictionary` to the `RTModel` by sending the `addPointOfInterest;` message. The method *geocodes* the point of interest — gets it GPS coordinates — and then creates the `PointOfInterest` object from the data, adds it to the `pointsOfInterestData` array, and stores it to the file system. It also sends itself the `addToItinerary:` message to add the newly created `PointOfInterest` to the itinerary. You can see how this works in Listing 2-8. (I cover this in more detail in Chapter 7 when you start to use a web service to get the points of interest.)

Listing 2-8: Adding a PointOfInterest

```
- (void)addPointOfInterest:(NSMutableDictionary *)
                                  pointOfInterestData {

  void (^clGeocodeCompletionHandler)(NSArray *, NSError *)
         = ^(NSArray *placemarks, NSError *error){
    CLPlacemark *placemark = [placemarks objectAtIndex:0];
    if (error!= nil || placemark == nil) {
      NSLog(@"Geocoder Failure! Error code: %u,
           description: %@, and reason: %@", error.code,
           [error localizedDescription],
                      [error localizedFailureReason]);
```

(continued)

Listing 2-8 ***(continued)***

```
      UIAlertView *alert = [[UIAlertView alloc]
           initWithTitle:@"Couldn't add"
           message:[pointOfInterestData
                             objectForKey:@"location"]
          delegate:self cancelButtonTitle:@"Thanks"
           otherButtonTitles:nil];
      [alert show];
    }
    else {

      [pointOfInterestData setObject:
             [NSNumber numberWithDouble:
                 placemark.location.coordinate.latitude]
          forKey:@"Latitude"];
      [pointOfInterestData setObject:
             [NSNumber numberWithDouble:
                placemark.location.coordinate.longitude]
          forKey:@"Longitude"];

      RTAppDelegate *appDelegate =
             [[UIApplication sharedApplication] delegate];
      NSString *fileComponent =
        [NSString stringWithFormat:@"%@%@%@", @"POI",
          appDelegate.destinationPreference, @".poi"];
      NSString *filePath =
                        [RTModel filePath:fileComponent];
      NSURL *pointsOfInterestDataURL =
                        [NSURL fileURLWithPath:filePath];
      [pointsOfInterestData
                          addObject:pointOfInterestData];
      [pointsOfInterestData writeToURL:
                 pointsOfInterestDataURL atomically:YES];

      PointOfInterest *addedPointOfInterest =
       [[PointOfInterest alloc]
                       initWithData:pointOfInterestData];
      [self addToItinerary:addedPointOfInterest];
    }
  };

  CLGeocoder* geocoder = [[CLGeocoder alloc] init];
  NSString* findLocation = [[pointOfInterestData
    objectForKey:@"Address"] isEqualToString:@""] ?
    [pointOfInterestData objectForKey:@"Name"]:
          [pointOfInterestData objectForKey:@"Address"];
  [geocoder geocodeAddressString:findLocation completionHa
          ndler:clGeocodeCompletionHandler];
}
```

Similarly, when the user removes a point of interest from his itinerary, the `RTModel` reverses the process in the `removePointOfInterest` method.

Part II
Adding iCloud

"We're still working out the kinks in our cloud computing environment."

In this part . . .

Now that you understand where you're coming from and where you want to go — a useful idea because, to paraphrase the Cheshire Cat in *Alice in Wonderland*, "If you don't know where you' re going, any road will get you there" — it's time to get started.

In this part, you start your trip off of Terra Firma by adding Core Data to RoadTrip and letting it manage all your iCloud synchronization for you.

Personally, I'm a big fan of letting someone else do all the drudge work leaving me to have all the fun.

Chapter 3

Setting Up Core Data

In This Chapter

- Discovering Core Data
- Looking at managed objects
- Understanding the Core Data architecture
- Adding a Core Data stack

As I explain in Chapter 1, the Application Ecosystem is based on two distinct technologies: iCloud and web services.

Although web services are very cool — so cool, in fact, that they were the original focus of this book — in some ways iCloud is actually more important. That's because if you believe in using the right device for the right job, then for many applications (RoadTrip, for example), you'll want to be able to work on different devices depending on what you're doing. For example, if you're traveling, you're probably going to be using your iPhone because it's mobile and easy to carry around. For sitting at home on the couch and planning your trip, the iPad is the more likely choice — with its larger screen, you can see a lot more at the same time, which makes it easier for you to really get into what you're doing.

When the ability to switch between multiple devices is a high priority, you need to make sure that data is synched among all devices. Of course, you could do this with web services, but that would mean creating a large infrastructure to support your users (you'll need to store their data, make sure it's secure, have lots of bandwidth, and so on), and why do that when Apple has already done all that work for you?

Managing Your Itinerary

As you can see in Figure 3-1, RoadTrip allows you to create (and save) an itinerary — the places you'd like to see on your trip — by tapping a point of interest in the popover (Figure 3-1, left). (I use iPad screen shots because they make it a little easier to see what's going on in the app, but keep in mind that, because RoadTrip is a universal app, the same functionality is found on the iPhone.) These places are represented by `PointOfInterest` objects in your code and are created from `PointsOfInterest` data included with RoadTrip in the Destinations plist (one set of `PointsOfInterest` data for each destination). In Chapter 14, the `PointsOfInterest` data will be downloaded using a web service instead of being bundled with the app, but for now just use it as is.

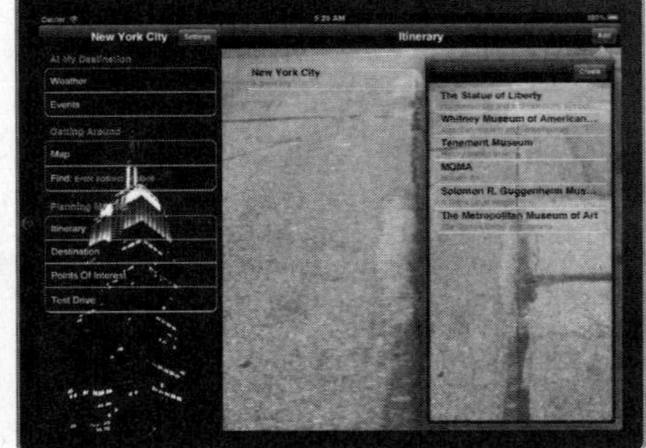

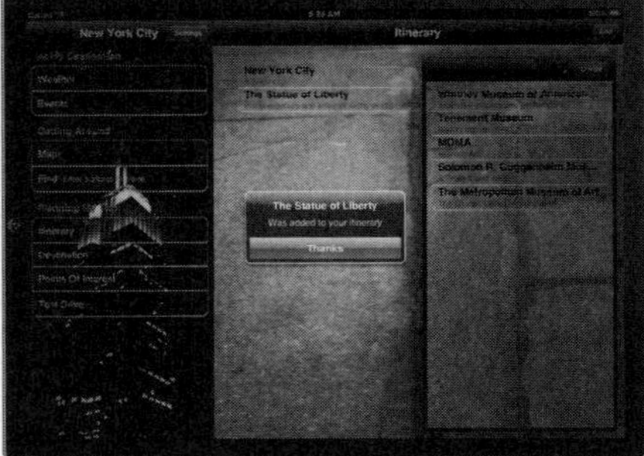

Figure 3-1: Your itinerary.

Being the firm believer in crowd sourcing (under some circumstances) that I am, I've set up RoadTrip in such a way that the user can also add a new point of interest to the `PointsOfInterest` data by tapping the Create button on the right side of the points of interest list toolbar, as shown in Figure 3-2, and then add that to his or her itinerary as well.

This is an obvious candidate for the Right Device for the Right Job approach. When I'm planning my trip, I like to be able to lie on my couch and scope out all the great places I want to see. (Did you know there are multiple claims to the world's largest ball of twine?) On the other hand, when I'm actually traveling, I like to have that same information on my iPhone because it fits in my pocket and is easier to carry around. What's more, I want the ability to update my itinerary on the iPhone and have it update the iPad accordingly, and vice versa.

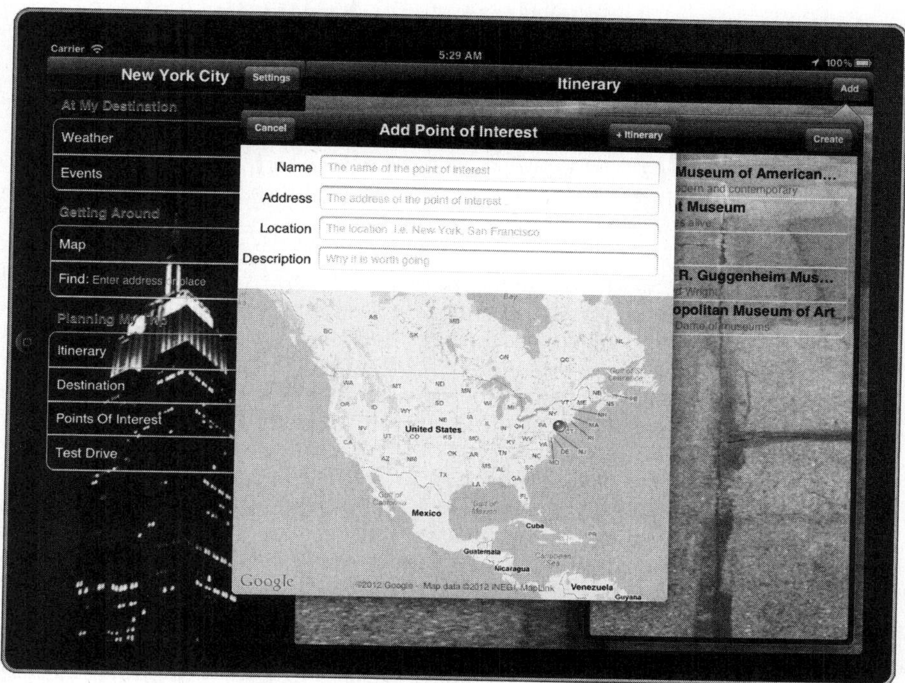

Figure 3-2: Adding a point of interest.

Apple provides a couple of basic approaches to implement iCloud's ability to share data between devices — the `UIDocument` class (which supports managing multiple documents) and Core Data (an *object persistence* framework where, instead of saving and retrieving an object's data, the object is saved and retrieved *as an object*). And even though both do work, I've found that, for applications such as RoadTrip, Core Data is hands-down the best choice, especially because RoadTrip isn't document-based. Hey, RoadTrip isn't a word processor, if you haven't noticed. And even if it were document-based, there's a Core Data `UIManagedDocument` class, which is a subclass of `UIDocument`. (Great stuff, but outside the scope of this book.)

So, the place to start is Core Data, and in this chapter, you start the migration of your itinerary from a saved file to Core Data — which, as explained in Chapter 4, offers some help when it comes to displaying the data as well.

Core Data Basics

Core Data is a deep, wide, and very mature technology, used on the Mac for years — a long and successful history that makes the iPhone version very attractive. Core Data not only makes it easy to create, manage, and delete objects, but it also incorporates the handy *shake* feature for undoing and redoing actions.

In this chapter and the next, I show you how to implement Core Data in RoadTrip to support the display, modification, and saving of your itinerary. You replace the way you currently display, modify, and save your itinerary in RoadTrip — where you're forced to save your itinerary as a file and then convert that data into objects — and vice versa — for any modifications. Because Core Data is very broad and deep, I don't get into all the bells and whistles of Core Data — it would take an entire book to do that. Instead, I focus on the basics as well as what you need to know to implement Core Data by using iCloud. I give you enough background and understanding so you'll be comfortable exploring Core Data on your own — and you'll be able to use the great sample code that Apple provides that shows you how to use Core Data to do most of what you want to do in your application.

Core Data makes it easy for a developer to do the two things you'll need to do in this book (actually, there is way more to Core Data than that, but that is beyond the scope of this book).

- Create, save, and fetch *objects as objects* — including their connections to other objects — from a persistent store, such as a file on disk. As explained in Chapter 4, going the traditional route of first turning objects into data to save them and *then* reconstructing them as objects can be quite a chore.
- Keep data synchronized between devices running the same application for the same user.

To do those two things you start by taking these steps:

1. Creating a *managed object* (data) *model* that describes the object's data and relationships to other objects.
2. Deriving your classes that are to be managed by Core Data from `NSManagedObject` instead of `NSObject`.
3. Creating a *managed object context* that manages your collection of objects — a context that would be responsible for lifecycle management, validation, maintaining relationships between objects, undo/redo, and managing *the persistent store*. This mechanism is for storing your objects to disk and is pretty much handled for you.

4. Creating your objects in the more or less usual way — within the managed object context, of course — and then saving them.
5. *Fetching* your saved objects, optionally using a `FetchedResultsController` to get your objects in a way that is optimized for Table views.

Before you go any further and get your hopes up, I want to explain what Core Data is *not:*

- Although Core Data can use a relational database — SQLite — as one of its persistent store types, it isn't in and of itself a relational database or a relational database management system. It's about providing an infrastructure for saving objects to (and retrieving them from) storage as well as Undo and Redo support.
- Core Data is not an application generator — you still have to write code.

You need to do quite a bit of (boilerplate) plumbing to set up Core Data. To start off, you need a managed object context, a managed object model, and a Persistent Store coordinator, all of which I explain in the sections that follow.

Before you go there, though, keep one thing in mind: In RoadTrip, you're already doing what you're going to use Core Data to do — managing a selection of `PointOfInterest` objects. (That's what you see displayed on the left side of Figure 3-1.) But as I explain, it's quite a chore to manage all that content. Core Data makes it all easier — including making it easier to take your itinerary list and making it more useful to the users by allowing them to access it from multiple devices.

Starting with the Objects — The Managed Object Model

Believe me, the idea of Core Data can be overwhelming at first — a lot of the documentation assumes that you're both an expert in object-oriented programming (which I am) and a database aficionado (which I am not). When it comes right down to it, though, after you wade through the mess (I personally have taken the bullet for you here), it actually makes sense.

So start at the beginning by understanding what you need done and how Core Data is going to do it for you.

You want to have Core Data manage your itinerary for you. That means you want to be able to create, save, and modify the `PointOfInterest` objects in your itinerary. (You could also support Undos, but that's not really necessary in this case.)

The right place to start is with a new object class, `SharedPointOfInterest`, which will eventually be shared between all of an individual user's devices running the RoadTrip app. The `SharedPointOfInterest` class is remarkably like the existing `PointOfInterest` class currently used in RoadTrip.

You continue to use `PointOfInterest` when you want to create a non-`ManagedObject` object. (I explain `ManagedObject` in a sec.)

If you were going to create a `SharedPointOfInterest` class on your own, it would sort of look like what you see in Listing 3-1.

Listing 3-1: A SharedPointOfInterest Class

```
#import <Foundation/Foundation.h>
#import <CoreData/CoreData.h>

@interface SharedPointOfInterest : NSObject

@property (nonatomic, retain) NSString * name;
@property (nonatomic, retain) NSString * address;
@property (nonatomic, retain) NSString * comment;
@property (nonatomic, retain) NSNumber * displayOrder;
@property (nonatomic, retain) NSString * latitude;
@property (nonatomic, retain) NSString * location;
@property (nonatomic, retain) NSString * longitude;
@property (nonatomic, retain) NSString * subtitle;
@property (nonatomic, retain) NSString * title;

@end
```

This code looks a lot like the other model objects I'd made use of in RoadTrip and, as I said, remarkably like the `PointOfInterest` class.

As you might have guessed, though, instead of having to manage these objects on my own, I'm going to let Core Data do it for me. But for Core Data to do it, it needs a description of its objects. You provide this description by creating a *managed object model* — a *schema* (a diagram that represents the elements in a system using symbols, in other words) that describes the *entities* (objects) your application uses and the relationships between them. Such a schema is illustrated in Figure 3-3 on the left, where you see the `SharedPointOfInterest` entity. Even though in your particular model you're going to go with only one entity, you can opt for more than one and can also set up relationships between entities. (The right side of Figure 3-3 shows an example). (As much as I would like this book to be an exhaustive study of Core Data, it just wasn't meant to be, so I leave you to explore this business of multiple entities on your own.)

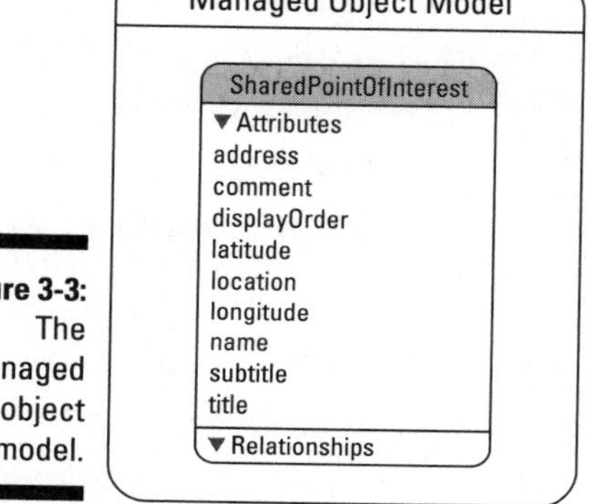

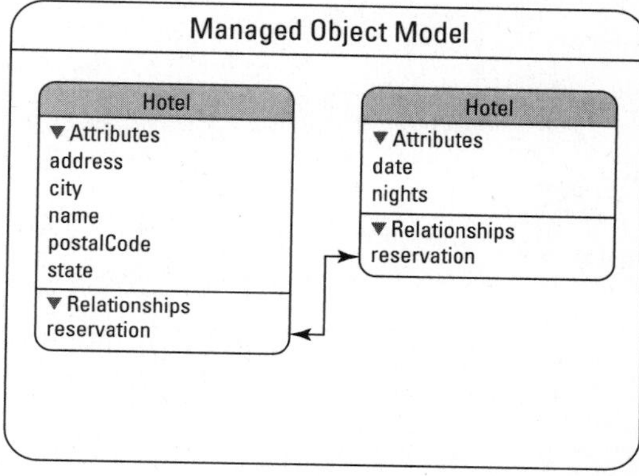

Figure 3-3: The managed object model.

Core Data uses the schema to map between the managed objects in your application and the records in a database used to create said objects. It's important to be aware that if you change the schema in your application, Core Data won't be able to read stores you created using the previous model — for that to work, you'd need to use a migration mechanism (which I explain in Chapter 5) or simply delete the application from the simulator or the device or iCloud and start over from scratch. (You'll need to take that step for now — at least until I explain your alternatives in Chapter 5.)

The managed object model is a collection of objects that provide Core Data with information, or *metadata* as it's called, about each entity. This data includes the entity's name, the class that represents it in your application (which doesn't have to be the same as its name), its attributes (which become class properties), and its relationships to other objects (which become pointers to other objects). Similarly, attribute and relationship description objects provide the information about attributes and relationships the Core Data needs, as illustrated in Figure 3-4. (Admittedly, I haven't covered all of what you see in Figure 3-4; I just want you to be aware of some of the possibilities, and as I said, there's a lot for you to explore in Core Data on your own.)

So, with that info in hand, you're ready to go build a managed object model for `SharedPointOfInterest` in the RoadTrip app.

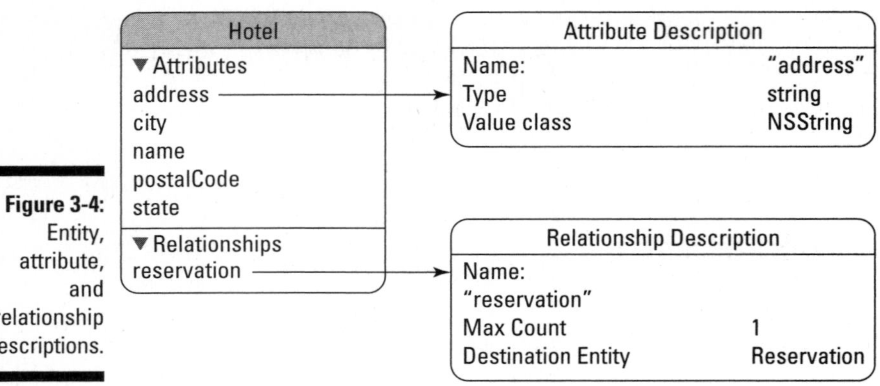

Figure 3-4: Entity, attribute, and relationship descriptions.

I show you how to use the Xcode modeling tool (one that's quite similar to Interface Builder) to create the model graphically.

I'm going to put my model in the Model Classes folder, so before you start, be sure to select that folder first.

1. **Choose File⇨New⇨File from the main menu (or press ⌘+N) to open the New File dialog.**
2. **In the leftmost column of the dialog, select Core Data under the iOS heading.**
3. **Select the Data Model template in the topmost pane (as I have in Figure 3-5) and then click Next.**

   You see a new dialog asking for some more information.

4. **In the new dialog that appears, leave the Model option selected in the Save As field, make sure Targets has RoadTrip selected and that the Group drop-down menu shows Model Classes (or wherever you want to put the model), and then click the Create button.**

   Your new managed object model, `Model.xcdatamodel`, gets placed in the Model Classes group. If you now close the Navigator area, you should see the same thing I see in Figure 3-6.

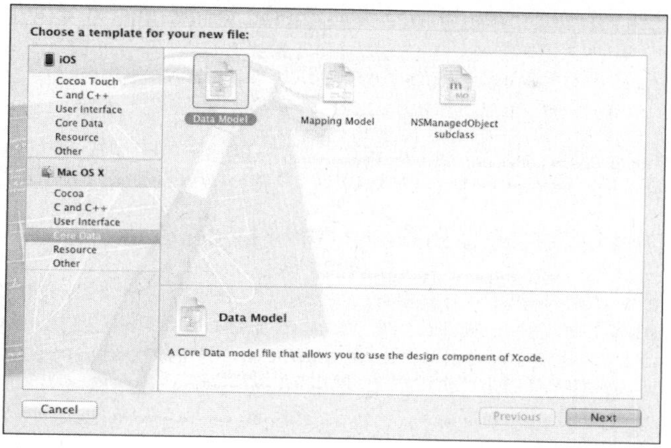

Figure 3-5: Create a data model.

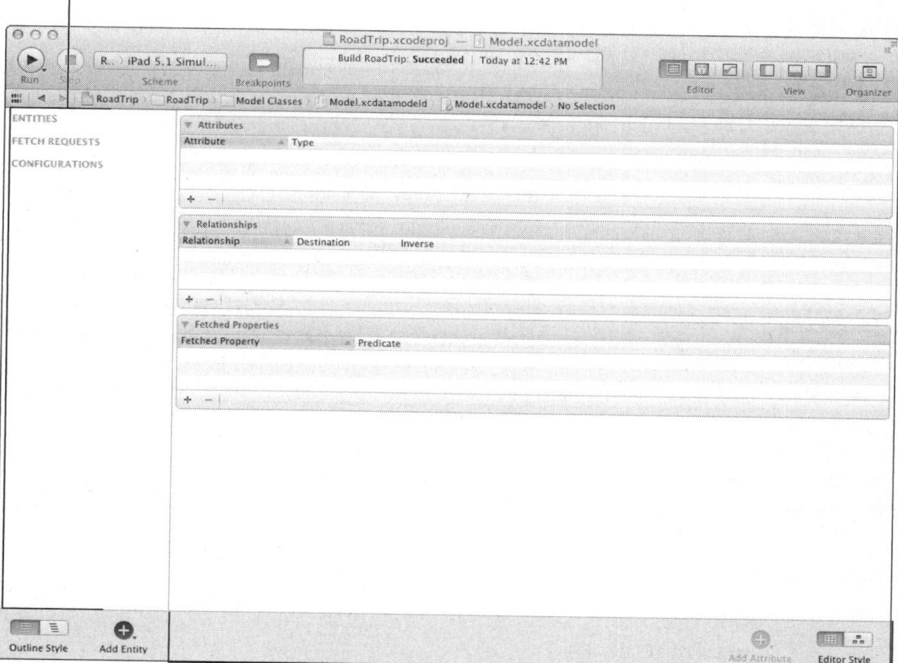

Figure 3-6: An empty model.

The Core Data Model editor is made up of two areas:

- **The Top-Level Components area,** showing the various entities, fetch requests, and configurations and
- **The Detail area,** showing the attributes, relationships, and fetched properties of the item selected in the Top-level Components area

Figure 3-6 shows the Core Data Model editor in all its glory.

The Core Data Model editor has two styles: Table style and Graph style. Figure 3-6 show the Table style, but you can switch to the Graph style (shown in Figure 3-7) by using the Editor Style segmented control you see in the bottom-right corner of the Core Data Model editor.

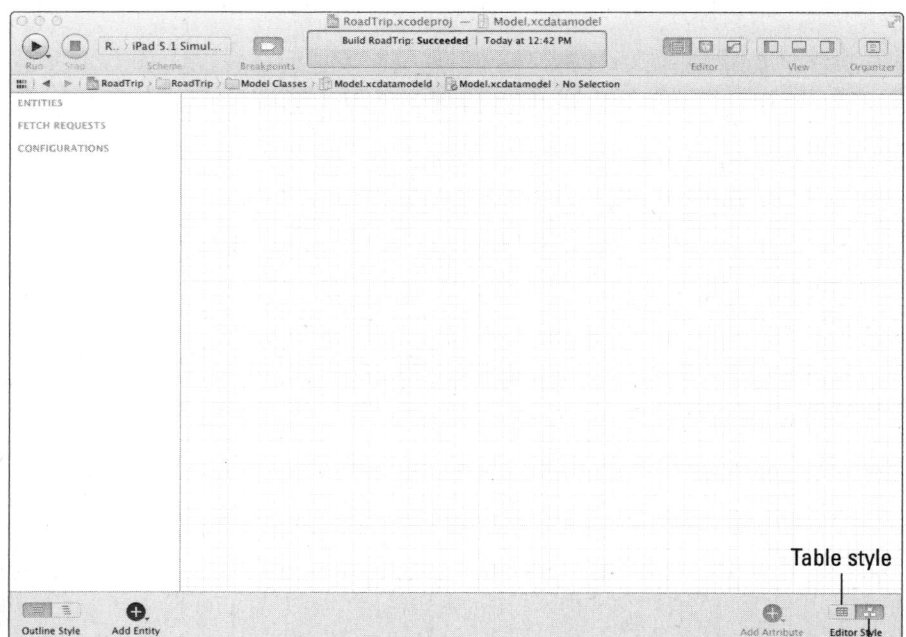

Figure 3-7: The Core Data Model editor in Graph style.

Now that you have your data model in place, it's time to add some actual content to it:

1. **With your brand-spanking-new (and empty) data model open, click the Add Entity button on the bottom toolbar of the Core Data Model editor.**

   You can alternatively choose Editor➪Add Entity from the main menu.

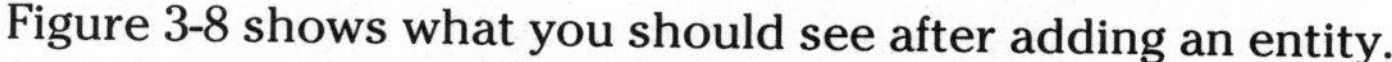

Figure 3-8 shows what you should see after adding an entity.

You also use the Add Entity button to add a fetch request or configuration. Just hold down the Add Entity button until it shows the other options. The button name will change to whatever option you choose — it remains in the state that you last used it in.

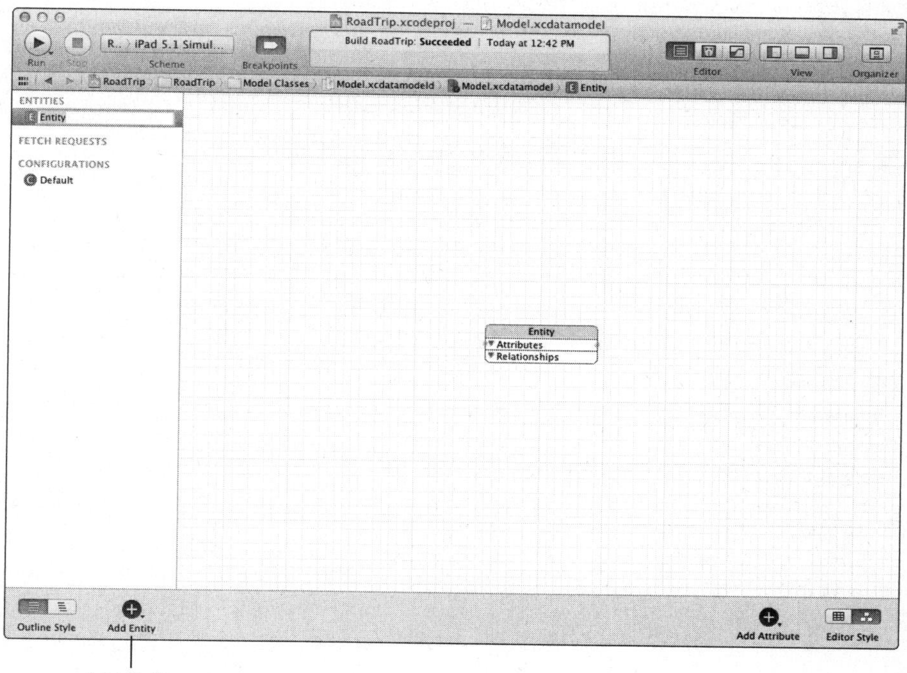

Figure 3-8: Your first entity.

You should see a new entry (called Entity) appear in the Entity section of the Top-Level Components area at the top left of the Core Data Model editor. Since you are in Graph style, a graphical representation of the entity (a rounded rectangle) appears in the Detail area.

Think of entities as classes in your application that become objects at runtime and hold the data that's described in their properties.

Now you can set the name for the new entity.

2. **Make sure you have the new entity selected in the Top-Level Components area and open the Core Data Model inspector by clicking the Hide or Show the Utilities button in toolbar (as I have in Figure 3-9) so that you see information about the entity.**
3. **Change the name of the entity to `SharedPointOfInterest`, as I have in Figure 3-9.**

Be sure to press Return after you enter the text and be sure not to change the class name — that will be filled in for you when you generate the `SharedPointOfInterest` class in the "Generating your classes" section, later in this chapter.

The Core Data Model inspector displays the information you select in the Detail area. By making a multiple selection in the Detail area, you can edit several properties at the same time — the Attribute Type for a number of attributes, for example.

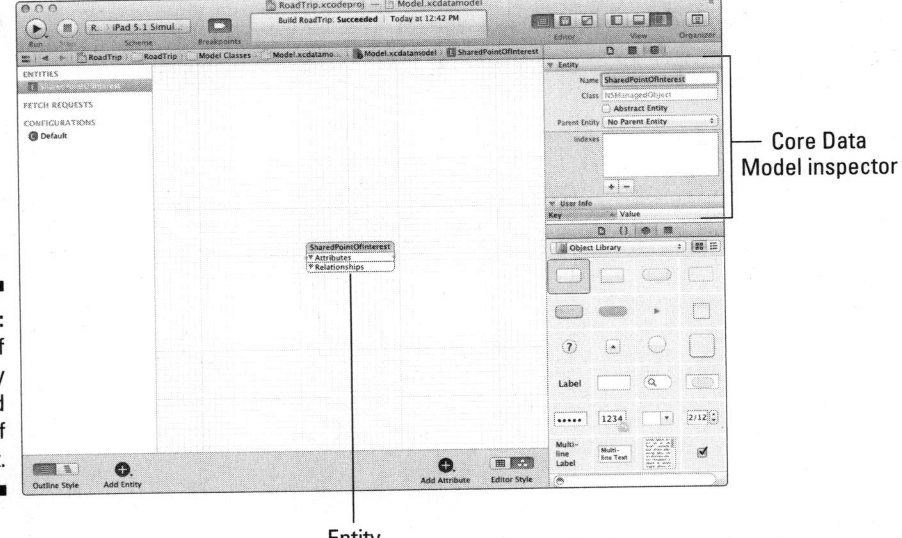

Figure 3-9: The name of your entity is SharedPointOfInterest.

The name of the entity and the name of the Objective-C class used to represent instances of the entity aren't the same thing. Core Data uses the entity name to manage its data objects, so that name doesn't have to be the same as its class name. In fact, you can often get away without really using any classes (although I use them in this example) other than `NSManagedObject`, which I explain later.

Adding the attributes

The next milestone on the road to managed object model nirvana comes when you add the attributes to the entity. These attributes correspond to the instance variables you're used to using, which correspond to the model's data.

You start by adding the `Name` attribute. To do that, you want to switch to the Table style in the Core Data Model editor.

I find Graph style is great for giving me the big picture of the whole schema, but Table style is better for editing. (Refer to Figure 3-6.)

1. **Make sure `SharedPointOfInterest` is selected in the Entities section of the Core Data Model editor.**

   I know it's the only entity listed, but if you've done a bit of exploring on your own you'll need to select an entity to get back to it.

2. **Click the Add Attribute button on the bottom toolbar of the Core Data Model editor.**

   You can also choose Editor⇨Add Attribute from the main menu, or you can even click the + control at the bottom of the Attributes section of the Detail area.

   No matter how you do this step, you end up seeing an attribute waiting for you in the Attributes section in the Detail area. (See Figure 3-10.) You also see information about the attribute in the Core Data Model inspector in the Utility area. All you have to do now is set the attribute's name and type.

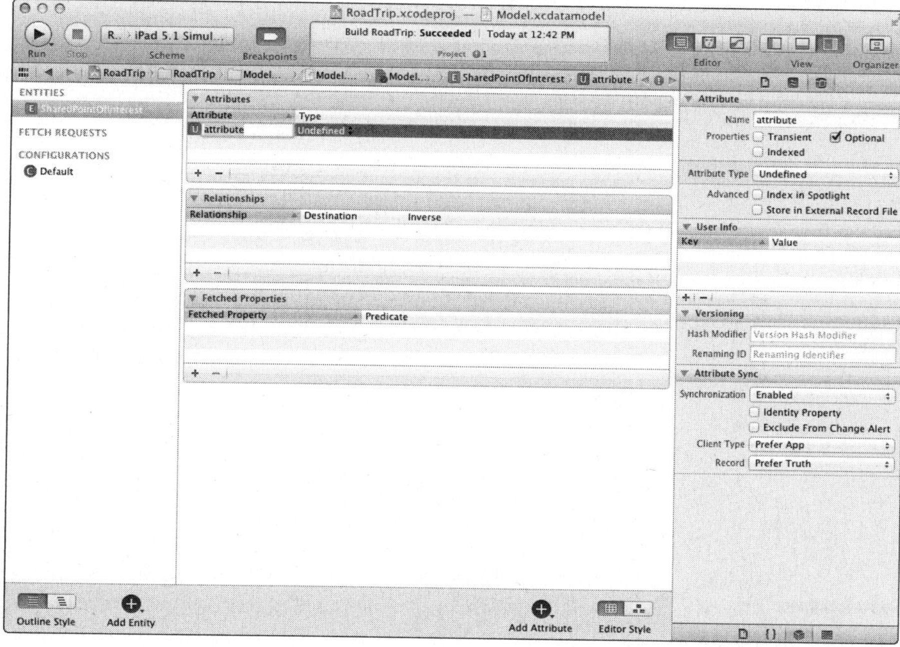

Figure 3-10: Table style with an attribute just waiting for you to set.

3. **Make sure you've selected the new attribute in the Attributes section. Then, in the Core Data Model inspector, change the name of the attribute to `name`, as I have in Figure 3-11.**

   You can also double-click the attribute in the Attributes section and enter the new name there.

   Next up, you need to tell Core Data what type of attribute this is. The warning in the Activity window in the Xcode toolbar is a subtle hint that you really need to take care of this.

4. **Choose String from the Attribute Type pop-up menu in the Attributes section of the Core Data Model inspector (or in the Attributes section of the Detail area), as shown in Figure 3-12.**

   You don't need to set any of the other values.

5. **Repeat Steps 1—3 to add attributes for**

   ```
   address
   comment
   displayOrder
   latitude
   location
   longitude
   name
   subtitle
   ```

   and

   ```
   title
   ```

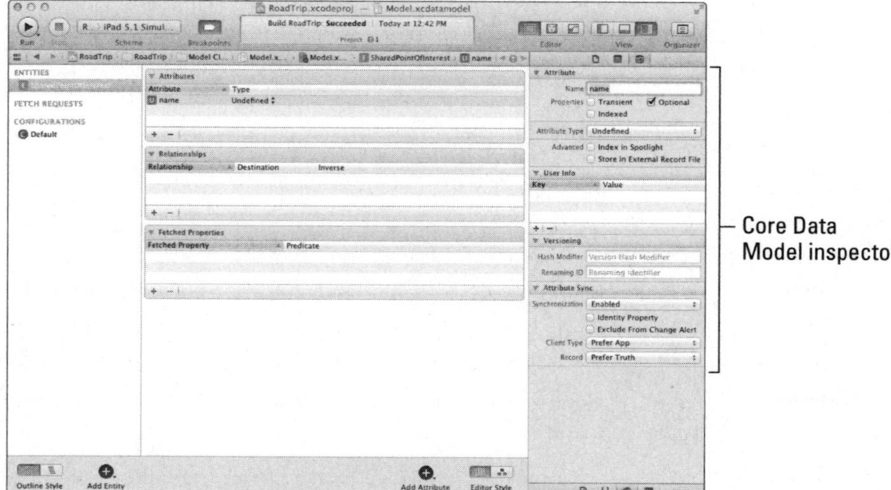

Figure 3-11: Setting the name.

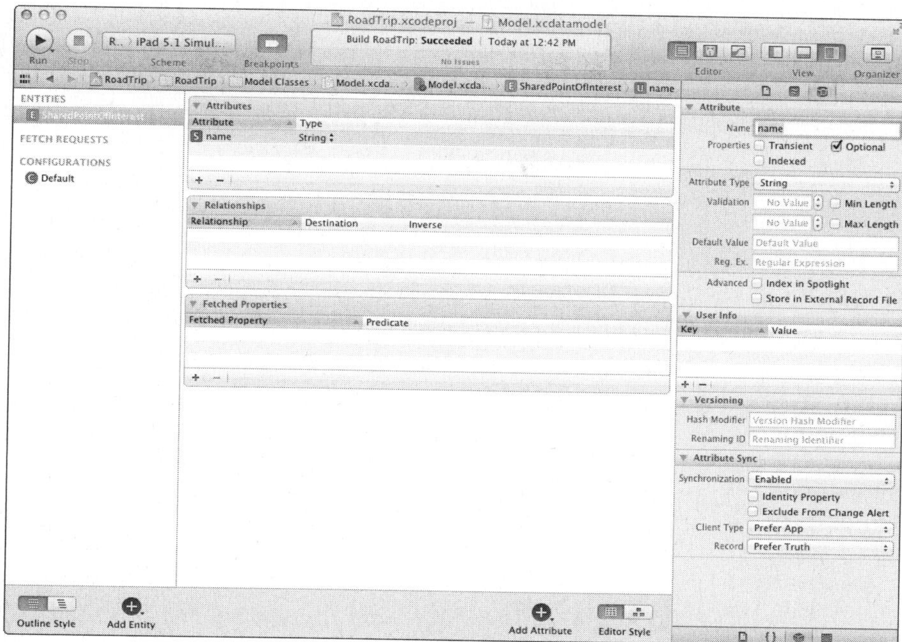

Figure 3-12: Setting the type.

All of them, except for `displayOrder` should be of type `String`. The `displayOrder` attribute should be of type `Integer 16`.

When you're done, your model should look like Figure 3-13.

Generating your classes

Of course, you still need the classes for your program. Remember, all you've done thus far is create a data model for Core Data to use to create, fetch, and save your `SharedPointOfInterest` objects. You still need the classes to describe them in your program.

Does that mean a lot of boring copying and pasting? Of course not. You can now use Xcode to generate the files for your `SharedPointOfInterest` class.

1. **Select `SharedPointOfInterest` in the Entities section and then choose Editor⇨Create NSManagedObject Subclass from the main menu.**
2. **In the dialog that appears (see Figure 3-14), select Model Classes from the Group drop-down menu and then click the Create button.**

   Core Data generates a class for you using the entity name as the class name and turning each of the attributes into properties.

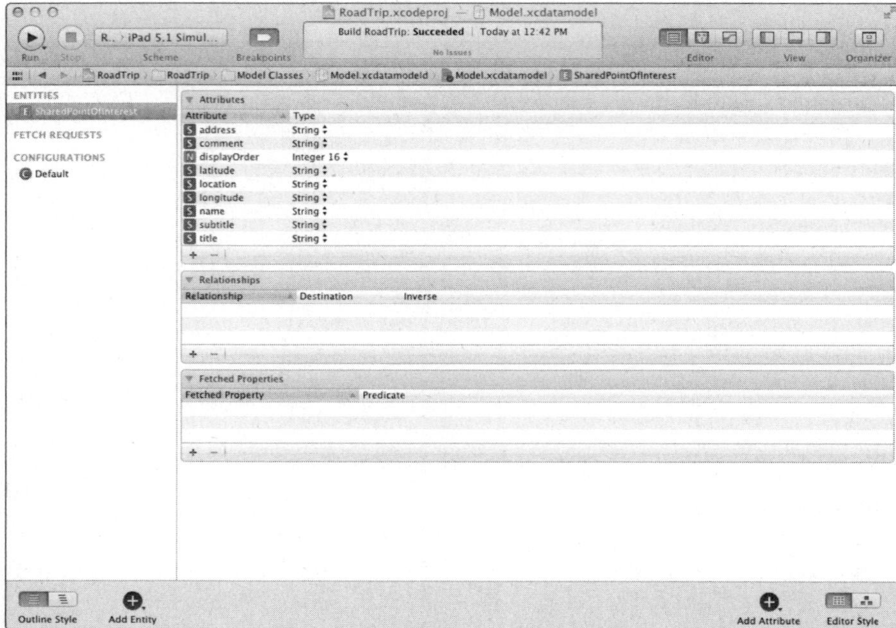

Figure 3-13: Your completed model.

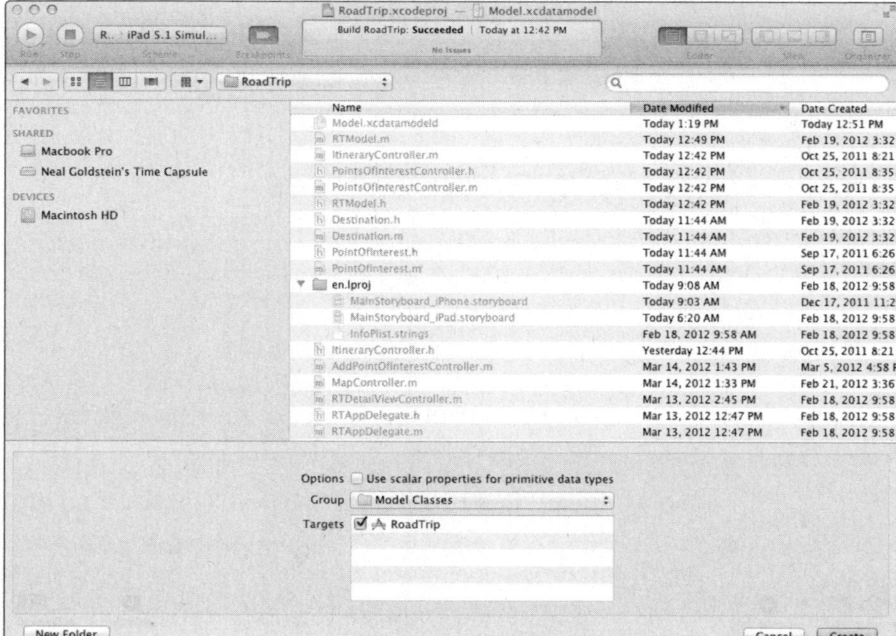

Figure 3-14: Creating a managed object class.

Although not a particular issue here, make sure that the Use Scalar Properties for Primitive Data Types check box is deselected — you want to be able to use objects (such as `NSNumber`) instead of single values (such as `int`). Note as well that you would have to also implement your own accessor methods if you selected this particular check box.

3. **Create a new Group in the Model Classes Group and move those classes in there.**

   See Figure 3-15, where I've selected the `SharedPointOfInterest` header file as well.

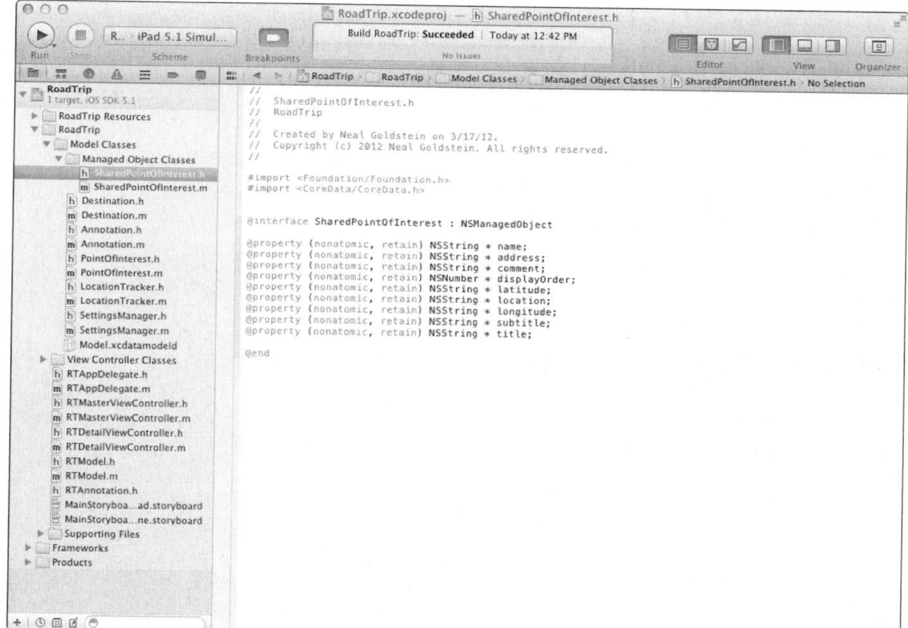

Figure 3-15: The generated managed object classes.

Take a look at Listings 3-2 and 3-3 which display the `.h` and `.m` files for `SharedPointOfInterest`

Listing 3-2: Generated SharedPointOfInterest.h Class File

```
#import <Foundation/Foundation.h>
#import <CoreData/CoreData.h>


@interface SharedPointOfInterest : NSManagedObject

@property (nonatomic, retain) NSString * name;
```

(continued)

Listing 3-2 *(continued)*

```
@property (nonatomic, retain) NSString * address;
@property (nonatomic, retain) NSString * comment;
@property (nonatomic, retain) NSNumber * displayOrder;
@property (nonatomic, retain) NSString * latitude;
@property (nonatomic, retain) NSString * location;
@property (nonatomic, retain) NSString * longitude;
@property (nonatomic, retain) NSString * subtitle;
@property (nonatomic, retain) NSString * title;

@end
```

Listing 3-3: Generated SharedPointOfInterest.m Class File

```
#import "SharedPointOfInterest.h"


@implementation SharedPointOfInterest

@dynamic name;
@dynamic address;
@dynamic comment;
@dynamic displayOrder;
@dynamic latitude;
@dynamic location;
@dynamic longitude;
@dynamic subtitle;
@dynamic title;

@end
```

You should take notice of a few things here:

- **The `SharedPointOfInterest` class is derived from `NSManagedObject`, not `NSObject`.** I explain that bit of business in the "Core Data Basics" section, earlier in the chapter.
- **In the implementation files, properties are implemented as `@dynamic`, not the usual `@synthesize`.** Core Data generates the accessor methods at runtime. `@dynamic` instructs the compiler not to generate a warning if it can't find implementations of accessor methods.
- **The model has been updated.** The `SharedPointOfInterest` entities are now `SharedPointOfInterest` classes instead of `NSManagedObject`. (You can double-check this by looking in the Core Data Model inspector in the Class field).

You also have to add a few things to `SharedPointOfInterest.h` if you want it to actually work in RoadTrip the way `PointOfInterest` does. Because each individual `SharedPointOfInterest` will appear on the map as an annotation, just as PointOfInterest does, you have to add a coordinate property. To do that, add the code in bold in Listing 3-4 to SharedPointOfInterest.h.

Listing 3-4: Updating the SharedPointOfInterest Interface

```
#import <Foundation/Foundation.h>
#import <CoreData/CoreData.h>
#import <MapKit/MapKit.h>

@interface SharedPointOfInterest : NSManagedObject

@property (nonatomic, retain) NSString * name;
@property (nonatomic, retain) NSString * address;
@property (nonatomic, retain) NSString * comment;
@property (nonatomic, retain) NSNumber * displayOrder;
@property (nonatomic, retain) NSString * latitude;
@property (nonatomic, retain) NSString * location;
@property (nonatomic, retain) NSString * longitude;
@property (nonatomic, retain) NSString * subtitle;
@property (nonatomic, retain) NSString * title;
@property (nonatomic, readwrite)
                          CLLocationCoordinate2D coordinate;

@end
```

The idea here is that you have to import the MapKit header so the compiler knows all about the CLLocationCoordinate2D type.

You also have a bit of work to do with SharedPointOfInterest.m. More specifically, you have to synthesize the accessor for the file's coordinate property. For good measure, I also have you add a get accessor. You have to override the accessor that will be synthesized for the coordinate property because you'll be creating the coordinate using the latitude and longitude properties. Adding the code in bold in Listing 3-5 to SharedPointOfInterest.m takes care of all that for you.

Listing 3-5: Synthesizing the New Accessor and Adding a Get Accessor

```
#import "SharedPointOfInterest.h"


@implementation SharedPointOfInterest

@dynamic name;
@dynamic address;
@dynamic comment;
@dynamic displayOrder;
@dynamic latitude;
```

(continued)

Listing 3-5 *(continued)*

```
@dynamic location;
@dynamic longitude;
@dynamic subtitle;
@dynamic title;
@synthesize coordinate;

- (CLLocationCoordinate2D) coordinate {

  CLLocationCoordinate2D theCoordinate;
  theCoordinate.latitude = [self.latitude doubleValue];
  theCoordinate.longitude = [self.longitude doubleValue];
  return theCoordinate;
}

@end
```

As I've mentioned a number of times, instead of being derived from `NSObject`, `SharedPointOfInterest` is derived from `NSManagedObject`. Read on to find out why `Managed` slipped its way between `NS` and `Object`.

Thinking managed objects through

`NSManagedObject` contains the methods and properties necessary to represent any entity. It has a reference to the entity description for the entity that it's an instance of — including the information in the entity description as well as its attributes and relationships descriptions. You can also create subclasses of `NSManagedObject` to implement additional behavior (as you just did with `SharedPointOfInterest`).

If you feel so inclined, you can think of a managed object as the object representation of a record in a table in a database. Each managed object represents the data you operate on in your application — in this case, `SharedPointOfInterest` objects and their associated data (name, location, and so on). You can even add in other properties (as you just did in Listing 3-5) and even methods. Just remember, though, that any properties you add will not be saved for you — to do that you would have to add the properties as attributes in the managed object model.

`NSManagedObject` connects your objects to the managed object context, as explained in the next section.

If you regenerate the classes because you made a change to the entity, all your work will be lost. If you need to regenerate, I suggest you rename the classes, generate the new ones, and then copy and paste your additions back in. (For more on this topic, see the "Generating your classes" section, earlier in this chapter.)

The Core Data Stack

After you've created the managed object model and generated your classes, you still need to set up what is known as the Core Data Stack in your application. This involves creating the following:

1. The `NSManagedObjectContext`
2. The `NSManagedObjectModel`
3. The `NSPersistentStoreCoordinator`

I run through the creation of each one of these in the next few sections, but quite frankly, for what you'll be doing in RoadTrip — and for quite a while in your own application — you'll probably be using the boilerplate I've provided.

The managed object context

Now that you have your Core Data managed object model as well as your classes, your next step is to create, save, and then restore your objects. (You can also implement Undos and Redos, although you won't be doing that in this book.)

Luckily for you, the `CoreData` framework provides most of this functionality for you automatically, primarily through a managed object context (or just plain context) object. Its primary responsibility is to manage a collection of managed objects. The managed object context is the way you'll use the Core Data objects that make up what's called the *persistence stack* — all the lower level plumbing objects that connect your object to its data. This is shown in Figure 3-16.

You add objects and remove objects using the managed object context. It tracks the changes you make, both to object attributes and to the relationships between objects. Because of that, the context is able to provide Undo and Redo support. It also ensures that if you change relationships between objects, the integrity of the relationship is maintained.

When you create a new managed object, you insert it into a context. You *fetch* existing records in the database into the context as managed objects. (I explain fetching in the next chapter when you actually put Core Data to work.)

In any application, you could have multiple managed object contexts. This would, for example, allow you to do things in one context in background while allowing the user to interact with objects in another context.

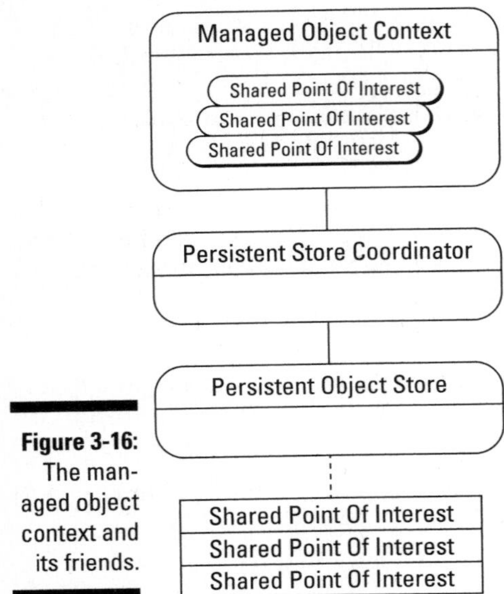

Figure 3-16: The managed object context and its friends.

When you fetch objects from a persistent store (I explain that next), you bring temporary copies into memory. You can then operate on these objects by changing their attributes and relationships and/or by adding and deleting objects. When you're done, you save the changes you've made, and the context ensures that your objects are in a valid state. Then the changes are written to the persistent store (or stores), new records are added (for objects you created), and records are removed (for objects you deleted). But unless you actually save those changes, the persistent store remains unchanged — persistent, isn't it?

The Persistent Store coordinator and persistent store

A Persistent Store coordinator (*persistent* here describes the store or file, not the coordinator) is an instance of `NSPersistentStoreCoordinator` and manages precisely what you'd think it would manage — a collection of *persistent object stores.* A persistent object store is simply an external store (file) of persisted data. The Persistent Store coordinator is the object that actually maps between objects in your application and records in the database. In iOS, you usually just have a single store, but in RoadTrip you'll have a separate store for each destination. (You could add all of them to a single store, but that could increase the iCloud overhead.) The Persistent Store coordinator manages these stores and makes them appear to the managed object contexts as a single store. (If you did have multiple managed object contexts, each of these would use the same coordinator.)

The Persistent Store coordinator handles the nitty gritty of reading and writing data files. You probably won't ever directly interact with the Persistent Store coordinator after you've specified the location of a new external data store to be associated with your application.

Adding the Core Data Stack

If you've been reading closely, you'll remember that I mention earlier that the Core Data Stack consists of the following:

1. The `NSManagedObjectContext`
2. The `NSManagedObjectModel`
3. The `NSPersistentStoreCoordinator`

Here's where I briefly explain the code in each of these puppies, although, as I mention earlier, for what you'll be doing in RoadTrip (and for quite a while in your own application), you'll probably just be using the boilerplate I'm about to provide.

I want to point out, though, that when you create a Master-Detail project, you can check a box in the "Choose Options for Your New Project" dialog and the stack will be generated for you. Note, however, that it gets generated in the `appDelegate` instead of in the model and you'll have to move it into the class you want to manage it.

Adding the properties needed by the Core Data stack

You're going to have to add some instance properties to the `RTModel.h` interface that will be used by the Core Data stack. It's a good idea to do that first to avoid a lot of compiler warnings/error messages. Make the modifications you see bolded in Listing 3-6 to `RTModel.h` to add the properties. When you're done with that, add the bolded code in Listing 3-7 to synthesize the accessors.

Listing 3-6: Adding the required Core Data properties to RTModel.h

```
#import <Foundation/Foundation.h>
#import <MapKit/MapKit.h>
#import <CoreData/CoreData.h>
@class Annotation;
@class PointOfInterest;

@interface RTModel : NSObject

+ (RTModel *)model;
- (id)initWithDestinationIndex:
                              (NSUInteger)destinationIndex;
- (void)loadItinerary;
- (NSArray *)returnItinerary;
- (void)addToItinerary:(PointOfInterest *)pointOfInterest;
- (void)removeFromItinerary:
                         (PointOfInterest *)pointOfInterest;
- (void)loadPointsOfInterest;
- (NSArray *)returnPointsOfInterest;
- (void)addPointOfInterest:
              (NSMutableDictionary *)pointOfInterestData;
- (UIImage *)destinationImage;
- (NSString *)destinationName;
- (CLLocationCoordinate2D)destinationCoordinate;
- (NSString *)weather;
- (void)loadEvents;
- (NSUInteger)numberOfEvents;
- (NSString *)getEvent:(NSUInteger)index;
- (NSArray *)returnPointsOfInterest;
- (NSString *)mapTitle;
- (NSArray *)createAnnotations;
- (void)addLocation:(NSString *)findLocation
    completionHandler:(void (^)(Annotation *annotation,
                              NSError* error)) completion;
- (CLLocation *)foundLocation;
+ (NSString *)filePath:(NSString *)fileComponent;
@property (readonly, strong, nonatomic)
            NSManagedObjectContext *managedObjectContext;
@property (readonly, strong, nonatomic)
                NSManagedObjectModel *managedObjectModel;
@property (readonly, strong, nonatomic)
 NSPersistentStoreCoordinator *persistentStoreCoordinator;

@end
```

Listing 3-7: Synthesizing the Accessors in RTModel.m

```
@implementation RTModel

@synthesize managedObjectContext = _managedObjectContext;
@synthesize managedObjectModel = _managedObjectModel;
@synthesize persistentStoreCoordinator =
                              _persistentStoreCoordinator;
```

Notice that the properties you just added are `readonly`. You do that because there is no reason for other objects to set those properties.

The managed object context

The managed object context does the creating, saving, and restoring of your objects for you. Listing 3-8 shows you the code for accessing the `managedObjectContext` property. It's actually an explicit implementation of the `managedObjectContext` property getter and is invoked every time you access the property.

`managedObjectContext` returns the `NSManagedObjectContext` for the application. If the context doesn't already exist, it's created and connected to the Persistent Store coordinator for the application — clever, isn't it?

Add the code in Listing 3-8 to `RTModel.m` to get `managedObjectContext` working for you.

Listing 3-8: Creating the managedObjectContext

```
- (NSManagedObjectContext *)managedObjectContext
{
  if (_managedObjectContext != nil) {
    return _managedObjectContext;
  }

  NSPersistentStoreCoordinator *coordinator =
                       [self persistentStoreCoordinator];

  if (coordinator != nil) {
    NSManagedObjectContext* managedObjectContext =
      [[NSManagedObjectContext alloc]
```

(continued)

Listing 3-8 *(continued)*

```
        initWithConcurrencyType:NSMainQueueConcurrencyType];

      [managedObjectContext performBlockAndWait:^{
        [managedObjectContext
                 setPersistentStoreCoordinator:
            coordinator];
      }];
      _managedObjectContext = managedObjectContext;
    }
    return _managedObjectContext;
  }
```

Listing 3-8 first gets the Persistent Store coordinator. Just as with the managed object context, if the Persistent Store coordinator hasn't been created yet, the getter method (which is added next in Listing 3-8) will add it for you.

```
  NSPersistentStoreCoordinator *coordinator =
                          [self persistentStoreCoordinator];

  if (coordinator != nil) {
```

Next in line in Listing 3-8, you create and initialize the `NSManagedObjectContext` using the Persistent Store coordinator:

```
     NSManagedObjectContext* managedObjectContext =
      [[NSManagedObjectContext alloc]
       initWithConcurrencyType:NSMainQueueConcurrencyType];

            [managedObjectContext performBlockAndWait:^{
       [managedObjectContext
                setPersistentStoreCoordinator: coordinator];
     }];
     _managedObjectContext = managedObjectContext;
   }
   return _managedObjectContext;
 }
```

I am going to have you use the new `NSManagedObjectContext` concurrency API. As you can see, you'll be using the `NSMainQueueConcurrencyType` because you'll be interacting with RoadTrip objects that are all running on the main thread.

Wait a second . . . unless you already understand concurrency in iOS (or OS X), you probably have no idea what I'm talking about. Maybe it's time for me to introduce you to concurrency in iOS?

Concurrency support for managed object contexts

Over the years, chip manufacturers have been adding more processor cores on each chip as part of their never-ending search for increased chip performance. But to take advantage of multiple cores, a computer needs software that can do multiple things simultaneously. Although that already does happen in modern multitasking operating systems (for system daemons or system background applications, for example), taking full advantage of multiple cores requires that individual applications use them as well.

In the past, the traditional way for an application to use multiple cores is to use multiple *threads*. Each application within iOS is made up of one or more threads, each of which represents a single path of execution through the application's code. Every application starts with a single thread, which runs the application's main function. The main thread encompasses the application's main run loop, and it's where the `NSApplication` object receives events. Applications can add (or *spawn* in tech lingo) additional threads, each of which executes the code you specify.

Threads, then, are simply a unit or stream of execution — an ordered sequence of instructions (some of your code). As I said, your program usually will be running on the *main* thread, but you can specify that pieces of your program (blocks of code) should run on other threads (which can be on other cores) — which results in doing more than one thing at once. However, there are some problems with actually implementing threads in a program — problems that are beyond the scope of this book.

Fortunately, in iOS (and OS X), rather than creating threads directly, all you have to do is define the task (in a block object) you want performed on a separate thread and tell the system to perform it. You do this by specifying a dispatch queue — a structure that manages the tasks you submit to it. There are three types of dispatch queues in iOS: Serial, Concurrent, and the Main Dispatch Queue. All three are first in, first out (i.e., first come first served), but with each one executing a task in a particular way. (The particularities, again, are out of scope for this book.) Trust me, though; dispatch queues provide a much simpler (and more efficient) programming model.

So why should you care?

Well if you run everything on the main thread, as most apps do in iOS, a task has to complete before the next task can start. And if the task that's running takes a long time to complete — such as downloading to your iPhone from iCloud the itinerary you created on your iPad — everything stops until that data is downloaded, which means the user can't do anything else with your application.

Threading has always been a part of Core Data, but the new concurrent Core Data model makes threading much easier. In the past, if you wanted to create multiple managed object contexts on different threads (to keep the user interface responsive while Core Data is executing a long running task, for example), you had to do all the work yourself. Now, all you have to do is associate a managed object context with a queue. Instead of *you* creating and managing a thread or queue, the *managed object context* manages all the details for you. But in the case of RoadTrip and other applications which use only a single managed object context on the main thread, you can also use threading to download the persistent store on a different thread, so the user can continue to interact with the app while the download (spun off on a different thread) happens. Of course, if the user actually wants to look at the itinerary, he or she has to wait for the download to complete (and handling that situation is elegantly managed by Core Data, as you see later), but that doesn't limit the user from doing other things in your app while waiting for the download to complete.

The Core Data `initWithConcurrencyType:` method from Listing 3-8 creates the managed object context in background, associating it with a queue you specify.

```
NSManagedObjectContext* managedObjectContext =
  [[NSManagedObjectContext alloc]
   initWithConcurrencyType:NSMainQueueConcurrencyType];
```

Queues, as I mention earlier, are beyond the scope of this book, but the queue you'll be using — `NSMainQueueConcurrencyType` — executes tasks on the application's main thread (where it will be used). You create RoadTrip's managed object context on the main thread because that enables you to link to your program objects (such as the model and view controllers) that are also running on that thread.

Making your way further down Listing 3-8, you see that the `performBlock AndWait:` block method sends the message to the managed object context that you want to set the Persistent Store coordinator:

```
[managedObjectContext performBlockAndWait:^{
  [managedObjectContext
             setPersistentStoreCoordinator: coordinator];
    }];
```

Using the `performBlockAndWait:` method, the managed object context executes the block on its own thread; the main thread in this case, but it could be a different thread if you were, for example, using multiple managed object contexts. The `performBlockAndWait:` method ensures that the messages you send to the managed object context are executed on the same thread as the managed object context itself. These messages include things like setting the Persistent Store coordinator as well as the post initialization that you will do later for iCloud. (Using the `performBlockAndWait:` method isn't really necessary here, because you'll be working on the main thread, but it's good to understand this more general form.)

The Persistent Store coordinator

Listing 3-9 shows the code for accessing the `persistentStoreCoordinator` property. It, too, is an explicit implementation of a getter, in this case of the `persistentStoreCoordinator` property getter which is invoked every time you access the property. Add it to `RTModel.m`.

It returns the `NSPersistentStoreCoordinator` for the application. If the coordinator doesn't already exist, it's created, and the application's store is added to it.

Listing 3-9: Creating the persistentStoreCoordinator

```
- (NSPersistentStoreCoordinator *)
                              persistentStoreCoordinator {

  if (_persistentStoreCoordinator != nil) {
    return _persistentStoreCoordinator;
  }
  _persistentStoreCoordinator =
   [[NSPersistentStoreCoordinator alloc]
    initWithManagedObjectModel:[self managedObjectModel]];

  RTAppDelegate *appDelegate =
            [[UIApplication sharedApplication] delegate];
  NSString *storePathComponent =
   [NSString stringWithFormat:@"%@%@%@",@"Model",
          appDelegate.destinationPreference, @".sqlite"];
  NSString *storePath = [RTModel
                             filePath:storePathComponent];
  dispatch_async(dispatch_get_global_queue(
                 DISPATCH_QUEUE_PRIORITY_DEFAULT, 0), ^{
    NSURL *storeUrl = [NSURL fileURLWithPath:storePath];
    NSDictionary* options = nil;
     NSError *error = nil;

    [_persistentStoreCoordinator lock];
    if (![_persistentStoreCoordinator
```

(continued)

Listing 3-9 *(continued)*

```
      addPersistentStoreWithType:NSSQLiteStoreType
       configuration:nil URL:storeUrl options:options
                                    error:&error]) {
      NSString *errorMessage = [error
                                 localizedDescription];
           UIAlertView *alertView = [[UIAlertView alloc]

          initWithTitle:@"Error in accessing your
            itinerary. Restart Road Trip and contact
            customer support if it continues."
          message:errorMessage delegate:nil
          cancelButtonTitle:@"OK"
          otherButtonTitles:nil];
      [alertView show];
      NSLog(@"Core Data Failure! Error code: %u,
          description: %@, and reason: %@", error.code,
           [error localizedDescription],
           [error localizedFailureReason]);
      return;
    }
    [_persistentStoreCoordinator unlock];
    dispatch_async(dispatch_get_main_queue(), ^{
      NSLog(@"Persistent store added");
      [[NSNotificationCenter defaultCenter]
        postNotificationName:@"PersistentStoreAdded"
                        object:self userInfo:nil];

    });
  });
  return _persistentStoreCoordinator;
}
```

This method returns the `NSPersistentStoreCoordinator` for the application. If the coordinator doesn't already exist, it's created, and the application's store is added to it.

```
if (_persistentStoreCoordinator != nil) {
    return _persistentStoreCoordinator;
  }
```

Although it's true that you're going to add the persistent store in background, you're actually going to create and assign the Persistent Store coordinator to `persistentStoreCoordinator` property *before* you add the persistent store proper. That's because in Core Data you can create the `NSManagedObjectContext` and fetch requests even if the Persistent Store coordinator doesn't (yet) have a store. In that case, a fetch request just returns an empty array. For example, the user may see an empty list when she initially taps the

Itinerary button. Creating and assigning the Persistent Store coordinator to the persistentStoreCoordinator property *before* you add the persistent store allows you, however, to bring up the user interface, which will require you to notify the view controllers when the persistent store is there so that they can tell their views to refresh themselves. That means that, as soon as the persistent store is created, the list will be refreshed, and the user will see her itinerary.

As I've stressed a number of times, doing things in background will be important when you implement iCloud, because any synchronizations or downloads can take some time.

```
_persistentStoreCoordinator =
  [[NSPersistentStoreCoordinator alloc]
   initWithManagedObjectModel: [self managedObjectModel]];
```

After creating and assigning the Persistent Store coordinator to persistent StoreCoordinator property, you need to create the path to the persistent store. You'll have to do that *before* you dispatch the task that will asynchronously (on another thread) create the persistent store, because NSBundle is not *thread safe* — meaning NSBundle can be used from any thread, but just one thread at a time (so use it from the main thread). (Code is thread safe when it can be executed simultaneously on multiple threads. This includes access to the same data and making sure when necessary — during an update, for example — a piece of data is accessed by only one thread at any given time.) Your path-creating goes as follows:

```
RTAppDelegate *appDelegate =
            [[UIApplication sharedApplication] delegate];
NSString *storePathComponent =
  [NSString stringWithFormat:@"%@%@%@",@"Model",
          appDelegate.destinationPreference, @".sqlite"];
NSString *storePath =
                   [RTModel filePath:storePathComponent];
```

Notice that I'm creating a separate Persistent Store path for each destination and hence a separate persistent store. I could have, of course, added an attribute that specified which destination an itinerary was attached to, but doing it this way allows me to show you how to create multiple persistent stores, and it makes the code simpler.

Notice here that the persistent store uses SQLite as its store. You can use other file formats if you like, but just be sure not to make any assumptions about the store. Core Data supports a number of file formats; if you don't make any assumptions about what the current format is, then you can change store implementation without causing all sorts of problems in your app.

Next, you create the persistent store on another thread for the simple reason that, if you're using iCloud and this is the first time this device is syncing with existing iCloud content, it may take a long, long time to download. While it's not important in RoadTrip the way it stands now (unless you are using iCloud), it could become a real issue as your application grows. So you might as well take care of business now.

```
dispatch_async(dispatch_get_global_queue
                (DISPATCH_QUEUE_PRIORITY_DEFAULT, 0), ^{
```

`dispatch_async` tells iOS to run this task in background using the global dispatch queue.

`dispatch_get_global_queue` returns a global concurrent queue of a given priority level. The queue has been created for you by Grand Central Dispatch, which implements the concurrency model I explain in the "Concurrency support for managed object contexts" section, earlier in the chapter. Grand Central Dispatch actually creates three queues for you:

> DISPATCH_QUEUE_PRIORITY_HIGH, DISPATCH_QUEUE_PRIORITY_DEFAULT, and DISPATCH_QUEUE_PRIORITY_LOW.

DISPATCH_QUEUE_PRIORITY_DEFAULT is the priority of the queue you want.

In order to run something on a separate thread, all you need to do is tell the system to do it (as you just did) and pass in a block with the task to run. In this case, the block is as follows:

```
^{
    NSURL *storeUrl = [NSURL fileURLWithPath:storePath];
    NSDictionary* options = nil;
    NSError *error = nil;

    [_persistentStoreCoordinator lock];
    if (![_persistentStoreCoordinator
      addPersistentStoreWithType:NSSQLiteStoreType
        configuration:nil URL:storeUrl options:options
                                      error:&error]) {
      NSString *errorMessage = [error
                                 localizedDescription];
      UIAlertView *alertView = [[UIAlertView alloc]
         initWithTitle:@"Error in accessing your
           itinerary. Restart Road Trip and contact
           customer support if the error continues."
         message:errorMessage delegate:nil
          cancelButtonTitle:@"OK" otherButtonTitles:nil];
     [alertView show];
```

```
        NSLog(@"Core Data Failure! Error code: %u,
            description: %@, reason: %@, recovery: %@",
            error.code, [error localizedDescription],
            [error localizedFailureReason],
            [error localizedRecoverySuggestion]);
    }
    [_persistentStoreCoordinator unlock];
    _persistentStoreCoordinator _async(dispatch_get_main_
            queue(), ^{
        NSLog(@"Persistent store added");
        [[NSNotificationCenter defaultCenter]
          postNotificationName:@"RefetchAllDatabaseData"
                                    object:self userInfo:nil];
    });
});
```

The first thing you do in this block is lock the Persistent Store coordinator, giving you exclusive access and ensuring no changes will be made to it while you're working with it. The `lock` method will keep your new thread from executing until the Persistent Store coordinator can be locked — meaning it can't be changed by another object.

```
[_persistentStoreCoordinator lock];
```

Then you add the persistent store

```
if (![_persistentStoreCoordinator
  addPersistentStoreWithType:NSSQLiteStoreType
    configuration:nil URL:storeUrl options:options
                                        error:&error]) {
```

Again, you're adding an `SQLLite` store, but as I mention earlier, Core Data supports several other file types (such as `NSBinaryStoreType` and `InMemoryStoreType`) as well as custom types. (`configuration` is used when you want to store different entities in different stores with a given Store coordinator and is beyond the scope of this book.)

`options` is a dictionary, and you won't need that until you start working with iCloud in Chapter 5.

Notice the error checking :

```
if (![psc addPersistentStoreWithType:NSSQLiteStoreType
  configuration:nil URL:storeUrl options:options
                                        error:&error]) {
```

You'll see this particular error (in addition to when the store is not accessible) when the schema for the persistent store is incompatible with current managed object model. That happens when you change the managed object model (which happens frequently during development) and either don't migrate to the new one (out of scope for this book) or delete the old one and start from scratch.

The current code merely posts an alert and logs the error. You'll want to go beyond merely posting an alert and logging the error in a shipping application by providing recovery options or retrying if that's possible.

```
NSString *errorMessage = [error localizedDescription];
UIAlertView *alertView = [[UIAlertView alloc]
  initWithTitle:@"Error in accessing your itinerary.
          Restart Road Trip and contact customer support
          if the error continues."
  message:errorMessage delegate:nil
  cancelButtonTitle:@"OK" otherButtonTitles:nil];
[alertView show];
NSLog(@"Core Data Failure! Error code: %u, description:
  %@, reason: %@, recovery: %@", error.code,
  [error localizedDescription],
  [error localizedFailureReason],
  [error localizedRecoverySuggestion]);
NSLog(@"Unresolved error %@, %@", error,
                                        [error userInfo]);
```

Then you unlock the Persistent Store coordinator.

```
  [_persistentStoreCoordinator unlock];
```

Finally, now that the persistent store has been added, you need to tell the view controllers (and the model) on the main thread that they can now load their data. But because you're doing all your executing on a different thread, you need to post that info on the main thread.

```
dispatch_async(dispatch_get_main_queue(), ^{
  NSLog(@"Persistent store added");
  [[NSNotificationCenter defaultCenter]
    postNotificationName:@"RefetchAllDatabaseData"
                             object:self userInfo:nil];
```

You post a notification that — as you'll soon see — may be subscribed to by RoadTrip objects. (I cover this in the next chapter, but you can guess what they are.) You need this because in Core Data you can create the `NSManagedObjectContext` and fetch requests even when the Persistent Store controller has no persistent store. (Again, setting it up this way allows you to bring up the user interface even when a RoadTrip user hasn't entered anything yet for the itinerary.)

Until you actually have a persistent store, fetch requests are going to return empty arrays. After the persistent store gets added, you'll be broadcasting that fact through the notification center so RoadTrip knows that the data should be refetched and will be displayable by the views.

Creating the persistent store synchronously

If you don't want to bother with creating the persistent store asynchronously (if you aren't even going to use iCloud, for example), you can get the code to do that by creating an application in Xcode using the Master-Detail template and selecting Use Core Data. You can then examine the generated code, which creates the store synchronously — it will look kind of like this:

```
- (NSPersistentStoreCoordinator *) persistentStoreCoordinator
{
    if (__persistentStoreCoordinator != nil) {
        return __persistentStoreCoordinator;
    }

    NSURL *storeURL =
      [[self applicationDocumentsDirectory]
                    URLByAppendingPathComponent:@"cdsynch.
  sqlite"];

    NSError *error = nil;
    __persistentStoreCoordinator =
       [[NSPersistentStoreCoordinator alloc]
             initWithManagedObjectModel:[self
  managedObjectModel]];
    if (![__persistentStoreCoordinator
       addPersistentStoreWithType:NSSQLiteStoreType
         configuration:nil URL:storeURL options:nil
  error:&error]) {
        /*
         Replace this implementation with code to handle the
  error
         appropriately.
        */
    }

    return __persistentStoreCoordinator;
}
```

I'd like to point out one other thing — the RTModel filePath class method. This class method simply creates the file path for you. (I got tired of the repetitious code, so I added this method, and it's used throughout the app.)

```
#pragma mark - Create the file path

+ (NSString *)filePath:(NSString *)fileComponent {

  return [[NSSearchPathForDirectoriesInDomains
   (NSDocumentDirectory, NSUserDomainMask, YES)
      lastObject] stringByAppendingPathComponent:
                                          fileComponent];
}
```

If you're an eagle-eyed reader, you might have noticed that the Persistent Store coordinator uses the managedObjectModel property:

```
_persistentStoreCoordinator =
   [[NSPersistentStoreCoordinator alloc]
    initWithManagedObjectModel:[self managedObjectModel]];
```

It's time now to take a closer look at this property and the managed object model behind it.

The managed object model

As I explain in the "Starting with the Objects — The Managed Object Model" section, earlier in this chapter, the managed object model describes the *entities* (objects) your application uses and the relationships between them.

Listing 3-10 shows you the code for accessing the managedObjectModel property. This code, like Listing 3-8 and Listing 3-9 before it, is an explicit implementation of the managedObjectModel property getter and is invoked every time you access the property — when you create the Persistent Store coordinator, for example. Add it to RTModel.m.

It returns the managed object model for the application. If the model doesn't already exist, it's created from the application's model (the one you created and named in the "Starting with the Objects — the Managed Object Model" section).

Listing 3-10: Creating the managedObjectModel

```
- (NSManagedObjectModel *)managedObjectModel
{
  if (_managedObjectModel != nil) {
    return _managedObjectModel;
  }

  NSURL *modelURL = [[NSBundle mainBundle]
          URLForResource:@"Model" withExtension:@"momd"];
  _managedObjectModel = [[NSManagedObjectModel alloc]
                       initWithContentsOfURL:modelURL];
  return _managedObjectModel;
}
```

There really isn't much going on here, other than the fact that you're creating a managed object model. The only thing you're wondering is, although you probably recognize the name `Model`, what's up with this `momd` extension business? In the Project navigator, notice that the extension stands revealed as the (relatively more straightforward) `xcdatamodel`. So why the name change?

When the data model is compiled (using the model compiler, `momc`), extraneous elements such as its layout are removed, and an `xcdatamodel` "source" directory is compiled into a `momd` deployment directory. In a model that supports versioning, as this one does, such a directory groups different versions of the model, each represented by an individual `.xcdatamodel` file, into one bundle. After you have all the versions tied together into one neat package, you load this particular `.momd` model bundle using the `initWithContentsOfURL:` method of `NSManagedObjectModel`.

Notifications

With RoadTrip — and with any app with any degree of complexity — it's often necessary to know that a certain kind of event has occurred. A `PointOfInterest` may be added to an `Itinerary`, or a `PointOfInterest` removed from the `PointsOfInterest` list, which means the view displaying the `Itinerary` or `PointsOfInterest` list would need to redraw itself using the newly updated data. In terms of the discussion in this chapter, you want to know when the persistent store has been downloaded, and it's now time for all those views that display data associated with that persistent store to go ahead and redraw themselves.

One way to send information to an object is by sending a message. Another way is by having the object become a delegate. Both of these methods require that the sender know all about the observer, which naturally increases the coupling in the system. Instead of going that route, you can use the *Notification Center* object (an `NSNotificationCenter`) which will broadcast information within a program, thereby decoupling the sender and the observer and making for a more flexible system. Every iOS application has a default Notification Center — all you have to do is use it.

The `UIKit` and `Foundation` frameworks make extensive use of notifications, and I suggest you explore this on your own. (You can usually find a listing of the notifications that a framework class posts in the Notifications section of its Class reference documentation.)

The beauty of the Notification Center is that any object can use it to post a notification and objects can register themselves with the Notification Center as observers so they receive notifications whenever they get posted. And this is what RoadTrip has done. Now, when a persistent store gets added, the Persistent Store coordinator posts a notification. (The `NSLog` is for your information.) The relevant code — shown here — can be found in Listing 3-9.

```
dispatch_async(dispatch_get_main_queue(), ^{
  NSLog(@"Persistent store added");
  [[NSNotificationCenter defaultCenter]
    postNotificationName:@"RefetchAllDatabaseData"
                              object:self userInfo:nil];
```

In a multithreaded application, notifications are always delivered in the thread in which the notification was posted — which may not necessarily be the same thread in which an observer registered itself. So the Persistent Store coordinator needs to post it on the main thread as well to ensure that it will be delivered on the main thread where the RoadTrip objects live.

```
dispatch_async(dispatch_get_main_queue(),
```

As for the syntax to use, posting a notification includes the notification name (`RefetchAllDatabaseData`), the object that is doing the posting (`self`), and an optional user information dictionary (`nil` in this case).

```
[[NSNotificationCenter defaultCenter]
    postNotificationName:@"RefetchAllDatabaseData"
                              object:self userInfo:nil];
```

To get a notification, an object registers with the Notification Center. You'll see an example of that in Chapter 4, when you have the `RTModel` register for the `RefetchAllDatabaseData` notification by doing the following:

```
__block __weak RTModel *weakSelf = self;

[[NSNotificationCenter defaultCenter]
  addObserverForName:@"PersistentStoreAdded" object:self
          queue:nil usingBlock:^(NSNotification *notif) {
  [weakSelf loadItinerary];
  [weakSelf loadPointsOfInterest];
  [[NSNotificationCenter defaultCenter] postNotificationNa
          me:@"DestinationChanged"
                          object:weakSelf userInfo:nil];
  }];
```

I know the declaration and references to _weakSelf look a bit odd — it has to do with how Automatic Reference Counting (ARC) handles references from within blocks. Let me explain notifications first and I'll get to that particular oddity.

addObserverForName:object:queue:usingBlock: is an NSNotificationCenter instance method that adds a block that is passed in as an argument. When the notification is posted, the block is added to the operation queue you specify to be executed — if you specify nil, the block is run synchronously on the posting thread.

The object parameter is the object whose notifications you want to register for. If you specify nil, the Notification Center will execute the block for any object that posts a notification with that name.

When the block is executed, the optional user information dictionary that is sent by the object that posts the notification is passed into the block as an argument.

```
^(NSNotification *notif) {
```

An object that registers for a notification needs to remove itself as an observer before it is de-allocated . For example, in RTDetailViewController — the base class for the view controllers in RoadTrip — that is done in the dealloc method:

```
-(void) dealloc {

  [[NSNotificationCenter defaultCenter]
                              removeObserver:self];
}
```

ARC and blocks

Although not explicitly explained in Apple's Transitioning to ARC Release Notes, there is a subtlety if you are using blocks and you refer to objects outside that block. While the whole topic really is outside of the scope of this book, I want to examine it because it has, in the past, caused me hours of pain, and I'll make a long boring story into a short boring one.

When you use a block, it has to be retained in order to be used later — think of it as becoming an object. All fine and good and when it is doing its thing it can be released. If, however, (and this is a big *however*) it needs to use something in the object within which it is declared (like `self` — the `RTModel` — to send the `loadItinerary` message above) then that object will also have to be retained. Whoops! This is known as the retain or reference cycle. I can't delete the `RTModel` because it is being retained by the block.

The solution is not to use `self` inside the block. To do that I define a `__block` variable

```
__block weak RTModel *weakSelf = self;
```

`weakSelf` is the same value as `self` — a reference to the `RTModel` — and since it has the `__block` storage type (which means it can be modified by the block) the `RTModel` will be retained so the block can use `weakSelf`. Once the block completes, however, it sets `weakSelf` to `nil` and both the `RTModel` and the block can be released.

`weakSelf` is the same value as `self` — a reference to the `RTModel` — and since it has the `__block` storage type (which means it can be modified by the block) the `RTModel` will be retained so the block can use `weakSelf`. Since the `weakSelf` variable has a weak pointer (has the `__weak` storage type) to the `RTModel`, however, once the block completes, both the `RTModel` and the block can be released.

There is actually, an easier way to deal with this in notifications. While I really like blocks, and use them whenever I can, you can also take advantage of notification without using blocks. For example, in Chapter 4 the `ItineraryController` adds itself as an observer for the `ItineraryChanged` notification in the following way:

```
[[NSNotificationCenter defaultCenter] addObserver:self
  selector:@selector(itineraryChanged:)
                     name:@"ItineraryChanged" object:nil];
```

`addObserver:selector:name:object:` is virtually identical to `addObserverForName:object:queue:usingBlock:` except you pass in a selector which does the same thing as the block.

```
- (void)itineraryChanged:(NSNotification *) notif {

  [self.itineraryTableView reloadData];
}
```

The only disadvantage here is that the selector can't use the originating method's local variables, which is not a problem in this particular case. So even though I prefer blocks, as you look through the code you'll see mostly the selector rather than block implementation of notifications

Adding the Core Data framework

Okay, you have a Core Data Stack, which — admit it — didn't require much heavy lifting. But to be able to actually use Core Data, you'll have to add the `CoreData` framework.

1. **In the Project navigator, select the Project icon (in this case, RoadTrip) at the top of the Project Navigator content area to display the Project editor.**
2. **In the TARGETS section in the Project editor, select RoadTrip.**
3. **In the Summary tab, scroll down to the Linked Frameworks and Libraries section.**
4. **Expand the Linked Frameworks and Libraries section (if it isn't already expanded) by clicking the disclosure triangle, as shown in Figure 3-17.**
5. **Click the + (plus sign) button underneath the list of current project frameworks.**

   A list of frameworks appears.
6. **Scroll down the list and select CoreData Framework, as shown in Figure 3-18.**
7. **Click the Add button.**

   You see the framework added to the Linked Frameworks and Libraries section.
8. **Click the disclosure triangle yet again to close the Linked Frameworks and Libraries section.**
9. **In the Project navigator (don't do this from the Linked Frameworks and Libraries section!), drag the `CoreData.framework` file to the Frameworks group to get it out of the way.**

You can also add a framework by clicking the Build Phases tab in the Project editor, expanding the Link Binary with Libraries section, and following the same procedure.

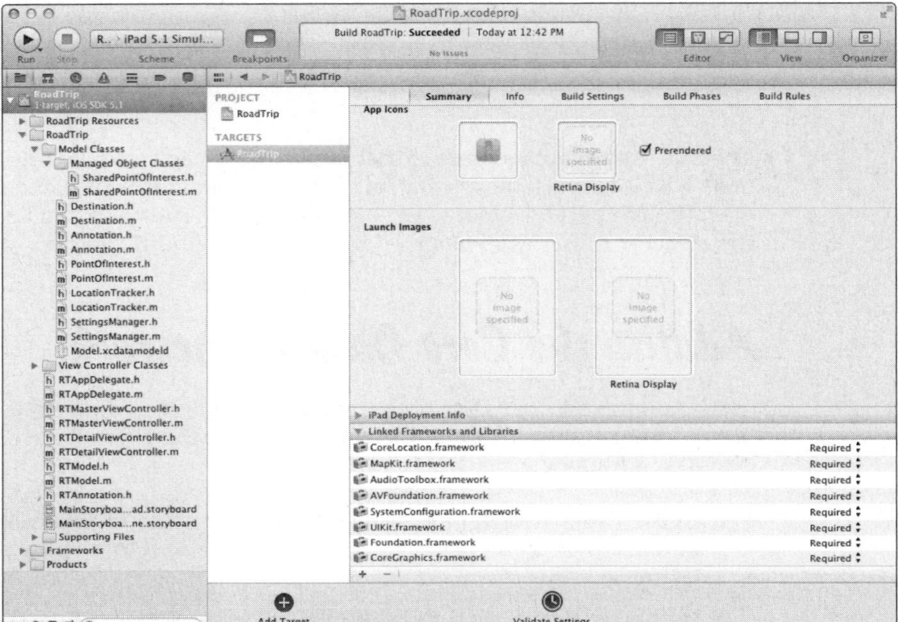

Figure 3-17: Adding a framework.

Figure 3-18: Adding a new framework.

You're now ready to actually use Core Data. Your project should compile and execute with no errors.

Putting Core Data to Work

At this point, you have what you need to start using Core Data. In the next chapter, you do just that by using Core Data to create, manage, and save `SharedPointOfInterest` objects which will make up your itinerary.

Chapter 4

Putting Core Data to Work

In This Chapter

- Using Core Data
- Figuring out fetch requests
- Adding, saving, and loading SharedPointOfInterest objects with Core Data

Chapter 3 is all about setting up Core Data. This chapter shows you how you can now use Core Data to manage your itinerary. Here, you move RoadTrip away from saving your itinerary in a file (the old way to do things) to storing it in Core Data (the new way to do things). Along the way, I have you add a new feature for displaying your data — displaying the points of interest in your itinerary by location. Actually, Core Data makes this little trick really easy, so it's not much to brag about.

The image on the left in Figure 4-1 shows you the way it works now. You can see that the pre-Core Data RoadTrip allows you to create (and save) an itinerary — the places you'd like to go. After Core Data, you can see from the middle image in Figure 4-1 that I've added a nice location heading to the itinerary. While that is certainly stylish, the real change occurs under the covers. All those itinerary objects that actually contain the information about each point of interest in my itinerary are now managed by Core Data.

You may think that making a change like that could bend your established code out of shape, but it turns out that the decision to update the model implementation to use Core Data doesn't bring with it a whole set of messy repercussions. Because I've been pretty obsessive all along about encapsulating all content-based functionality in a loosely coupled model, the changes you'll need to make to `ItineraryController` will be minor and transparent to `MapController`, which — as you can see from the image on the right in Figure 4-1 — actually takes all of those points of interest and plots them on a map.

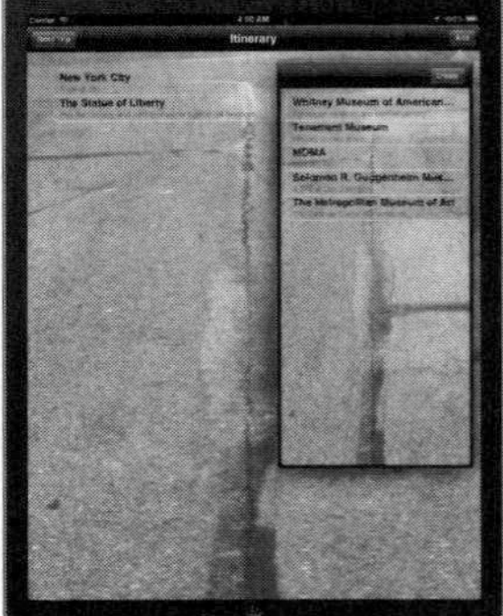

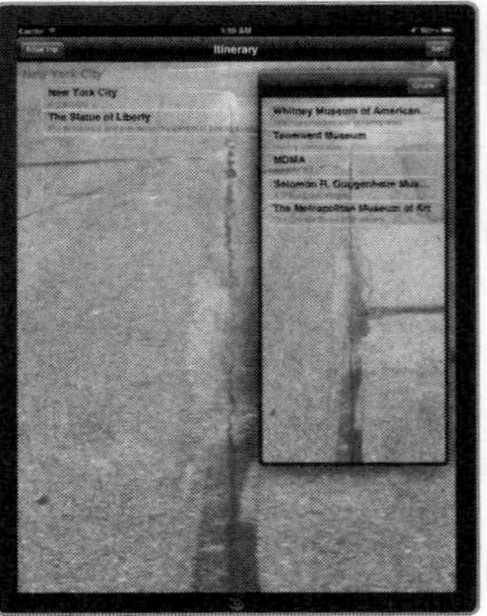

Figure 4-1: Your itinerary before and after Core Data.

Okay, nice overview, but how does that actually work?

In this chapter, I start off by explaining how this works in the old school version of RoadTrip — the pre–Core Data one. Now, I don't necessarily go into excruciating detail, especially when you're going to replace the current implementation with one that uses Core Data, but you get the general outline. After that, I highlight the changes you need to make to the old version of RoadTrip for it to handle the new way of doing things.

Core Data has a lot to it — enough to write a book about — so I can't explain everything. I do, however, make suggestions for things you might want to explore on your own.

As I mention in Chapter 2, the RoadTrip application is a bit complex. That's kind of the point. I want to show you how to use iCloud and web services in the context of a real application, and by using RoadTrip in particular, I can also illustrate some of the issues that arise when dealing with a more complex application (like the ones you're likely to build). On the other hand, I've architected the app by obsessively making sure the model is loosely coupled, making it easier to evolve, and also much easier for you to follow. As a result, it turns out (as it should) that all the changes you'll be making in order to incorporate Core Data and iCloud capabilities are limited to two classes — `RTModel` and `ItineraryController`.

Adding a Point of Interest to the Itinerary

In the RoadTrip application, the `PointsOfInterestController` is what's behind the display of `PointOfInterest` objects in the list you saw in the popover back in 4-1.These `PointOfInterest` objects are created by the

RTModel — initially from the RoadTrip's Destinations.plist file — and stored in the PointsOfInterest array. The PointsOfInterest array is accessed by the PointsOfInterestController using its pointsOf Interest instance variable.

When the user selects a row in the PointsOfInterestController's Table view, as shown back in Figure 4-1, the PointsOfInterestController tableView:didSelectRowAtIndexPath: method sends the addToItinerary:objectAtIndex: message to the RTModel, as you can see in Listing 4-1.

Listing 4-1: The User Selects a Point of Interest to Add to His Itinerary

```
- (void)tableView:(UITableView *)tableView
        didSelectRowAtIndexPath:(NSIndexPath *)indexPath
{
  [tableView deselectRowAtIndexPath:
                                   indexPath animated:YES];

  [[RTModel model] addToItinerary:
        [pointsOfInterest objectAtIndex:indexPath.row]];
}
```

The PointsOfInterestController deselects the row and then sends the RTModel the addToItinerary:objectAtIndex: message to add the selected point of interest to the itinerary.

In the RTModel's addToItinerary:objectAtIndex: method, shown in Listing 4-2, the selected point of interest is added to the itinerary array. The returnPointOfInterestData method returns the object's data in a dictionary, which is added to the itineraryData array and then saved to the file system.

Listing 4-2: Adding to the Itinerary

```
- (void)addToItinerary:
                   (PointOfInterest *)pointOfInterest {

  [itinerary addObject:pointOfInterest];
  [pointsOfInterest removeObject:pointOfInterest];

  [itineraryData addObject:
          [pointOfInterest returnPointOfInterestData]];
  RTAppDelegate *appDelegate =
          [[UIApplication sharedApplication] delegate];
  NSString *fileComponent = [NSString
        stringWithFormat:@"%@%@%@", @"Itinerary",
        appDelegate.destinationPreference, @".poi"];
```

(continued)

Listing 4-2 *(continued)*

```
  NSString *filePath = [RTModel filePath:fileComponent];

  NSURL *itineraryDataURL =
                    [NSURL fileURLWithPath:filePath];
  [itineraryData writeToURL:
                    itineraryDataURL atomically:YES];

  [[NSNotificationCenter defaultCenter] postNotific
         ationName:@"ItineraryChanged" object:self
         userInfo:nil];
  [[NSNotificationCenter defaultCenter] postNotificatio
         nName:@"PointsOfInterestChanged" object:self
         userInfo:nil];
  UIAlertView *alert = [[UIAlertView alloc]
      initWithTitle:pointOfInterest.title
      message:@"Was added to your itinerary"
      delegate:self cancelButtonTitle:@"Thanks"
      otherButtonTitles:nil];
  [alert show];
}
```

Walking through Listing 4-2, you can see that, to add a point of interest to the itinerary, the `RTModel` adds the `pointOfInterest` object to the `itinerary` array and removes it from the `pointsOfInterest` array. As a result, when the `ItineraryController` and `PointsOfInterestController` reload their table data, the `PointOfInterest` will appear in the Itinerary list (shown in the main window in the leftmost image in Figure 4-1) and disappear from the Points of Interest list (the popover window in the leftmost image in Figure 4-1).

```
 [itinerary addObject:pointOfInterest];
[pointsOfInterest removeObject:pointOfInterest];
```

Then the selected `PointOfInterest` data is used to create a dictionary, which will be added to the `itineraryData` array and also saved in the Itinerary file (which will be loaded at application launch). `returnPointOfInterestData` does what it says, and I leave you to investigate it on your own, because you'll replace it in Listing 4-6 when you implement the Core Data functionality:

```
 [itineraryData addObject:
            [pointOfInterest returnPointOfInterestData]];
RTAppDelegate *appDelegate =
            [[UIApplication sharedApplication] delegate];
NSString *fileComponent = [NSString
         stringWithFormat:@"%@%@%@", @"Itinerary",
         appDelegate.destinationPreference, @".poi"];
NSString *filePath = [RTModel filePath:fileComponent];

NSURL *itineraryDataURL =
```

```
                        [NSURL fileURLWithPath:filePath];
[itineraryData writeToURL:
                        itineraryDataURL atomically:YES];
```

One of the more interesting parts of Listing 4-2 is the fact that the `RTModel` posts notifications telling the world that both the `Itinerary` and `PointsOfInterest` arrays have changed. This ends up being the primary mechanism to make sure that if something changes in the data, all views that are visible have the opportunity to redisplay themselves with that new data. (I explain notifications in Chapter 3.)

```
  [[NSNotificationCenter defaultCenter] postNotific
          ationName:@"ItineraryChanged" object:self
          userInfo:nil];
  [[NSNotificationCenter defaultCenter] postNotificationNa
          me:@"PointsOfInterestChanged" object:self
```

Both the `PointsOfInterestController` and the `ItineraryController` have added themselves as observers of those notifications in their `viewDid-Load` methods and as a result will reload their views when they receive the appropriate notifications. As I explain in Chapter 3, each controller starts off by sending the `addObserver:selector:name:object:` message:

```
[[NSNotificationCenter defaultCenter] addObserver:self
    selector:@selector(itineraryChanged:)
                    name:@"ItineraryChanged" object:nil];
```

The `object` parameter is `nil`, which means that it wants to be registered for an `ItineraryChanged` notification posted by any object out there.

The selector sends a message to the Table view to reload said data:

```
- (void)itineraryChanged:(NSNotification *)notif {

[self.itineraryTableView reloadData];
}
```

Finally, the `addToItinerary:` method posts an alert to inform the user that the addition to the itinerary has been carried out.

```
UIAlertView *alert = [[UIAlertView alloc]
        initWithTitle:pointOfInterest.title
        message:@"Was added to your itinerary"
        delegate:self cancelButtonTitle:@"Thanks"
        otherButtonTitles:nil];
[alert show];
```

All eminently doable, I suppose, but take a look at how you could do all this by using Core Data.

Adding a Point of Interest to the Itinerary Using Core Data

When you work with Core Data, you (necessarily) work with managed objects. (Chapter 3 has more on the whole managed objects topic.) So, you'll need to modify the `RTModel` to use the new `NSManagedObject` that you created in Chapter 3 — `SharedPointOfInterest`. To do that, add the code in bold in Listing 4-3 to `RTModel.m`.

Listing 4-3: Updating the RTModel.m Implementation

```
#import "RTModel.h"
#import "RTAppDelegate.h"
#import "Destination.h"
#import "PointOfInterest.h"
#import "Annotation.h"
#import "SharedPointOfInterest.h"
```

After importing `SharedPointOfInterest`, you're going to implement a new method in it which will take a dictionary and update its properties accordingly. You take care of all that by adding the code in bold in Listing 4-4 to `SharedPointOfInterest.h`.

Listing 4-4: Updating the SharedfPointOfInterest.h Interface

```
#import <Foundation/Foundation.h>
#import <CoreData/CoreData.h>
#import <MapKit/MapKit.h>

@interface SharedPointOfInterest : NSManagedObject

@property (nonatomic, retain) NSString * name;
@property (nonatomic, retain) NSString * address;
@property (nonatomic, retain) NSString * comment;
@property (nonatomic, retain) NSNumber * displayOrder;
@property (nonatomic, retain) NSString * latitude;
@property (nonatomic, retain) NSString * location;
@property (nonatomic, retain) NSString * longitude;
@property (nonatomic, retain) NSString * subtitle;
@property (nonatomic, retain) NSString * title;
@property (nonatomic, readwrite)
                        CLLocationCoordinate2D coordinate;
- (void)loadData:(NSDictionary *)data;
@end
```

Add the code in Listing 4-5 to SharedPointOfInterest.m to implement the loadData: method.

Listing 4-5: Adding the loadData: Method

```
- (void)loadData:(NSDictionary *)data {

  self.latitude =
            [[data objectForKey:@"Latitude"] stringValue];
  self.longitude =
           [[data objectForKey:@"Longitude"] stringValue];
  self.title = [data objectForKey:@"Name"];
  self.name = [data objectForKey:@"Name"];
  self.address = [data objectForKey:@"Address"];
  self.location = [data objectForKey:@"Location"];
  self.comment = [data objectForKey:@"Description"];
  self.subtitle = [data objectForKey:@"Description"];
}
```

As I mention earlier, in this method, you take a dictionary and use it to initialize the SharedPointOfInterest properties. You don't have to do anything with the coordinate property. That's because back in Chapter 3 you created an accessor for it that constructs the CLLocationCoordinate2D from the latitude and the longitude properties.

In a bit, you'll be modifying addToItinerary so that instead of creating a PointOfInterest object and adding it to the itinerary array, you'll have the managed object context create a new SharedPointOfInterest all on its own, which the managed object context will then manage. (The object's data will be added in the loadData: method as you'll see in Listing 4-9.) You'll also execute a fetch request to reload the list of SharedPointOfInterest objects that you'll use to display the point of interest information.

So what is a fetch request? I'm glad you asked.

The fetch request

In Listing 4-7, you're going to be creating a Fetch Request accessor following the same process you used to create the other Core Data stack accessors — persistentStoreCoordinator for example — back in Chapter 3. Before you take that step, however, you need to prepare the ground a bit by adding the bolded code in Listing 4-6 to RTModel.m so you can get the property added and synthesize the accessors.

You're making the reference to the fetch request a property to take advantage of the same kind of accessor plumbing you used to create the other Core Data stack accessors in Chapter 3, but you aren't making this property accessible to other objects. Rather, you're ensuring that the property is *private* — OK, sort of private — by being hidden in the `RTModel.m` implementation rather than published in the interface. You're also making it `readonly` to be consistent with the other properties.

Listing 4-6: Adding the sharedPointOfInterestFetchRequest Instance Property

```
#import "RTModel.h"
#import "RTAppDelegate.h"
#import "Destination.h"
#import "PointOfInterest.h"
#import "Annotation.h"
#import "SharedPointOfInterest.h"

typedef void (^addLocationCompletionHandler)(Annotation
          *annotation, NSError* error);

@interface RTModel () {
  NSDictionary *destinationData;
  Destination* destination;
  NSMutableArray *events;
  NSMutableArray *pointsOfInterest;
  NSMutableArray *itinerary;
  NSMutableArray *itineraryData;
  NSMutableArray *pointsOfInterestData;
  addLocationCompletionHandler
                       addFindLocationCompletionHandler;
  CLLocation *foundLocation;
}
@property (readonly, strong, nonatomic)
        NSFetchRequest *sharedPointOfInterestFetchRequest;
@end

@implementation RTModel

@synthesize managedObjectContext = _managedObjectContext;
@synthesize managedObjectModel = _managedObjectModel;
@synthesize persistentStoreCoordinator =
                            _persistentStoreCoordinator;
@synthesize sharedPointOfInterestFetchRequest =
                      _sharedPointOfInterestFetchRequest;
```

Keep things moving along by adding the code in Listing 4-7 to `RTModel.m` to add the needed Fetch Request accessor.

Listing 4-7: Adding the sharedPointOfInterestFetchRequest Accessor

```
- (NSFetchRequest *)sharedPointOfInterestFetchRequest {

  if (_sharedPointOfInterestFetchRequest != nil) {
    return _sharedPointOfInterestFetchRequest;
  }

  _sharedPointOfInterestFetchRequest = [NSFetchRequest
     fetchRequestWithEntityName:@"SharedPointOfInterest"];

  return _sharedPointOfInterestFetchRequest;
}
```

A *fetch request* is an object that specifies what data you want from the persistent store. You could, for example, specify that you want "all `SharedPointOfInterest` objects ordered by location," or "all `SharedPointOfInterest` objects in New York."

A fetch request must specify an entity to search for. `fetchRequestWithEntityName:` creates a fetch request with the entity name you specify — `SharedPointOfInterest`. It also can contain one (or both) of the following:

- **A predicate object that specifies conditions that objects must match (for example, "last name begins with an 'X'"):** If you don't specify a predicate (and you won't be using predicates in RoadTrip), you'll get all instances of the entity.
- **An array of Sort Descriptor objects that specifies the order in which the objects should appear:** For example, by `location` then by `sortOrder`. (Both are `SharedPointOfInterest` attributes.)

You can also specify other things, such as the maximum number of objects that a request should return, even distinct property values and attribute values that satisfy a given function — all of which are out of scope for this book.

One thing you might want to think about, though, is the batch size. `setFetchBatchSize:` allows you to control the memory footprint of your application. The default value of `0` is treated as infinite. But, if you set a non-zero batch size, the collection of objects returned when the fetch is executed is broken into batches, and no more than the set `batchSize` objects' data will be fetched from the persistent store at a time. If you need an object that isn't in the batch, Core Data will go out and get it for you *transparently* — no need for you to tell it what to do, in other words.

You send a fetch request to a managed object context, which gets the objects that match your request (possibly none), adds them to the managed object context, and returns them to the application. If a context already contains a managed object for an object returned from a fetch, then the existing managed object is returned in the fetch results.

The framework tries to be as efficient as possible — you get only the objects you asked for. If you follow a relationship to an object that hasn't yet been fetched, it's fetched automatically for you. If you stop using an object, by default it will be de-allocated. (This is, of course, not the same as deleting it.)

And, as I mention earlier, unless you really need *all* the objects of a particular entity, you can also use a predicate to limit the number of objects returned to those you're actually interested in.

Your fetch request can also cache the results so that if the same data is subsequently needed, the work doesn't have to be repeated. Core Data also uses a mechanism called *faulting,* which reduces the amount of memory your application requires by using a placeholder object that represents a managed object until the data is actually accessed.

If you're displaying objects in a Table view, you can use a *Fetched Results controller,* `NSFetchedResultsController`. It, too, tries to minimize the amount of data held in memory. It efficiently manages the results returned from a Core Data fetch request to provide data for a `UITableView` object. You use this class to get the objects you need in order to create the cells in in a Table View, as well as to determine the number of sections you need and the number of rows in each section. (By the way, you just happen to create and use a Fetched Results controller in the "Add the Fetched Results Controller" section, later in this chapter.) A Fetched Results controller can also monitor changes to objects and report changes to a delegate, which can then do what's necessary to update the Table view accordingly, including reloading the data.

Predefining fetch requests in a managed object model

While I'll keep on using the code you just entered, you can also just predefine fetch requests in your managed object model. To do that, take these steps:

1. **Open the `Model.xcdatamodel` in the Core Data Model editor and select the `SharedPointOfInterest` entity in the top-level components area.**

   For an overview of how the Core Data Model editor works, check out Chapter 3.

2. **Hold down the Add Entity button until you see the pop-up menu and then select Add Fetch Request, as I have in Figure 4-2. (The button retains the selection you make here, so it functions as the default.)**

   You can also choose Editor➪Add Fetch Request.

3. **Using the Core Data Model inspector, name the Fetch Request `SharedPointOfInterestFetchRequest`, as I have in Figure 4-3, and set any other fetch request properties you'd like.**

   For your purposes, you won't need to select any additional filtering properties; you want all the objects.

   I clicked the + button in the `SharedPointOfInterestFetchRequest` entry in the Core Data Model Editor Detail area (see Figure 4-4) to show you what kinds of things you can specify in a fetch request, either in the template or in your own code.

To actually use the new fetch request you just created in the managed object model, you need to modify `sharedPointOfInterestFetchRequest`. To do that, delete the ***bolded-underlined-italicized*** code in Listing 4-8 and then add the listing's **bolded** code to `sharedPointOfInterestFetchRequest` in `RTModel.m`.

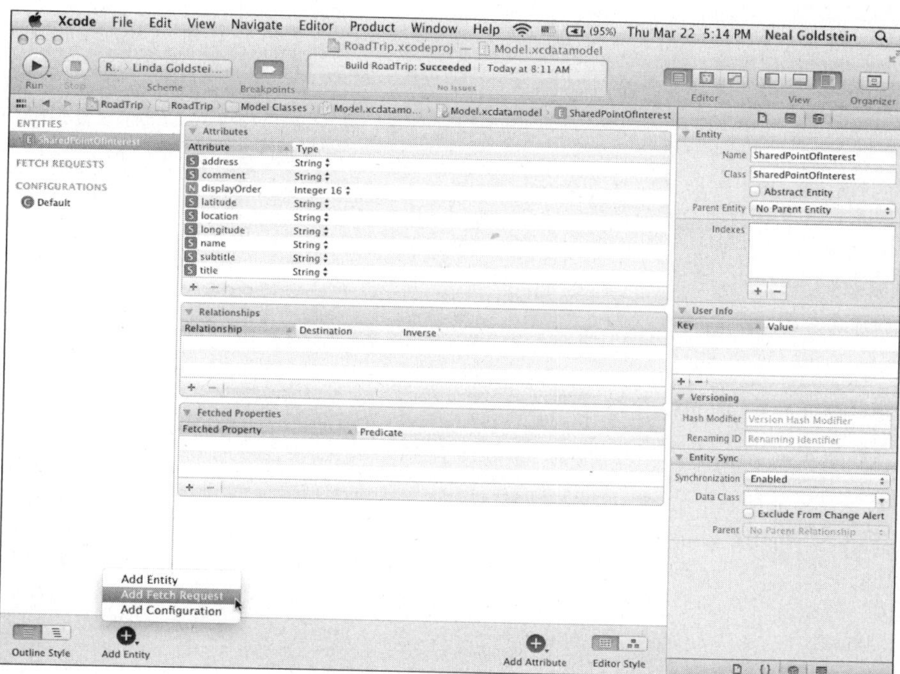

Figure 4-2: Creating a fetch request.

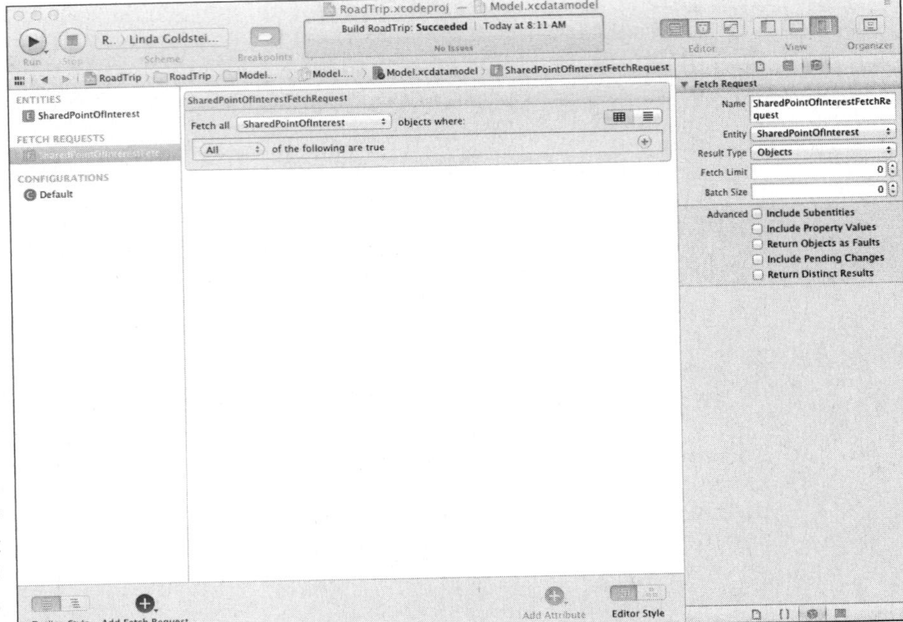

Figure 4-3: The Shared PointOf Interest Fetch Request.

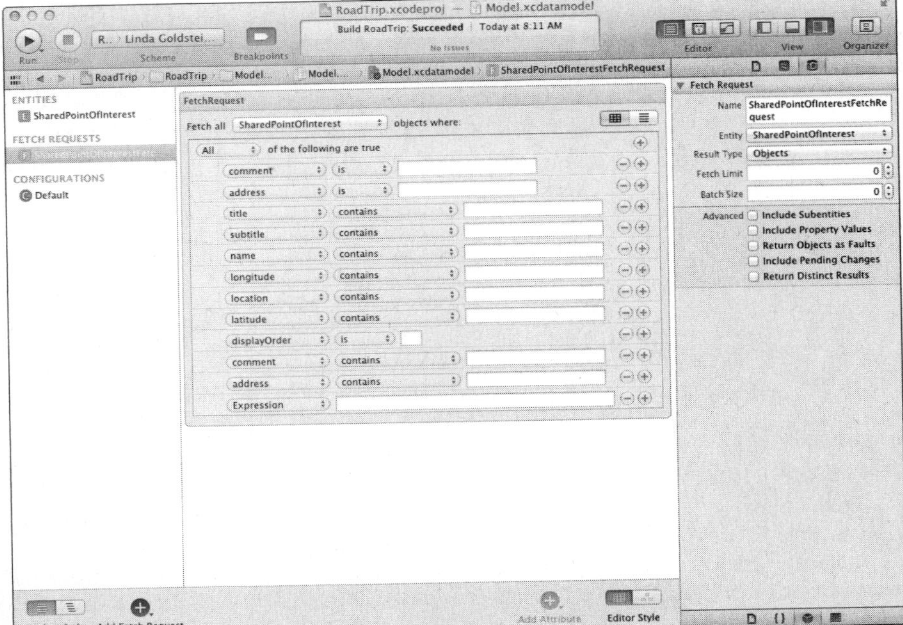

Figure 4-4: Further nailing down the request.

Listing 4-8: Using a Fetch Request Predefined in the Managed Object Model

```
- (NSFetchRequest *)sharedPointOfInterestFetchRequest {

  if (_sharedPointOfInterestFetchRequest != nil) {
    return _sharedPointOfInterestFetchRequest;
  }
  _sharedPointOfInterestFetchRequest = [NSFetchRequest
     fetchRequestWithEntityName:@"SharedPointOfInterest"];

  _sharedPointOfInterestFetchRequest =
     [self.managedObjectModel fetchRequestTemplateForName:
                    @"SharedPointOfInterestFetchRequest"];
  return _sharedPointOfInterestFetchRequest;
}
```

If you do go down this road, understand that this code creates a fetch request that you can't modify. If you want to set any properties; either you'll need to use `fetchRequestFromTemplateWithName:substitutionVariables:` or you'll have to copy the result.

Creating a SharedPointOfInterest

With fetch requests out of the way, you can now modify `addToItinerary` so that, instead of going to the trouble of creating a `PointOfInterest` object and adding it to the `itinerary` array, you have the managed object context create a new `SharedPointOfInterest`, which the managed object context will in turn manage. To do that bit of modification, delete the ***bolded-underlined-italicized*** code and add the **bolded** code in Listing 4-9 to `addToItinerary` in `RTModel.m`.

Listing 4-9: Updating addToItinerary: in RTModel.m

```
- (void)addToItinerary:
                      (PointOfInterest *)pointOfInterest {

  [itinerary addObject:pointOfInterest];

  [pointsOfInterest removeObject:pointOfInterest];

  [itineraryData addObject:[pointOfInterest
                             returnPointOfInterestData]];
  RTAppDelegate *appDelegate =
           [[UIApplication sharedApplication] delegate];
  NSString *fileComponent =
```

(continued)

Listing 4-9 *(continued)*

```
    [NSString stringWithFormat:@"%@%@%@", @"Itinerary",
              appDelegate.destinationPreference, @".poi"];
  NSString *filePath = [RTModel filePath:fileComponent];
  NSURL *itineraryDataURL =
                          [NSURL fileURLWithPath:filePath];
  [itineraryData
              writeToURL:itineraryDataURL atomically:YES];

  NSManagedObjectContext* context =
                              self.managedObjectContext;
  SharedPointOfInterest *sharedPointOfInterest =
   [NSEntityDescription insertNewObjectForEntityForName:
     @"SharedPointOfInterest"
                         inManagedObjectContext:context];
  [sharedPointOfInterest loadData:
             [pointOfInterest returnPointOfInterestData]];
  sharedPointOfInterest.displayOrder =
          [NSNumber numberWithInteger:[itinerary count]];
  NSError *error = nil;
  if ([[[context persistentStoreCoordinator]
        persistentStores] count] > 0) {
    if (![context save:&error]) {
      NSString *errorMessage =
                          [error localizedDescription];
      UIAlertView *alertView = [[UIAlertView alloc]
      initWithTitle:@"Error in accessing your itinerary.
           Restart Road Trip and contact customer support
           if the error continues."
      message:errorMessage delegate:nil
      cancelButtonTitle:@"OK" otherButtonTitles:nil];
      [alertView show];
      NSLog(@"Core Data Failure! Error code: %u,
           description: %@, and reason: %@", error.code,
             [error localizedDescription],
             [error localizedFailureReason]);
      return;
    }
    itinerary = [NSMutableArray arrayWithArray:
      [context executeFetchRequest:
        self.sharedPointOfInterestFetchRequest
                                        error:&error]];
    if (error)
      NSLog(@"Core Data Failure! Error code: %u,
           description: %@, and reason: %@", error.
           code, [error localizedDescription], [error
           localizedFailureReason]);
}
  [[NSNotificationCenter defaultCenter] postNotific
          ationName:@"ItineraryChanged" object:self
          userInfo:nil];
```

```
  [[NSNotificationCenter defaultCenter] postNotificatio
          nName:@"PointsOfInterestChanged" object:self
          userInfo:nil];
  UIAlertView *alert = [[UIAlertView alloc]
       initWithTitle:pointOfInterest.title
       message:@"Was added to your itinerary"
       delegate:self cancelButtonTitle:@"Thanks"
       otherButtonTitles:nil];
  [alert show];
}
```

Looking at the changes, you see that the first thing you do is delete the instruction that added the `PointOfInterest` to the `itinerary` array.

```
[itinerary addObject:pointOfInterest];
```

You can get away with doing this because you'll be using a Core Data *fetch request* to load the array instead.

Next, you keep the instruction that removes the `PointOfInterest` from the `pointsOfInterest` array because the `PointsOfInterestController` is going to remain the way it is.

```
[pointsOfInterest removeObject:pointOfInterest];
```

You then delete the block of code that adds the object to the `itineraryData` array and then saves it as a file, like so:

```
[itineraryData addObject:[pointOfInterest
                           returnPointOfInterestData]];
RTAppDelegate *appDelegate =
             [[UIApplication sharedApplication] delegate];
NSString *fileComponent =
    [NSString stringWithFormat:@"%@%@%@", @"Itinerary",
             appDelegate.destinationPreference, @".poi"];
NSString *filePath = [RTModel filePath:fileComponent];
NSURL *itineraryDataURL =
                        [NSURL fileURLWithPath:filePath];
itineraryData writeToURL:itineraryDataURL atomically:YES];
```

All that code is now moot because you'll have the managed object context create a new `SharedPointOfInterest` managed object instead.

```
NSManagedObjectContext* context =
                          self.managedObjectContext;
SharedPointOfInterest *sharedPointOfInterest =
  [NSEntityDescription insertNewObjectForEntityForName:
      @"SharedPointOfInterest"
                       inManagedObjectContext:context];
```

insertNewObjectForEntityForName:inManagedObjectContext: is an NSEntityDescription method that creates an instance of the class you specify — in this case, a SharedPointOfInterest — in the managed object context you specify. (Okay, you have only one here, so that's a bit of a no-brainer.) NSEntityDescription describes a Core Data entity and is where you find all that metadata I describe back in Chapter 3.

Again, back in Chapter 3 when I was doing similar managed object context stuff, I used the performBlockAndWait: block method to send the necessary message to the managed object context to set the Persistent Store coordinator. I went that route because using the performBlockAndWait: method results in the managed object context executing the block on its own thread:

```
[managedObjectContext performBlockAndWait:^{
  [managedObjectContext
             setPersistentStoreCoordinator:coordinator];
    }];
```

I admitted back in Chapter 3 that this wasn't *really* necessary because the managed object context was created on the main thread. In Chapter 3, I just wanted to show you how to work with a managed object context on a different thread. Because I don't need to use performBlockAndWait:, I don't from here on out, and I just send the message directly to the managed object context.

After you have the new SharedPointOfInterest, you initialize its properties with the properties from the selected PointOfInterest.

```
 [sharedPointOfInterest loadData:
              [pointOfInterest returnPointOfInterestData]];
```

You'll also add a display order — it can be used to order the list of SharedPointsOfInterest. (Its inner workings are outside the scope of this book, but I encourage you to explore that on your own.) When you create the SharedPointsOfInterest, you end up adding it to the end of the list.

```
sharedPointOfInterest.displayOrder =
          [NSNumber numberWithInteger:[itinerary count]];
```

Finally, you save SharedPointsOfInterest to the managed object context.

```
  NSError *error = nil;
  if ([[[context persistentStoreCoordinator]
        persistentStores] count] > 0) {
    if (![context save:&error]) {
      NSString *errorMessage =
```

```
                                [error localizedDescription];
    UIAlertView *alertView = [[UIAlertView alloc]
      initWithTitle:@"Error in accessing your itinerary.
        Restart Road Trip and contact customer support
        if the error continues."
    message:errorMessage delegate:nil
    cancelButtonTitle:@"OK" otherButtonTitles:nil];
    [alertView show];
    NSLog(@"Core Data Failure! Error code: %u,
        description: %@, and reason: %@", error.code,
          [error localizedDescription],
          [error localizedFailureReason]);
    return;
  }
```

The idea here is that you need to make sure that there is at least one store; with that fact established, you then save the new `SharedPointOfInterest`. Keep in mind that, although the `SharedPointOfInterest` object was *created* by `insertNewObjectForEntityForName`, it isn't *added to the store* until you save it.

If you get an error, you post an alert and log the error. (You'll want to expand this in a shipping application.) Then you execute a fetch request you created to reload the itinerary data used by the `RTModel` in its methods. This array is used by several methods in the `RTModel` class and especially by `loadPointsOfInterest`, as you will soon see. Because that's the case, whenever you make changes to the `SharedPointOfInterest` object in your itinerary — as you most definitely do in `addToItinerary` — you need to reload the array.

```
itinerary = [NSMutableArray arrayWithArray:
  [context executeFetchRequest:
    self.sharedPointOfInterestFetchRequest error:&error]];
}
```

Again, if you get an error, you log the error. You'll want to expand this in a shipping application. (I'll stop saying that now — I'm sure you get the point.)

```
NSLog(@"Core Data Failure! Error code: %u, description:
 %@, and reason: %@", error.code,
   [error localizedDescription],
   [error localizedFailureReason]);
```

The last little bit of Listing 4-9 stays the same: You continue to post the notification to inform anyone interested that both the itinerary and the Points of Interest list have changed.

Now, I do explain notifications in Chapter 3, but look at what's happening here. The *Notification Center* (an `NSNotificationCenter` object) will broadcast information within the program, thereby decoupling the sender and the observer and making for a more flexible system. Every iOS application has a default Notification Center — all you have to do is use it.

In this case, the `RTModel` posts the notifications, which include the notification name (`ItineraryChanged` and `PointsOfInterestChanged`), the object that is doing the posting (`self`), and an optional user information dictionary (`nil` in this case).

In the "Displaying the SharedPointOfInterests" section, later in this chapter, you see what happens when the `ItineraryController` (which has subscribed for this notification) is notified.

Displaying Your Itinerary

After you have the data you need safely stored in the `SharedPointOfInterest` managed objects, you need to make some changes to the `ItineraryController` in order to display them. It turns out you'll still be displaying them in the `ItineraryController` Table view, but you'll be getting a little help from `NSFetchedResultsController` to make that possible.

You have to get your head around two aspects of `NSFetchedResultsController`. The first is the fetch part — getting the objects you want and need. The second is the controller part — how the controller helps you when it comes to displaying managed objects in a Table view.

First, the fetching part. You make the `ItineraryController` an `NSFetchedResultsControllerDelegate` and import the Core Data header file. To do that, add the bolded code in Listing 4-10 to `ItineraryController.h`.

Listing 4-10: Updating the ItineraryController.h Interface

```
#import <UIKit/UIKit.h>
#import "RTDetailViewController.h"
#import <CoreData/CoreData.h>

@class PointOfInterest;

@interface ItineraryController : RTDetailViewController
  <UITableViewDelegate, UITableViewDataSource,
     UIPopoverControllerDelegate,
```

```
                          NSFetchedResultsControllerDelegate>
@property (strong, nonatomic)NSMutableArray  *itinerary;
@property (weak, nonatomic)
                   IBOutlet UITableView *itineraryTableView;
- (IBAction)add:(id)sender;
@end
```

Next, you need to create the Fetched Results controller, just as you created a `SharedPointOfInterstFetchRequest` in the section entitled "The fetch request," earlier in the chapter, to take advantage of the same kind of accessor plumbing that you used to create the other Core Data stack accessors in Chapter 3.

Before you can do that, though, you need to add the bolded code in Listing 4-11 to `ItineraryController.m` in order to import the `SharedPointOfInterest` header file. (You need that to access the `SharedPointOfInterest` properties.) The bolded code also adds the `fetchedResultsController` property and synthesizes the accessors.

Listing 4-11: Updating the ItineraryController Interface and Implementation in ItineraryController.m

```
#import "RTDefines.h"
#import "ItineraryController.h"
#import "RTAppDelegate.h"
#import "RTModel.h"
#import "PointsOfInterestController.h"
#import "PointOfInterest.h"
#import "AddPointOfInterestController.h"
#import "SharedPointOfInterest.h"

@interface ItineraryController () {
  NSDictionary* POIEntry;
  NSArray *itineraryPointsOfInterest;
  UIPopoverController *popover;
}
@property (readonly, strong, nonatomic)
     NSFetchedResultsController *fetchedResultsController;

@end

@implementation ItineraryController
@synthesize itinerary = _itinerary;
@synthesize itineraryTableView = _tableView;
@synthesize fetchedResultsController =
                              _fetchedResultsController;
```

Adding the Fetched Results controller

One of the things that makes Core Data so useful, besides being able to store and retrieve objects, is its ability to retrieve objects based on certain criteria, as you saw when you created the SharedPointOfInterestFetchRequest in "The fetch request" section, earlier in the chapter.

As I mention earlier in the chapter, if you plan on displaying objects in a Table view, you can use a Fetched Results controller — NSFetchedResultsController to be precise — to take care of that for you. NSFetchedResultsController, like any good controller, tries to minimize the amount of data held in memory. It efficiently manages the results returned from a Core Data fetch request to provide data for a UITableView object. You use this class to get the objects you need in order to create cells in a Table view, as well as to determine the number of sections you need as well as the number of rows in each section. (I pointed out how Fetch Results controller can be used to monitor changes to objects and report changes to a delegate, which can then do what's necessary to update the Table view accordingly — including reloading the data.)

You create the Fetched Results controller in the same way you create all the other Core Data properties you need. Just as you did with the sharedPointOfInterestFetchRequest back in "The fetch request" section, you set it up as a property with an accessor that you code.

Add the code in Listing 4-12 to ItineraryController.m.

Listing 4-12: The fetchedResultsController Accessor

```
#pragma mark - Fetched results controller

- (NSFetchedResultsController *)fetchedResultsController {

  if (_fetchedResultsController == nil) {
    NSFetchRequest *fetchRequest =
      [NSFetchRequest fetchRequestWithEntityName:
                           @"SharedPointOfInterest"];
    NSSortDescriptor *sectionSortDescriptor =
     [[NSSortDescriptor alloc] initWithKey:@"location"
                                       ascending:YES];
    NSSortDescriptor *sharedPointOfInterestDescriptor =
     [[NSSortDescriptor alloc] initWithKey:@"displayOrder"
                                       ascending:YES];
    NSArray *sortDescriptors = [[NSArray alloc] initWithOb
           jects:sectionSortDescriptor,
                  sharedPointOfInterestDescriptor, nil];
    [fetchRequest setSortDescriptors:sortDescriptors];

    NSFetchedResultsController *aFetchedResultsController
```

```
      = [[NSFetchedResultsController alloc]
           initWithFetchRequest:fetchRequest
           managedObjectContext:
                    [RTModel model].managedObjectContext
  sectionNameKeyPath:@"location" cacheName:nil];
    aFetchedResultsController.delegate = self;
    _fetchedResultsController = aFetchedResultsController;

  }
  NSError *error = nil;
  if (![_fetchedResultsController performFetch:&error]) {
    NSString *errorMessage = [error localizedDescription];
    UIAlertView *alertView = [[UIAlertView alloc]
       initWithTitle:@"Error in accessing your itinerary.
           Restart Road Trip and contact customer support
           if the error continues."
       message:errorMessage delegate:nil
       cancelButtonTitle:@"OK" otherButtonTitles:nil];
    [alertView show];
    NSLog(@"Core Data Failure! Error code: %u,
           description: %@, and reason: %@", error.code,
          [error localizedDescription],
          [error localizedFailureReason]);
    NSLog(@"Unresolved error %@, %@", error,
                                        [error userInfo]);
    return nil;
  }
  return _fetchedResultsController;
}
```

Looking at Listing 4-12, the first thing you do to set up your very own Fetched Results controller is create the fetch request for the entity.

```
NSFetchRequest *fetchRequest =
      [NSFetchRequest fetchRequestWithEntityName:
                              @"SharedPointOfInterest"];
```

If you think this looks familiar, that's probably because it is. This is (pretty much) the same thing you did in "The fetch request" section, earlier in the chapter. (If you aren't clear on exactly what you've just accomplished here by creating a fetch request accessor, refer to the discussion following Listing 4-7.)

Note one slight difference, however. In this case, you're adding a set of sort descriptors.

```
NSSortDescriptor *sectionSortDescriptor =
 [[NSSortDescriptor alloc] initWithKey:@"location"
                                   ascending:YES];
NSSortDescriptor *sharedPointOfInterestDescriptor =
 [[NSSortDescriptor alloc] initWithKey:@"displayOrder"
                                   ascending:YES];
```

The first sort descriptor specifies that you want the returned fetch to be sorted by location (`initWithKey:@"location"`) in ascending order (`ascending:YES`). Within that sorted order, the second sort descriptor specifies sort `SharedPointOfInterest` objects by display order — this was an attribute I had you add in the original managed object model which, right now, is simply the order in which you added a `SharedPointOfInterest` to the itinerary. You can, however, use the Table View delegate methods to allow the user to reorder `SharedPointOfInterest` objects within a location (or even reorder the location), but I leave that up to you.

Then, you add the sort descriptors to an array and add it to the fetch request, as follows:

```
NSArray *sortDescriptors =
  [[NSArray alloc] initWithObjects:sectionSortDescriptor,
                     sharedPointOfInterestDescriptor, nil];
[fetchRequest setSortDescriptors:sortDescriptors];
```

After that's done, you create the Fetched Results controller and initialize it with the fetch request and then the section name key path and cache. You finish up by setting `self` as the delegate:

```
NSFetchedResultsController *aFetchedResultsController =
  [[NSFetchedResultsController alloc]
          initWithFetchRequest:fetchRequest
          managedObjectContext:
                 [RTModel model].managedObjectContext
          sectionNameKeyPath:@"location" cacheName:nil];
aFetchedResultsController.delegate = self;
_fetchedResultsController = aFetchedResultsController;
```

`sectionNameKeyPath:` is what you use to create the section information. `cacheName` is the name of the cache that should (eventually) be used. If there isn't one with that name, one is created for you. If you pass in `nil`, as you have here, no caching is done. Given the amount of data you have, you really don't need to cache, but as your itinerary grows, you should consider it.

To keep things in perspective, Figure 4-5 shows you what all this code leads up to, practically speaking — assuming, of course, that you add Hoboken of all places as a point of interest by tapping Add in the Points of Interest popover shown back in left-most image of Figure 4-1 to see how the points of interest are neatly placed in their location.

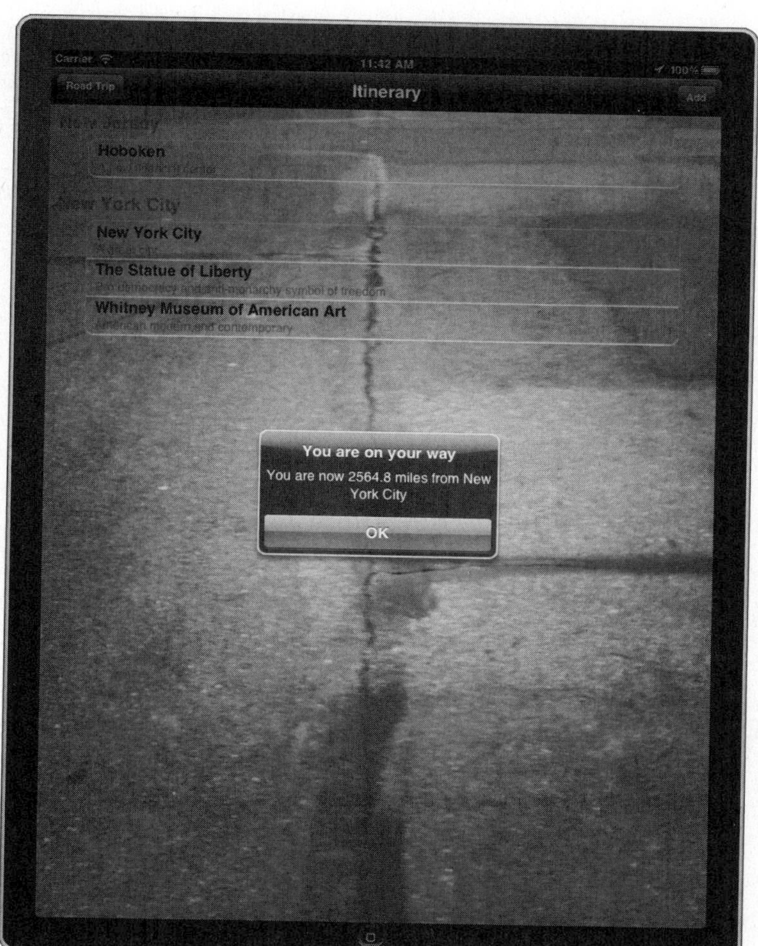

Figure 4-5: Adding location and sorting to your itinerary.

The Fetched Results controller delegate

Even though you made `ItineraryController` a delegate of the Fetched Results controller, you aren't implementing any of the delegate methods . . . but I do suggest you explore them on your own.

For example, the NSFetchedResultsController always sends the following controllerWillChangeContent: message to the NSFetchedResultsControllerDelegate method before the Fetched Results controller has completed processing of an Add, Remove, Move, or Update.

```
- (void)controllerWillChangeContent:
              (NSFetchedResultsController *) controller {
  [self.itineraryTableView doSomething];
}
```

Along the same lines, the following controllerDidChangeContent: message is sent after the Fetched Results controller has completed processing of an Add, Remove, Move, or Update.

```
- (void)controllerDidChangeContent:

  [self.itineraryTableView doSomethingElse];
}
```

Although they're beyond the scope of this book, the NSFetchedResultsController and its delegate methods come with a lot of functionality that allows you to deal not only with content changes, but also with moving rows and sections in a Table view.

Displaying the SharedPointOfInterests

Currently, RoadTrip is set up so that the ItineraryController displays its data in a Table view using the following UITableViewDataSource methods:

```
tableView:numberOfSectionsInTableView:
tableView:numberOfRowsInSection:
update tableView:cellForRowAtIndexPath:
```

In this section, you make the changes necessary to use the Fetched Results controller. For good measure, you also add two methods that take advantage of one of the things a Fetched Results controller makes easy — displaying entries by section.

Currently, the ItineraryController displays the SharedPointOfInterests in a single section. Because you initialized the Fetched Results controller with sectionNameKeyPath:@"location", you need to change that. To do so, delete the ***bolded-underlined-italicized*** code and add the **bolded** code in Listing 4-13 to tableView:numberSectionsInTableView: in ItineraryController.m.

Listing 4-13: Updating tableView:numberSectionsInTableView: in ItineraryController.m

```
- (NSInteger)numberOfSectionsInTableView:
                                    (UITableView *)tableView
{
  return 1;
  return [self.fetchedResultsController.sections count];
}
```

sections is an NSFetchedResultsController property — an array of objects that contains information about each section. (You don't need to use that information in RoadTrip — all you care about is how many sections there are.)

Each object in the sections arrays adopts the NSFetchedResultsSectionInfo protocol, which has as a required method numberOfObjects. You'll use numberOfObjects to determine the number of rows in each section instead of the total number of objects in the itineraryPointsOfInterest array.

To get this working for you, delete the ***bolded-underlined-italicized*** code and add the **bolded** code in Listing 4-14 to tableView:numberOfRowsInSection: in ItineraryController.m.

Listing 4-14: Updating tableView:numberOfRowsInSection: in ItineraryController.m

```
- (NSInteger)tableView:(UITableView *)tableView numberOfRo
          wsInSection:(NSInteger)section
{
  return [itineraryPointsOfInterest count];
  id<NSFetchedResultsSectionInfo> sectionInfo = [[self.
          fetchedResultsController sections]
                                   objectAtIndex:section];
  return [sectionInfo numberOfObjects];
}
```

Because you now have section information, you can also display section headers. The default header view doesn't work the way I want it to, however, so I have you create your own by implementing the UITableViewDataSource methods tableView:viewForHeaderInSection: (which allows you to create and return a view for each section) and tableView:heightForHeaderInSection: method (which allows you to specify the height). Add these two methods as spelled out in Listing 4-15 to ItineraryController.m.

Listing 4-15: Adding tableView:viewForHeaderInSection: and tableView: heightForHeaderInSection:

```
- (UIView *)tableView:(UITableView *)tableView viewForHead
           erInSection:(NSInteger)section {

  UIView *headerView = [[UILabel alloc] initWithFrame:
      CGRectMake (0,0,tableView.frame.size.width-10,40)];
  headerView.backgroundColor = [UIColor clearColor];

  UILabel *labelView = [[UILabel alloc] initWithFrame:
   CGRectMake (tableView.frame.origin.x+10,0,
                        tableView.frame.size.width-20,40)];
  labelView.numberOfLines = 2;
  labelView.font = [UIFont boldSystemFontOfSize:21];
  labelView.textColor = [UIColor darkGrayColor];
  labelView.opaque = YES;
  labelView.alpha = 1.0;
  labelView.backgroundColor = [UIColor clearColor];
  id <NSFetchedResultsSectionInfo> sectionInfo =
     [self.fetchedResultsController.sections
                                 objectAtIndex:section];
  labelView.text = sectionInfo.name;
  [headerView addSubview:labelView];
  return headerView;
}

- (CGFloat)tableView:(UITableView *)tableView heightForHea
           derInSection:(NSInteger)section {

  return 40;
}
```

All you do to create the header in Listing 4-15 is create a label (with a transparent background) that uses the text you get from the section object that has implemented the required `name` property.

Finally, to display the cell containing the header, you use the title and subtitle of the `SharedPointOfInterest` returned by the Fetched Results controller instead of the `PointOfInterest` in the `itineraryPointsOfInterest` array.

To do that, delete the ***bolded-underlined-italicized*** code and add the **bolded** code in Listing 4-16 to `tableView:cellForRowAtIndexPath:` in `ItineraryController.m`.

Listing 4-16: Updating tableView:cellForRowAtIndexPath: in ItineraryController.m

```
- (UITableViewCell *)tableView:(UITableView *)tableView
          cellForRowAtIndexPath:(NSIndexPath *)indexPath
{
  UITableViewCell *cell = [tableView
        dequeueReusableCellWithIdentifier:kItineraryCell];
  PointOfInterest *pointOfInterest =
    [itineraryPointsOfInterest
                              objectAtIndex:indexPath.row];
  SharedPointOfInterest *sharedPointOfInterest =
  (SharedPointOfInterest *)
            [self.fetchedResultsController
                              objectAtIndexPath:indexPath];
  cell.textLabel.text = pointOfInterest.title;
  cell.textLabel.text = sharedPointOfInterest.title;
  cell.detailTextLabel.text = pointOfInterest.subtitle;
  cell.detailTextLabel.text =
                            sharedPointOfInterest.subtitle;
  return cell;
}
```

`objectAtIndexPath:` is an `NSFetchedResultsController` method that returns the object for a row within a section (index path).

As you can see, between providing section information, doing the necessary sorting, and gaining access to an object by way of its index path, the `NSFetchedResultsController` controller does make your life a lot easier.

If you just can't wait to see what changes you've wrought, you can run the app as is, which produces an empty Itinerary. You need to add the destination as a `SharedPointOfInterest`. (Refer to Figure 4-5.) You also can add a point of interest, as shown in Figure 4-6 — you just can't *delete* one, but you find out how to do that next. (Hey, it's a start.)

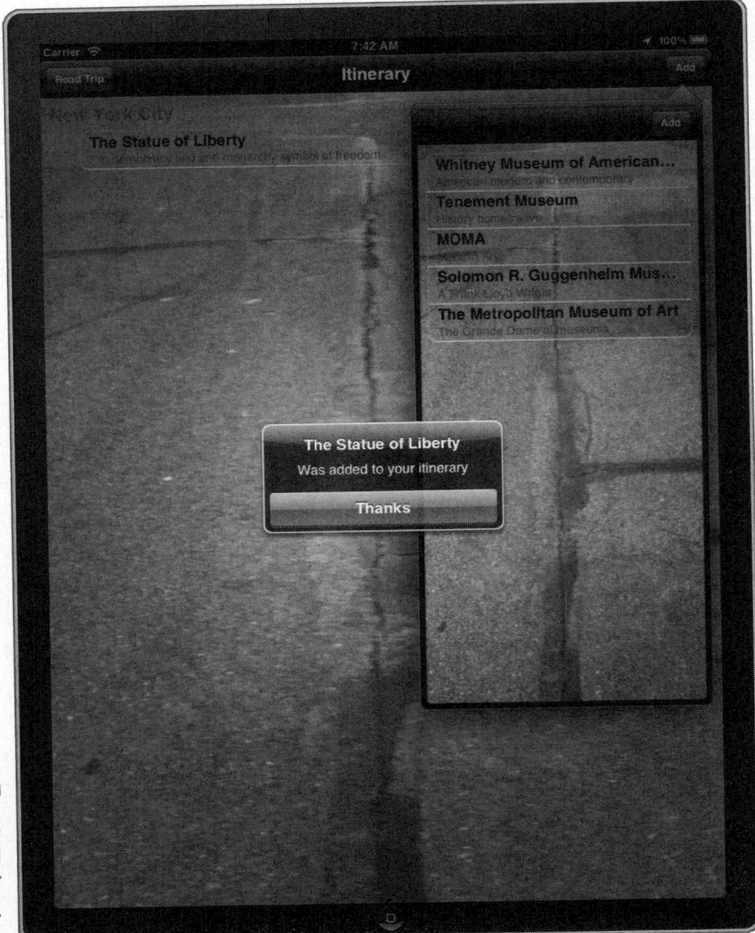

Figure 4-6: Adding to your itinerary.

Cleaning Up the ItineraryController and RTModel Classes

Because you've changed the `ItineraryController` around a bit so you can use `SharedPointOfInterest` objects managed by Core Data instead of having to do it yourself in the `RTModel` class, feel free to get rid of the code in the `ItineraryController` that uses the `RTModel` methods as well as the code that does all the `SharedPointOfInterest` managing in `RTModel`. (A little spring cleaning can't hurt, can it?)

You'll want to delete the message in `ItineraryController` `viewDidLoad` to the `RTModel` that updates the `itineraryPointsOfInterest` array. Core Data is doing that for you via the `NSFetchedResultsController`.

To do that, delete the ***bolded-underlined-italicized*** code in `viewDidLoad` in `ItineraryController.m`, as shown in Listing 4-17.

Listing 4-17: Updating viewDidLoad

```
- (void)viewDidLoad
{
  [super viewDidLoad];
  self.title = @"Itinerary";

  itineraryPointsOfInterest =
                          [[RTModel model] returnItinerary];

  ...
}
```

Now, because the `RTModel` no longer has to manage your `itinerary` array, you can delete the methods associated with doing that. Delete the ***bolded-underlined-italicized*** code in both Listing 4-18 (to delete the `returnItinerary` declaration in `RTModel.h`) and in Listing 4-19 (to delete implementation in `RTModel.m`).

Listing: 4-18: Deleting returnItinerary from the RTModel Interface

```
@interface RTModel : NSObject

+ (RTModel *)model;
- (id)initWithDestinationIndex:(NSUInteger)
          destinationIndex;
- (void)loadItinerary;
- (NSArray *)returnItinerary;
...
@end
```

Listing: 4-19: Deleting returnItinerary from the RTModel Implementation

```
-(NSArray *)returnItinerary {

  return itinerary;
}
```

Loading the Itinerary

Understanding the mechanics of adding something to the itinerary (see the previous section) is only half the battle. You also need to know how the file gets created to start with.

Listing 4-20 shows you how it all starts — with the `RTModel`'s `loadItinerary` method that's used to load the saved itinerary at application `startup`.

Listing 4-20: Loading the Itinerary, Part I

```
- (void)loadItinerary {

  RTAppDelegate *appDelegate =
            [[UIApplication sharedApplication] delegate];
  NSString *fileComponent = [NSString
          stringWithFormat:@"%@%@%@", @"Itinerary",
            appDelegate.destinationPreference, @".poi"];
  NSString *filePath = [RTModel filePath:fileComponent];
  NSURL *itineraryDataURL =
                     [NSURL fileURLWithPath:filePath];
  itineraryData = [NSMutableArray arrayWithContentsOfURL:
                                    itineraryDataURL];

  if (itineraryData) {
    itinerary = [NSMutableArray arrayWithCapacity:[itinera
          ryData count]];
    for (NSDictionary *pointOfInterestData in
                                      itineraryData) {
      PointOfInterest *pointOfInterest =
        [[PointOfInterest alloc]
                      initWithData:pointOfInterestData];
      [itinerary addObject:pointOfInterest];
    }
  }
  else {
    NSDictionary *destinationPointOfInterestData =
       [destinationData objectForKey:
                           @"DestinationLocation"];
    itineraryData = [NSMutableArray
          arrayWithObject:destinationPointOfInterestData];
    [itineraryData writeToURL:
                   itineraryDataURL atomically:YES];
    PointOfInterest *destinationPointOfInterest =
          [[PointOfInterest alloc]
            initWithData:destinationPointOfInterestData];
    itinerary = [NSMutableArray arrayWithObject:destinatio
          nPointOfInterest];
  }
}
```

Listing 4-20 starts by loading the `itineraryData` file using its URL:

```
RTAppDelegate *appDelegate =
          [[UIApplication sharedApplication] delegate];
NSString *fileComponent =
  [NSString stringWithFormat:@"%@%@%@", @"Itinerary",
           appDelegate.destinationPreference, @".poi"];
NSString *filePath = [RTModel filePath:fileComponent];
NSURL *itineraryDataURL =
                      [NSURL fileURLWithPath:filePath];
itineraryData = [NSMutableArray arrayWithContentsOfURL:
                                    itineraryDataURL];
```

The filename is a concatenation of `Itinerary` and the destination (identified as an integer). The file type is `.poi` (short for *p*oint *o*f *i*nterest), and the `filePath` method simply adds the filename and type (file component) to the file path for the application's Documents directory.

```
+ (NSString *)filePath:(NSString *)fileComponent {

return [[NSSearchPathForDirectoriesInDomains
 (NSDocumentDirectory, NSUserDomainMask, YES)
 lastObject]stringByAppendingPathComponent:fileComponent];
}
```

Next, you turn the file path into a URL. This change isn't necessarily a requirement, but Apple encourages the use of URLs to access files. You then load the contents into the `itineraryData` array instance variable.

If there's already a file present, you create the `itinerary` array and then create a `PointOfInterest` object for each dictionary in the file.

```
if (itineraryData) {
  itinerary = [NSMutableArray arrayWithCapacity:
                              [itineraryData count]];
  for (NSDictionary *pointOfInterestData in
                                   itineraryData) {
    PointOfInterest *pointOfInterest =
      [[PointOfInterest alloc]
                 initWithData:pointOfInterestData];
    [itinerary addObject:pointOfInterest];
  }
}
```

If there isn't a file yet (there won't be the first time RoadTrip is launched), you create a `PointOfInterest` object from the `DestinationLocation` data in the `Destinations` plist. Go on and create the `itineraryData` array, and then save it to the file system.

```
  else {
    NSDictionary *destinationPointOfInterestData =
      [destinationData objectForKey:
                             @"DestinationLocation"];
    itineraryData = [NSMutableArray arrayWithObject:
                           destinationPointOfInterestData];
    [itineraryData writeToURL:
                          itineraryDataURL atomically:YES];
    PointOfInterest *destinationPointOfInterest =
     [[PointOfInterest alloc]
           initWithData:destinationPointOfInterestData];
    itinerary = [NSMutableArray
            arrayWithObject:destinationPointOfInterest];
  }
```

The good news is that, with your handy managed object model, you no longer need to do any of that. (Okay, the first time through, you still need to add the `DestinationLocation` as `SharedPointOfInterest`, but that's not asking too much.) Instead, you do a fetch (the one you created in "The fetch request") to load the `SharedPointOfInterest` objects into the `itinerary` array that you can now access in the `RTModel`.

The `itinerary` array is used by several methods in the `RTModel` class — most importantly by `loadPointsOfInterest`, as you soon see. Because that's the case, when you make any changes to `itinerary` array — as you did, for example, in `addToItinerary` — you need to reload the array.

To start working with your new and improved version of `loadItinerary`, delete the ***bolded-underlined-italicized*** code and add the **bolded** code in Listing 4-21 to the `loadItinerary` method in `RTModel.m`.

Listing 4-21: Loading the Itinerary, Part II

```
- (void)loadItinerary {

  RTAppDelegate *appDelegate = [[UIApplication
          sharedApplication] delegate];
  NSString *fileComponent = [NSString
          stringWithFormat:@"%@%@%@", @"Itinerary",
          appDelegate.destinationPreference, @".poi"];
  NSString *filePath = [RTModel filePath:fileComponent];
  NSURL *itineraryDataURL = [NSURL
          fileURLWithPath:filePath];
  itineraryData = [NSMutableArray arrayWithContentsOfURL:i
          tineraryDataURL];

  if (itineraryData) {
    itinerary = [NSMutableArray arrayWithCapacity:[itinera
          ryData count]];
```

```
    for (NSDictionary *pointOfInterestData in
            itineraryData) {
      PointOfInterest *pointOfInterest = [[PointOfInterest
            alloc] initWithData:pointOfInterestData];
      [itinerary addObject:pointOfInterest];
    }
  }
  else {
    NSDictionary *destinationPointOfInterestData =
            [destinationData objectForKey:@"DestinationLoca
            tion"];
    itineraryData = [NSMutableArray arrayWithObject:destin
            ationPointOfInterestData];
    [itineraryData writeToURL:itineraryDataURL
            atomically:YES];
    PointOfInterest *destinationPointOfInterest =
            [[PointOfInterest alloc]initWithData:destinatio
            nPointOfInterestData];
    itinerary = [NSMutableArray arrayWithObject:destinatio
            nPointOfInterest];
  }

  NSManagedObjectContext *context =
                              self.managedObjectContext;
  NSError *error = nil;
  itinerary = [NSMutableArray arrayWithArray:
    [context executeFetchRequest:
    self.sharedPointOfInterestFetchRequest error:&error]];
  if (error)
      NSLog(@"Core Data Failure! Error code: %u,
           description: %@, and reason: %@", error.code,
           [error localizedDescription],
           [error localizedFailureReason]);
  if (![itinerary count]) {
    SharedPointOfInterest *sharedPointOfInterest =
     [NSEntityDescription insertNewObjectForEntityForName:
                               @"SharedPointOfInterest"
        inManagedObjectContext:self.managedObjectContext];
    NSDictionary *destinationDataDictionary =
      [destinationData objectForKey:
                               @"DestinationLocation"];
    [sharedPointOfInterest
                    loadData:destinationDataDictionary];
    sharedPointOfInterest.displayOrder =
         [NSNumber numberWithInteger:[itinerary count]];
    itinerary = [NSMutableArray arrayWithArray:
     [context executeFetchRequest:
       self.sharedPointOfInterestFetchRequest
                                      error:&error]];
```

(continued)

Listing 4-21 *(continued)*

```
    if (error)
      NSLog(@"Core Data Failure! Error code: %u,
           description: %@, and reason: %@", error.code,
           [error localizedDescription],
           [error localizedFailureReason]);

    if ([[[context persistentStoreCoordinator]
                         persistentStores] count] > 0) {
      if (![context save:&error]) {
        NSString *errorMessage = [error
           localizedDescription];
        UIAlertView *alertView = [[UIAlertView alloc]
           initWithTitle:@"Error in accessing your
           itinerary. Restart Road Trip and contact
           customer support if the error continues."
           message:errorMessage delegate:nil
           cancelButtonTitle:@"OK" otherButtonTitles:nil];
        [alertView show];
        NSLog(@"Core Data Failure! Error code: %u,
           description: %@, and reason: %@", error.code,
           [error localizedDescription],
           [error localizedFailureReason]);
        return;
      }
    }
  }
}
```

You start off by fetching the `SharedPointOfInterests`.

```
itinerary = [NSMutableArray arrayWithArray:
 [context executeFetchRequest:
   self.sharedPointOfInterestFetchRequest error:&error]];
```

Notice here that, if I get an error, all I do is log it and merrily continue on. Although this works for development, you need to add more robust error handling in any project that you actually end up shipping.

With all that fetching out of the way, you then check to see whether you've already added the Destination `SharedPointOfInterest`.

```
   if (![itinerary count]) {
```

You do this because, if no Destination `SharedPointOfInterest` is there, you definitely want to add one, but if you already have one in place, you don't want to confuse things by adding a new one. After you add the Destination `SharedPointOfInterest` for the first time, your fetch will have at least `SharedPointOfInterest` in it.

This is similar to the old way of doing things illustrated in Listing 4-20 — you'd simply add a new Destination `PointOfInterest` if the `itinerary` array was empty.

So, if no Destination `SharedPointOfInterest` has been added yet, you create a `SharedPointOfInterests` for the `DestinationLocation` and add it to the managed object context:

```
SharedPointOfInterest *sharedPointOfInterest =
  [NSEntityDescription insertNewObjectForEntityForName:
    @"SharedPointOfInterest" inManagedObjectContext:
                          self.managedObjectContext];
NSDictionary *destinationDataDictionary =
    [destinationData objectForKey:@"DestinationLocation"];
[sharedPointOfInterest
                      loadData:destinationDataDictionary];
sharedPointOfInterest.displayOrder =
          [NSNumber numberWithInteger:[itinerary count]];
itinerary = [NSMutableArray arrayWithArray:
  [context executeFetchRequest:
    self.sharedPointOfInterestFetchRequest error:&error]];
if (error)
  NSLog(@"Core Data Failure! Error code: %u, description:
     %@, and reason: %@", error.code,
     [error localizedDescription],
     [error localizedFailureReason]);
```

Then you save the new `SharedPointOfInterest`:

```
if ([[[context persistentStoreCoordinator]
                        persistentStores] count] > 0) {
  if (![context save:&error]) {
    NSString *errorMessage = [error localizedDescription];
      UIAlertView *alertView = [[UIAlertView alloc]
         initWithTitle:@"Error in accessing your
           itinerary. Restart Road Trip and contact
           customer support if the error continues."
         message:errorMessage delegate:nil
         cancelButtonTitle:@"OK" otherButtonTitles:nil];
      [alertView show];
      NSLog(@"Core Data Failure! Error code: %u,
          description: %@, and reason: %@", error.code,
          [error localizedDescription],
         [error localizedFailureReason]);
        return;
    }
  }
```

Because you're now using `SharedPointOfInterest` objects in the itinerary instead of `PointOfInterest` objects, you need to tweak the `loadPointsOf`

Interest method — the method you'll use to compare your PointOfInterest objects to the SharedPointOfInterest objects. If a PointOfInterest is already in the itinerary, you don't want it to display in the Points of Interest list that displays the points of interest you can add to your itinerary.

To do that tweaking, delete the ***bolded-underlined-italicized*** code and add the **bolded** code in Listing 4-22 to the loadPointsOfInterest method in RTModel.m.

Listing 4-22: Updating loadPointsOfInterest

```
- (void) loadPointsOfInterest {

  RTAppDelegate *appDelegate =
           [[UIApplication sharedApplication] delegate];
  NSString *fileComponent = [NSString
         stringWithFormat:@"%@%@%@", @"POI",
         appDelegate.destinationPreference, @".poi"];
  NSString *filePath = [RTModel filePath:fileComponent];

NSURL *pointsOfInterestDataURL =
                        [NSURL fileURLWithPath:filePath];
  pointsOfInterestData = [NSMutableArray
         arrayWithContentsOfURL:pointsOfInterestDataURL];
  if (!pointsOfInterestData) {
    pointsOfInterestData = [NSMutableArray arrayWithArray:
      [destinationData objectForKey:@"PointsOfInterest"]];
    NSDictionary *destinationPointOfInterestData =
    [destinationData objectForKey:@"DestinationLocation"];
    [pointsOfInterestData insertObject:
             destinationPointOfInterestData atIndex:0];
    [pointsOfInterestData writeToURL:
          pointsOfInterestDataURL atomically:YES];
  }
  pointsOfInterest =
    [NSMutableArray arrayWithCapacity:
                         [pointsOfInterestData count]];
  BOOL isInItinerary = NO;
  for (NSDictionary *aPointOfInterest in
                                pointsOfInterestData) {
    for (PointOfInterest *pointOfInterest in itinerary) {
      if ([pointOfInterest.title isEqualToString:
               [aPointOfInterest objectForKey:@"Name"]])
    for (SharedPointOfInterest *sharedPointOfInterest
                                      in itinerary) {
      if ([sharedPointOfInterest.title isEqualToString:
               [aPointOfInterest objectForKey:@"Name"]])
       isInItinerary = YES;
    }
    if (!isInItinerary) {
          [pointsOfInterest addObject:[[PointOfInterest
        alloc]initWithData:aPointOfInterest]];
```

```
      }
      else {
        isInItinerary = NO;
      }
    }
  }
```

The idea here is that you simply replace a PointOfInterest with a SharedPointOfInterest. Not a big deal, right?

To see what you've accomplished so far, delete the old RoadTrip from the simulator or your device and then load the new RoadTrip. If you run it now, you'll see that you have the destination in the list, just like in Figure 4-7.

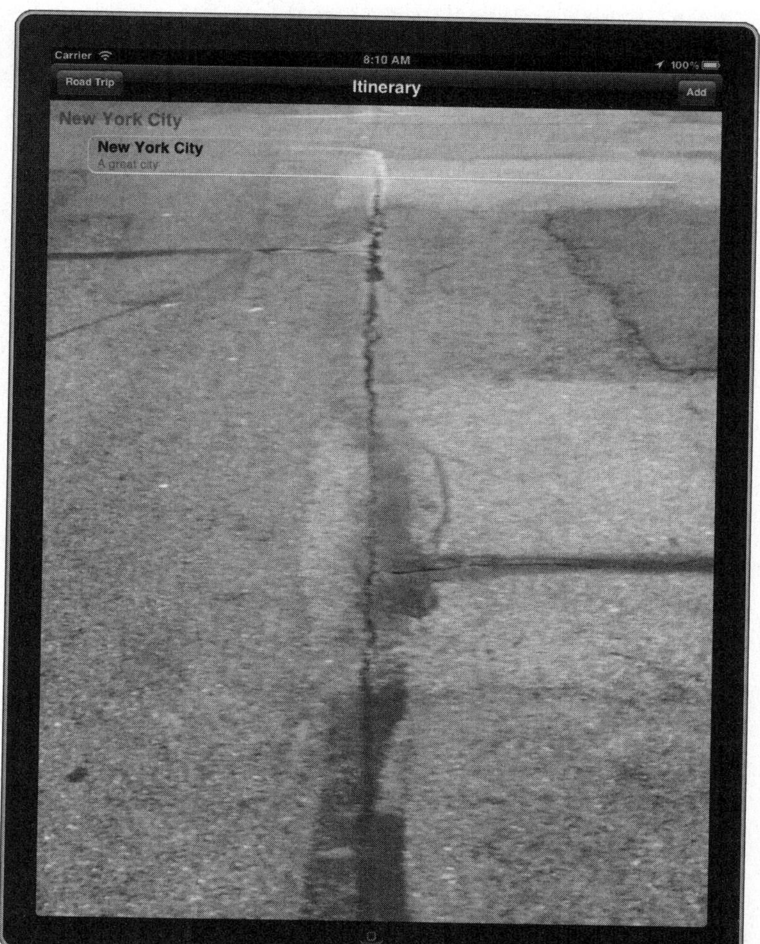

Figure 4-7: Now you're going someplace.

Because Core Data does a very good job of being persistent, you need to delete RoadTrip, which will delete the persistent store, whenever you make any significant changes (those that impact what is (or should be) in the Core Data store).

Timing is Everything

You want to be sure to add the `SharedPointOfInterest` managed object you created from the destination information to the persistent store right when you load the itinerary for the very first time. To be sure you get your timing right, wait until the store is actually loaded before you create the itinerary (and then the points of interest).

Luckily for you, you're going to know when the persistent store has been created because, in the `persistentStoreCoordinator` accessor that you added in Chapter 3, you post a notification that lets you know when that happens:

```
dispatch_async(dispatch_get_main_queue(), ^{
  NSLog(@"Persistent store added");
  [[NSNotificationCenter defaultCenter]
       postNotificationName:@"PersistentStoreAdded"
                                object:self userInfo:nil];
});
```

You could use the `destinationAddedKey` in `NSUserDefaults` to decide whether you should wait for the adding of the Destination `SharedPointOfInterest` before loading the itinerary. However, to make things simpler, I just have you wait anyway.

To set it up so that your timing jibes, delete the ***bolded-underlined-italicized*** code and add the **bolded** code in Listing 4-23 to `initWithDestinationIndex:` in `RTModel.m`.

Listing 4-23: Updating initWithDestinationIndex:

```
- (id)initWithDestinationIndex:
                         (NSUInteger)destinationIndex {

  if ((self = [super init])) {

    NSURL *destinationsURL = [[NSBundle mainBundle]
          URLForResource:@"Destinations"
          withExtension:@"plist"];
```

```
    NSDictionary *destinations = [NSDictionary dictionaryW
          ithContentsOfURL:destinationsURL];
    NSArray *destinationsArray = [destinations objectForKe
          y:@"DestinationData"];
    destinationData = [destinationsArray objectAtIndex:des
          tinationIndex];
    destination = [[Destination alloc] initWithDestination
          Index:destinationIndex];
    [self loadEvents];
    [self loadItinerary];
    [self loadPointsOfInterest];
    [[NSNotificationCenter defaultCenter] postNotific
          ationName:@"DestinationChanged" object:self
          userInfo:nil];
    NSManagedObjectContext *context =
                            self.managedObjectContext;

    NSError *error = nil;
    itinerary = [NSMutableArray arrayWithArray:
      [context executeFetchRequest:self.
         sharedPointOfInterestFetchRequest error:&error]];
    if (error)
      NSLog(@"Core Data Failure! Error code: %u,
          description: %@, and reason: %@", error.
          code, [error localizedDescription], [error
          localizedFailureReason]);

    __block weak RTModel *weakSelf = self;

    [[NSNotificationCenter defaultCenter] addObserver
          ForName:@"PersistentStoreAdded" object:self
          queue:nil usingBlock:^(NSNotification *notif) {
      [weakSelf loadItinerary];
      [weakSelf loadPointsOfInterest];
      [[NSNotificationCenter defaultCenter] postNotifica
          tionName:@"DestinationChanged" object:weakSelf
          userInfo:nil];
    }];
  }
  return self;
}
```

Here you're simply deferring the sending of any and all `loadItinerary` and `loadPointsOfInterest` messages until you get notification that the persistent store had been loaded.

Because you're using a block here that references `RTModel` methods using `self`, you need to be concerned about the Retain cycle and declare `__block weak weakSelf` and use `weakSelf` instead of `self`. (I explain this fully in Chapter 3, where I talk about notifications in greater depth.)

```
__block weak RTModel *weakSelf = self;

 [[NSNotificationCenter defaultCenter]
     addObserverForName:@"PersistentStoreAdded"
         object:self queue:nil
                  usingBlock:^(NSNotification *notif) {
     [weakSelf loadItinerary];
     [weakSelf loadPointsOfInterest];
     [[NSNotificationCenter defaultCenter] postNotificati
         onName:@"DestinationChanged"
                         object:weakSelf userInfo:nil];
   }];
```

Note that you're also moving the DestinationChanged notification into that block. Because it's possible for the ItineraryController to be visible when you change the destination (see Figure 4-8), you notify it of any relevant change. (You, of course, have planned ahead and have registered it for the DestinationChanged notification.)

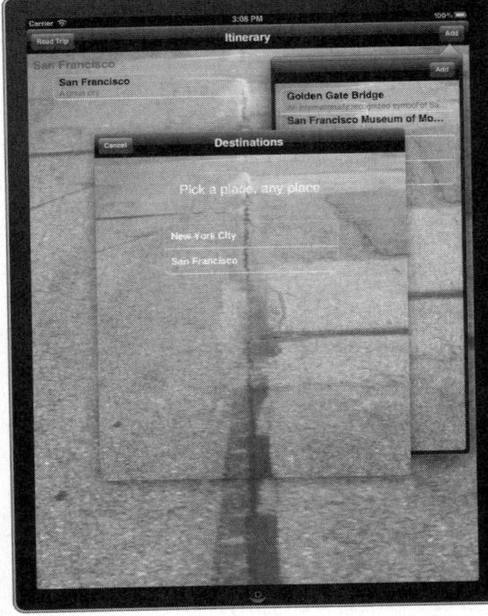

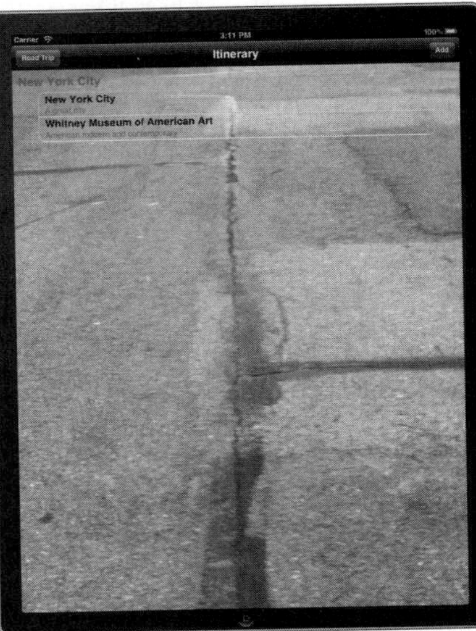

Figure 4-8: Changing the destination while the Itinerary Controller is visible.

You also need to update the ItineraryController destinationChanged: selector used by the Notification Center. When the destination changes, you need to create a new Fetched Results controller for the new managed object context; setting the fetchedResultsController property to nil will cause that to happen.

To do that, add the **bolded** code in Listing 4-24 to `destinationChanged:` in `ItineraryController.m`.

Listing 4-24: Updating destinationChanged:

```
- (void)destinationChanged:(NSNotification *)notif {

  _fetchedResultsController = nil;
  if (popover) {
    [popover dismissPopoverAnimated:YES];
    popover = nil;
  }
 [self.itineraryTableView reloadData];
}
```

When the data is reloaded, the `fetchedResultsController` is accessed by the Table View delegate methods. Because it's `nil`, the accessor method will create a new one using the current (new) managed object context.

Removing a Point Of Interest From the Itinerary

Currently, you can remove a point of interest from your itinerary by selecting any point of interest in the list, holding it down for two seconds to show the editing controls (or hide the editing controls if they're visible), tapping the Delete icon (Figure 4-9, left), and then tapping Delete (Figure 4-9, middle). The point of interest is then put back in the Points of Interest list (Figure 4-9, right). Although this isn't necessarily the best user experience, it's good enough for me to be able to show you how to delete a managed object from the managed object context.

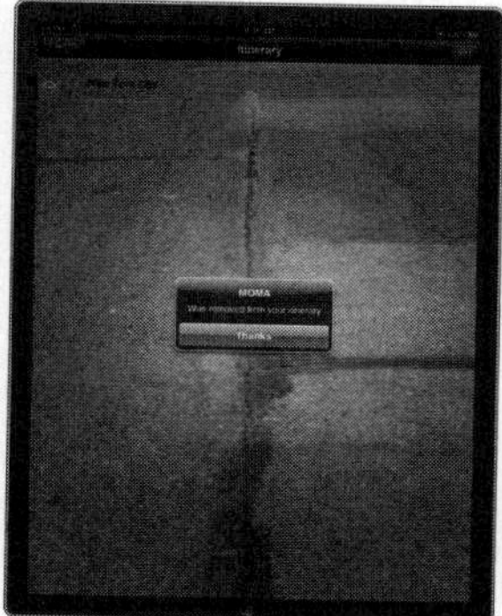
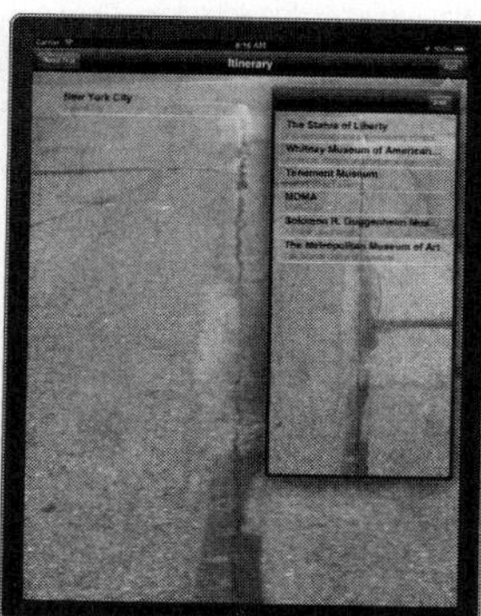

Figure 4-9: I changed my mind about MOMA.

How it works now

Pressing in the cell in the `ItineraryController` is recognized as a long press gesture. This was added to the view in the `ItineraryController`'s `viewDidLoad` method, as shown in Listing 4-25.

Listing 4-25: Creating the Gesture Recognizer in viewDidLoad

```
  - (void)viewDidLoad
{
…
UILongPressGestureRecognizer *longPressGesture =
  [[UILongPressGestureRecognizer alloc]
          initWithTarget:self action:@selector(handleLong
          PressGesture:)];
  longPressGesture.minimumPressDuration = 2;
[self.view addGestureRecognizer:longPressGesture];
..
}
```

Then, in the `handleLongPressGesture` method, editing is toggled — turned on if it's off or turned off if it's on — as shown in Listing 4-26.

Listing 4-26: Working with the handleLongPressGesture

```
- (void)handleLongPressGesture:
                      (UIGestureRecognizer *)sender {

  if (sender.state == UIGestureRecognizerStateEnded)
  [self.itineraryTableView
    setEditing:!self.itineraryTableView.editing
                                      animated:YES];
}
```

`[self.itineraryTableView setEditing:!self.itinerary TableView.editing animated:YES]` toggles the Table View editing mode. If you send the Table view the `setEditing:` message with a value of `YES`, the Table view goes into editing mode. Sending a value of `NO`, turns off editing mode. In editing mode, the cells of the table might show an insertion or deletion control on the left side of each cell and a reordering control on the right side — what is displayed is controlled by various `UITableViewDataSourceDelegate` methods. `editing` is a Table View property and indicates if the Table view is in editing mode.

You can also control whether a row can be edited. In RoadTrip, I don't want the user to be able to delete the Destination PointOfInterest because it is used to focus the map on the destination. I disable editing for that row in the Table View delegate method tableView:canEditRowAtIndexPath:indexPath, as you can see in Listing 4-27.

Listing 4-27: You can't delete the first row

```
- (BOOL)tableView:(UITableView *)tableView canEditRowAtInd
            exPath:(NSIndexPath *)indexPath
{
  if ((indexPath.section == 0) && (indexPath.row == 0))

  return NO;

  else
    return YES;
}
```

Here all I do is check to see if the selection is in the first row of the first (and only) section, and if it is I simply return NO

The Fetched Results controller has an array of its sections and the interface for a section is defined in the NSFetchedResultsSectionInfo protocol. name is a required property of that protocol. Here you check to see if destinationName, and the section name are the same. If it is, you won't allow the user to delete the first entry in that section — the destination — by returning NO.

When the Table view is in editing mode and the user first taps the Deletion control and then the Delete button, the UITableViewDataSourceDelegate tableView:commitEditingStyle:forRowAtIndexPath: message is sent to the delegate and, as you can see in Listing 4-28, the selected PointOfInterest is sent to the RTModel for deletion.

Listing 4-28: Using tableView:commitEditingStyle:forRowAtIndexPath:

```
- (void)tableView:(UITableView *)tableView
    commitEditingStyle:
      (UITableViewCellEditingStyle)editingStyle
          forRowAtIndexPath:(NSIndexPath *)indexPath {

  PointOfInterest *pointOfInterest =
    [itineraryPointsOfInterest
                              objectAtIndex:indexPath.row];
  [[RTModel model] removeFromItinerary:pointOfInterest];
}
```

Updating for Core Data

When you start using the Fetched Results controller and displaying multiple sections, determining which SharedPointOfInterest is the one that represents the destination is a bit trickier. To finesse that bit of business, start by deleting the ***bolded-underlined-italicized*** code and adding the bolded code in Listing 4-29 to tableView:canEditRowAtIndexPath:indexPath in ItineraryController.m.

Listing 4-29: You can't delete the first row, part II

```
- (BOOL)tableView:(UITableView *)tableView
        canEditRowAtIndexPath:(NSIndexPath *)indexPath {

  if ((indexPath.section == 0) && (indexPath.row == 0))

 id <NSFetchedResultsSectionInfo> section  =
     [[self.fetchedResultsController sections]
                          objectAtIndex:indexPath.section];

 if ([section.name isEqualToString:[[RTModel model]
          destinationName]] && indexPath.row == 0)
    return NO;

  else
    return YES;
}
```

The Fetched Results controller has an array of its sections, and the interface for any particular section is defined in the NSFetchedResultsSectionInfo protocol. name is a required property of that protocol. Here you check to see if the destinationName, and the section name are the same. If it is, you won't allow the user to delete the first entry in that section — the destination — by returning NO.

But because you're now using SharedPointOfInterest, you need to update tableView:commitEditingStyle:forRowAtIndexPath: to use that class.

To do that, delete the ***bolded-underlined-italicized*** code and add the **bolded** code in Listing 4-30 to tableView:commitEditingStyle:forRowAtIndexPath: ItineraryController.m.

Listing 4-30: Updating tableView:commitEditingStyle: forRowAtIndexPath:

```
- (void)tableView:(UITableView *)tableView
   commitEditingStyle:
        (UITableViewCellEditingStyle)editingStyle
             forRowAtIndexPath:(NSIndexPath *)indexPath {

  PointOfInterest *pointOfInterest =
    [itineraryPointsOfInterest
                      objectAtIndex:indexPath.row];
  [[RTModel model] removeFromItinerary:pointOfInterest];
  SharedPointOfInterest *sharedPointOfInterest =
      (SharedPointOfInterest *)
          [self.fetchedResultsController
                        objectAtIndexPath:indexPath];
  [[RTModel model] removeFromItinerary:sharedPointOfInter
          est];
}
```

Close but no cigar. You still need to update `RTModel.h` to use the `SharedPointOfInterest` in `removeFromItinerary:` (in fact there will be a compiler warning to inform you of that). To take care of that, delete the ***bolded-underlined-italicized*** code and add the **bolded** code in Listing 4-31 to `RTModel.h`.

Listing 4-31: Change the removeFromItinerary: declaration

```
#import <Foundation/Foundation.h>
#import <MapKit/MapKit.h>
#import <CoreData/CoreData.h>
@class Annotation;
@class PointOfInterest;
@class SharedPointOfInterest;

@interface RTModel : NSObject

+ (RTModel *)model;
- (id)initWithDestinationIndex:(NSUInteger)
           destinationIndex;
- (void)loadItinerary;
- (void)addToItinerary:(PointOfInterest *)pointOfInterest;
- (void)removeFromItinerary:
                        (PointOfInterest *)pointOfInterest;
- (void)removeFromItinerary:
                 (SharedPointOfInterest *)pointOfInterest;
...
@end
```

You're getting there, but you still need to update the `removeFromItinerary` method in `RTModel.m` so that it can use a `SharedPointOfInterest`.

Delete the ***bolded-underlined-italicized*** code and add the **bolded** code in Listing 4-32 to `removeFromItinerary:` in `RTModel.m`.

Listing 4-32: Updating removeFromItinerary:

```
- (void)removeFromItinerary:
                        (PointOfInterest *)pointOfInterest {
- (void)removeFromItinerary:
          (SharedPointOfInterest *)sharedPointOfInterest {

  UIAlertView *alert = [[UIAlertView alloc]
    initWithTitle:pointOfInterest.title
    initWithTitle:sharedPointOfInterest.title
    message:@"Was removed from your itinerary"
    delegate:self cancelButtonTitle:@"Thanks"
    otherButtonTitles:nil];
  [alert show];

  NSDictionary *itineraryItemToRemove;
  for (NSDictionary *itineraryItem in itineraryData) {
    if ([[itineraryItem objectForKey:@"Name"]
          isEqualToString:pointOfInterest.title]) {
      itineraryItemToRemove = itineraryItem;
      break;
    }
  }

  [itineraryData removeObject:itineraryItemToRemove];
  [itinerary removeObject:pointOfInterest];
  RTAppDelegate *appDelegate =
            [[UIApplication sharedApplication] delegate];
  NSString *fileComponent =
    [NSString stringWithFormat:@"%@%@%@", @"Itinerary",
            appDelegate.destinationPreference, @".poi"];
  NSString *filePath = [RTModel filePath:fileComponent];
  NSURL *itineraryDataURL =
                      [NSURL fileURLWithPath:filePath];
  [itineraryData writeToURL:
                      itineraryDataURL atomically:YES];

  NSManagedObjectContext* context = sharedPointOfInterest.
          managedObjectContext;
  [context deleteObject:sharedPointOfInterest];
  NSError *error = nil;
  if ([[[context persistentStoreCoordinator]
          persistentStores] count] > 0) {
```

```
    if (![context save:&error]) {
      NSString *errorMessage =
                              [error localizedDescription];
      UIAlertView *alertView = [[UIAlertView alloc]
           initWithTitle:@"Error in accessing your
            itinerary. Restart Road Trip and contact
            customer support if the error continues."
            message:errorMessage delegate:nil
            cancelButtonTitle:@"OK" otherButtonTitles:nil];
      [alertView show];
      NSLog(@"Core Data Failure! Error code: %u,
            description: %@, and reason: %@", error.
            code, [error localizedDescription], [error
            localizedFailureReason]);
      return;
    }
    itinerary = [NSMutableArray arrayWithArray:
       [context executeFetchRequest:
          self.sharedPointOfInterestFetchRequest
                                     error:&error]];
    NSLog(@"Core Data Failure! Error code: %u,
            description: %@, and reason: %@", error.code,
            [error localizedDescription],
           [error localizedFailureReason]);
  }
  [self loadPointsOfInterest];

  [[NSNotificationCenter defaultCenter]
     postNotificationName:@"ItineraryChanged"
                                object:self userInfo:nil];
  [[NSNotificationCenter defaultCenter]
     postNotificationName:@"PointsOfInterestChanged"
                                object:self userInfo:nil];
}
```

This pretty much does the same thing as the `addToItinerary:` method I highlight in Listing 4-9, except in reverse so I don't go through the logic here.

Deleting a managed object is also similar to adding one, as you'll soon see.

To delete a managed object:

```
[context deleteObject:sharedPointOfInterest];
```

To add a managed object:

```
[NSEntityDescription insertNewObjectForEntityForName:
 @"SharedPointOfInterest" inManagedObjectContext:context];
```

Because you won't need `itineraryData` any more, you can delete it from `RTModel.m`. Just delete the ***bolded-underlined-italicized*** code in Listing 4-33 in `RTModel.m`.

Listing 4-33: Update RTModel.m

```
#import "RTModel.h"
#import "RTAppDelegate.h"
#import "Destination.h"
#import "PointOfInterest.h"
#import "Annotation.h"
#import "SharedPointOfInterest.h"

typedef void (^addLocationCompletionHandler)
                (Annotation *annotation, NSError* error);

@interface RTModel () {
  NSDictionary *destinationData;
  Destination* destination;
  NSMutableArray *events;
  NSMutableArray *pointsOfInterest;
  NSMutableArray *itinerary;
  NSMutableArray *itineraryData;
  NSMutableArray *pointsOfInterestData;
  addLocationCompletionHandler
          addFindLocationCompletionHandler;
  CLLocation *foundLocation;
  NSFetchRequest *sharedPointOfInterestFetchRequest;
}
@end
```

Now what you have is a situation where Core Data is managing the `SharedPointOfInterest` objects in your itinerary. But what that really means is that, once you have created your `SharedPointOfInterest` objects, you never have to worry about them again — even when the application is terminated. When the user re-launches RoadTrip, Core Data will re-instantiate the `SharedPointOfInterest` objects, instead of you reading in the file and doing it yourself. And that's what a persistent object store is all about.

What's more, as you'll see in Chapter 5, Core Data will also manage to keep your itinerary and `SharedPointOfInterest` objects synchronized across devices.

Chapter 5

Adding iCloud Support

In This Chapter

- Seeing how iCloud works
- Using Core Data to implement iCloud support
- Managing iCloud provisioning and entitlements
- Testing your iCloud implementation

The fact that the iPhone and the iPad are *mobile* isn't what makes them so beloved — hey, there are lots of mobile devices available after all. What people really like is the fact that the iPhone and iPad *make it easier for them to be mobile.*

One thing that increases mobility is the ability to share your data among devices without having to manually sync them. Of course, the applications built into the iPhone and iPad (Contacts and Calendars, for example) or built by Apple (Keynote and Pages, for example) already do the sharing thing using iCloud. But while that works great for the Apple apps, what about data sharing for all the non-Apple apps — apps such as RoadTrip?

Well, just as the Apple apps are built on top of iCloud, you can also build your apps on top of iCloud. In this chapter, you get introduced to the features in Core Data that let you do precisely that.

Of course, you have another alternative — you can build the infrastructure to do all the data sharing work. All you would have to do is take these steps:

1. Set up and configure servers.
2. Create a protocol.
3. Write a lot of code to make it efficient.
4. Implement push notifications.
5. Add replication for high availability and disaster recovery.
6. Pay for the storage and bandwidth.
7. Be on call 24/7.

The choice is yours. But having done it on my own, before iCloud was available, I want to tell you that this task isn't for the faint of heart — or for anyone who wants a life for that matter. Unless you have lots of money to hire people to do it for you, iCloud is the way to go.

iCloud

iCloud is an Apple technology that provides a way for you to share data among instances of your app running on different devices. Your app (usually) will continue to store its data on the device it's currently running on, but a copy of your data will also reside on iCloud (except for SQLite files in Core Data, where transaction files are stored instead). When your app makes a change to its data on one device, the changes are seamlessly sent to iCloud, where iCloud then updates its copy (or its transaction files) and then sends updates to all other instances of your app on different devices. If the app isn't currently running, those changes are made available when it's launched. While all this is going on, your app continues to operate on the file as if it's simply sitting there and not being sent hither and yon.

iCloud is free to all users (along with 5GB of storage) and is part of the iOS setup. If you need to use more than that amount of storage, you can (of course) buy more storage or choose to delete some of the files being stored there.

Apple has worked hard at optimizing iCloud's performance. For example, if both devices are on the same wireless network, data transfer will go peer-to-peer rather than through the Apple servers.

In RoadTrip, I show you how to use iCloud to share your itinerary among devices. To see what that would like, check out Figure 5-1.

Figure 5-1 makes the advantages of iCloud clear: no more explicit user synchronization features or having to use a computer as a hub.

You have two flavors of iCloud storage:

- **Document storage:** You can share documents as well as app data. Document storage is the way to go if you want to coordinate your app's user-oriented data files, but it can be used to synchronize any files your app uses internally.
- **Key-value data storage:** As the name implies, key-value data storage lets you share small amounts of relatively stable (key) data among instances of your app — things such as preferences come to mind here.

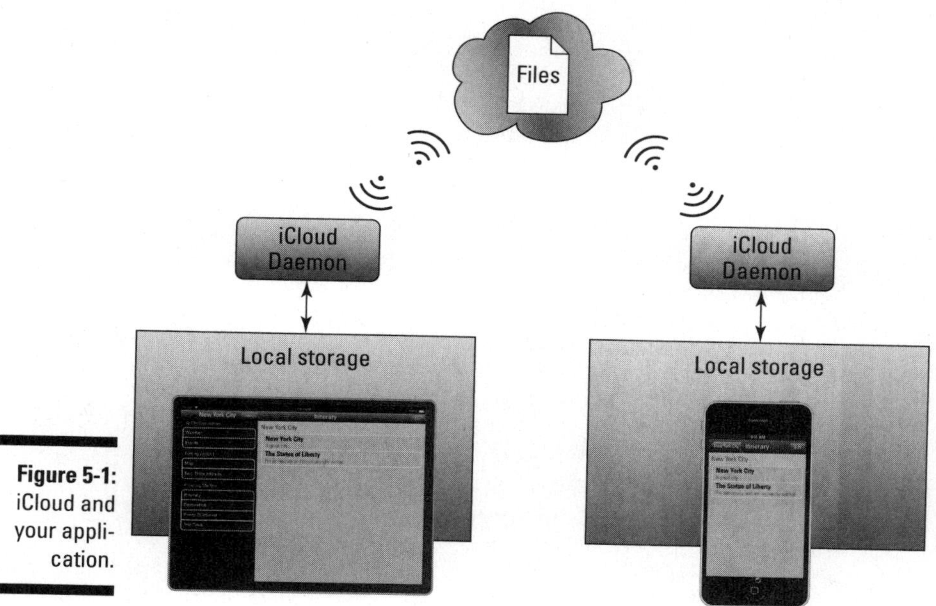

Figure 5-1: iCloud and your application.

Putting iCloud to work for you

Implementing iCloud can require a bit of work on your part, but as you see in the upcoming "Enter Core Data" section, you can have Core Data do most of that work for you. The following step list gives you an overview of the task ahead:

1. Determine whether iCloud is enabled by sending the `NSFileManager` the `URLForUbiquityContainerIdentifier:` message.
2. Add file presenters, which manage the files stored in iCloud. A file presenter must adopt the `NSFilePresenter` protocol and make all changes through an `NSFileCoordinator` object that locks the file to keep it from being changed by the iCloud *daemons* — programs that run in the background under control of the system as opposed to being controlled by the end user.

   The easiest way to do all that is to use the `UIDocument` class, which implements the `NSFilePresenter` protocol methods to handle file management and leaves you to read and write the data when required.
3. Explicitly move your files to iCloud. After you create your file (or directory) in your app's sandbox, you'll use the `NSFileManager` `URLForUbiquityContainerIdentifier:` method to get a URL for

the iCloud container directory that you want to use in order to store a file, build a new URL that specifies the iCloud path, and then send the `NSFileManager` the `setUbiquitous:itemAtURL:destinationURL:error:` message to move the files. (This process will have to be done on a separate thread.) You then manage files and directories in iCloud the same way you'd manage your local files and directories — the only difference is the URLs you use to access them are relative to the iCloud container directory rather than being relative to your app's sandbox.

4. Handle version conflicts for a file — conflicts that arise when two instances of an app change their copy of the file and transfer both to iCloud. When this happens, both versions of the file are stored and iCloud tells your app's file presenters that they need to resolve the issue.
5. Use running `NSMetadataQuery` objects to receive notifications as files are added or removed from other devices.
6. Handle cases where files are in iCloud but not fully downloaded to the local device. Files aren't fully downloaded until your app either A) attempts to open or access the file or B) sends the `NSFileManager` the `startDownloadingUbiquitousItemAtURL:error:` message to download the changes explicitly. So, be sure to check the download status of a file before trying to open it (and if it's a large file, let the user know this may take some time). Although the user should not have to care whether his or her file is in the cloud (or even that there is such a thing as a file), if something is going to impact the user experience, it behooves you to keep the user informed of what's going on.

Enter Core Data

I realize this whole Putting iCloud to Work for You thing must seem pretty daunting. In fact, I know from personal experience how daunting it can actually be because I went through all those steps listed in the preceding section when I started working with iCloud. You do have an alternative, however, and that is to use Core Data. In fact, if you've worked through the Core Data discussion back in Chapters 3 and 4, adding iCloud support is pretty easy.

So, even though it's true that the `UIDocument` class does support iCloud and you can thus put it to use for your iCloud file management needs, what you really want to do is use Core Data even for document storage — and that means you want to use the new `NSManagedDocument` class instead of the `UIDocument` class. (In any event, `NSManagedDocument` has all the functionality of `UIDocument` and then some.)

And because RoadTrip already uses Core Data, adding iCloud support is remarkably easy.

You do need to understand that when you use Core Data with an SQLite store (which is what you have been doing), the actual database file is never transferred to the iCloud server. Each device has its own copy of the SQLite store and synchronizes changes by writing them to a transaction file. The transaction files are what then get transferred to and from iCloud from each device. Core Data uses the transaction files to update its local database. The result is that each local database ends up with the exact same set of changes. This situation is illustrated in Figure 5-2.

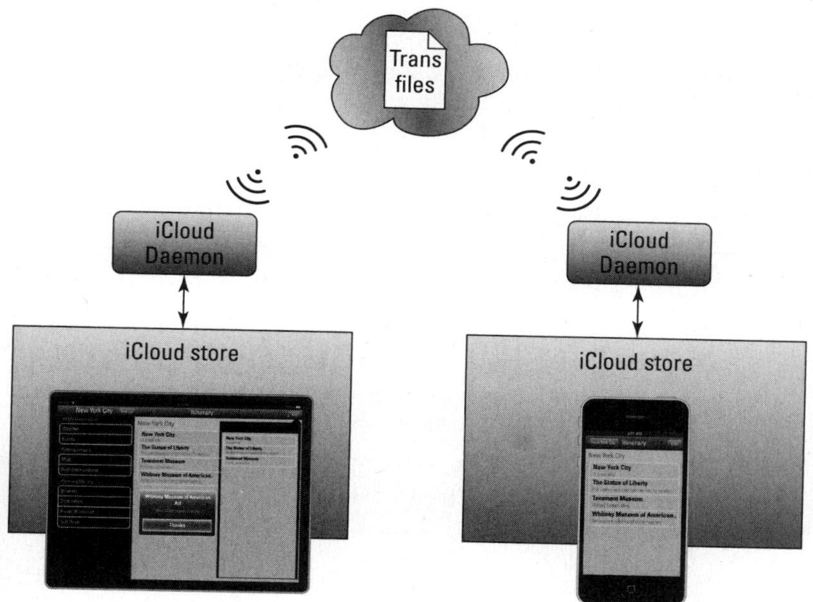

Figure 5-2: Core Data and iCloud.

Before you can move your transaction file into the cloud, the first thing your app needs to do is get a URL that points to the iCloud storage container — called the *ubiquity container* by Apple. You need the URL because you must tell Core Data where to store the transaction logs associated with changes to the store. This URL will look something like the following:

```
/private/var/mobile/Library/Mobile
    Documents/N42E42A42L.com.nealgoldstein.RoadTrip/
                                RoadTripSharedPointsOfInterest
```

I'll be referring to this as the *iCloud Container Directory URL*. The key here is the `N42E42A42L.com.nealgoldstein.RoadTrip` business, where the `N42E42A42L` is my Developer program *Team ID* (assigned by Apple and part of your provisioning profile) and the `com.nealgoldstein.RoadTrip` part is my application's (RoadTrip) *Bundle ID* — the two together make up the path to my app's ubiquity container in iCloud. (Note that the `RoadTripShared PointsOfInterest` part refers to a subdirectory I have specified in that container — this will come from something called an Entitlements file that I explain in the "Configuring Your App's iCloud Entitlements" section, later in this chapter.)

Setting up Core Data for iCloud

You need to do two things to set up iCloud:

1. Provide a value for the `NSPersistentStoreUbiquitousContentNameKey`. This key is used to identify your persistent store and needs to be used by all the devices that want to use that file (in this case, the transaction logs for the local SQLite database).

2. Provide a value for the `NSPersistentStoreUbiquitous ContentURLKey`. This key identifies the directory in the ubiquity container where the transaction logs will be stored. (This is the `N42E42A42L.com.nealgoldstein.RoadTrip/ RoadTripSharedPointsOfInterest` that I showed you in the "Enter Core Data" section, earlier in this chapter.)

   As far as you're concerned, while this step has to be done, you may not be the one having to do it. If you don't provide a value for the `NSPersistentStoreUbiquitousContentURLKey`, Core Data will create a default value by using your Bundle ID — the ID listed in the `RoadTrip-Info.plist` as the Bundle Identifier Key. Core Data takes the Bundle ID and then slaps on your team ID — a unique 10-character string generated by Apple, also known as the *Bundle Seed ID* — in front of it. These two pieces put together are known as your App ID. (You can read more on App IDs in the "Provisioning Your App for iCloud" section, later in this chapter.)

   Using the default Bundle ID is fine for iOS devices for the simple reason that your app will stick with the same Bundle ID across all devices. However, if you also want to access your files and container on non-iOS devices (such as the Mac), you may run into trouble because it's unlikely that such a device will have this same Bundle ID. In Listing 5-1, I have you create a value yourself using your Team ID, Bundle ID, and a subdirectory just to show you how it's done, and later — in the "Configuring Your App's iCloud Entitlements" section, later in this chapter, to be specific — I explain how you can specify that this is the ID you want to use on another device with a different Bundle ID.

Oh, and by the way, sometimes your Bundle ID is case sensitive and sometimes not, so treat it always as case sensitive.

Both of these things are really easy to do. In fact, all you have to do is add the code in bold to the `persistentStoreCoordinator` in `RTModel.m`, as shown in Listing 5-1.

Listing 5-1: Updating persistentStoreCoordinator

```
- (NSPersistentStoreCoordinator *)
                              persistentStoreCoordinator {

  if (_persistentStoreCoordinator != nil) {
    return _persistentStoreCoordinator;
  }

  _persistentStoreCoordinator =
   [[NSPersistentStoreCoordinator alloc]
    initWithManagedObjectModel:[self managedObjectModel]];

  RTAppDelegate *appDelegate =
          [[UIApplication sharedApplication] delegate];
  NSString *storePathComponent =
     [NSString stringWithFormat:@"%@%@%@",@"Model",
         appDelegate.destinationPreference, @".sqlite"];
  NSString *storePath =
                 [RTModel filePath:storePathComponent];
  dispatch_async(dispatch_get_global_queue(
                 DISPATCH_QUEUE_PRIORITY_DEFAULT, 0), ^{
    NSURL *storeUrl = [NSURL fileURLWithPath:storePath];
    NSDictionary* options = nil;

#if !TARGET_IPHONE_SIMULATOR
    NSFileManager *fileManager =
                       [NSFileManager defaultManager];
    NSURL *persistentStoreUbiquitousContentURL =
     [fileManager URLForUbiquityContainerIdentifier:nil];

    NSString *ubiquityContainerIdentifierPath =
          [[persistentStoreUbiquitousContentURL path]
          stringByAppendingPathComponent:
                    @"RoadTripSharedPointsOfInterest"];
    persistentStoreUbiquitousContentURL =
      [NSURL fileURLWithPath:
                     ubiquityContainerIdentifierPath];
    options = [NSDictionary dictionaryWithObjectsAndKeys:
      [NSString stringWithFormat:
        @"%@%@",@"com.nealgoldstein.coredata.
        itineraryR01.",appDelegate.destinationPreference],
         NSPersistentStoreUbiquitousContentNameKey,
       persistentStoreUbiquitousContentURL,
```

(continued)

Listing 5-1 *(continued)*

```
          NSPersistentStoreUbiquitousContentURLKey,
        [NSNumber numberWithBool:YES],
          NSMigratePersistentStoresAutomaticallyOption,
        [NSNumber numberWithBool:YES],
          NSInferMappingModelAutomaticallyOption,nil];
#endif

...
}
```

The bolded part starts with you using the following preprocessor directive:

```
#if !TARGET_IPHONE_SIMULATOR
```

This directive tells the compiler to check to see whether you're building for the actual device or just the simulator — and if you're building for the device to include the statements up to the `#endif`.

I go to the trouble of doing this because, if you're using iCloud, you of course need to be running on the device, but it's also handy to be able to run on the simulator so you can work on other parts of your app using a non-shared Core Data store.

Looking at the statements that get included, you start by setting up the value for the `NSPersistentStoreUbiquitousContentURLKey` — the iCloud Container Directory URL. To do that, you first get the `URLForUbiquityContainerIdentifier` from the file manager — this is the URL for your app's iCloud Container Directory. (Refer to Step 3 in the section "Putting iCloud to work for you," earlier in this chapter.)

```
NSFileManager *fileManager =
                              [NSFileManager defaultManager];
NSURL *persistentStoreUbiquitousContentURL =
     [fileManager URLForUbiquityContainerIdentifier:nil];
```

By specifying `nil` for the `URLForUbiquityContainerIdentifier`, you're telling this method to use the first container listed in the `com.apple.developer.ubiquity-container-identifiers` entitlement — explained in due course in the "Configuring Your App's iCloud Entitlements" section, later in this chapter. This first container corresponds to `N42E42A42L.com.nealgoldstein.RoadTrip`.

You then create the path to the container directory:

```
NSString *ubiquityContainerIdentifierPath =
  [[persistentStoreUbiquitousContentURL path]
          stringByAppendingPathComponent:
                           @"RoadTripSharedPointsOfInterest"];
```

Then comes the `NSPersistentStoreUbiquitousContentURLKey` value — the NSURL that contains the path you just created. (This is the second of two things you need to do in order to set up iCloud, as spelled out at the beginning of this section.)

```
persistentStoreUbiquitousContentURL =
      [NSURL fileURLWithPath:
                         ubiquityContainerIdentifierPath];
```

Now all the pieces are in place for you to set up iCloud. You do that by creating and passing in an Options directory to the `addPersistentStoreWithType:configuration:URL:options:error:` message, which adds the persistent store. When you weren't using iCloud, that message looked like the following:

```
  [_persistentStoreCoordinator
    addPersistentStoreWithType:NSSQLiteStoreType
      configuration:nil URL:storeUrl options:options
                                              error:&error]
```

In that iCloud-less world, what you were doing was setting up an SQLite store. With iCloud in the picture, you'll be still doing that, but passing in an Options dictionary (previously it was `nil`) means you can now specify the values and keys needed by Core Data to implement iCloud support (and some additional non-iCloud support as well). I've bolded the keys to make them easier to see:

```
options =
  [NSDictionary dictionaryWithObjectsAndKeys:
    [NSString stringWithFormat:@"%@%@",
        @"com.nealgoldstein.coredata.itineraryR01.",
                 appDelegate.destinationPreference],
      NSPersistentStoreUbiquitousContentNameKey,
    persistentStoreUbiquitousContentURL,
      NSPersistentStoreUbiquitousContentURLKey,
    [NSNumber numberWithBool:YES],
      NSMigratePersistentStoresAutomaticallyOption,
    [NSNumber numberWithBool:YES],
      NSInferMappingModelAutomaticallyOption,nil];
```

The first bolded bit — `NSPersistentStoreUbiquitousContentNameKey` — is the name of the persistent store. (Providing a value for `NSPersistentStoreUbiquitousContentNameKey` is the first of two things you need to do in order to set up iCloud, as spelled out in the beginning of this section.) Here, you're naming it `com.nealgoldstein.coredata.itineraryR01`, followed by the destination identifier (0 for New York for example, 1 for San Francisco, and so on). As I explain in Chapter 3, I'm adding a separate store for each destination and do the same for the transaction files.

The second bolded bit — NSPersistentStoreUbiquitousContent URLKey — was just explained and is what you have just constructed.

The last bolded bits — NSMigratePersistentStoresAutomatically Option and NSInferMappingModelAutomaticallyOption — work together. As you might have found out already (if not, I find it out for you in Chapter 3), you can't just change your managed object model and then run the app. I've been having you delete the model, but as you go through development, that may not be convenient. The alternative is to *migrate* the model. You can do that by specifying a mapping model, but if you're just making simple changes to your model (such as adding a new attribute to an entity), Core Data can perform automatic data migration, referred to as *lightweight migration,* for you. In lightweight migration, Core Data infers a mapping model from differences between the old and new models. If the boolValue of the number in the NSMigratePersistentStores AutomaticallyOption key is YES, Core Data will perform the migration, and if the boolValue of the number in the NSInferMappingModel AutomaticallyOption is YES, Core Data will infer the mapping model from the perceived differences — that is, it will perform a lightweight migration.

I leave this to you to explore on your own, but be aware of this fact: If you're using iCloud, lightweight migration is the only game in town.

Handling changes

Although Core Data will do its job by keeping your data up to date, you need to do your part as far as the user interface is concerned. At this point, the notifications you have in place will work fine — just be sure to use them! For example, you have to post a notification in situations where your app is running on one device and the data is changed on another and Core Data has updated your store accordingly.

To get the notifications process started, you need to register for one particular notification: NSPersistentStoreDidImportUbiquitous ContentChangesNotification. You get this notification for each Persistent Store coordinator whose store has been modified by the import. To register, update managedObjectContext in RTModel.m with the bolded code in Listing 5-2.

Listing 5-2: Registering for the NSPersistentStoreDidImportUbiquitous ContentChangesNotification

```
- (NSManagedObjectContext *)managedObjectContext
{
  if (_managedObjectContext != nil) {
    return _managedObjectContext;
  }

  NSPersistentStoreCoordinator *coordinator =
                          [self persistentStoreCoordinator];

  if (coordinator != nil) {
    NSManagedObjectContext* managedObjectContext =
     [[NSManagedObjectContext alloc]
      initWithConcurrencyType:NSMainQueueConcurrencyType];

    [managedObjectContext performBlockAndWait:^{
       [managedObjectContext
               setPersistentStoreCoordinator:coordinator];
#if !TARGET_IPHONE_SIMULATOR
      [[NSNotificationCenter defaultCenter]
           addObserver:self selector:@selector(iCloudChang
           esReceived:) name:NSPersistentStoreDidImportUbi
           quitous
                                 ContentChangesNotification
           object:coordinator];
#endif
    }];
    _managedObjectContext = managedObjectContext;
  }
  return _managedObjectContext;
}
```

Although it doesn't fit on one line in the code on the printed page here, `NSPersistentStoreDidImportUbiquitousContentChanges Notification` is one word.

After registering, you also need to add the selector you specified when you added yourself as an observer — in this case, the `iCloudChangesReceived:` selector. Add the code in Listing 5-3 to `RTModel.m`.

Listing 5-3: Adding iCloudChangesReceived:

```
- (void)iCloudChangesReceived:(NSNotification *)
                                          notification {

  NSManagedObjectContext* context =
                         self.managedObjectContext;

  [context performBlock:^{
    [self persistentStoreChanged:notification
                               forContext:context];
  }];
}
```

Because notifications are posted on the callers' thread, you need to make sure that they're sent to the main thread, where the view controllers and your model live. (If this talk of different threads doesn't ring a bell, take a look at Chapter 3, where you can find a handy concurrency discussion.) To implement what you need to do as a result of the notification, you add a new method, `persistentStoreChanged:`, to the mix (you'll be getting a compiler error until you do that). Start by adding the method declaration to `RTModel.h` with the help of the bolded code in Listing 5-4.

Listing 5-4: Updating RTModel.h

```
@interface RTModel : NSObject

+ (RTModel *)model;
- (id)initWithDestinationIndex:
                       (NSUInteger)destinationIndex;
- (void)loadItinerary;
- (void)addToItinerary:(PointOfInterest *)pointOfInterest;
- (void)removeFromItinerary:(SharedPointOfInterest *)
                                     pointOfInterest;
- (void)loadPointsOfInterest;
- (NSArray *)returnPointsOfInterest;
- (void)addPointOfInterest:(NSMutableDictionary *)
                                 pointOfInterestData;
- (UIImage *)destinationImage;
- (NSString *)destinationName;
- (CLLocationCoordinate2D)destinationCoordinate;
- (NSString *)weather;
- (void)loadEvents;
- (NSUInteger)numberOfEvents;
- (NSString *)getEvent:(NSUInteger)index;
- (NSString *)mapTitle;
- (NSArray *)createAnnotations;
```

```
- (void)addLocation:(NSString *)findLocation
          completionHandler:(void (^)(Annotation
          *annotation, NSError* error)) completion;
- (CLLocation *)foundLocation;
+ (NSString *)filePath:(NSString *)fileComponent;
- (void)persistentStoreChanged:
     (NSNotification*)notification forContext:(NSManagedOb
          jectContext*)context;

@property (readonly, strong, nonatomic)
          NSManagedObjectContext *managedObjectContext;
@property (readonly, strong, nonatomic)
              NSManagedObjectModel *managedObjectModel;
@property (readonly, strong, nonatomic)
          NSPersistentStoreCoordinator
                              *persistentStoreCoordinator;
@end
```

With the method declaration in place, you can now add the method itself by adding the code in Listing 5-5 to RTModel.m.

Listing 5-5: Add persistentStoreChanged:

```
- (void)persistentStoreChanged:
     (NSNotification*)notification forContext:(NSManagedO
          bjectContext*)context {

  [context mergeChangesFromContextDidSaveNotification:
                                            notification];

  [[NSNotificationCenter defaultCenter]
     postNotificationName:@"PersistentStoreChanged"
          object:self userInfo:[notification userInfo]];
}
```

mergeChangesFromContextDidSaveNotification: is a managed object context method that will merge the changes you get from the iCloudChangesReceived notification. The notification you get includes a dictionary that contains the object IDs of the objects that have been changed, added, or deleted. You then post a notification to let your other objects know that the persistent store has changed. The userInfo method used here simply returns the dictionary associated with that notification, which is then used in the userInfo parameter of the postNotificationName:object:userInfo: method.

Finally, you have to actually *respond* to the notification. To do that, update initWithDestinationIndex: with the bolded code in Listing 5-6.

Listing 5-6: Updating initWithDestinationIndex:

```
- (id)initWithDestinationIndex:
                          (NSUInteger)destinationIndex {

  if ((self = [super init])) {

    NSURL *destinationsURL = [[NSBundle mainBundle]
       URLForResource:@"Destinations"
                           withExtension:@"plist"];
    NSDictionary *destinations =
       [NSDictionary dictionaryWithContentsOfURL:
                                  destinationsURL];
    NSArray *destinationsArray =
           [destinations objectForKey:@"DestinationData"];
    destinationData =
       [destinationsArray objectAtIndex:destinationIndex];
    destination = [[Destination alloc] initWithDestination
          Index:destinationIndex];
    [self loadEvents];
    NSManagedObjectContext *context =
                          self.managedObjectContext;
    NSError *error = nil;
    itinerary = [NSMutableArray arrayWithArray:
        [context executeFetchRequest:
           self.sharedPointOfInterestFetchRequest
                                   error:&error]];
    if (error)
      NSLog(@"Core Data Failure! Error code: %u,
           description: %@, and reason: %@", error.
           code, [error localizedDescription], [error
           localizedFailureReason]);

    __block weak RTModel *weakSelf = self;

    [[NSNotificationCenter defaultCenter] addObserver
           ForName:@"PersistentStoreAdded" object:self
           queue:nil usingBlock:^(NSNotification *notif) {
      [weakSelf loadItinerary];
      [weakSelf loadPointsOfInterest];
      [[NSNotificationCenter defaultCenter] postNotifica
           tionName:@"DestinationChanged" object:weakSelf
           userInfo:nil];
    }];
#if !TARGET_IPHONE_SIMULATOR
    [[NSNotificationCenter defaultCenter] addObserver:self
           selector:@selector(persistentStoreChanged:)
           name:@"PersistentStoreChanged" object:nil];
#endif
  }
  return self;
}
```

Then add the selector you specified in the `addObserver:selector:name:object:` message — `persistentStoreChanged:` — by adding the code in Listing 5-7 to `RTModel.m`.

Listing 5-7: Adding persistentStoreChanged

```
#if !TARGET_IPHONE_SIMULATOR
- (void)persistentStoreChanged:(NSNotification *)notif {

  NSManagedObjectContext *context =
                                self.managedObjectContext;
  NSError *error = nil;

  itinerary = [NSMutableArray arrayWithArray:
     [context executeFetchRequest:self.
         sharedPointOfInterestFetchRequest error:&error]];
  NSString *destinationName =
    [[destinationData objectForKey:@"DestinationLocation"]
                                    objectForKey:@"Name"];
  SharedPointOfInterest
                *destinationSharedPointOfInterest = nil;
  for (SharedPointOfInterest* sharedPointOfInterest in
                                           itinerary) {
    if (([sharedPointOfInterest.name
      isEqualToString:destinationName]) &&
        ([sharedPointOfInterest.displayOrder intValue] ==
                                                 0 )) {
      if (destinationSharedPointOfInterest) {
        [self.managedObjectContext
                  deleteObject:sharedPointOfInterest];
        if (![context save:&error]) {
          NSString *errorMessage =
                         [error localizedDescription];
          UIAlertView *alertView = [[UIAlertView alloc]
            initWithTitle:@"Error in accessing your
              itinerary. Restart Road Trip and contact
              customer support if the error continues."
             message:errorMessage delegate:nil
             cancelButtonTitle:@"OK"
             otherButtonTitles:nil];
          [alertView show];
          NSLog(@"Core Data Failure! Error code: %u,
            description: %@, and reason: %@", error.code,
            [error localizedDescription],
            [error localizedFailureReason]);
          return;
        }
      }
      destinationSharedPointOfInterest =
                               sharedPointOfInterest;
```

(continued)

Listing 5-7 *(continued)*

```
        }
    }
    [self loadPointsOfInterest];
    [[NSNotificationCenter defaultCenter]
        postNotificationName:@"PointsOfInterestChanged"
        object:self userInfo:nil];
    [[NSNotificationCenter defaultCenter]
        postNotificationName:@"ItineraryChanged"
        object:self userInfo:nil];
}
#endif
```

`persistentStoreChanged:` is an interesting method because it makes explicit some things about working with iCloud that may be a bit subtle at this point.

Note that a network is involved here — which means that, as with all things network-related, there's a chance that it may take some time for any changes to the store to be downloaded. This is normally not a problem (aside from user annoyance) except for the very first time you launch the app on a device. That's because we've set it up so that you add a `SharedPointOfInterest` managed object to represent the destination in the `loadItinerary` method, as spelled out in the following excerpt from Listing 5-6. If the app has already been launched on another device, when the timing is right your store will already have been updated with that `SharedPointOfInterest` *before* you load your itinerary. When you then check to see whether any objects are in your itinerary, there will be one courtesy of the other device, and you won't have to create one on your own.

```
itinerary = [NSMutableArray arrayWithArray:
   [context executeFetchRequest:
    self.sharedPointOfInterestFetchRequest error:&error]];
  if (error)
    NSLog(@"Core Data Failure! Error code: %u,
          description: %@, and reason: %@", error.code,
          [error localizedDescription],
          [error localizedFailureReason]);
  if (![itinerary count]) {
```

But, if your slow-as-molasses network does bring about a lag, you'll end up with nothing in the fetch, which means you'll add the object only to later have that very same object sent to you as an update (as will the other device).

So, in your code what you want to do is check to see whether there are two destination `SharedPointOfInterest` objects (by definition, the destination `SharedPointOfInterest displayOrder` is 0); if there are, you delete any others. There is, of course, a statistical possibility (albeit small) that if two people are working on two devices simultaneously, both objects will be deleted — you can take that into account in your code, but I leave that to you to figure out. In that case, the user will have to add the destination `SharedPointOfInterest` object back.

This is by no means a problem unique to Core Data. It has to do with the fact that I wanted to go with asynchronous processing and that I chose to add an object to the store outside of the normal flow. I could have done this differently by creating a unique object to represent the destination outside of Core Data, or I could have even created a separate managed object context, but I leave it to you to work that out on your own.

Configuring Your App's iCloud Entitlements

You probably know all about those provisioning profiles Apple makes you do if you want to actually run your app on a device. I talk about some of those provisioning requirements in a bit, but it turns out that, in order to use iCloud, you also need to sign your app with iCloud-specific entitlements. This section shows you how to deal with that.

In the "Setting up Core Data for iCloud" section, earlier in this chapter, you had the `URLForUbiquityContainerIdentifier:` method use the first container listed in the `com.apple.developer.ubiquity-container-identifiers` entitlement (by specifying `nil`).

```
NSFileManager *fileManager =
                            [NSFileManager defaultManager];
NSURL *persistentStoreUbiquitousContentURL =
      [fileManager URLForUbiquityContainerIdentifier:nil];
```

The thing is, you could have specified a different container if you wanted to, but to do that you would have to add the container to your app's entitlements.

All fine and dandy, but what exactly are these things called entitlements?

In general, *entitlements* enable your app to do certain things. In iOS and on the Mac, you have entitlements designed to enable iCloud storage and push notification, whereas on the Mac alone you have an additional entitlement for sandboxing. In the RoadTrip app, you're going to take advantage of the Enabling iCloud Storage and Push Notifications aspects of entitlements.

You're going to keep all your iCloud entitlements in a file named `RoadTrip.entitlements`, which I'll have you add to your app shortly. The `RoadTrip.entitlements` file is a property list file like the `RoadTrip-info.plist` file, and includes the keys and values for your application's entitlements. When you're building for the device, Xcode checks to make sure that your entitlements are consistent with your Provisioning Profile (more on that in the "Provisioning Your App for iCloud" section, later in this chapter) and your app will be able to run on the device. If everything isn't consistent, you'll get the dreaded "The executable was signed with invalid entitlements" message, shown in Figure 5-3.

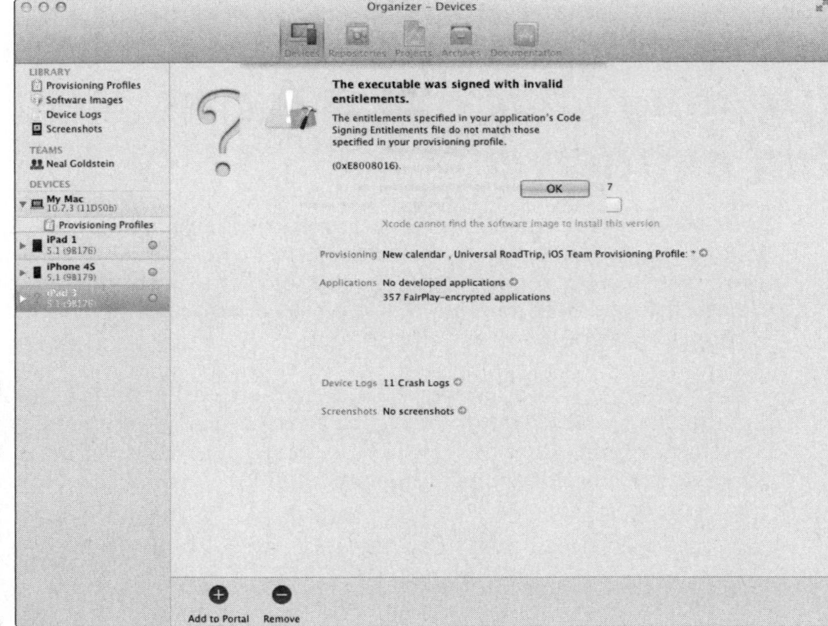

Figure 5-3: See what happens when you mess up your entitlements.

With definitions of iCloud entitlements now dancing in your head, it's time to talk about iCloud storage.

There are two keys in your `RoadTrip.entitlements` file that have to do with iCloud storage:

- `com.apple.developer.ubiquity-container-identifiers`
- `com.apple.developer.ubiquity-kvstore-identifier`

There's also another key that comes along for the ride when you create an entitlements file, and that is `keychain-access-groups`, which is a list of the keychain access groups to which the app belongs. (You — and any other application that needed to share keychain data — would use this list to determine the keychain items the app has access to, which is nice in and of itself but is not relevant to iCloud.)

Way back in the "iCloud" section at the beginning of this chapter, I mention that iCloud storage has two flavors: document storage and key-value data storage. iCloud Key-Value Store is the unique identifier for the key-value store in iCloud. As I said, you won't use it here, but it can be useful, and it's easy to figure out — it works just like `NSUserDefaults` on the device.

The iCloud Containers section represents directories in the cloud your application can use to read and write documents. In fact, the first `com.apple.developer.ubiquity-container-identifier` for RoadTrip is your Apple team identifier followed by your Bundle ID. So, if my team identifier were N42E42A42L, my `com.apple.developer.ubiquity-container-identifier` would be that ID combined with my Bundle ID (`com.nealgoldstein.RoadTrip`, if you're curious), which would be `N42E42A42L.com.nealgoldstein.RoadTrip`. When you get around to generating your entitlement files, you'll see a value that looks more or less like that in the `Value` field (actually the `Value` field array) for the `com.apple.developer.ubiquity-container-identifiers` key. And if you recall, when you created `NSPersistentStoreUbiquitousContentURLKey` back in the "Setting Up Core Data for iCloud" section, earlier in this chapter, you used the `com.apple.developer.ubiquity-container-identifier` as the first part of the iCloud container directory URL you created.

Another piece of the puzzle in place.

Although you can use a different value than your Bundle ID for the key (which is what you'd have to do to get to access your iCloud container from a Mac), you have to maintain the Team ID in place or you'll get a repeat of the dreaded "The executable was signed with invalid entitlements" message. (Refer to Figure 5-3.) If that fate does befall you, for this or any other reason, you need to examine all the working parts, including the provisioning profile I explain in "Provisioning Your App for iCloud."

Now that you have an idea about what entitlements are all about, all you need to do is enable iCloud entitlements in your app. Start by selecting your project in the Project Navigator and then select the RoadTrip target. Select the Summary tab, scroll down to the Entitlements section, and then check the Enable Entitlements check box, as I have in Figure 5-4. Also select the iCloud Key-Value Store check box and click the + button in the iCloud Containers section. (When you do that, the name initially looks truncated, but just press Return and you see what's shown in Figure 5-4 — `com.nealgoldstein.RoadTrip`.)

If you take a close look at Figure 5-4, you can see that the `RoadTrip.entitlements` file has added to the project as well.

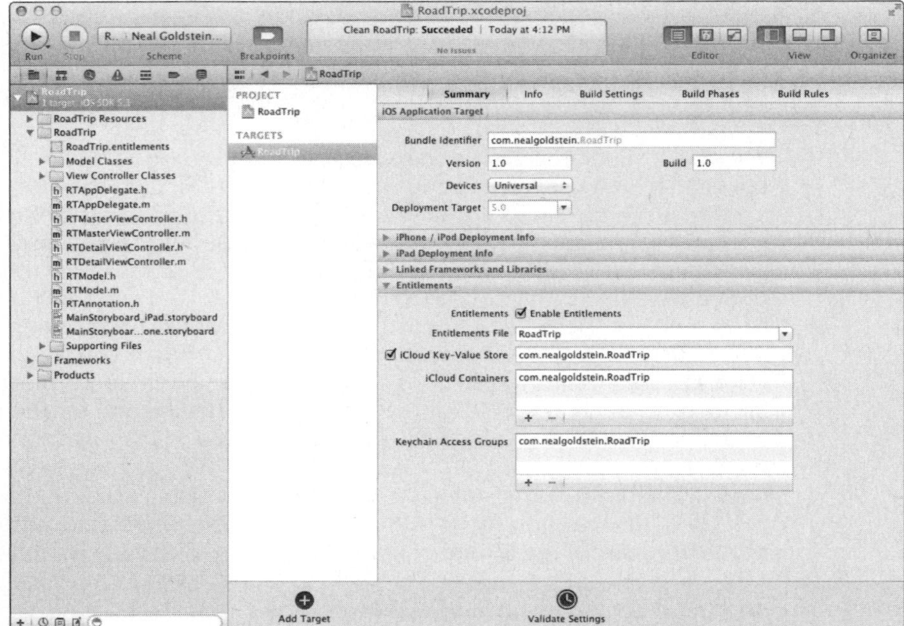

Figure 5-4: Enabling entitlements.

When you enable entitlements for your app target, Xcode automatically configures both the Document Storage and Key-Value Data Storage entitlements for your app using the Team ID and Bundle ID combination I just explained — and which you can change, as I also just explained.

You can always find your Team ID in the Member Center on the Apple Developer website (`http://developer.apple.com/membercenter`). When you get to the main page, select the Your Account tab, and if you're an individual, you see your Team ID in Your Account Summary. If you're part of a company, select Organization Profile from the column on the left of that tab, and you find your Team ID in the Company/Organization ID field.

This Team ID is also the first part of a Provisioning Profile name, which I explain next.

Provisioning Your App for iCloud

If you have any history with Apple in creating provisioning profiles to enable your app to run on a device, you know that it can easily turn into a nightmare — even though, to be fair, the whole process has gotten much better.

After jumping through the hoops for what seems like hundreds of thousands of times, it finally does make sense to me and actually is rather simple. So let me take you through it. The key to provisioning bliss is to understand that your provisioning profile, your App ID, your Bundle ID, and the value of the `com.apple.developer.ubiquity-container-identifiers` key in your Entitlements file are inexorably tied together, and one little mistake in referring to any one piece can cost you hours of frustration.

One way Apple has made provisioning simple is through the use of its Development Provisioning Assistant. Although you can't use it if you want to use an existing App ID with a custom Bundle Identifier, doing it on your own is actually pretty simple, and I take you through the process here.

From the iOS Dev Center at `https://developer.apple.com/devcenter/ios`, select the iOS Provisioning Portal under the iOS Developer Program. (Note that you only see the iOS Provisioning Portal if you're a member of the Developer Program, which is required if you want to run your app on a device.)

I assume that you already have your iOS Development Certificate. If not, you need to take care of that first. Just follow the instructions in the Certificates section of the iOS Provisioning Portal.

To start the provisioning process proper, go ahead and create an App ID for your application. To do that, do the following:

1. **Select App IDs under the Provisioning Portal section of the iOS Provisioning Portal.**

   The home page of the iOS Provisioning Portal site appears.

2. **Select the Manage tab and then select the New App ID button.**

   The page refreshes to show the Create App ID section of the Manage tab.

3. **In the tab's Description subsection, enter a name for your ID in the name field.**

   Try to come up with a name that makes sense to you, rather than just some random word. (I used Universal RoadTrip, as shown in Figure 5-5.)

4. **In the Bundle Seed ID section of the tab, select the Use Team ID option from the Bundle ID drop-down list.**

5. **In the Bundle Identifier section of the tab, enter what you find in the `Value` field of the `com.apple.developer.ubiquity-container-identifiers` key in your Entitlements file.**

   The `Value` field should contain something like `$(TeamIdentifierPrefix)com.nealgoldstein.RoadTrip)`, leaving off the `$(TeamIdentifierPrefix)` bit, which is your Team ID and which you already specified in Bundle Seed ID.

   If you look at Figure 5-5, you see that my Bundle Identifier is `com.nealgoldstein.RoadTrip`. This is also what you find as the value for the Bundle Identifier Key in `RoadTrip-Info.plist`, but with the app name (product name) acting as a variable there. (`com.nealgoldstein.${PRODUCT_NAME:rfc1034identifier}`)

6. **Click Submit.**

   If you filled in all your fields correctly, you're now the proud owner of an App ID.

Be sure that your entries match precisely. ***Spelling and case are important.*** Minor mismatches are the main cause of most provisioning problems.

After creating a new App ID, you still need to configure it. Here's how you do it:

1. **Find the newly created App ID in the App ID list in the Manage tab and select its Configure link in the Action column.**

   Doing that brings up what you see Figure 5-6.

2. **Select the Enable for iCloud check box, read the nice Warning message that appears as shown in Figure 5-7, and then click OK.**

   The warning applies to you if you are enabling iCloud for an existing App ID you're already using in existing Provisioning Profiles.

   Clicking OK should mean that your App ID is now enabled for iCloud. To double-check, look for the Enabled message, as shown in Figure 5-8.

Next, you need to create a Provisioning Profile using the App ID you just created:

1. **From the menu on the left in the iOS Provisioning Portal, choose Provisioning.**

2. **Make sure the Development tab is selected in the new page that appears, and then click the New Profile button.**

   Doing so brings up what you see in Figure 5-9.

3. **In the Create iOS Development Provisioning Profile section, enter a name for your Provisioning Profile in the Profile Name field.**

   Be sure to use a descriptive name — something like Universal RoadTrip,

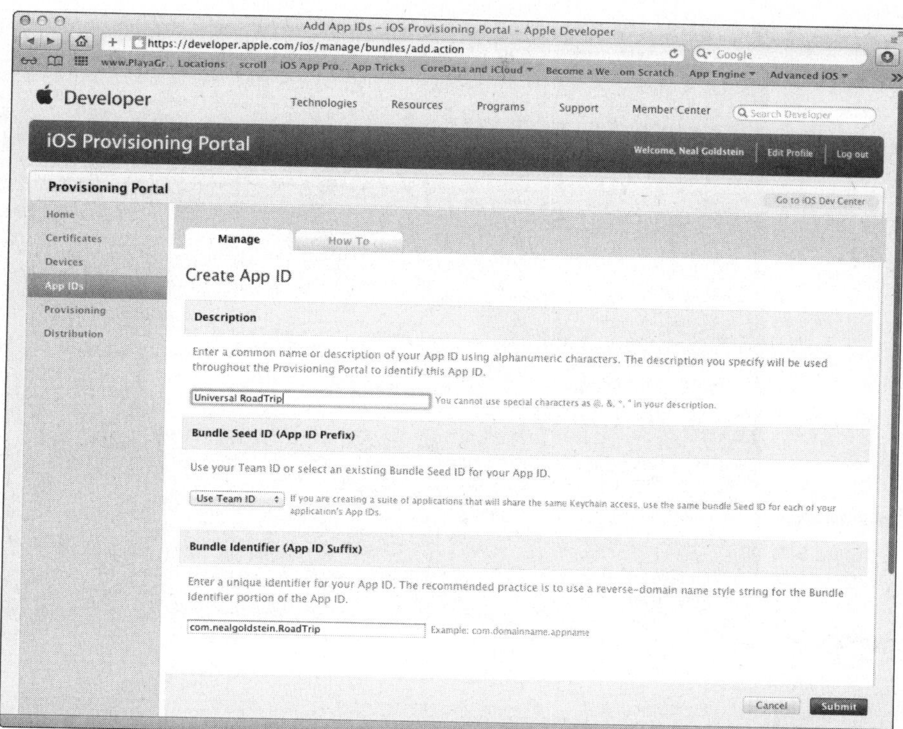

Figure 5-5: Create the App ID.

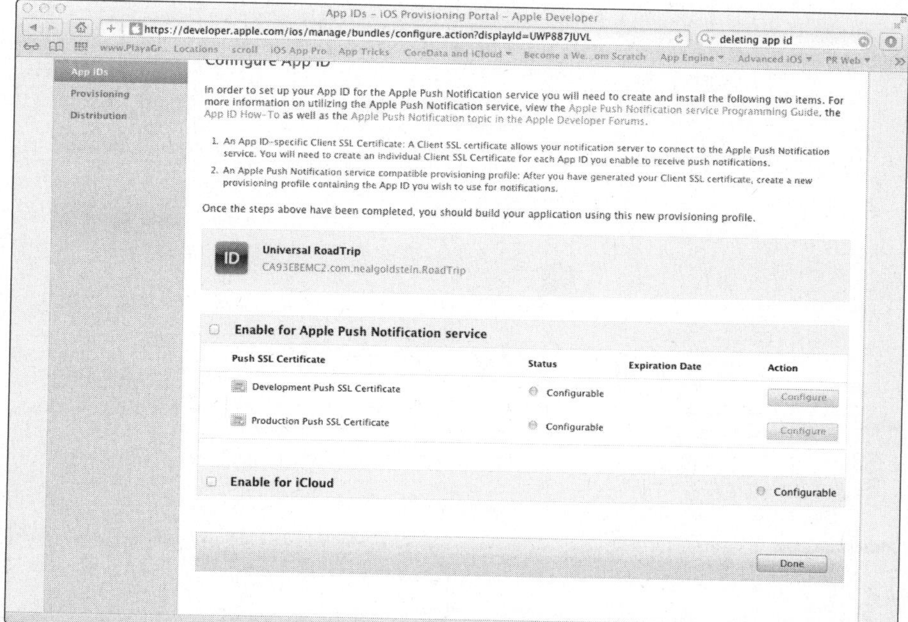

Figure 5-6: You need to enable iCloud.

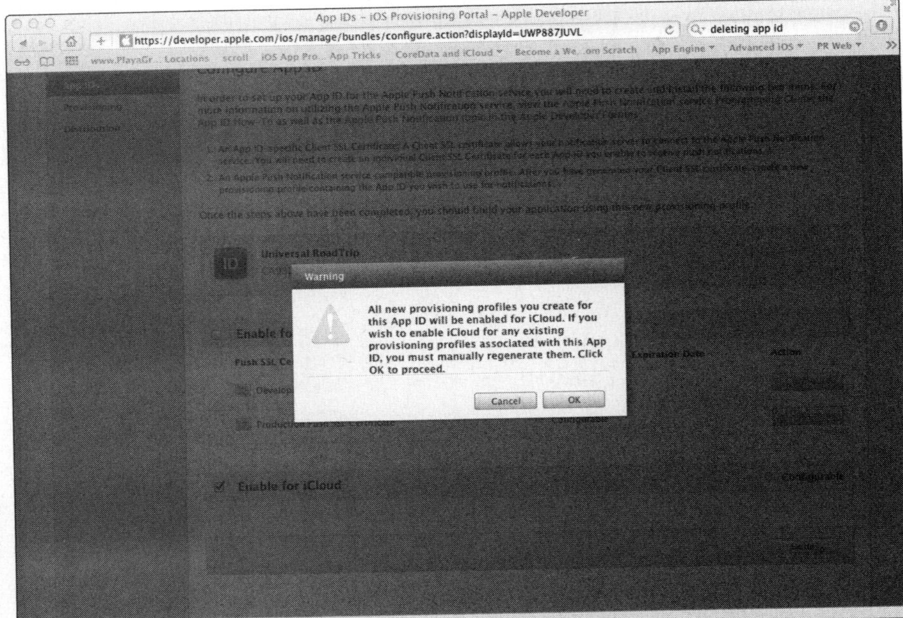

Figure 5-7: Read the warning.

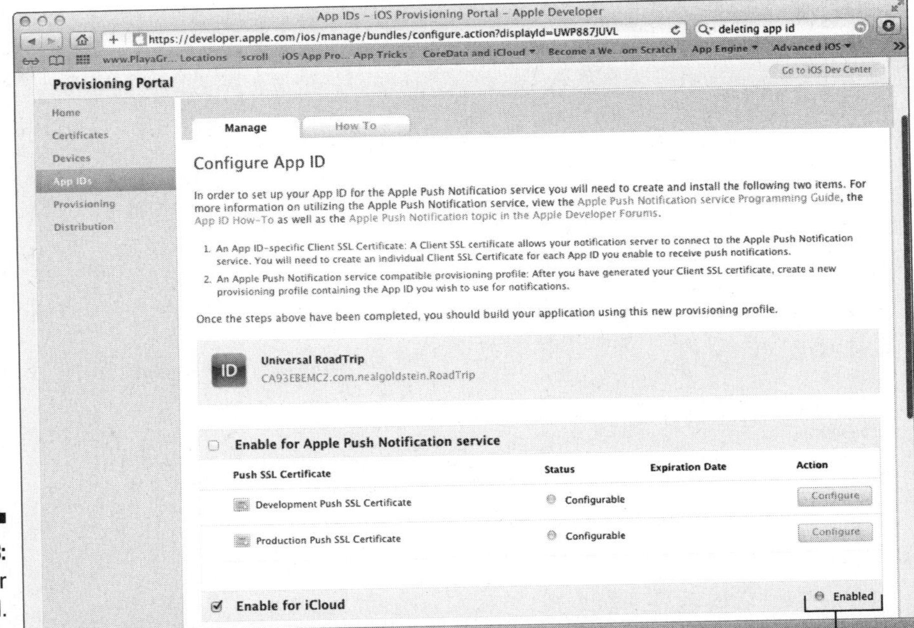

Figure 5-8: Enabled for iCloud.

4. **Still in the Create iOS Development Provisioning Profile section, select the Certificates check box, select the App ID you just created from the App ID drop-down list, and then select the devices you want the app to run on.**
5. **Click Submit.**

After creating the profile, keep refreshing the page until it's ready for download (see Figure 5-10) and then click the Download button to download it to your computer.

After the profile downloads, drag it into Xcode (or simply double-click it) and verify that it's visible in the Xcode Organizer, as you see in Figure 5-11.

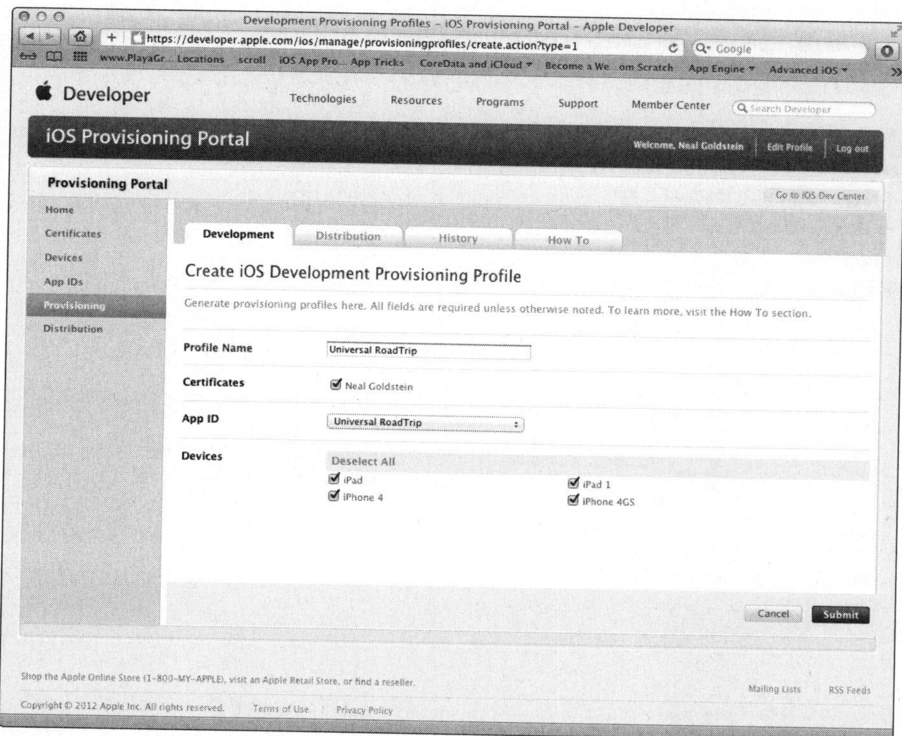

Figure 5-9: Your new profile.

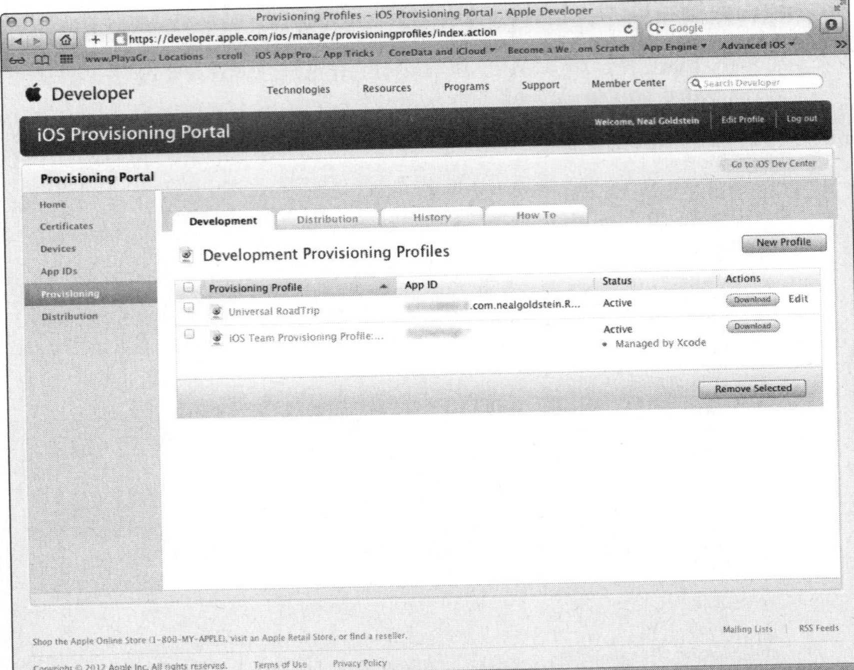

Figure 5-10: Ready for download.

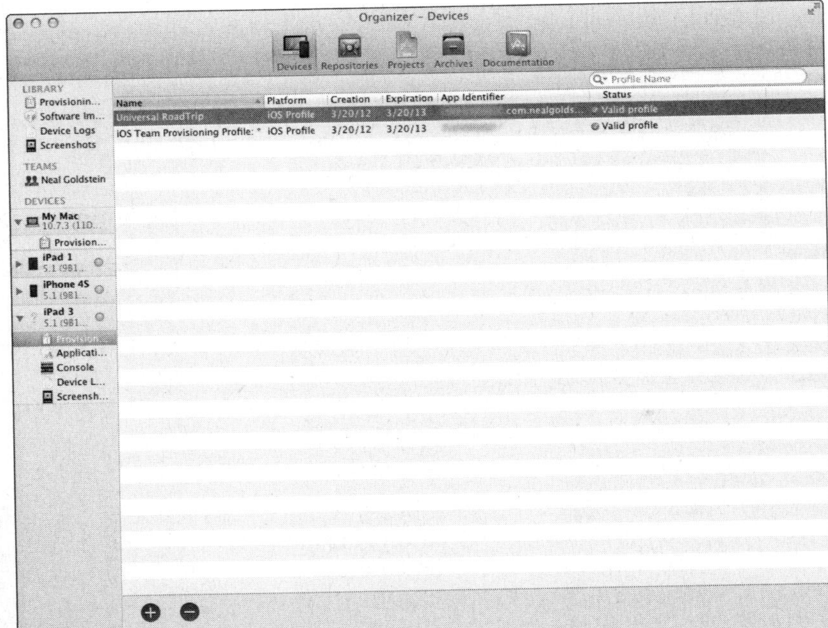

Figure 5-11: Yes, it's there.

Testing

With all the various IDs and Provisioning Profiles out of the way, you can now build and run your app.

You need two devices to make sure that the iCloud support you enabled actually works.

First, delete all existing copies of the app on both devices. If you have an existing persistent store, it won't be shared.

On Device 1:

1. Build and run your app.
2. Tap the Home button.
3. Select the Stop button in the Xcode toolbar.
4. Delete the app from the multitasking bar.
5. Tap the app on the Home screen to re-launch it.

Do the same thing for Device 2. There are no shortcuts here.

If you add a point of interest to your itinerary on one device, it should eventually show up on the second device. The amount of time it can take can run from seconds to many minutes. Have patience!

If you made any mistakes and want to restart the whole thing, take these steps:

1. **Delete the apps from both devices.**
2. **Delete the iCloud store for your app.**

   You can do that on the Mac by selecting iCloud in System Preferences and selecting the Manage button. In the screen that appears, select the storage you want to delete (it will be named Unknown until your app is live in the store), and then select Delete.

   On either device, use the Settings app, tap iCloud, tap Storage and Backup, tap Manage Storage, select the storage you want to delete (it will be named Unknown until your app is live in the store), tap the Edit button, and then tap the big red Delete All button.
3. **If you're as paranoid as I am, change the name of your iCloud file.**

   Although Step 2 will delete your iCloud container, if you run the app again right away, the deletion may not have propagated through all the servers. If you're concerned about that (as I am), simply change the name of your store (transactions) file in iCloud in the `persistentStoreCoordinator` method in `RTModel.m`. I've highlighted the changes you need to make in bold for you in Listing 5-8.

Listing 5-8: Updating persistentStoreCoordinator

```
- (NSPersistentStoreCoordinator *)
                                persistentStoreCoordinator {

…

#if !TARGET_IPHONE_SIMULATOR
    NSFileManager *fileManager =
                       [NSFileManager defaultManager];
    NSURL *persistentStoreUbiquitousContentURL =
     [fileManager URLForUbiquityContainerIdentifier:nil];

    NSString *ubiquityContainerIdentifierPath =
           [[persistentStoreUbiquitousContentURL path]
           stringByAppendingPathComponent:
                       @"RoadTripSharedPointsOfInterest"];
    persistentStoreUbiquitousContentURL =
      [NSURL fileURLWithPath:
                        ubiquityContainerIdentifierPath];
    options = [NSDictionary dictionaryWithObjectsAndKeys:
      [NSString stringWithFormat:
        @"%@%@",@"com.nealgoldstein.coredata.
        itineraryR01.",appDelegate.destinationPreference],
       NSPersistentStoreUbiquitousContentNameKey,
      persistentStoreUbiquitousContentURL,
       NSPersistentStoreUbiquitousContentURLKey,
      [NSNumber numberWithBool:YES],
       NSMigratePersistentStoresAutomaticallyOption,
      [NSNumber numberWithBool:YES],
       NSInferMappingModelAutomaticallyOption,nil];
#endif

…
}
```

Part III

Web Services

In this part . . .

Now that you're able to share data among devices, it's probably a good idea to figure out where that data is going to come from.

In this part, you find out all about consuming web services (yum yum).

You discover how to use the Google Geocoding web service, and along the way you build yourself a couple of classes that you'll be able to take home with you — to the envy of all your friends. Not only will these classes be able to construct your web services requests for you, but they will then make the request and then download the response asynchronously.

You'll also find out all you need to know about XML and JSON, which will make you multilingual in the blink of an eye.

Chapter 6

Living in the Cloud

In This Chapter

- Getting familiar with how web services work
- Understanding the nuts and bolts of network access
- Taking a look at web service architectures
- Deploying web services to a server

Being able to share data among all your devices is only half the battle. You also need to look at where your data comes from.

Take RoadTrip, for example. In the old-school version of RoadTrip, the points of interest are bundled with the RoadTrip app in the Destinations plist. The problem here is that as you, the developer, discover more and more points of interest that your users might enjoy, the only way you could pass that on to your devoted users would be by sending out a new version of the app — a time-consuming and often painful process.

Instead, I have you create web services that allow RoadTrip to download the points of interest from a server. I also show you how to create web services that allow you as the developer to add and delete those server-based points of interest.

But for you to really understand how to create those web services, you need to understand the entire enchilada — the Internet, the web, and networks. For you to be successful and go off and add web services to your apps, you need to understand not only how to develop a web service, but also why you're doing what you're doing.

I know that most people are at least familiar with things like the web, the Internet, and maybe even the HTTP protocol. But because these things are the foundation upon which you'll build your web services, I want to spend some time taking you past familiarity to real understanding.

The place to start is with the very basics — networks. I start with some very elementary stuff, but by the time you're done here, you'll have the in-depth knowledge you need to take what you learned in this book and apply it any number of ways to your own apps.

Understanding How Networks Work

A computer network is simply a bunch of computers and other devices interconnected by communications channels. The network is the way computers can send messages to one another. Of course, computers can ask a lot of things of one another, but here I focus on requests to get (or upload) some data.

One network we're all familiar with is the Internet, and you'll be using the Internet to access and deliver web services. But before we continue, I want to make sure you understand the difference between the Internet and the World Wide Web.

Although the terms *Internet* and *World Wide Web* are often used synonymously, *they are not one and the same.* The Internet is a global system of interconnected governmental, academic, corporate, public, and private computer networks, whereas the web is a system of interlinked hypertext documents that people can access via the Internet. The web is really an application running on the Internet — the Internet being the communications backbone underlying the World Wide Web. I get back to the web after explaining the Internet.

The Internet

The Internet is a network of networks — millions of individual networks (private, public, academic, business, and government) of local to global scope, which are linked by a broad array of electronic, wireless, and optical networking technologies that use the standard Internet Protocol Suite (TCP/IP) to communicate with each other. Not only is the Internet home to the World Wide Web (WWW), but it's also the infrastructure that supports electronic mail and voice over IP (VoIP).

The *Internet Protocol Suite* is the set of communications protocols used for the Internet and other similar networks. "What exactly," you may ask, "is a communications protocol?" Well, thanks for asking. A *communications protocol* is a formal description of message formats and the rules for exchanging those messages in or between computing systems and in telecommunications. This is where the term *TCP/IP* comes in — what the standard Internet Protocol Suite is commonly called. The Transmission Control Protocol (TCP) and the Internet Protocol (IP) are two of the suite's most important protocols.

The Internet Protocol Suite consists of four layers (starting at the bottom), as shown in Figure 6-1:

- **The Link layer:** Here you can find the connectivity functions at the networking hardware level of the computer. This is home to Ethernet and its cohorts.
- **The Internet layer:** Look here for the communication methods between multiple computers that create a network (and multiple networks) — this layer establishes the Internet. Here's where you find IP, which defines the fundamental addressing namespaces — Internet Protocol version 4 [IPv4] and Internet Protocol version 6 [IPv6], used to identify and locate hosts on the network — and that thing called the IP address, which looks like xxx.xxx.xxx.xxx.
- **The Transport layer:** Home to a general framework for transmitting data between hosts. Here you can find TCP.
- **The Application layer:** Look no further for the protocols for application-based interaction on a process-to-process level between communicating Internet hosts. This is where HTTP lives. It's the HTTP protocol, running in the application layer of the Internet Protocol Suite, which you use to request and receive data from a web service.

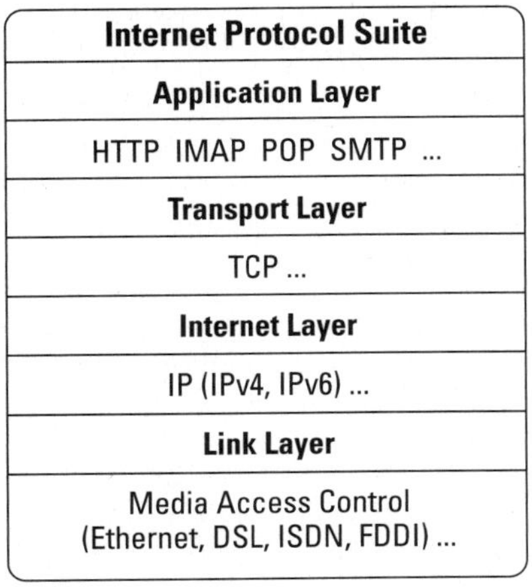

Internet Protocol Suite
Application Layer
HTTP IMAP POP SMTP ...
Transport Layer
TCP ...
Internet Layer
IP (IPv4, IPv6) ...
Link Layer
Media Access Control (Ethernet, DSL, ISDN, FDDI) ...

Figure 6-1: The Internet Protocol Suite.

The origins of the Internet reach back to the 1960s, when the United States government collaborated with private commercial interests to build robust and fault-tolerant distributed computer networks. If you're interested in the history, you can explore it on your own. What's important about this structure is that no one is in charge of the Internet as a whole. There is, however, oversight (someone is in charge) in two areas:

- The Domain Name System is directed by the Internet Corporation for Assigned Names and Numbers (ICANN).
- The standardization of the core protocols (IPv4 and IPv6) is directed by the Internet Engineering Task Force (IETF).

The work of these two groups is critical for doing something people take for granted — the mundane task of finding a computer on the Internet that you want to interact with. You need to understand that "finding" in this case has two aspects to it. First, you need to know the name of the computer, and second, you need to know how to access it on the network. Think of a name and phone number — for example, the domain name `example.com` translates to the addresses 192.0.32.10 (IPv4) and 2620:0:2d0:200::10 (IPv6). This is where the Domain Name System (DNS) comes in, which is simply a distributed database that links together the domain name and how to access it.

For your development purposes, the Internet itself consists of four types of components:

- **Clients:** A *client* is an application or system that accesses a remote service on another computer system, known as a *server*, by way of a network. Hello client-server (again).

  Web browsers, for example, are clients that connect to web servers and retrieve web pages for display. Most people use e-mail clients to retrieve their e-mail from their Internet service provider's mail servers. Online games run as clients on each user's computer.

- **Hosts (aka servers):** A *host* may offer information resources, services, and applications to users or other nodes on the network. A host is what serves up your web page or web service. Hosts can provide services to clients or other hosts. One of the important things about a host is that it can provide, as you'll see, a generic services interface to its resources. This is the familiar structure of the URL (actually URI and I'll get to that distinction shortly) with a base address and all those slashes after the `.com`. For example, to download the source code for this book, you can go to my website:

  ```
  www.nealgoldstein.com/support/downloads
  ```

  What's more, the host can hide all the implementation details from the user behind this simple interface.

  You won't be using the next two components, but you may want to know what they do because you've probably heard somebody somewhere refer to them. They're both intermediary components that act as both a client and a server.

- **Gateways (also known as a reverse proxy):** A gateway is a network node that interfaces one network with another — they're imposed by the network or origin server.
- **Proxies (more accurately, proxy servers):** Proxy servers are client facing nodes that act as an intermediary for requests from clients seeking resources from other servers. Most proxies are web proxies, mediating access to content on the World Wide Web, and they provide services such as data translation, security, and caching to improve performance.

The World Wide Web

The World Wide Web (as big and important as it appears) is only one of the services that run on the Internet. The World Wide Web, abbreviated as WWW and commonly known as the web, is a system of interlinked hypertext documents accessed via the Internet. With a web browser, people can view web pages that may contain text, images, videos, and other multimedia, and they can navigate among them via hyperlinks. The history is interesting, and if you look into it, you'll hear a lot about Sir Tim Berners-Lee and Robert Cailliau. I leave you to explore that on your own, though.

What "made" the web was using hypertext on the Internet. URLs and the HyperText Markup Language (HTML) form a system of interlinked resources, called *hypertext documents.*

Hypertext is text (okay, sometimes images) with references (hyperlinks) to other text (or images) that the reader can immediately access, usually by a mouse click or key sequence. For most folks, hypertext is what makes the web the web — it's an easy-to-use and flexible way you can share and access information over the Internet.

This particular form of linking is accomplished through the use of a URL (really the URI as you'll see later). Viewing a web page on the World Wide Web usually follows the pattern spelled out here:

1. You either type the URL of the page into a web browser or follow a hyperlink to the page or resource that has the URL embedded.
2. The web browser submits an HTTP request message to the server for a particular page. (Note that this is the way a web service works as well.)
3. The server-name portion of the URL (shown in bold here) is resolved into an IP address using the Domain Name System (DNS). This IP address is necessary to contact the web server.

```
http://www.nealgoldstein.com/support/downloads/
```

4. The browser then makes a request by sending an HTTP request (I explain that in detail shortly) to the web server at that particular IP address. In the case of a typical web page, the HTML text of the page is requested first and parsed immediately by the web browser, which then makes additional requests for images and any other files that complete the page image.
5. While receiving these files from the web server, browsers may progressively render the page onto the screen as specified by its HTML, Cascading Style Sheets (CSS), or other page composition languages. Any images and other resources are incorporated to produce the onscreen web page that the user sees.

Web pages usually also have hyperlinks to other pages or even downloadable files, documents, and other web resources. This creates the web of information that users almost take for granted.

This pattern illustrates (pretty much) how a web service works as well, which will become abundantly clear in the next sections.

What Exactly Is a Web Service?

A web service is a way for one device to request of another device (over a network) that it do something for the first device — for example, return some data or do a computation and return the result. To put it another way, a web service is a method of communication between two electronic devices.

The W3C (the World Wide Web Consortium that develops web standards) defines a web service as "a software system designed to support interoperable machine-to-machine interaction over a network." The W3C also states,

> "We can identify two major classes of Web services, REST-compliant Web services, in which the primary purpose of the service is to manipulate XML representations of Web resources using a uniform set of 'stateless' operations; and arbitrary Web services, in which the service may expose an arbitrary set of operations."

Perfectly clear, right? Okay, maybe not. I need to both translate their gibberish for you and expand on their somewhat out-of-date definitions.

To reduce it to its essences, a web service is simply the server end of a client-server interaction.

With all due respect to the W3C, it's not that there two are different kinds of web services; it's easier to understand if you look at it as two different styles of implementation. The first is *message-oriented* (the W3C arbitrary), and the second is *resource based* (the W3C REST-compliant).

Message-oriented web services

Message-oriented web services (also referred to as Big web services) generally follow a set of standards, such as these:

- **UDDI (Universal Description Discovery and Integration):** A directory service which tells you what services are available
- **WSDL (Web Services Description Language):** Describes its interface in a way that can be processed by a computer
- **SOAP:** Defines the messages and used to stand for Simple Object Access Protocol but now stands for nothing

This kind of web service is often used to expose the services available in an enterprise-level architecture to remote clients not part of the local network. It allows an enterprise to communicate with other enterprises and clients while encapsulating the details of their IT systems behind a firewall. Listing 6-1 shows you an example of a SOAP request for Apple's stock price. (Notice the XML.)

Listing 6-1: A SOAP Request for a Stock Price

```
POST /StockQuote HTTP/1.1
Host: www.stockquoteserver.com
Content-Type: text/xml; charset="utf-8"
Content-Length: nnnn
SOAPAction: "Some-URI"

<SOAP-ENV:Envelope
  xmlns:SOAP-ENV="http://schemas.xmlsoap.org/soap/
          envelope/"
  SOAP-ENV:encodingStyle="http://schemas.xmlsoap.org/soap/
          encoding/">
   <SOAP-ENV:Body>
       <m:GetLastTradePrice xmlns:m="Some-URI">
           <symbol>APPL</symbol>
       </m:GetLastTradePrice>
   </SOAP-ENV:Body>
</SOAP-ENV:Envelope>
```

I mention the big web services here only because you may have heard the term somewhere, but I don't explain them any further because you aren't going to use them.

Resource-based web services

So how does a web API differ from your run-of-the-mill web interaction? Well, when you visit a website, the web server returns a web page. A web page is essentially HTML, CSS, and JavaScript. And the browser renders the page text into a nice-looking page.

However, this HTML data format would never be another program's first choice when it comes to processing or consuming information. This is where web services come in. Because web services have a well-defined API — what parameters they accept and the response you can expect, usually in program-friendly XML or JSON format — other programs can make better use of them because such programs can be set up to process the responses programmatically.

A resource-based web service (also called a web API) is typically a set of HTTP request messages along with a set of response messages, typically in eXtensible Markup Language (XML) or JavaScript Object Notation (JSON) format with the request defined in a URI. (I explain JSON in detail in Chapter 10.)

The resource-based web service moves away from the message-oriented approach (all that SOAP/WSDL/UDDI stuff from the previous section) to what is often referred to as Representational State Transfer (REST) based communications. Although resource-based web services have become synonymous with Representational State Transfer (REST), as I explain in the section "Representational State Transfer (REST)," it isn't really the same thing!

Curious how a resource-based (HTTP API) web service would tackle that Apple stock price request I highlighted in the previous section? Check out Listing 6-2.

Listing 6-2: A Resource-Based (HTTP API) Web Service

```
http://stockquoteserver.example/query?symbol=APPL
```

As Listing 6-2 makes clear, even though some people swear by the SOAP/WSDL/UDDI approach to web services, for your purposes the resource-based (HTTP API) web service is a better solution, so that's what you'll work with.

A Web Service Request

The best place to start learning about web services is by making an actual web service request. For example, enter the following URL into your web browser of choice:

```
http://maps.googleapis.com/maps/api/geocode/json
   ?sensor=false&address=1 Infinite Drive, Cupertino, CA
```

You're rewarded with what you see in Figure 6-2.

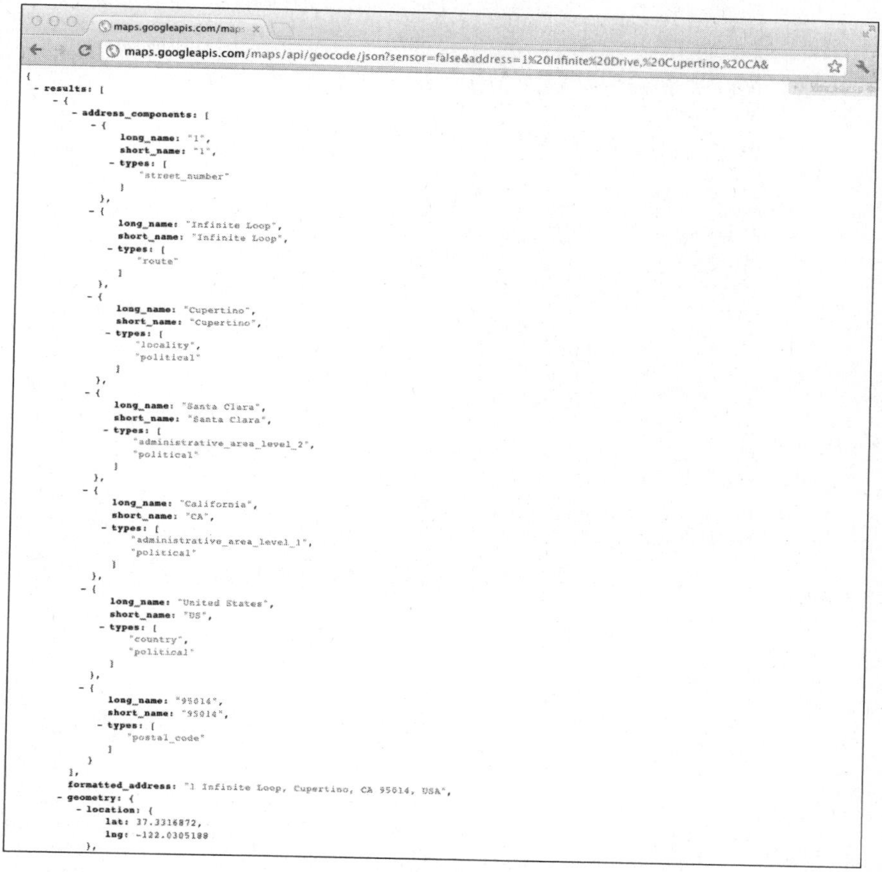

maps.googleapis.com/maps/api/geocode/json?sensor=false&address=1%20Infinite%20Drive,%20Cupertino,%20CA&


```
{
 - results: [
   - {
     - address_components: [
       - {
             long_name: "1",
             short_name: "1",
           - types: [
                "street_number"
             ]
         },
       - {
             long_name: "Infinite Loop",
             short_name: "Infinite Loop",
           - types: [
                "route"
             ]
         },
       - {
             long_name: "Cupertino",
             short_name: "Cupertino",
           - types: [
                "locality",
                "political"
             ]
         },
       - {
             long_name: "Santa Clara",
             short_name: "Santa Clara",
           - types: [
                "administrative_area_level_2",
                "political"
             ]
         },
       - {
             long_name: "California",
             short_name: "CA",
           - types: [
                "administrative_area_level_1",
                "political"
             ]
         },
       - {
             long_name: "United States",
             short_name: "US",
           - types: [
                "country",
                "political"
             ]
         },
       - {
             long_name: "95014",
             short_name: "95014",
           - types: [
                "postal_code"
             ]
         }
     ],
     formatted_address: "1 Infinite Loop, Cupertino, CA 95014, USA",
   - geometry: {
     - location: {
           lat: 37.3316872,
           lng: -122.0305188
       },
```


Figure 6-2: A web service in the browser.

What you just did was make a *request* to the geocode web service to return you the latitude and longitude coordinates for 1 Infinite Drive, Cupertino, CA in JSON format. (I explain JSON and how to use it in Chapter 10.) The service obliged you with a *response*, which was even more kindly displayed for you by your browser.

Since the response is in an application-friendly format, you can see it's not too much of a leap to imagine using this in RoadTrip. Figure 6-3 gives you an idea what that may look like. Think of Figure 6-3 as a foretaste of what you'll actually be doing in Chapters 7-10 when you change from using the iOS SDK geocoder class to using a Google Geocoder web service.

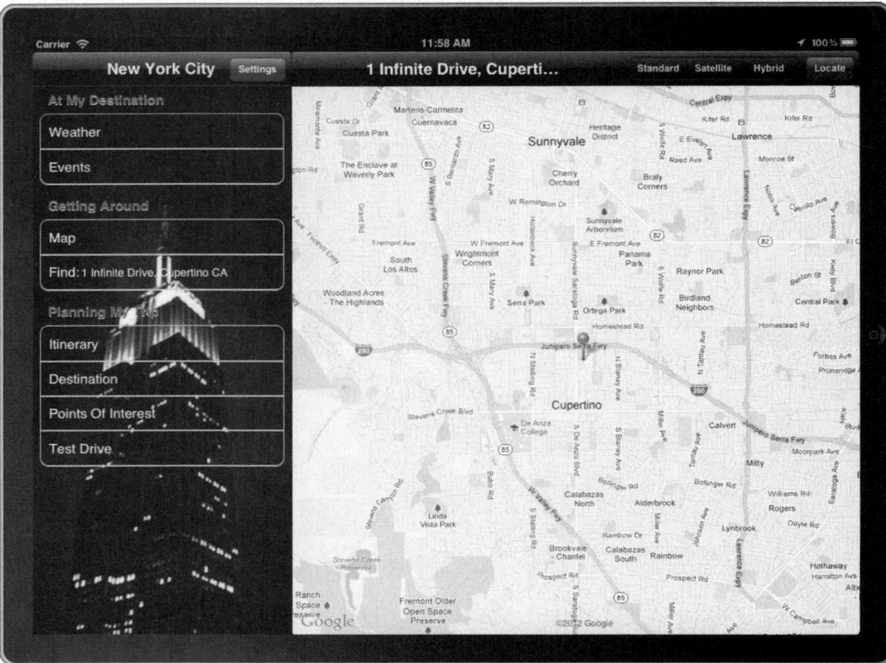

Figure 6-3: A web service on the iPad.

So what actually happened when you typed that `http://` stuff in your web browser and pressed Enter?

Figure 6-4 gives you the (schematic) overview:

1. A request is sent from your browser to a URL address — the same kind you normally enter into a browser with a few more parameters. (I explain that shortly.)
2. The URL request gets routed to a web server running in the cloud. The web server processes the request and sends it to the right program.
3. In that program (which can be written in any one of a number of languages), a handler processes the request, interacts with its model, and packages a response.
4. That response is then returned back to your browser.

That's all there is to it. Basically, this whole interaction takes place within the framework of that long-established workhorse of the Internet, the client-server architecture.

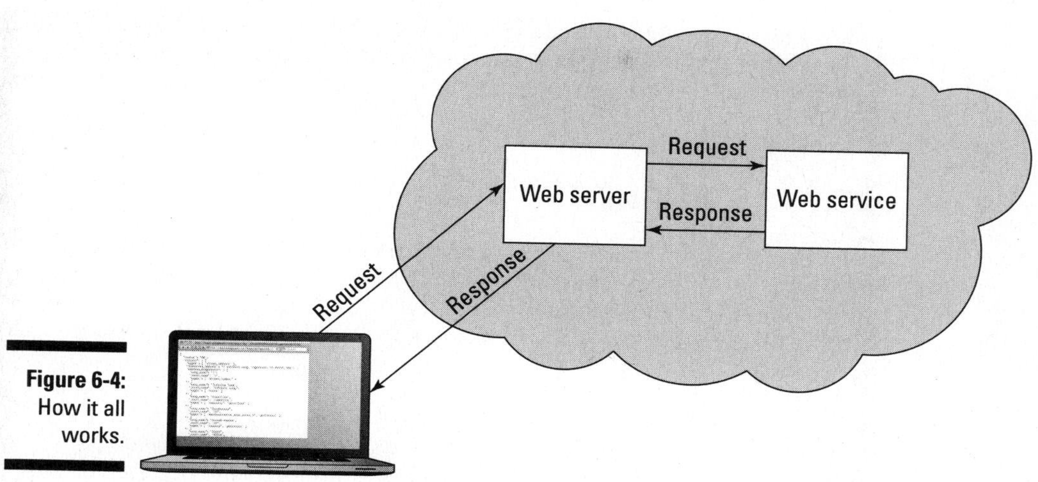

Figure 6-4: How it all works.

It's about client-server

The *client-server* model of computing distributes the tasks of an application between the providers of a resource or service, called *servers,* and service requesters, called *clients.* It has been around for quite a while — since the 1980s, to be (a bit more) precise — where it was used in reference to personal computers on a network (usually a LAN). From its humble beginnings, it has evolved over time to where it is now recognized as one of the central ideas of network computing. In fact, the Internet's main application protocols — HTTP, SMTP, Telnet, and DNS — proudly use client-server. Web browsers and web servers function as part of a client-server relationship, and many of the apps you use every day follow a client-server model — e-mail and banking services, to name just two. The client-server model has become one of the central ideas of network computing.

I talk even more about client-server when I explain web service design in Chapter 11.

The client-server model is, of course, at the heart of the Model Application Controller Architecture that I describe in Chapter 1. And, if it's not clear by now, it's also exactly what you'll end up doing with a web service — offloading computation or data storage from your iPhone to a server in the cloud (and getting all the other benefits I explain in Chapter 1). Think about the *reverse geocoding* you just did in the last section (using your browser to turn a GPS coordinate address into an address). It's almost impossible to store all those addresses and coordinates on the phone. So the phone sends the GPS location, and the server returns a location.

In short, client-server is about the relationship of cooperating programs in an application with the server providing a service to one or many clients making requests for such services.

And it's about the URL

At the beginning of this section — a section labeled appropriately enough "A Web Service Request" — you entered a URL to request a web service. The URL (Uniform Resource Locator) is central to the kind of web services you'll be using because it's the tool you use to specify where something is and how to access it.

Every URL consists of some of the following: the scheme name (commonly called *protocol*) followed by a colon; then, depending on the scheme, a domain name (alternatively, *IP address*); a port number; the path to the service requested; and an optional query string. (There's also an optional fragment identifier which you won't be using in RoadTrip.) Put them all together and it looks like the following:

```
scheme://domain:port/path?query_string#fragment_id
```

You can see a more user-friendly version in Figure 6-5.

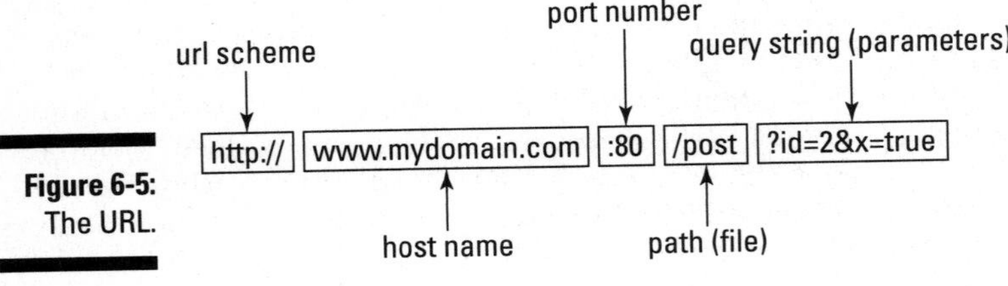

Figure 6-5: The URL.

A bit off-putting isn't it? Let me deconstruct it for you.

The *scheme* name defines what you need to know in order to process the rest of the URL. It is the communication protocol you want to use. You've seen things like `http:`, `https:`, and `ftp:` in the URL in your browser? Those are scheme names.

```
http://example.org:80
```

Next comes the *domain*. Here you can use a domain name (such as Apple.com) or its IP address of 17.251.200.70 (which is paired with Apple.com by the Domain Name System eventually anyway) to reach Apple's domain.

The domain name portion of a URL is not case sensitive because DNS ignores case: `http://example.org/` and `HTTP://EXAMPLE.ORG/` both open the same page. (Try it — you may be surprised by what you find there.)

The domain you just used in your browser to request a web service was `maps.googleapis.com`.

Next in line comes the *port* number, a term you may not be familiar with. Port numbers work like telephone extensions. A computer has a main address and a set of port numbers to handle incoming and outgoing connections. In the following example, `localhost` refers to the domain name and `8080` represents the port number:

```
http://localhost:8080/pointsofinterest?destination=0
```

The port number is optional; if omitted, the default for the scheme is used. For example, `http://example.com:80` connects to port 80 of `example.com`. This also happens to be the default for an `http:` URL, with the default port for an `https:` request being 443. (You get some practical experience using port numbers when you start testing your Google App Engine Application in Chapter 12.) Regardless, the specified or default port number has to match the port that the web server is listening to.

The *path* is used to specify (and perhaps find) the resource requested. It's all that stuff with the slashes after the domain name. (Remember, the port number is optional, so you usually won't see it.) Treat the path as case-sensitive, even though some servers — some based on Microsoft Windows, for example — treat it as case-insensitive.

For example, in the following URL

```
http://maps.googleapis.com/maps/api/geocode/json
    ?sensor=false&address=1 Infinite Drive, Cupertino, CA
```

`maps/api/geocode/` is the path to the JSON geocode web service you just used in your web service request.

The *query string* contains data to be passed to the software running on the server. It may contain name/value pairs separated by ampersands. The query string you entered in your web service request was:

```
?sensor=false&address=1 Infinite Drive, Cupertino, CA
```

The *fragment identifier,* if present, specifies a part or a position within the overall resource or document. When used with HTTP, it usually specifies a section or location within the page, and the browser may scroll to display that part of the page.

I began this section with the scheme — the communication protocol you want to use. In an upcoming section, I give you a look at the scheme you'll be using — HTTP.

But first, it's time to clean up the URI versus URL confusion.

URI or URL?

URI stands for Uniform Resource Identifier as opposed to URL which stands for Uniform Resource Locator.

Uniform Resource Identifier (URI) is a compact string of characters used to identify or name a resource. The main purpose of this identification is to enable interaction with representations of the resource over a network (typically the World Wide Web) using specific protocols. URIs are defined in schemes that call for a specific *syntax* and associated *protocols.*

URIs can be classified as a Uniform Resource Locator (URL) or a Uniform Resource Name (URN) or both.

```
www.nealgoldstein.com
```

A Uniform Resource Locator (URL) is a URI that, in addition to identifying a resource, provides a way to access that resource by describing its network "location." For example, the URL `http://www.nealgoldstein.com/` is a URI that identifies a resource (my home page) and implies that you can get a representation of that resource (such as my home page's HTML code) via HTTP from a network host named `www.nealgoldstein.com`.

A Uniform Resource Name (URN) is a URI that identifies a resource by name in a particular namespace, but it does not imply its location or how to access it. For example, the URN `urn:isbn:0-395-36341-1` is a URI that, like an

International Standard Book Number (ISBN), allows one to talk about an identifiably specific book, but doesn't suggest where and how to obtain an actual copy of it.

In this naming universe, `http:` is a URI scheme, but `urn:` is also a URI scheme. It defines subspaces — called *namespaces*. For example, the set of URNs of the form `urn:isbn:n-nn-nnnnnn-n` is a URN namespace. (`isbn` is a URN namespace identifier — it is neither a URN scheme nor a URI scheme.)

Over time, the importance of this additional level of hierarchy seemed to lessen; the view became that an individual scheme (`http` or `urn`) doesn't need to become a URI type such as URL, URN, or any other type people may come up with.

Furthermore, according to what has become the contemporary view, the term *URL* doesn't refer to a formal partition of URI space; it is merely a useful but informal concept. In this brave new world, a URL is merely a type of URI that identifies a resource via a representation of its primary access mechanism (that is, its network 'location'), rather than by other attributes it may have. In this context, `http:` is best referred to as a URI scheme and an `http` URI is a URL. The phrase "URL scheme" is now used infrequently, usually to refer to some subclass of URI schemes which exclude URNs.

So according to the cognoscenti, *URI* is the correct term to use when referring to the location of resources on the WWW.

The only problem with that is that most people are unaware of the distinction and doggedly continue to use URL. And, in that spirit, I also (mostly) use URL in this book when explaining things in less technical terms.

HTTP

Accordingly to both written and unwritten rules, the first part of any URI specifies the scheme. A word to the wise: The schemes you really want to pay attention to — at least for the purpose of this book — are `http://` (primarily) and `https://` — the HyperText Transfer Protocol (HTTP) and HTTP Secure, respectively. URIs with this scheme are called URLs.

The scheme is the networking protocol used by your browser (mostly) to access information on the web. Back in "The Internet" section, earlier in this chapter, I point out that HTTP is an application layer protocol designed within the framework of the Internet Protocol Suite and is a formal description of message formats and the rules for exchanging those messages.

In this context, HTTP is the request-response protocol in the client-server computing model on the web. A web browser acts as a client, submitting an HTTP *request* message to the server. Somewhere on the server is an application that provides a service or hosts a website that also has content or resources. This application returns a *response* message to the client. A response contains the content requested by the client in its message body as well as request status information.

HTTP is the network protocol used to deliver most of the HTML files, image files, query results, or anything else (collectively called *resources*) on the web. A resource is defined as information that can be identified by a URL. (It's the R in URL.) The most common kind of resource is a file, but a dynamically generated query result is also considered a resource. But whereas a URL's roots are in web pages, a web service can also be considered a resource.

`https` is syntactically identical to the `http` scheme, but it tells the browser to use an added encryption layer of SSL/TLS to protect the traffic. Transport Layer Security (TLS) and its predecessor, Secure Sockets Layer (SSL), are security protocols that provide communications security over the Internet. If you're interested in Internet security, I leave you to investigate that on your own, but I discuss it further in Chapter 15.

The HTTP session

Your web page is downloaded (or your web service is used) in an HTTP *session* — a sequence of network request-response transactions.

An HTTP client opens a connection and sends a request message to an HTTP server; the server then returns a response message, usually containing the resource that was requested. Keep in mind that the request URI isn't necessarily a resource to download; it can also be a program to handle the data you're sending. The response message may contain a static file (such as a web page) or program output.

After delivering the response, the server closes the connection making HTTP a *stateless* protocol — one that does not maintain any connection information between transactions. The current version of HTTP is HTTP/1.1 and it does provide *persistent* connections. That means a connection between a browser and the hosting server is kept open for multiple requests. This is done to improve the page loading speed. Establishing the connection is expensive in processing terms, so once a connection is open, you want to keep it open for the successive requests.

Be that as it may, there is *no* state maintained between each request, which makes HTTP a stateless protocol.

When an HTTP client initiates a request, it establishes a Transmission Control Protocol (TCP) connection to a particular port on a server. An HTTP server listening on that port waits for a client's request message. Upon receiving the request, the server sends back a status line, such as `"HTTP/1.1 200 OK"`, and a message of its own, the body of which is perhaps the requested resource, an error message, or some other information.

The formats of the request and response messages are similar and oriented to the languages humans speak, as opposed to being in hexadecimal or some binary format. Both kinds of messages consist of the following:

1. <initial line, different for request versus response>
2. Header1: value1

   . . .

   Header*n*: value*n*
3. <optional message body>

Although I *am* going to explain the structure of the message in the next few sections, it's not something you particularly have to worry about. Both the web service and iOS frameworks take care of constructing the messages for you (`NSURLRequest` and `NSURLResponse`, in the case of iOS), and all you'll have to do is provide the right content.

Initial line — Request

The initial line is different for the request than for the response (which I cover in the next section). A request line has three parts, separated by spaces: a *method name,* the *local path of the requested resource,* and the *version of HTTP* being used. Here's a typical request line:

```
GET /images/neal.png HTTP/1.1
```

It requests a resource (GET), called `/images/neal.png` from the domain you specified in the URL using HTTP/1.1.

Method name

HTTP defines nine *methods* (sometimes referred to as *verbs*) indicating the desired action to be performed on the identified resource. These *method names* are always uppercase. The most common ones are shown in Table 6-1.

Table 6-1 The Most Common HTTP Methods

Method	*Description*	*Safe*	*Idempotent*
`GET`	Requests a specific representation of a resource	Yes	Yes
`PUT`	Creates or updates a resource with the supplied representation	No	Yes
`DELETE`	Deletes the specified resource	No	Yes
`V`	Submits data to be processed by the identified resource	No	No
`HEAD`	Similar to `GET` but retrieves only headers and not the body	Yes	Yes
`OPTIONS`	Returns the methods supported by the identified resource	Yes	Yes

Of those nine methods, you really have to care about only these four:

- `GET`, which is the most common `HTTP` method; it says "give me this resource." You use `GET` in Chapters 3–5 to make a web service request of an existing web server.
- `POST`, which submits data to be processed that is included in the body of the request. You use `POST` in Part IV when you add a new point of interest.
- `PUT`, which creates or updates a resource.
- `DELETE`, which deletes the specified resource.

You should also know a few characteristics of methods. Some methods (for example, `GET`) are defined as *safe,* which means they should not change the state of the server other than logging, caching, and so on. Because they're safe, they're also considered to be *idempotent* — multiple identical requests should have the same effect as a single request.

Other methods (`POST` and `DELETE`) are not safe because they're intended to make changes to the server — updating a user's location, for example, or changing a username. These methods are also not necessarily idempotent, and therefore sending an identical `POST` request multiple times may further affect the state or cause further side effects. This can turn into a major issue when, for example, a user doesn't get feedback from an action and then tries it again (and again).

The local path of the requested resource

The path is the part of the URL after the host name, also called the request URI.

The HTTP version

The HTTP version always takes the form `HTTP/x.x`, uppercase.

Initial line — Response (Status line)

The initial response line, called the *status line,* also has three parts separated by spaces: the HTTP version, a response status code that gives the result of the request, and an English phrase describing the status code. Typical status lines are

```
HTTP/1.0 200 OK
```

and

```
HTTP/1.0 404 Not Found
```

Headers

Header lines provide information either about the request/response or about the object sent in the message body. HTTP 1.1 defines 46 headers, and only one (`Host:`) is required in requests, although to be polite, the following are also included:

- The `From` header gives the e-mail address of whoever's making the request or running the program making the request.
- The `User-Agent` header identifies the program that's making the request.

On the server side:

- The `Server` header is analogous to the `User-Agent:` header.
- The `Last-Modified` header gives the modification date of the resource that's being returned.
- The `ETag` (entity tag) header is used to determine whether a cached version of the requested resource is identical to the current version of the resource on the server.

If an HTTP message includes a body, you can usually find header lines in the message that describe the body. In particular,

- The `Content-Type:` header gives the Internet media type of the data in the body. (The Internet media type was originally called a MIME type. MIME, or Multipurpose Internet Mail Extensions, is a two-part identifier for file formats on the Internet.) You use the `Content-Type:` header in the Bonus Chapter, "Adding and Deleting Points of Interest," available for download from this book's website.
- The `Content-Length:` header gives the number of bytes in the body. You use this one in the Bonus Chapter as well.

An optional message body

The message body, if included, comes after the header lines. In a response, it contains either the data the client requested or information if there's an error. In a request, the message body is where user-entered data or uploaded files are sent to the server.

You don't need to be concerned about the message body in the `GET` request, but you have to be aware of it in the response. Fortunately, it gets handled by the `NSURLConnection` class you're using, which will deconstruct the response for you. You do, however, use the message body in a `POST` request in the Bonus Chapter when you add and delete points of interest.

A `POST` request is used to send data to the server to be processed in some way — that data is included in the message body of the request. A `POST` request usually has extra headers to describe this message body, like `Content-Type:` and `Content-Length:`.

Next I want to wade into the swamp known as RESTful web services.

The RESTful Web Service Architecture

A web service is essentially a way for one device to request of another device (over a network) that it do something for the first device — for example, return some data or do a computation and return the result. As you may expect, you can accomplish that goal a number of different ways.

As I mention earlier in this chapter, the web service world is divided into two major camps: message-oriented web services, which follow a particular set of standards (such as SOAP, WSDL, or UDDI, as described earlier); and resource-based web services, which came to life along with Web 2.0 and moved away from SOAP/WSDL/UDDI to a variant of Representational State Transfer (REST) based communications. (You use the resource-based approach in this book.)

You may have heard a lot about RESTful web services, but note that I'm talking about a *variant* on REST. I stress that fact because most people refer to any web service that uses HTTP request messages and JSON or XML response messages as REST.

In fact, there's much more to REST than that.

REST is a style of web service architecture for distributed resources such as the World Wide Web — an architecture style for networked systems, in other words. It also happens to be the underlying architectural model of the web. (*Fun Fact:* A Ph.D. student named Roy Fielding coined the term REST in his Ph.D. dissertation, `www.ics.uci.edu/~fielding/pubs/dissertation/top.htm`, which — wonder of wonders — is available online.)

That's all fine and dandy, but the crucial thing you need to understand about REST is that it was created in order to meet the web's requirements — the requirements for an Internet-scale distributed hypermedia system.

Although there are nuances to what the web is about, the web is primarily about delivering lots of information to lots of users; it has to work in a rapidly growing and evolving heterogeneous environment where you can't count on the client or the server to do anything more than meet some very minimal requirements. There are intentionally very low barriers to entry — information is transferred in a standardized form rather than one which is specific to an application's needs, text-based protocols, and hypermedia as the user interface.

Although an architecture capable of accomplishing those goals will obviously have a lot of moving parts to it, and even though I would love to linger over every aspect of its awesomeness, I'm not going to dive too deeply into REST in this book, just because there's really no need to. I'm going to limit myself to highlighting three aspects of REST that I think warrant your attention:

- **Optimization:** Because the web is an Internet-scale distributed hypermedia system, any web architecture you come up with must be optimized for large-grain hypermedia data transfer. That is what the web is really all about after all — large amounts of data (in different formats, including hyperlinks to even more data) displayed in a browser.
- **Flexibility:** Because of the heterogeneous nature of the clients and faced with the reality that both the client and server side are rapidly evolving, the architecture must build in maximum flexibility to allow for the independent evolution of client and server components.
- **Scalability:** And finally, since the web is growing rapidly and you really have no idea what the demands will be on servers down the road, components must be *scalable*.

REST, as you'll soon see, is optimized for the common case of the web (i.e., browsers and downloading of data) but results in an interface that isn't optimal for other forms of architectural interaction (like applications that use web services). That's why you don't usually find applications that are truly RESTful. (I explain more about this state of affairs in the next section.)

REST requirements

Requirements for being a fully compliant RESTful web service are detailed in the Roy Fielding dissertation I mention in the previous section. (Again, it's there for the reading at `www.ics.uci.edu/~fielding/pubs/dissertation/top.htm`.) Requirements like optimizing large-grain hypermedia data transfer, allowing independent evolution of client and server components, and enabling scalable components should ring a bell. His additional requirements — some useful to us and some not — are summarized here:

- **Client-server:** In REST, clients are consumers that request representations using a well-defined interface. Clients are not concerned with mechanics such as how something is done or how it's stored, which allows you to isolate the client code from those kinds of changes. Servers, on the other hand, are not concerned with the user interface or user state, so servers can be simpler and less concerned with implementation side effects. (There won't be any as far as user interface or user state are concerned.) Servers and clients may also be replaced and developed independently, as long as the interface is not altered.
- **Stateless:** No client context is stored on the server between requests. (That does *not* mean that clients cannot send data to update the server.) Each request from any client contains all the information necessary to service the request, and any session state is held in the client.
- **Cacheable:** Responses must implicitly or explicitly define themselves as cacheable or not to prevent clients from reusing stale or inappropriate data in response to further requests. (This is really about reducing the amount of data that needs to be downloaded.)
- **Layered:** Although intermediaries (such as proxy servers, cache servers, gateways, and so on) can be inserted between clients and resources, a client shouldn't ordinarily be able to tell whether it's connected directly to the end server or to an intermediary along the way.
- **Code On Demand:** Code On Demand is the only optional constraint of REST. If a client component has access to a set of resources but not the know-how on how to process them, it sends a request to a remote server for the code representing that know-how, receives that code, and executes it locally. Code On Demand can be used to provide the code to render a content type as needed.

- **Uniform Interface (between Components):** As Roy Fielding says, "The central feature that distinguishes the REST architectural style from other network-based styles is its emphasis on a uniform interface between components." This is *the* major characteristic of REST and the one that most RESTful applications are lacking.

  The uniform interface is what implements the requirements for the independent evolution of servers and clients by imposing four requirements. I explain each in more detail in their respective sections, but the basics are as follows:

  - *Identification of resources:* The resource is the key abstraction of information in REST — any information that can be named can be a resource.
  - *Manipulation of resources through representations:* Each resource has one or more representations — resources themselves are conceptually separate from the representations that are returned to the client.
  - *Self-descriptive messages:* A message includes enough information necessary for the receiver to process the message.
  - *Hypermedia as the engine of application state:* A RESTful application moves from one state to the next by using the alternatives (hyperlinks) embedded in the content (or representation).

Those are the basics. Read on for a bit more detail.

Identification of resources

The resource is the key abstraction of information in REST — and any information that can be named can be a resource. In fact, a resource can be defined pretty broadly — in essence, it is simply a concept based on whatever is needed to meet the needs of a client.

The web is made up of resources, which are named using a logical URL — there doesn't have to be an HTML page associated with every URL. Using a logical URL enables you to hide the implementation behind the concept. This means, for example, that I can deliver you that resource in one of any number of ways, based upon negotiations. It also means I can change the way I implement that resource without any impact on the clients — think encapsulation.

Manipulation of resources through representations

Each resource has one or more representations — resources themselves are conceptually separate from the representations that are returned to the client. For example, the server doesn't send its database, but rather, perhaps, some HTML, XML, or JSON that represents some database records.

In more technical terms, a representation consists of data, metadata describing the data, and, on occasion, metadata to describe the metadata.

This means that a client can request a representation (view) of a resource that the client knows how to process and is appropriate to the way it will be used. The following, for example, requests a particular representation — geocoded location information with the response in JSON format:

```
http://maps.googleapis.com/maps/api/geocode/json
```

You may also want to know the last time the points of interest for the RoadTrip was updated (you'll get to that in Part IV), or you may want to get all the points of interest for a destination, or even all the points of interest for *all* destinations. Using representations makes this possible.

The data format of a representation is known as a *media type*, and as you'll see, the ability to return self-describing messages (as I explain in the next section) is what makes REST so powerful. The client needs to know nothing about how the user will use the content or even about the content itself — it just needs to be able to render (work with) the media type it is represented in. The app is merely a vehicle for accessing and displaying information.

In addition, providing the same data using an assortment of media types makes it possible to support lots of different clients. As you recall, this is one of the requirements for the web architecture that Fielding was trying to develop.

The request for a representation of a resource is what is being called a web service. This is similar, but not the same as a class's method in an Objective-C application.

Self-describing messages

If you want to support clients that are merely vehicles for delivering and requesting information, the message itself must contain information about how to "display" its content — that is, a message has to include the information necessary to process the message.

What self-describing messages really do is reduce the amount of coupling between components throughout the system and facilitate independent evolution of client and server components.

For example, an HTTP request for a web service (resource) is self-describing since it contains all the information a server needs to process the request in the request line (such as the version, HTTP method, and so on) and its header (as is also the case with the response). The particulars are as follows:

- The available methods are limited to the HTTP Methods with neither the client nor the server (resource) free to redefine what an HTTP GET means for example.
- HTTP messages contain information about the message in the headers and the body.
- The client can specify the set of resource representations it can handle using HTTP Accept header(s).
- The server describes the format of the message body using HTTP Content-type header(s).

The self-describing messages requirement is why most web services are not truly RESTful. An XML or JSON response, for example, is not self-describing. The client needs to know the JSON or XML schema in order to make sense of the representation being returned.

Hypermedia as the engine of application state

A RESTful application moves from one state to the next by choosing from among the alternative state transitions embedded in the content (representation). Again, the client need know nothing about the application because it merely acts as a vehicle to display information and take the user's response — in the form of clicking a link — to display the next step in the application.

So, if you can get past the self-describing messages business, hypermedia as the engine of application state become your next formidable hurdle to RESTfulness, and this one, too, is a challenge for most applications.

For an application to be truly RESTful, it would need to be only about rendering the response, but in reality, most applications are about operating on, or using, the data rather than just rendering it.

The rationale behind the requirements

Although some of Roy Fielding's requirements serve multiple purposes, it's a lot easier to think about them by categorizing them in accordance with three broad principles:

- **For you to have scalability,** you can't link together a resource and a server. A series of requests for the same resource needs to be able to be responded to by any available server, which is why servers have to be stateless.

- **To be able to support large scale hypermedia transfer,** you have to minimize the amount of data that's being transferred. (I know that spends like an oxymoron, but network transfers are expensive, so paring things down is a good thing.) Caching data minimizes the number of times you have to download the same data.
- **For clients and servers to be able to evolve independently (and limit the requirements for clients and servers),** there has to be as little coupling as possible between clients and servers. This requirement of course is not only a web or network requirement; it is the basis of all good software engineering and one of the basic principles of object-oriented programming. Client-server, layering, identification of resources, and manipulation of resources through representations all result in loose coupling, and you can apply those principles (or some variation on them) as you design your web services.

Admittedly, the requirements Roy Fielding came up with are applicable (in broad terms) to almost any kind of software system you could come up with and are ones you can and should use when you design your web services. But because of some unique aspects of the Internet, Fielding is able to go beyond the "normal" approach to reducing coupling.

On the web, the ultimate consumer of the information is not the client; it is the user — *the user is the information (content) processor.* That means that you can remove from the client any dependency or behavior based on content and reduce the coupling any further. And Fielding (and REST) do that superbly with his last two constraints: The (dual) insistence on self-descriptive messages and hypermedia as the engine of application state.

Having these two constraints on board means that the client can simply act as a conduit to the end user. You can change the content at will because all you need to be able to do is make sure that the client can display that content in the way described by the message. That's where HTTP comes in because it gives the client and server the ability to negotiate on what each is capable of doing (the content negotiation mechanism). For example, although a client may not be capable of displaying a particular media type (and this is where Code on Demand comes in), that fact does not break the client in the sense that the client may still be able display other media types. (If you were looking for the reason why plain vanilla versions of JSON or XML aren't going to fly in these circumstances, here's your answer.) This business about things not "breaking" is also true of the server when it comes to delivering resources. And because the state transitions are built into the content, the client is blissfully unaware of them. A client simply has to be able to process the "standard" request.

This is where REST and the needs of the web begin to diverge from what you're going to be doing (most of the time) with web services. In most service scenarios, the consumer of the information is the client — *and the client is the information (content) processor.* This means that, for the majority of the time, messages aren't going to be self-descriptive — the web service provider takes over the task of message description by publishing some kind of schema to tell you how to interpret the message — and the content of the message (or some processing of it, or some user action other than clicking on a link) determines state rather than hypermedia.

This is why most applications are not RESTful, nor should they be — their purpose in life is not the same as the (web browser-like) RESTful client.

But don't let that fact distract you from the main point: You can still be guided by the rest of the architectural requirements of REST because it is simply good design. Taking a (more or less) RESTful approach to things like HTTP, resources, and resource representations actually does eliminate some of the complexity and overhead found in message-based services.

It doesn't matter that most web services aren't really RESTful

I'll admit it: Most of the web services that bill themselves as RESTful are fibbing just a tad; they usually break down when it comes to self-describing messages and hypermedia as an engine of the application state. And yet, it is precisely those last two requirements that enable the independent evolution of client and server components, which (as I've mentioned before) would seem to be a pretty big deal.

But then again, that doesn't really matter.

All those other requirements for REST are basically sound software engineering and work well to create web services that are scalable and extensible, and furthermore, easy to develop and use.

So even though I personally have a problem calling all those web services (the ones you will develop here included) RESTful, go ahead and call them whatever you'd like. At the end of the day, it's the value that this approach delivers that's important, not the label, and the basic REST architecture (which is not unique to REST) does deliver a lot of value and will be the basis of the web services in this book.

Chapter 7

Exploring an Existing Web Service

In This Chapter

- Seeing how web services work
- Having Google Geocoding do the heavy lifting for you
- Creating a class to make web service requests

Although my ultimate goal in this book is to teach you how to build your own web service — a goal I tackle with a vengeance in Part IV — the best place to start is by having you use an *existing* web service. In doing that, you create a program infrastructure that will enable you to add any web service to RoadTrip — which in turn will make it easy to use the web service that you'll create in Part IV. That web service will provide the user with the new and up-to-date points of interest instead of using the current list that came prepackaged with RoadTrip in the Destinations plist.

So, which existing web service should you go with? How about the Google Geocoding API that is part of Google Maps API Web Services? Yes, I know, RoadTrip already does geocoding quite well, thanks to the `CLGeocoder` that's part of the iOS SDK, and after this bit of business is taken care, you will continue to use it. But I'm having you use the Google Geocoding API for this brief space of time for several reasons:

- Because you're already having RoadTrip do geocoding, you don't have to do anything to the basic structure of the app; you're just replacing one implementation with another. The idea here is to make things as easy as possible allowing you to focus on the web **service** access piece without having to complicate things by also extending the app functionality.
- The Google Geocoding API Response is both in JSON and XML (more on both of those technologies in just a bit), allowing me to explain how to work with both. Even though JSON is becoming more popular, XML is still a major player, and you should know how to process an XML response.
- The response is sufficiently complex to give a real introduction to using web services.
- The way the Google Geocoding API works is pretty standard for a web service.

The Google Geocoding API

The Google Geocoding API web service is part of the Google Maps API Web Services. You can find out all about it at `http://code.google.com/apis/maps/documentation/geocoding`. Figure 7-1 shows this particular corner of the web.

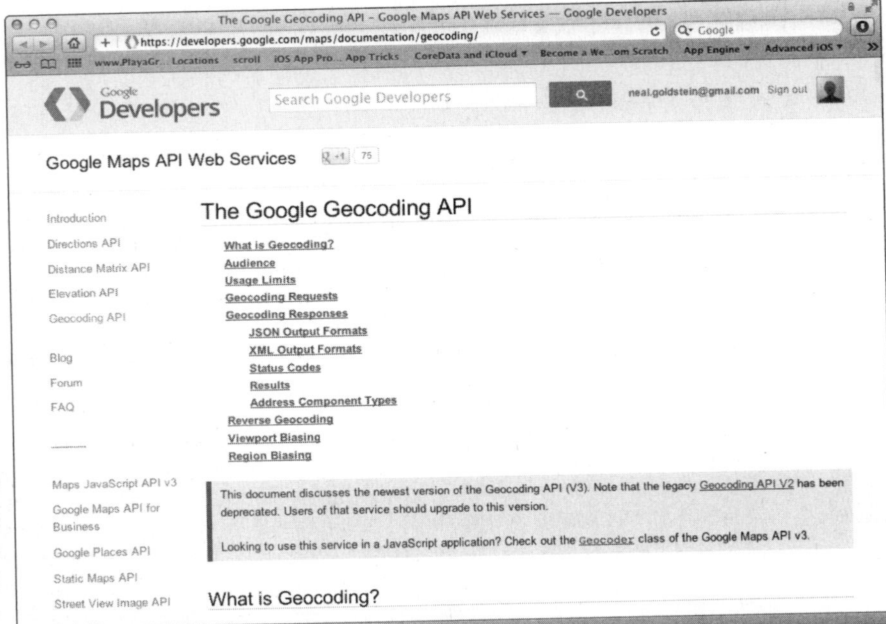

Figure 7-1: The Google Geocoding API.

Although painfully boring, the place to start is with the usage limits and terms of service.

If you were to click the Usage Limits link on the Google Maps API Web Services page (shown in Figure 7-1), you would find that use of the Google Geocoding API is subject to a query limit of 2,500 geolocation requests per day. (Not bad, right?)

Still in the Usage Limits section, you'd see a nice little Note highlighted with a touch of red that lets you know that the Geocoding API can be used only in conjunction with a Google map; you'd also see a nice link to the Maps API Terms of Service License Restrictions.

If you were to click that link, you'd be taken to another page outlining all the other Google rules you have to follow. For your purposes, neither the usage limits nor the terms of service present a problem, because you're not planning to use this in production, but it is something you need to pay attention to if you're planning to use APIs (web services) provided by third parties. You'll also need to publish your own terms of service if you're creating a web service for others to use, so it wouldn't hurt to see what the big boys came up with.

The request

I want you to start by getting your head around a couple aspects of request requirements:

- A resource-based (HTTP API) web service is a defined set of HTTP request messages with response messages that have a defined structure. (For more on resource-based (HTTP API) web services, see Chapter 6.)
- The request for a resource-based (HTTP API) web service is defined in a URI (Uniform Resource Identifier).
- The response to a request is typically in Extensible Markup Language (XML) or JavaScript Object Notation (JSON) form.

In Chapter 6, I introduced you to the URI (Uniform Resource Identifier), which is used to specify where something is and how to access it; it's central to the kind of web services you'll be using. I also explain that URI is generally preferred to URL (Uniform Resource Locators). Unfortunately, URI usage hasn't been adopted by Apple, and you can see URL throughout the iOS frameworks. So as not to confuse you, I refer to the URI as URL as well.

Every URL consists of at least some of the following: the scheme name (commonly called the *protocol*) followed by a colon, then, depending on the scheme, (HTTP for example)

- A domain name (alternatively, an *IP address*)
- A port number
- The path to the service requested
- An optional query string

(There is also an optional fragment identifier which you won't be using.) What you end up with is something like the following:

```
scheme://domain:port/path?query_string#fragment_id
```

The various pieces are shown in Figure 7-2.

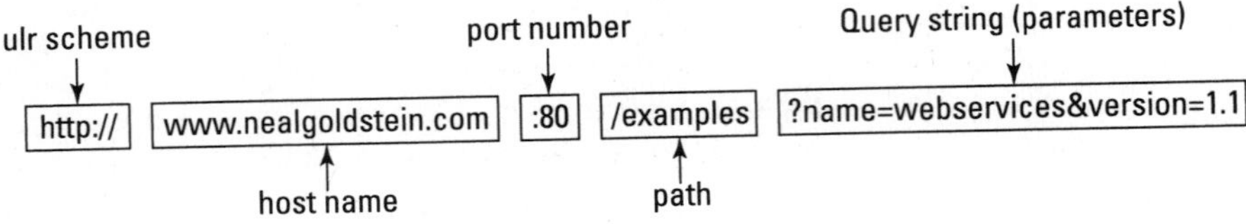

Figure 7-2: The URL structure.

If you were to click the Geocoding Requests link on the Google Maps API Web Services page (refer to Figure 7-1), you'd see the detailed information, including the tidbit that a Geocoding API request must have the following form

```
http://
    maps.googleapis.com/maps/api/geocode/output?parameters
```

where *output* may be either of the following values:

- json (recommended) indicates output in JavaScript Object Notation (JSON)
- xml indicates output as XML

In the Geocoding Requests section of the page (see Figure 7-3) you'd also find an explanation of the "*output?parameters*" business. Parameters are separated using the ampersand character (&), and as you may have guessed, some parameters are required, whereas some are optional.

The required parameters are:

- **address:** The address that you want to geocode.

  or

  latlng: The textual latitude/longitude value for which you wish to obtain the closest, human-readable address.
- **sensor:** Indicates whether or not the geocoding request comes from a device with a location sensor. This value must be either `true` or `false`.

In this case, you can pass either an `address` or a `latlng` to lookup. (If you pass a `latlng`, the geocoder performs what is known as a *reverse geocode*. I leave that to you to explore.)

You can look through this section of the documentation to see the other parameters.

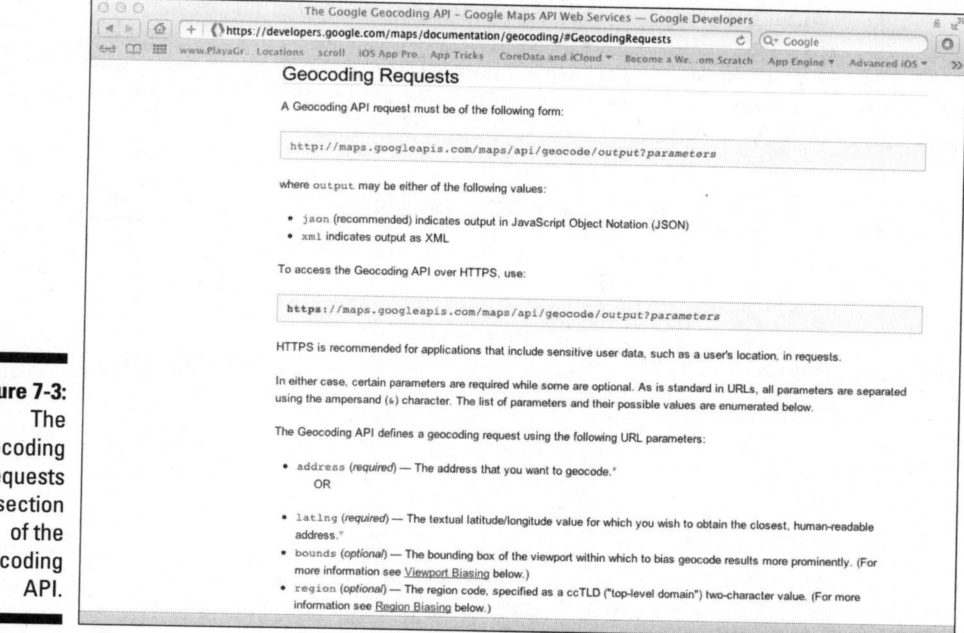

Figure 7-3: The Geocoding Requests section of the Geocoding API.

You can also access the Geocoding API over HTTPS, by using this:

```
https:
  //maps.googleapis.com/maps/api/geocode/output?parameters
```

As I explain in Chapter 6, you should use HTTPS if you're including sensitive data in your request — for example, if you were sending the user's current location.

The response

Send out a request and you get a response, right? Looking at your trusty Google Maps API Web Services page, you see a Geocoding Responses — XML Output Formats link. (Refer to Figure 7-1.) If you were to click that link, you'd discover that the documentation explains that the following request

```
http://maps.googleapis.com/maps/api/geocode/xml?
address=1600+Amphitheatre+Parkway,+Mountain+View,+CA&
sensor=true_or_false
```

would get the XML response shown in Listing 7-1. Of course, you'll need to replace `true_or_false` with either `true` or `false`. (I'll explain which is which in a bit.) I don't spend a lot of time on XML, because the web service you create in Part IV will have a JSON response, but along the way I explain enough so that what you're doing makes sense.

Listing 7-1: The Documented Response from the Geocoding Web Service


```
<GeocodeResponse>
 <status>OK</status>
 <result>
  <type>street_address</type>
  <formatted_address>
      1600 Amphitheatre Pkwy, Mountain View, CA 94043, USA
  </formatted_address>
  <address_component>
   <long_name>1600</long_name>
   <short_name>1600</short_name>
   <type>street_number</type>
  </address_component>
  <address_component>
   <long_name>Amphitheatre Pkwy</long_name>
   <short_name>Amphitheatre Pkwy</short_name>
   <type>route</type>
  </address_component>
  <address_component>
   <long_name>Mountain View</long_name>
   <short_name>Mountain View</short_name>
   <type>locality</type>
   <type>political</type>
  </address_component>
  <address_component>
   <long_name>San Jose</long_name>
   <short_name>San Jose</short_name>
   <type>administrative_area_level_3</type>
   <type>political</type>
  </address_component>
  <address_component>
   <long_name>Santa Clara</long_name>
   <short_name>Santa Clara</short_name>
   <type>administrative_area_level_2</type>
   <type>political</type>
  </address_component>
  <address_component>
   <long_name>California</long_name>
   <short_name>CA</short_name>
   <type>administrative_area_level_1</type>
   <type>political</type>
  </address_component>
```

```
    <address_component>
     <long_name>United States</long_name>
     <short_name>US</short_name>
     <type>country</type>
     <type>political</type>
    </address_component>
    <address_component>
     <long_name>94043</long_name>
     <short_name>94043</short_name>
     <type>postal_code</type>
    </address_component>
    <geometry>
     <location>
      <lat>37.4217550</lat>
      <lng>-122.0846330</lng>
     </location>
     <location_type>ROOFTOP</location_type>
     <viewport>
      <southwest>
       <lat>37.4188514</lat>
       <lng>-122.0874526</lng>
      </southwest>
      <northeast>
       <lat>37.4251466</lat>
       <lng>-122.0811574</lng>
      </northeast>
     </viewport>
    </geometry>
   </result>
</GeocodeResponse>
```


Now, just for fun, try entering the following request in your browser. Notice that I've changed the `sensor=true_or_false` to `sensor=true`. (If you don't pick `true` or `false`, you'll get an error, which I illustrate in the "Status codes" section, later in this chapter.) I also, for now, explain things in terms of the XML response. I explain the JSON response in Chapter 10.

```
http://maps.googleapis.com/maps/api/geocode/xml?
address=1600+Amphitheatre+Parkway,+Mountain+View,+CA&
sensor=true
```

I use Google Chrome when I explore web service requests and responses because I like the JSON output formatting in the browser window better.

When you enter the preceding request in your browser, you can see that the actual response you get (see Listing 7-2) is a little different than the documented response (shown in Listing 7-1). This discrepancy (which I won't get into because you won't be using it) brings up a point. In "free" web services, things may change, and because they're free, the documentation may take a little while to catch up. The only way to really see what the response is going to be is to look at the actual response using the documented response as a guide.

Listing 7-2: The Actual Response

```
<GeocodeResponse>
 <status>OK</status>
 <result>
  <type>street_address</type>
  <formatted_address>
      1600 Amphitheatre Pkwy, Mountain View, CA 94043, USA
  </formatted_address>
  <address_component>
   <long_name>1600</long_name>
   <short_name>1600</short_name>
   <type>street_number</type>
  </address_component>
  <address_component>
   <long_name>Amphitheatre Pkwy</long_name>
   <short_name>Amphitheatre Pkwy</short_name>
   <type>route</type>
  </address_component>
  <address_component>
   <long_name>Mountain View</long_name>
      <short_name>Mountain View</short_name>
   <type>locality</type>
   <type>political</type>
  </address_component>
  <address_component>
   <long_name>Santa Clara</long_name>
   <short_name>Santa Clara</short_name>
   <type>administrative_area_level_2</type>
   <type>political</type>
  </address_component>
  <address_component>
   <long_name>California</long_name>
   <short_name>CA</short_name>
   <type>administrative_area_level_1</type>
   <type>political</type>
  </address_component>
  <address_component>
   <long_name>United States</long_name>
   <short_name>US</short_name>
```

```
    <type>country</type>
    <type>political</type>
   </address_component>
   <address_component>
    <long_name>94043</long_name>
    <short_name>94043</short_name>
    <type>postal_code</type>
    </address_component>
   <geometry>
    <location>
     <lat>37.4229181</lat>
     <lng>-122.0854212</lng>
    </location>
    <location_type>ROOFTOP</location_type>
    <viewport>
     <southwest>
      <lat>37.4215691</lat>
      <lng>-122.0867702</lng>
     </southwest>
     <northeast>
      <lat>37.4242671</lat>
      <lng>-122.0840722</lng>
     </northeast>
    </viewport>
   </geometry>
  </result>
 </GeocodeResponse>
```

Oh, and by the way, by the time you read this book, the code underlying both Listings 7-1 and 7-2 may have changed as well.

The documentation for the Google Geocoding web service explains that the XML response consists of a single `<GeocodeResponse>` (refer to Listing 7-1) and two top-level elements:

- `<status>`, which contains metadata on the request. (Again refer to Listing 7-1.) I explain the status codes next.
- `<result>` elements (zero or more), which each contain a single set of geocoded address information and geometry information.

The documentation also points out that the XML response is much longer than the JSON response and that Google recommends you use JSON as the preferred output flag unless your service requires XML for some reason. For good measure, it also lets you know that processing the XML "requires some care." No wonder, then, that I eventually nudge you to JSON, which I explain in Chapter 10.

Interestingly enough, when I first started working with the Google Geocoding web service, XML was the preferred response. This gives you at least a small indication of where things seem to be going.

I'll have you work only with a very small part of the response; as for the rest — what's a `location_type` or `viewport`, for example — you can find that out in the Google Geocoding API Geocoding Responses documentation.

Status codes

Most web services return some sort of status code to let you know about your request. I mention in "The response" section, earlier in this chapter, that if you don't change `sensor=true_or_false` to either `sensor=true` or `sensor=false`, you're sure to get an error. Try entering the following in your browser. (I've left out the sensor parameter entirely.)

```
http://maps.googleapis.com/maps/api/geocode/xml?
     address=1600+Amphitheatre+Parkway,+Mountain+View,+CA
```

In Listing 7-3, you can see the response.

Listing 7-3: You Can't Do This

```
<GeocodeResponse>
 <status>REQUEST_DENIED</status>
</GeocodeResponse>
```

In the case of the Google Geocoding web service, `status` can have the following values:

- `OK` indicates that no errors occurred; the `address` was successfully parsed, and at least one geocode was returned.
- `ZERO_RESULTS` indicates that the geocode was successful but returned no results. This situation may occur if the geocode was passed a non-existent `address` or a `latlng` in a remote location.
- `OVER_QUERY_LIMIT` indicates that you're over your quota.
- `REQUEST_DENIED` indicates that your request was denied, generally because of lack of a required sensor parameter (as you can see in Listing 7-3).
- `INVALID_REQUEST` generally indicates that the query (`address` or `latlng`) is missing.

With all this information, you now have what it takes — conceptually, at least — to use the Google Geocoding API web service in RoadTrip.

I do want to point out that when you're working with a web service's `GET` requests you often can test the response by using your browser. You take advantage of that in Part IV. (In case you're unclear regarding what `GET` requests are all about, I explain them in Chapter 12.)

How RoadTrip Currently Does Geocoding

Before you tackle grafting web services into RoadTrip, take a look at how RoadTrip currently does geocoding. Now, geocoding actually happens in more than one place in RoadTrip, but the most convenient corner to scrutinize it in action is `RTModel`, which eventually does the geocoding at the behest of the `FindController` when you enter a place to find in the Find row of the Main view.

The idea is that it's pretty useful when traveling to be able to enter a location and have that location display on a map. Although you can do that in many of the map applications currently available, having to use a different application does take you out of the app you're using. What's more, you can't just take that point displayed on the other application's map and then do something with it in your own app, such as display it with all your other annotations.

Forward geocoding, which is the most popular type of geocoding — in fact, whoever just says *geocoding* means *forward geocoding* — allows you to take an address and turn it into a map coordinate. Being able to take an address and turn it into a map coordinate enables the feature in RoadTrip that allows the user to enter an address, or even just the name of a well-known landmark, and display it on the map. (*Reverse geocoding* allows you to take a map coordinate — your current location, for example — and turn it into an address.)

I don't drill down too deeply into the mechanics of how the user interface works other than to say that when a user taps in an enabled `UITextField`, it becomes the first responder and the keyboard automatically rises to allow the user to enter text — you don't have to do a thing to make that happen. (Although normally you're responsible for scrolling the view if the keyboard will cover the Text field — which in this case will only happen when running the app on the iPhone; because the Text field is in a Table View cell, scrolling the view is done by the Table view.)

When the user is done entering text (which will be sent to the geocoder), he taps the Return key (which has been relabeled Go).

When the user taps the Go key, the Text field determines whether it has a delegate and whether the delegate has implemented a `textFieldShouldReturn:` method — one of the optional `UITextFieldDelegate` protocol methods. If the delegate has done so, it sends the delegate the `textFieldShouldReturn:` message. In `textFieldShouldReturn:` the text is captured and the `FindController` is instantiated and launched.

In its `viewDidLoad` method, the `FindController` sends a message to the `RTModel` to create an annotation to display on the map, as you can see in Listing 7-4. (I've bolded the message for you.)

Listing 7-4: Sending a Message to the RTModel

```
- (void)viewDidLoad
{
  [super viewDidLoad];
  self.title = self.findLocation;

  void (^addFindLocationCompletionHandler)(Annotation *,
   NSError *) = ^(Annotation *annotation, NSError *error){
    if (error!= nil || annotation == nil) {
      NSLog(@"Geocoder Failure! Error code: %u,
           description: %@, and reason: %@", error.
           code,[error localizedDescription],
                          [error localizedFailureReason]);
    }
    else {
      MKCoordinateRegion region;
      region.center.latitude =
                           annotation.coordinate.latitude;
      region.center.longitude =
                          annotation.coordinate.longitude;
      region.span.latitudeDelta = .05;
      region.span.longitudeDelta = .05;
      [self.mapView setRegion:region animated:NO];
      [self.mapView addAnnotation:annotation];
    }
  };
  [[RTModel model] addLocation:self.findLocation
      completionHandler:addFindLocationCompletionHandler];
  }
}
```

The message includes a completion block, which I don't need to explain here, but it's in the `RTModel addLocation:completionHandler:` method where the actual geocoding occurs, as you can see bolded in Listing 7-5.

Listing 7-5: The Geocoding Request

```
- (void)addLocation: (NSString *)findLocation
    completionHandler:(void (^)(Annotation  *annotation,
                              NSError* error)) completion {

  void (^clGeocodeCompletionHandler)(NSArray *, NSError *)
        = ^(NSArray *placemarks, NSError *error){
    CLPlacemark *placemark = [placemarks objectAtIndex:0];
    Annotation *foundAnnotation;
    if (error!= nil || placemark == nil) {
      NSLog(@"Geocoder Failure! Error code: %u,
           description: %@, and reason: %@", error.
           code, [error localizedDescription], [error
           localizedFailureReason]);
    }
    else {
      foundAnnotation = [[Annotation alloc]init];
      foundAnnotation.coordinate = placemark.location.
           coordinate;
      foundAnnotation.subtitle = [NSString
           stringWithFormat:@"Lat:%f Lon:%f", placemark.
           location.coordinate.latitude, placemark.
           location.coordinate.longitude];
      foundAnnotation.title = findLocation;
    }
    foundLocation = [[CLLocation alloc]
      initWithLatitude:foundAnnotation.coordinate.latitude
         longitude:foundAnnotation.coordinate.longitude];
    addFindLocationCompletionHandler(
                                foundAnnotation, error);
  };
  addFindLocationCompletionHandler = completion;
  CLGeocoder* geocoder = [[CLGeocoder alloc] init];
  [geocoder geocodeAddressString:findLocation completionHa
         ndler:clGeocodeCompletionHandler];
}
```

The way it works now — and the way it will work again when you're done with this part — is that a `CLGeocoder`, which is part of the `CoreLocation.framework`, is instantiated,

```
CLGeocoder* geocoder = [[CLGeocoder alloc] init];
```

and the geocoding request is made, again passing in a completion block, like so:

```
[geocoder geocodeAddressString:findLocation completionHand
         ler:clGeocodeCompletionHandler];
```

Interesting as it is, I'm neither going to explain iOS geocoding further nor say any more about using blocks. If either or both interest you, check out my *iPhone Application Development For Dummies* and *iPad Application Development For Dummies* books, where you can find an extensive explanation of both topics. For now, though, simply comment out the iOS geocoding request and the completion block (*comment out,* not *delete*; you'll want to restore it later) and add a new method to the `RTModel` that makes a Google Geocoding web service request instead.

But before you do that, I have you add a new class with the apt name of `WSManager` — an infrastructure class which will construct and manage not only the Google Geocoding web service request and response, but also any resource-based (HTTP API) web service, including the one you will build in Part IV. This class is very handy.

If you want to use this web service in an app you're creating, you're in luck because most of the work you're about to do will transfer, with the exception of the actual creation of the `Annotation` object unique to RoadTrip. In fact, the `WSManager` that you're about to add will be the basis of Part IV, where you create your own web service, and it's pretty similar to the general web service manager I use in my apps.

Creating the Plumbing: The WSManager

On the long road to web services nirvana, you start by adding the `WSManager.m` and `.h` files:

1. **Create a new group to contain your model classes by going to the Project navigator, selecting the RoadTrip group (not the RoadTrip project, which is at the top), right-clicking, and then choosing New Group from the menu that appears.**

   Alternatively, you can select the RoadTrip group and then choose File➪New➪New Group from the main menu.

   Whichever method you choice, you see a new group (it looks like a folder) under the RoadTrip group heading.

2. **Name your new group** Web Service Classes.

   To change a file's group, select the file and drag it to the group you want it to occupy. The same goes for groups as well. (After all, they can go into other groups.)

3. **In the Project navigator, select the (newly created) Web Service Classes group, right-click the selection, and then choose New File from the menu that appears to open the New File dialog.**

   Or you can select the Model Classes group and choose File➪New➪New File from the main menu (or press ⌘+N).

   You see a dialog that enables you to select a file type.

4. **In the left column of the dialog, select Cocoa Touch under the iOS heading, select the Objective-C class template in the top-right pane, and then click Next.**

5. **In the Class field, enter** WSManager, **choose NSObject from the Subclass Of pop-up menu, and then click Next.**

   A Save sheet appears.

6. **In the Save sheet, click Create.**

You start with a single method in this class — `geocodeSynchronouslyXML:`. It will create and manage a Google Geocoding web services request set up to work with an XML response. As you can see from the name, the request will be made synchronously. I explain that and how to make the request asynchronously in Chapter 9.

Add the bolded code in Listing 7-6 to `WSManager.h`.

Listing 7-6: Updating the WSManager.h Interface

```
#import <Foundation/Foundation.h>

@interface WSManager : NSObject

- (void)geocodeSynchronouslyXML:(NSMutableDictionary *)
                                                  userParams
    successBlock:(void (^)(NSDictionary *))success
    failureBlock:(void (^)())failure;
@end
```

You also need some instance variables, and you need to declare a few methods private to the class's implementation. To do that, add the bolded code in Listing 7-7 to `WSManager.m`.

Listing 7-7: Updating the WSManager Interface in the WSManager.m Implementation File

```
#import "WSManager.h"

@interface WSManager () {

  void (^returnSuccess)(NSDictionary *);
  void (^returnFail)();
  NSString *webService;
  NSMutableDictionary *params;
}
- (void)setupGeocodingWebService;
- (NSMutableURLRequest *)createGETRequest:
                  (NSString *)baseURL withParams:
                           (NSDictionary *)userParams;
- (void)requestSynchronousWebService:
                       (NSMutableURLRequest *)request;
@end
```

The first method I have you add is `setupGeocodingWebService`. This method creates a dictionary with the required sensor parameter and its associated value (`true` here, because you'll be using a mobile device that does have a location sensor). The dictionary is used by the `createGETRequest:withParams:` method as it constructs the URL you'll need for the Geocoding web service.

To do all that, add the code in Listing 7-8 to `WSManager.m`.

Listing 7-8: Adding setupGeocodingWebService to WSManager.m

```
- (void)setupGeocodingWebService {

  params = [[NSMutableDictionary alloc] init];
  [params setValue:@"true" forKey:@"sensor"];
}
```

The dictionary key here — `sensor` — corresponds to the required parameter in the request. As you'll soon see in Listing 7-10, having the keys correspond to the required parameters will enable you to use the `NSDictionary`'s `for...in` enumerator, which in turn makes it a lot easier to add the key and its value to the web service request (string).

Next, you set up the actual web service request. Although this one is specific to the Google Geocoding web service in its XML Response mode, as you'll see, it uses a set of methods applicable to any web service request. Add the geocodeSynchronouslyXML:successBlock:failureBlock in Listing 7-9 to WSManager.m.

Listing 7-9: Adding geocodeSynchronouslyXML:successBlock:failureBlock to WSManager.m

```
- (void)geocodeSynchronouslyXML:(NSMutableDictionary *)
    userParams successBlock:(void (^)(NSDictionary *))
                success failureBlock:(void (^)())failure {


  returnSuccess = success;
  returnFail = failure;
  [self setupGeocodingWebService];
  webService =
      @"http://maps.googleapis.com/maps/api/geocode/xml?";
  [params addEntriesFromDictionary:userParams];
  NSMutableURLRequest *request =
     [self createGETRequest:webService withParams:params];
  [self requestSynchronousWebService:request];
}
```

In Listing 7-9, you start by saving the success and failure blocks that you'll use later (see Listing 7-11) and then sending the setupGeocodingWebService message to set up the required sensor parameter. This is saved in the params instance variable:

```
  returnSuccess = success;
  returnFail = failure;
  [self setupGeocodingWebService];
```

You then create the first part of the Google Geocoding web service request string:

```
webService =
      @"http://maps.googleapis.com/maps/api/geocode/xml?";
```

You add any caller-specified parameters (in this case, you'll pass in the address or point of interest from the RTModel method) to the params dictionary you just created in setupGeocodingWebService.

```
[params addEntriesFromDictionary:userParams];
```

You then send the createGETRequest:withParams: message, which will construct the request:

```
NSMutableURLRequest *request =
     [self createGETRequest:webService withParams:params];
```

Finally, you send the `requestSynchronousWebService:` message to actually make the request. (Not bad for a few minutes' work.)

Next, I explain the inner workings of the `createGETRequest:withParams:` method that constructs the request. (I get to `requestSynchronousWebService:` in a bit.)

Start by adding the code in Listing 7-10 to `WSManager.m`.

Listing 7-10: Adding createGETRequest:withParams: in WSManager.m

```
- (NSMutableURLRequest *)createGETRequest:(NSString *)
         baseURL withParams:(NSDictionary *)userParams {

  NSMutableString *queryString = [NSMutableString string];
  if (userParams != nil) {
    for (id key in userParams) {
      id value = [userParams valueForKey:key];
      NSString *paramString =
        [NSString stringWithFormat:@"%@=%@&", key, value];
      paramString = [paramString
          stringByAddingPercentEscapesUsingEncoding:
                                NSASCIIStringEncoding];
      [queryString appendString:paramString];
    }
  }
  NSString *urlString = [NSString stringWithFormat:
                           @"%@%@", baseURL, queryString];
  NSURL *url = [NSURL URLWithString:urlString];
  NSMutableURLRequest *request  =
                 [NSMutableURLRequest requestWithURL:url];
  [request setHTTPMethod:@"GET"];
  return request;
}
```

This method shows you all you need to do in order to create a web service request. As I explain in Chapter 6, all you really have to do is create a URL that includes a `GET` "verb" and the necessary parameters needed by the web service. `createGETRequest:withParams:` does that for you quite nicely.

I take you through Listing 7-10 slowly.

You start here by creating an empty string that you'll use to create the URL:

```
NSMutableString *queryString = [NSMutableString string];
```

The Geocoding web service is a resource-based (HTTP API) web service. (If you're not sure what that means, refer back to Chapter 6.)

To access the Geocoding web service, you call `HTTP GET` on the base URL, specifying the input location with one or more URL parameters. The response from the Geocoder contains geographic data, including latitude and longitude, as well as address information such as street, state, and country. The sensor parameter and at least one location parameter are required for all requests.

So what is `HTTP GET`? To refresh your memory, a `GET` request refers to sending information to the server using parameters tacked on to the web service's URL. This task can be done by directly adding more info to the URL. Luckily for you, you don't actually have to create the `GET` request yourself; that's done when you create the `NSURL` (which you'll do next). What you *do* have to do now, however, is provide a string with the base URL and the query (the parameters, in other words).

You started this process back in Listing 7-9 by creating the base URL in `geocodeSynchronouslyXML:successBlock:failureBlock:`.

```
webService =
      @"http://maps.googleapis.com/maps/api/geocode/xml?";
```

The question mark at the end is a separator and specifies that what follows is a query string. The query string is composed of a series of name-value pairs, each separated by an equals sign. The query allows you to pass data (the URL parameters) from you (the client) to the web service.

Next, you extract the parameters using the `for…in` construct I spoke of at the beginning of this section. In this construct, you are returned each key in a dictionary. You then get the value for that key and then format and add both to a string, which is then concatenated with the base URL string:

```
if (userParams != nil) {
    for (id key in userParams) {
      id value = [userParams valueForKey:key];
      NSString *paramString =
         [NSString stringWithFormat:@"%@=%@&", key, value];
      paramString = [paramString
           stringByAddingPercentEscapesUsingEncoding:
                                   NSASCIIStringEncoding];
      [queryString appendString:paramString];
    }
  }
```

When you read the documentation for the Geocoding web service, it tells you that certain parameters are required and some are optional and that parameters are separated using the ampersand (`&`) character.

As you see when you finally get to Listing 7-14, you'll send the `geocodeSynchronouslyXML:successBlock:failureBlock:` message, passing that method a dictionary that you create with a key of `address` and the location you want to geocode as the key's corresponding value.

Because you're using the `address` parameter, the Geocoding web service will do a forward geocoding. (Using a `latlng` key would result in a reverse geocode.)

`stringByAddingPercentEscapesUsingEncoding:` takes the string and turns it into a legal URL string with the required *escapes* — instructions that say "ignore this character." This step is necessary because the specification for URLs limits the use of allowed characters in URLs to a subset of the US-ASCII character set. This means ASCII Control characters, non-ASCII characters, and characters that might be misunderstood (such as space) need to be "escaped." Fortunately, this escaping is done for you by the method so you don't have to think about it.

You construct the string by starting with the base URL (the `webService` string created in `geocodeSynchronouslyXML:successBlock:failureBlock`) and then you add the query string

```
NSString *urlString = [NSString stringWithFormat:
                         @"%@%@", baseURL, queryString];
NSURL *url = [NSURL URLWithString:urlString];
```

Actually, what you're doing is creating an `NSURL` object. The `NSURL` class provides a way to manipulate `URLs` and the resources they reference. `NSURL` objects can be used to refer to files; in fact, they are the preferred way to do so. (I talk about this more in Chapter 4 when I explain the URL loading system.)

```
NSURLRequest *request = [NSURLRequest requestWithURL:url];
```

Finally, you take the `NSURL` object and use it to create an `NSMutableURLRequest`. (An `NSURLMutableRequest` object is a URL load request.)

```
NSMutableURLRequest *request  =
                 [NSMutableURLRequest requestWithURL:url];
```

One of the methods in the `NSMutableURLRequest` is `setHTTPMethod:`. The default method is `GET`, so it isn't necessary to set that property, but I want to show you how to explicitly set it, which you'll have to do when you do a `POST` in Part IV:

```
[request setHTTPMethod:@"GET"];
```

And then you return the request:

```
return request;
```

The `request` is used by `geocodeSynchronouslyXML:successBlock:failureBlock`: to send the service request:

```
[self requestSynchronousWebService:request];
```

You need to implement `requestSynchronousWebService:` next. To do so, add the code in Listing 7-11 to `WSManager.m`.

Listing 7-11: Adding requestSynchronousWebService: to WSManager.m

```
- (void)requestSynchronousWebService:
                          (NSMutableURLRequest *)request {

  NSURLResponse *response = nil;
  NSError *error = nil;
  NSData *synchronousData = [NSURLConnection
          sendSynchronousRequest:request
          returningResponse:&response error:&error];

  if (error != nil) {
    UIAlertView *alert = [[UIAlertView alloc]
       initWithTitle:@"Error getting response from server"
       message:[error localizedDescription] delegate:nil
       cancelButtonTitle:@"OK" otherButtonTitles:nil];
    [alert show];
    returnFail (nil);
  }
  else {
    if (!synchronousData) {
      UIAlertView *alert = [[UIAlertView alloc]
          initWithTitle:
                 @"Your request could not be carried out"
          message:
                @"There is a problem on the cloud server"
          delegate:nil
          cancelButtonTitle:@"OK" otherButtonTitles:nil];
      [alert show];
      returnFail (nil);
    }

    else {
      NSDictionary *responseDict =
        [NSDictionary dictionaryWithObject:synchronousData
                         forKey:@"response"];
      returnSuccess (responseDict);
    }
  }
}
```

Walking through the code, you see that the first thing you do is initialize a couple of variables used by the request:

```
NSURLResponse *response = nil;
NSError *error = nil;
```

Then you make the actual request by sending the `sendSynchronousRequest:returningResponse:error:` message:

```
NSData *data =
[NSURLConnection sendSynchronousRequest:request
          returningResponse:&response error:&error];
```

`response` will point to the URL response returned by the server and `error` will point to error information if an error occurs while processing the request. `data` will point to the data that is returned.

In this case, you're using the `NSURLConnection` to perform a synchronous load of the specified URL request (`sendSynchronousRequest:returningResponse:error:`), which means everything grinds to a halt while you wait for a response. And if the server is on coffee break or something like that, well, you know how it is. (This delay is, as you'd expect, unacceptable in a robust application, which means you'll have to move to asynchronous loads as you further develop the app — in Chapter 8, to be precise.)

With the request out of the way, you then check for errors:

```
if (error != nil) {
  UIAlert *alertView = [[UIAlertView alloc]
    initWithTitle:@"Error getting response from server"
    message:[error localizedDescription] delegate:nil
    cancelButtonTitle:@"OK" otherButtonTitles:nil];
  [alert show];
  returnFail (nil);
}
```

When everything works out, you still check for errors — you want to make sure that there is actually some data returned.

```
if (!synchronousData) {
  UIAlertView *alert = [[UIAlertView alloc]
    initWithTitle:@"Your request could not be carried out"
    message: @"There is a problem on the cloud server"
    delegate:nil
    cancelButtonTitle:@"OK" otherButtonTitles:nil];
    [alert show];
    returnFail (nil);
}
```

And then, if everything really has worked out, you simply create a dictionary, add the response to it with a key of `data`, and then call the success block you saved earlier, passing in the newly created dictionary. (I use a dictionary because that's the way the JSON data is usually returned, and I can show you how to work with data returned that way.)

```
NSDictionary *responseDict = [NSDictionary dictionaryWithO
          bject:synchronousData forKey:@"response"];

returnSuccess (responseDict);
```

Having the Model Use the Geocoding Web Service

With the plumbing in place, you're ready to update RoadTrip's `RTModel` to use the Geocoding web service. Start by adding the necessary headers, instance variables, and method declaration — the bolded code in Listing 7-12 — to `RTModel.m`.

Listing 7-12: Updating the RTModel Interface in the RTModel.m Implementation

```
#import "RTModel.h"
#import "RTAppDelegate.h"
#import "Destination.h"
#import "PointOfInterest.h"
#import "Annotation.h"
#import "SharedPointOfInterest.h"
#import "WSManager.h"

typedef void (^addLocationCompletionHandler)(Annotation
          *annotation, NSError* error);

@interface RTModel () {
  NSDictionary *destinationData;
  Destination* destination;
  NSMutableArray *events;
  NSMutableArray *pointsOfInterest;
  NSMutableArray *itinerary;
  NSMutableArray *pointsOfInterestData;
  addLocationCompletionHandler
          addFindLocationCompletionHandler;
  CLLocation *foundLocation;
  NSMutableData *data;
  NSString *latitude;
  NSString *longitude;
  NSString *responseStr;
  NSUInteger errorCode;
  NSString *responseErrorMessage;
  NSString *address;
}
@property (readonly, strong, nonatomic) NSFetchRequest
          *sharedPointOfInterestFetchRequest;
- (void)geocodeSynchronouslyXML:(NSString *)findLocation;
@end
```

Next, add the bolded code in Listing 7-13 to `RTModel.m` to have `RTModel` use the Geocoding web service.

Listing 7-13: Updating addLocation:completionHandler: in RTModel.m

```
- (void)addLocation:(NSString *)findLocation
          completionHandler:(void (^)(Annotation
          *annotation, NSError* error)) completion {
  /*
  void (^clGeocodeCompletionHandler)(NSArray *, NSError *)
          = ^(NSArray *placemarks, NSError *error){
    CLPlacemark *placemark = [placemarks objectAtIndex:0];
    Annotation *foundAnnotation;
    if (error!= nil || placemark == nil) {
      NSLog(@"Geocoder Failure! Error code: %u,
          description: %@, and reason: %@", error.
          code, [error localizedDescription], [error
          localizedFailureReason]);
    }
    else {
      foundAnnotation = [[Annotation alloc]init];
      foundAnnotation.coordinate = placemark.location.
          coordinate;
      foundAnnotation.subtitle = [NSString
          stringWithFormat:@"Lat:%f Lon:%f", placemark.
          location.coordinate., placemark.location.
          coordinate.longitude];
      foundAnnotation.title = findLocation;
    }
    foundLocation = [[CLLocation alloc]
     initWithLatitude:foundAnnotation.coordinate.latitude
        longitude:foundAnnotation.coordinate.longitude];
    addFindLocationCompletionHandler
                              (foundAnnotation, error);
  };
   */
  addFindLocationCompletionHandler = completion;
//CLGeocoder* geocoder = [[CLGeocoder alloc] init];
//[geocoder geocodeAddressString:findLocation completionHa
          ndler:clGeocodeCompletionHandler];
  [self geocodeSynchronouslyXML:findLocation];
}
```

I'm having you comment out the existing code here so that it's easy to return to it when you're done with this section.

Now you need to add the code in Listing 7-14 to `RTModel.m`. (This code does what `addLocation:completionHandler` did, except it does so using the Geocoding web service instead of the `CLGeocoder`.)

Listing 7-14: Add geocodeSynchronouslyXML:completionHandler: in RTModel.m

```
- (void)geocodeSynchronouslyXML:(NSString *)findLocation {

  void (^success) (NSDictionary *) =
```

```
                                ^(NSDictionary *response) {

    data = [response objectForKey:@"response"];
    responseStr = [[NSString alloc] initWithData:data
                        encoding: NSUTF8StringEncoding];
    NSLog(@"XML response:\n%@\n", responseStr);

    CLLocationCoordinate2D coordinate;
    coordinate.latitude = [latitude doubleValue];
    coordinate.longitude = [longitude doubleValue];

    Annotation *foundAnnotation =
                            [[Annotation alloc] init];
    foundAnnotation.coordinate = coordinate;
    foundAnnotation.subtitle =
      [NSString stringWithFormat:@"Lat:%f Lon:%f",
         [latitude doubleValue], [longitude doubleValue]];
    foundAnnotation.title = findLocation;

    foundLocation = [[CLLocation alloc]
      initWithLatitude:foundAnnotation.coordinate.latitude
          longitude:foundAnnotation.coordinate.longitude];
    responseStr = [[NSString alloc]
        initWithData:data encoding:NSUTF8StringEncoding];
    addFindLocationCompletionHandler
                              (foundAnnotation, nil);
  };

  void (^failure) (NSError *) = ^(NSError *error ){
    NSString *errorMessage = [error localizedDescription];
    UIAlertView *alertView = [[UIAlertView alloc]
      initWithTitle:@"Error getting response from server"
         message:errorMessage delegate:nil
         cancelButtonTitle:@"OK" otherButtonTitles:nil];
    [alertView show];
    return;
  };

  latitude = @"n/a";
  longitude = @"n/a";
  errorCode = 0;
  responseErrorMessage = @"";
  NSMutableDictionary *params =
                    [[NSMutableDictionary alloc] init];
  [params setObject:findLocation forKey:@"address"];
  WSManager *wsManager = [[WSManager alloc] init];
  [wsManager geocodeSynchronouslyXML:params
             successBlock:success failureBlock:failure];
}
```

With this code — after taking the time to initialize a few variables — you create the parameter dictionary with the key name (`address`) and value that will become part of the URL query that you send to `geocodeSynchronouslyXML:successBlock:failureBlock:failure`.

```
NSMutableDictionary *params =
                    [[NSMutableDictionary alloc] init];
[params setObject:findLocation forKey:@"address"];
```

You then allocate a new `WSManager` to handle the request and send the `geocodeSynchronouslyXML:successBlock:failureBlock:failure` message.

```
WSManager *wsManager = [[WSManager alloc] init];
[wsManager geocodeSynchronouslyXML:params
            successBlock:success failureBlock:failure];
```

In the success block, you get the data from the dictionary returned to you, which you then log to the console.

```
data = [response objectForKey:@"response"];
responseStr = [[NSString alloc] initWithData:data
                        encoding: NSUTF8StringEncoding];
NSLog(@"XML response:\n%@\n", responseStr);
```

The idea here is that documentation is like many things in life — you can trust but you also need to verify.

In the rest of the block, you actually do what you had done in the completion block for a successful geocode request in the `RTModel addLocation:completionHandler:`. I'm not going to go into it here because it stays the same, and you even can copy and paste it to save some typing. The same thing is true of the failure block and the failure handling code in the `addLocation:completionHandler:` block. I'm using separate failure and success blocks here because two blocks separate out your response to the response and make it easier to follow.

Now build and run the app, select Travel, and then enter *Empire State Building* in Find.

In Figure 7-4, you can see a new annotation in the Atlantic Ocean with a latitude and longitude of 0.0 and 0.0 respectively. That's because you haven't done anything with the response except log it, so the longitude and latitude both end up 0.0, their initialized values. (You'll fix that next chapter.)

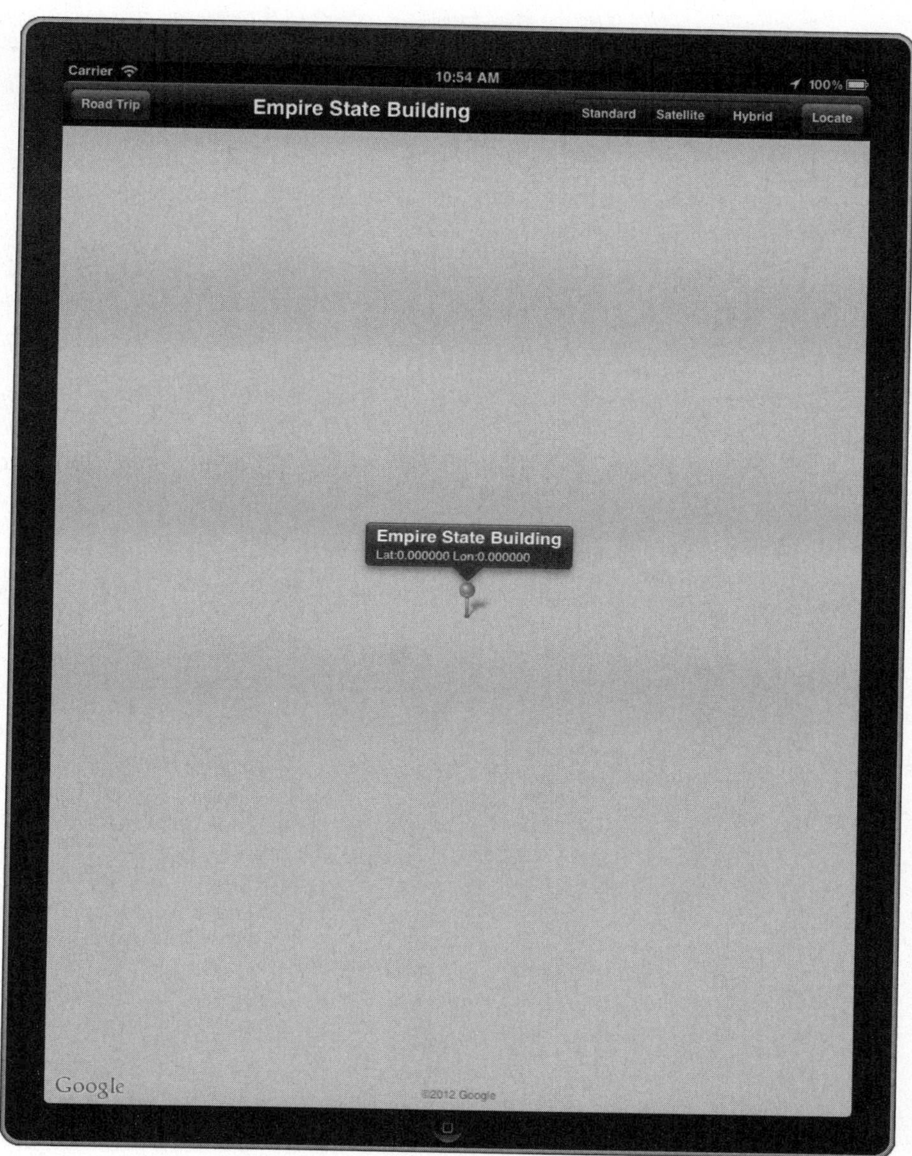

Figure 7-4: No, this isn't really the location of the Empire State Building.

If you look in the Debug area console pane (courtesy of the `NSLog` statement you added in Listing 7-14), you should see something like what's shown in Listing 7-15.

Listing 7-15: The XML Response


```
<?xml version="1.0" encoding="UTF-8"?>
<GeocodeResponse>
 <status>OK</status>
 <result>
  <type>point_of_interest</type>
  <type>courthouse</type>
  <type>establishment</type>
  <formatted_address>Empire State, 350 5th Avenue Suite
          300, New York, NY 10118, USA</formatted_
          address>
  <address_component>
   <long_name>Empire State</long_name>
   <short_name>Empire State</short_name>
   <type>point_of_interest</type>
   <type>establishment</type>
  </address_component>
  <address_component>
   <long_name>350</long_name>
   <short_name>350</short_name>
   <type>street_number</type>
  </address_component>
  <address_component>
   <long_name>5th Avenue Suite 300</long_name>
   <short_name>5th Avenue Suite 300</short_name>
   <type>route</type>
  </address_component>
  <address_component>
   <long_name>Midtown</long_name>
   <short_name>Midtown</short_name>
   <type>neighborhood</type>
   <type>political</type>
  </address_component>
  <address_component>
   <long_name>Manhattan</long_name>
   <short_name>Manhattan</short_name>
   <type>sublocality</type>
   <type>political</type>
  </address_component>
  <address_component>
   <long_name>New York</long_name>
   <short_name>New York</short_name>
   <type>locality</type>
   <type>political</type>
  </address_component>
  <address_component>
   <long_name>New York</long_name>
   <short_name>New York</short_name>
   <type>administrative_area_level_2</type>
   <type>political</type>
```

```
   </address_component>
   <address_component>
    <long_name>New York</long_name>
    <short_name>NY</short_name>
    <type>administrative_area_level_1</type>
    <type>political</type>
   </address_component>
   <address_component>
    <long_name>United States</long_name>
    <short_name>US</short_name>
    <type>country</type>
    <type>political</type>
   </address_component>
   <address_component>
    <long_name>10118</long_name>
    <short_name>10118</short_name>
    <type>postal_code</type>
   </address_component>
   <geometry>
    <location>
     <lat>40.7485584</lat>
     <lng>-73.9857465</lng>
    </location>
    <location_type>APPROXIMATE</location_type>
    <viewport>
     <southwest>
      <lat>40.7401048</lat>
      <lng>-74.0017539</lng>
     </southwest>
     <northeast>
      <lat>40.7570109</lat>
      <lng>-73.9697391</lng>
     </northeast>
    </viewport>
   </geometry>
  </result>
 </GeocodeResponse>
```


Lot's of information here, most of which you won't be using. But to actually make what you *will* be using useful to your app, you'll need to parse the XML. You'll do that in the next chapter.

Chapter 8

Working With XML

In This Chapter

- Seeing how the XML parser works
- Using the XML parser delegates
- Processing the XML response

The state of play at the end of Chapter 7 had the Empire State Building floating in the mid-Atlantic. This of course will never do, especially if you're in New York and want to visit it. In this chapter, I show you how to take the XML data returned from the Geocoding web service request and use the XML parser that's part of the SDK to extract the data you need to place it where it really belongs on the map.

Parsing the XML Response

The whole point of using the Geocoding web service in RoadTrip is to be able to quickly get accurate (and usable) location information whenever you request it. You send the request in the form of an address or point of interest. What you get back from the request is a response, which is a lot of data in XML format. For you to be able to use the data you get back, you are going to have to parse the XML response to extract the data (latitude and longitude) you are interested in.

The key factor here is the XML parser — being able to download XML from a web service is pointless unless you can access the data within it.

To do that, you'll use the `NSXMLParser` class. (Note that, as is the case with most of these kinds of framework classes, you also have to implement delegate methods, so start by making the `RTModel` an `NSXMLParserDelegate` by adding the bolded code in Listing 8-1 to `RTModel.h`.

Listing 8-1: Updating the RTModel.h Interface

```
@interface RTModel : NSObject <NSXMLParserDelegate>

+ (RTModel *)model;
- (id)initWithDestinationIndex:
                        (NSUInteger)destinationIndex;
- (void)loadItinerary;
- (void)addToItinerary:(PointOfInterest *)pointOfInterest;
- (void)removeFromItinerary:(SharedPointOfInterest *)
                                     pointOfInterest;
- (void)loadPointsOfInterest;
- (NSArray *)returnPointsOfInterest;
- (void)addPointOfInterest:(NSMutableDictionary *)
                                 pointOfInterestData;
- (UIImage *)destinationImage;
- (NSString *)destinationName;
- (CLLocationCoordinate2D)destinationCoordinate;
- (NSString *)weather;
- (void)loadEvents;
- (NSUInteger)numberOfEvents;
- (NSString *)getEvent:(NSUInteger)index;
- (NSString *)mapTitle;
- (NSArray *)createAnnotations;
- (void)addLocation:(NSString *)findLocation
   completionHandler:(void (^)(Annotation *annotation,
                         NSError* error)) completion;
- (CLLocation *)foundLocation;
+ (NSString *)filePath:(NSString *)fileComponent;
#if !TARGET_IPHONE_SIMULATOR
- (void)persistentStoreChanged:
     (NSNotification*)notification forContext:(NSManagedOb
           jectContext*)context;
#endif

@property (readonly, strong, nonatomic)
           NSManagedObjectContext *managedObjectContext;
@property (readonly, strong, nonatomic)
           NSManagedObjectModel *managedObjectModel;
@property (readonly, strong, nonatomic)
 NSPersistentStoreCoordinator *persistentStoreCoordinator;
@end
```

You also need to add instance variables you'll be using in the NSXMLParserDelegate delegate methods. Add the bolded code in Listing 8-2 to GeocoderViewController.m.

Listing 8-2: Updating the RTModel Interface in the RTModel.m Implementation

```
#import "RTModel.h"
#import "RTAppDelegate.h"
#import "Destination.h"
#import "PointOfInterest.h"
#import "Annotation.h"
#import "SharedPointOfInterest.h"
#import "WSManager.h"

typedef void (^addLocationCompletionHandler)(Annotation
            *annotation, NSError* error);

@interface RTModel () {
  NSDictionary *destinationData;
  Destination* destination;
  NSMutableArray *events;
  NSMutableArray *pointsOfInterest;
  NSMutableArray *itinerary;
  NSMutableArray *pointsOfInterestData;
  addLocationCompletionHandler
                            addFindLocationCompletionHandler;
  CLLocation *foundLocation;
  NSMutableData *data;
  NSString *latitude;
  NSString *longitude;
  NSString *responseStr;
  NSUInteger errorCode;
  NSString *responseErrorMessage;
  NSString *address;

  BOOL inLocation;
  BOOL foundFirstLocation;
  BOOL accumulatingParsedCharacterData;
  NSMutableString *currentParsedCharacterData;
}
@property (readonly, strong, nonatomic)
       NSFetchRequest *sharedPointOfInterestFetchRequest;
- (void)geocodeSynchronouslyXML:(NSString *)findLocation;
@end
```

Looking at the bolded bit, the `currentParsedCharacterData` property is there to assemble the data as it is returned from the parser. (I explain that and the `BOOL` instance variable when I explain how the parser works.)

Now that that's all set up, you can set up the XML parser, get it started, and then display the result.

Putting the parser through its paces

To use the parser to parse the response, add the bolded code in Listing 8-3 to `geocodeSynchronouslyXML:` in `RTModel.m`.

Listing 8-3: Updating geocodeSynchronouslyXML:

```
- (void)geocodeSynchronouslyXML:(NSString *)findLocation {

  void (^success) (NSDictionary *) =
                              ^(NSDictionary *response) {

    data = [response objectForKey:@"response"];
    responseStr = [[NSString alloc]
       initWithData:data encoding: NSUTF8StringEncoding];
    NSLog(@"XML response:\n%@\n", responseStr);

    inLocation = NO;
    foundFirstLocation = NO;
    accumulatingParsedCharacterData = NO;

    NSXMLParser *xmlParser =
                 [[NSXMLParser alloc] initWithData:data];
    [xmlParser setDelegate:self];
    [xmlParser parse];


    CLLocationCoordinate2D coordinate;
    coordinate.latitude = [latitude doubleValue];
    coordinate.longitude = [longitude doubleValue];

    Annotation *foundAnnotation =
                              [[Annotation alloc] init];
    foundAnnotation.coordinate = coordinate;
    foundAnnotation.subtitle =
      [NSString stringWithFormat:@"Lat:%f Lon:%f",
         [latitude doubleValue], [longitude doubleValue]];
    foundAnnotation.title = findLocation;

    foundLocation = [[CLLocation alloc]
     initWithLatitude:foundAnnotation.coordinate.latitude
          longitude:foundAnnotation.coordinate.longitude];
    responseStr =  [[NSString alloc] initWithData:data
                        encoding:NSUTF8StringEncoding];
    addFindLocationCompletionHandler
    (foundAnnotation, nil);
  };

  void (^failure) (NSError *) = ^(NSError *error ){
```

```
    NSString *errorMessage = [error localizedDescription];
    UIAlertView *alertView = [[UIAlertView alloc]
       initWithTitle:@"Error getting response from server"
       message:errorMessage delegate:nil
       cancelButtonTitle:@"OK" otherButtonTitles:nil];
    [alertView show];
    return;
  };

  latitude = @"n/a";
  longitude = @"n/a";
  errorCode = 0;
  responseErrorMessage = @"";
  NSMutableDictionary *params =
                     [[NSMutableDictionary alloc] init];
  [params setObject:findLocation forKey:@"address"];
  WSManager *wsManager = [[WSManager alloc] init];
  [wsManager geocodeSynchronouslyXML:params
               successBlock:success failureBlock:failure];
}
```

With the bolded code here, you start by initializing a few of the variables and then create an NSXMLParser and tell it to start parsing

```
inLocation = NO;
foundFirstLocation = NO;
accumulatingParsedCharacterData = NO:

NSXMLParser *xmlParser =
             [[NSXMLParser alloc] initWithData:data];
[xmlParser setDelegate:self];
[xmlParser parse];
```

The `geocodeSynchronouslyXML:` method creates an `NSXMLParser` (thoughtfully supplied by the iOS SDK) and sets the `RTModel` as the delegate. The parser, as you'll soon see, uses delegate methods as it parses the data. You'll use the `BOOL` instance variables to control whether to parse a particular tag of the data.

When the parser completes its job, the parsed data will be found in the `latitude` and `longitude` instance variables. You'll use that data to create the annotation you place on your RoadTrip map.

Next, you add the delegate methods used by the parser. The next section deals with that.

The `NSXMLParser` delegate methods

There are four `NSXMLParser` delegate methods you will be implementing to parse the XML response you get back from a Geocoding web service request

```
parser:didStartElement:namespaceURI:qualifiedName:
                                            attributes:
parser:foundCharacters:
parser:didEndElement:namespaceURI:qualifiedName:
parser:parseErrorOccurred:
```

To remind you, the XML response you'll need to parse is going to look like Listing 7-15 in the last chapter and what you see in the Debug area console pane when you run the program.

XML is a well-defined language and can be pretty complex. Because you won't actually be using XML for your web service, I don't go very deeply into the messy details. For our purposes, all you really need to know is that XML is made up of elements that have start and end tags.

For example, you are interested in the latitude element which has a start (also called opening) tag of `<lat>`, and a corresponding end (also called closing) tag of `</lat>`. Between the tags you have the content. You find similar tags for each data element in the XML document. You may have tags within tags, like `<lat>` within `<location>` or `<location>` within `<geometry>`, as shown below. But what you are interested in is the content — 40.7485584 for example — between the start tag, `<lat>` and its corresponding end tag, `</lat>` in the following:

```
<geometry>
   <location>
    <lat>40.7485584</lat>
    <lng>-73.9857465</lng>
   </location>
   <location_type>APPROXIMATE</location_type>
   <viewport>
    <southwest>
     <lat>40.7401048</lat>
     <lng>-74.0017539</lng>
    </southwest>
    <northeast>
     <lat>40.7570109</lat>
     <lng>-73.9697391</lng>
    </northeast>
   </viewport>
  </geometry>
```

When the XML parser recognizes a start tag, you'll want it to send you the `parser:didStartElement:namespaceURI:qualifiedName:attributes:` message. To make sure that happens, add the code in Listing 8-4 to `RTModel.m`.

Listing 8-4: Adding parser:didStartElement:namespaceURI:qualifiedName:

```
#pragma mark - Parsing methods

- (void)parser:(NSXMLParser *)parser
         didStartElement:(NSString *)elementName
         namespaceURI:(NSString *)namespaceURI
         qualifiedName:(NSString *)qName
             attributes:(NSDictionary *)attributeDict {

  if ([elementName isEqualToString:@"status"]) {
    accumulatingParsedCharacterData = YES;
    currentParsedCharacterData =
                          [[NSMutableString alloc] init];
  }
  if ([elementName isEqualToString:@"location"] &&
                                     !foundFirstLocation)
    inLocation = YES;
  if (inLocation) {
    if ([elementName isEqualToString:@"lat"] ||
                [elementName isEqualToString:@"lng"]) {
      accumulatingParsedCharacterData = YES;
      currentParsedCharacterData =
                          [[NSMutableString alloc] init];
    }
  }
}
```

In this method, you're looking for one of four tags. The `status` tag contains (surprise, surprise) the status of your request, whereas `location` acts as the container tag that houses the separate `lat` and `lon` tags that correspond to the latitude and longitude of the address or point of interest the user entered.

If the tag the XML parser comes across is `status`, you want to start accumulating the parsed data, so you set `accumulatingParsedCharacterData` to `YES` and create a string to accumulate the data. (You'll use the accumulated data in the next method.)

If the tag the parser came up with is `location` *and* the `foundFirstLocation` is `NO`, you set `inLocation` to `YES` and you let loose the hounds to start looking for the `lat` and `lon` tags. The reason you generally want to do that is the fact that the Geocoding web service can return multiple results (try entering Springfield here). Admittedly, in this working example, you're going to settle for the very first result you get, but if you were doing this in a production environment, you'd need to be a bit more discerning.

I found this out the hard way by reading the documentation (after the fact, as it were), which clearly states:

> *Generally, only one entry in the "results" array is returned for address lookups, though the Geocoder may return several results when address queries are ambiguous.*

The next method you need to implement is `parser:foundCharacters:`. To do that, add the code in Listing 8-5 to `RTModel.m`.

Listing 8-5: parser:foundCharacters:

```
- (void)parser:(NSXMLParser *)parser
                    foundCharacters:(NSString *)string {

  if (accumulatingParsedCharacterData) {
    [currentParsedCharacterData appendString:string];
  }
}
```

After the parser finishes with the tag, the parser then sends the delegate the `parser:foundCharacters:` message to let it know whether or not the parser has found parsed character data in an element. Keep in mind that the parser is not guaranteed to deliver all the parsed character data for an element all at once, so it's necessary to accumulate character data until the end of the element is reached. (That's why you created a mutable string.) Check to see whether this is something you wanted to accumulate (`accumulatingParsedCharacterData` is set to `YES`), and if it is, you add it to the string

```
if (accumulatingParsedCharacterData) {
         [currentParsedCharacterData appendString:string];
```

Finally, when the XML parser finds the end tag for an element, it sends the delegate the `parser:didEndElement:` message. Add the code in Listing 8-6 to `RTModel.m` to implement that method.

Listing 8-6: parser:didEndElement:namespaceURI:qualifiedName:

```
- (void)parser:(NSXMLParser *)parser
        didEndElement:(NSString *)elementName
        namespaceURI:(NSString *)namespaceURI
        qualifiedName:(NSString *)qName {

  if ([elementName isEqualToString:@"status"]) {
    if ([currentParsedCharacterData
         caseInsensitiveCompare:@"ok"] != NSOrderedSame) {
      UIAlertView *alertView = [[UIAlertView alloc]
        initWithTitle:@"Error when invoking web service"
        message:elementName delegate:nil
        cancelButtonTitle:@"OK" otherButtonTitles:nil];
      [alertView show];
    }
    accumulatingParsedCharacterData = NO;
  }
  if ([elementName isEqualToString:@"lat"] &&
                                        inLocation) {
    latitude = [[NSString alloc] initWithString:currentPar
          sedCharacterData];
    accumulatingParsedCharacterData = NO;
  }
  else if ([elementName isEqualToString:@"lng"] &&
                                        inLocation) {
    longitude = [[NSString alloc] initWithString:currentPa
          rsedCharacterData];
    accumulatingParsedCharacterData = NO;
  }
  if ([elementName isEqualToString:@"location"])  {
    inLocation = NO;
    foundFirstLocation = YES;
  }
}
```

When you get this message, you check to see whether it was the end tag for something you're interested in.

If it happens to be the end tag associated with the `status` tag, you check to see if the status was `ok`. If not, you post an alert and then set `accumulatingParsedCharacterData` to `NO`.

If `inLocation` is `YES` and the end tag is a `lat` or `lon`, you initialize the corresponding instance variable (`latitude` or `longitude`) with the resulting data and then set `accumulatingParsedCharacterData` to `NO`.

```
if ([elementName isEqualToString:@"lat"] &&
                                          inLocation) {
    latitude = [[NSString alloc] initWithString:currentPar
           sedCharacterData];
    accumulatingParsedCharacterData = NO;
  }
  else if ([elementName isEqualToString:@"lng"] &&
                                          inLocation) {
    longitude = [[NSString alloc] initWithString:currentPa
           rsedCharacterData];
    accumulatingParsedCharacterData = NO;
```

If the end tag is `location`, you set `inLocation` to `NO` and `foundFirstLocation` to `YES` and you're done.

When the parser finds another tag, it sends the `didStartElement:namespaceURI:qualifiedName:attributes:` message again for the next tag until it runs out of tags.

Dealing with errors

For an error condition, the delegate (in this case the `RTModel`) is sent the `parseErrorOccurred:parseError::`, message and all you will do is post an alert — so do that by adding the code in Listing 8-7 to `RTModel.m`. (In a production environment however, you might want to do more or even try some sort of error recovery.)

Listing 8-7: parser:parseErrorOccurred:

```
- (void)parser:(NSXMLParser *)parser
          parseErrorOccurred:(NSError *)parseError {

  NSString *errorMessage = [parseError
          localizedDescription];
  UIAlertView *alertView = [[UIAlertView alloc]
        initWithTitle:@"Geocode error"
        message:errorMessage delegate:nil
        cancelButtonTitle:@"OK" otherButtonTitles:nil];
  [alertView show];
}
```

Time to take RoadTrip for another spin. Now build and run the app and in the Find: text field enter *Empire State Building*.

You should see an annotation in the correct place on the New York City Map, as shown in Figure 8-1.

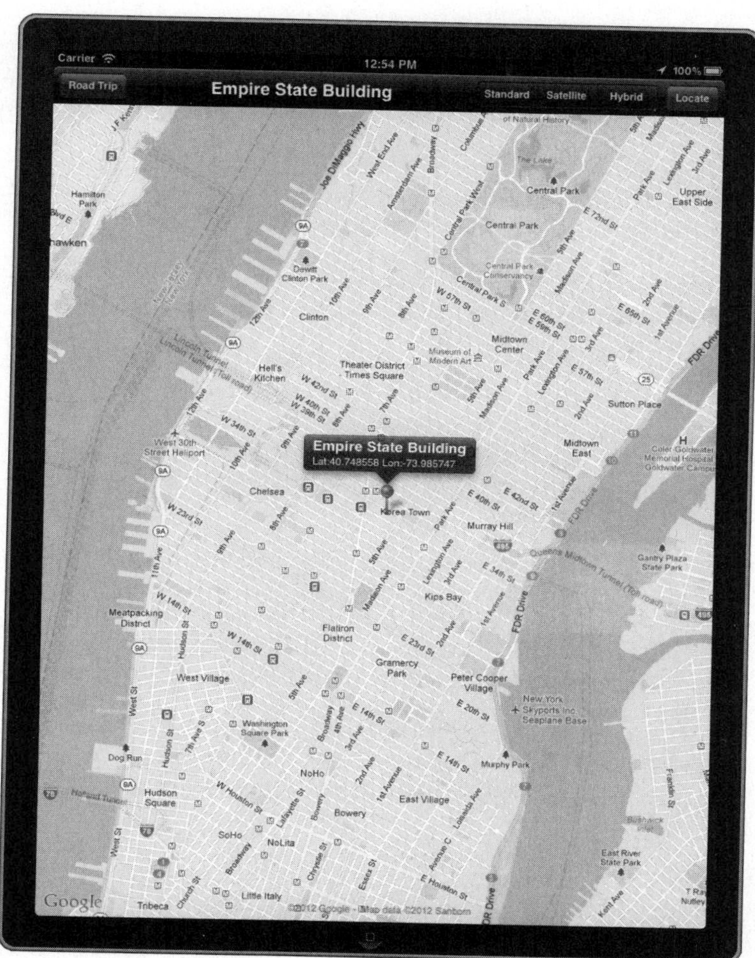

Figure 8-1: An Empire State of mind.

Good, But Not Good Enough

Although the use of the Geocoding web service I came up with here works, and works well, it really isn't the kind of implementation you would want to go forward with.

First, as I mention back in Chapter 7, the web service request is being done synchronously. That means from the time you make the request to the time you receive the response, your application just sits there waiting. I wouldn't normally do it this way myself, but as a learning exercise it makes it much easier for you if you have to concentrate on only the basics of using a web service.

In the case of my ongoing example, the fact that the web service request is being done synchronously wouldn't tend to pose a problem, but if you were to employ a more complex web service, your users might get really annoyed about having to wait for it to finish, especially if they could be doing other things with your app in the meantime. You can imagine, then, how annoyed the users will be when you start downloading lots of images and text in a "real" application. Users may even have to get themselves another iPhone to keep themselves amused while waiting for the data to finish downloading.

The solution to that is to make the request asynchronously, and in the next chapter, you do precisely that by using the URL Loading system to handle load requests.

Plus you're not doing a heck of a lot of error checking, either. You're just assuming that every little thing goes well and that you will naturally get latitude and longitude. In real applications, not only do you need to expect errors, but you also need to handle them gracefully when they inevitably do arrive.

But before you get introduced to the URL Loading system, I want to close out this chapter by addressing one more issue. One of the easiest ways to get your app rejected by Apple is to fail to make sure that you have an Internet connection when your app needs it, and therefore fail to notify the user that the functionality that requires the connection will be unavailable (or even worse, have your app just hang there).

To check for network availability, I have included the Reachability sample code from Apple in RoadTrip (which I cover in *iPad Application Development For Dummies* and *iPhone Application Development For Dummies*).

But while this code does check at application launch for an Internet connection it does not do anything if the status of the connection changes. Doing that in the Reachability sample code is straightforward, and I leave it as an exercise for the reader.

Chapter 9

Asynchronous URL Loading

In This Chapter

- Understanding synchronous and asynchronous processing
- Working with the URL loading system
- Adding a class to manage asynchronous loading

In the grand scheme of things, downloading only a small bit of data from the Internet has no impact on your app's performance, but when the amount that you download begins to increase, you're going to run into trouble. That's because right now — the way our RoadTrip app is working — when the downloading is taking place, you can't really do anything else in the app.

Again, this isn't an issue in small, simple apps, but it's something you must address if you're creating industrial-strength applications. By this I mean not just business applications, but anything that uses web services that respond with a significant amount of content.

When it comes to solving your problem, you have three choices: a) take advantage of the asynchronous capabilities of the URL loading system, b) do your downloading in another thread, or c) do both.

Reviewing Your Choices

In Chapter 7, you sent your data request to a web service (and received the response) by using the following:

```
NSData *data = [NSURLConnection
         sendSynchronousRequest:request
         returningResponse:&response error:&error];
```

This snippet of code makes the request and waits for the response to be downloaded *synchronously* — which means that the main thread (the one driving the user interface) waits until the network request completes. During that time, no other main thread activity can take place. So, the screen is essentially frozen. If the network request takes a while to complete (a fair chance, because network delays are just a fact of life), the user experience will suffer.

Clearly, you need to address this. You can do one of two things:

- Use `NSURLConnection`'s asynchronous loading functionality.
- Continue using the synchronous request response, but do it in a background thread.

The first approach has clear pluses and minuses. The URL loading system requires you as a developer to adopt a protocol and implement certain delegate methods just like you did for the `XMLParser` (`didStartElement`, for example, or `foundCharacters`, `didEndElement`, and `parseError Occurred`). Asynchronous URL loading works exactly (well, almost exactly) the same way as the XML parser worked. Using delegate methods adds a bit more complexity to the app and makes it a little harder to follow, but that's pretty much the (small) price you have to pay whenever asynchronous processing is done on a single thread. Going this route also allows you to work with partial downloads (although you won't do that here). That's all good, but a definite downside comes with the fact that when you're doing all your asynchronous processing, you're going to be using valuable main thread processing resources.

Looking at the second option, it's clear that using a background thread doesn't impose any protocol implementation on the developer and consumes little in the way of main thread processing resources. However, you still have to create a structure to manage the asynchronous response, switch threads to post alerts, or do anything that accesses the user interface, because no user interface access is allowed from the background thread. In addition, if you're downloading synchronously, you won't be able to work with partial downloads.

So, the bottom line is that one approach is not better than the other . . . they're just two distinct options with their own set of pluses and minuses.

In the RoadTrip scenario (the one where you're geocoding a location the user wants to display on a map), asynchronous processing really doesn't buy you much. The user still has to wait for the data to finish downloading to see the location they had specified, no matter what. But at least if you're doing it asynchronously, they'll see a map to keep them amused — a map that will eventually center on the found location and display the annotation.

In this chapter, I explain the URL loading system which — besides all the asynchronous processing stuff — includes quite a bit of additional functionality and control that are tailored for the kinds of things you'll want to do when you use web services. I have to keep the explanations of all the Big Picture items relatively brief, given the page constraints my editors impose on me, but that means I have more room to show you (in detail) how to implement the URL loading system's asynchronous processing capabilities.

You used background threads when you set up Core Data back in Chapters 3 and 4 — a relatively uncomplicated task.

URL Loading System Overview

The URL loading system is a set of classes and protocols that provide the underlying capability for an application to access the data pointed to by a URL.

The most commonly used classes in the URL loading system allow an application to create a request for the contents of that URL and then download it from there.

A request for the contents of a URL is represented by an `NSURLRequest` object — something you're already using as part of RoadTrip. The `NSURLRequest` class encapsulates a URL and any protocol properties in a way that is independent of the protocol itself.

An `NSURLRequest` contains two basic data elements of a load request: the URL to load and instructions on what to do with any cached data. It also enables you to set the timeout for a connection.

Because you're already using an `NSURLRequest`, all I have to do now is show you how to include some additional functionality provided by the URL loading system to make the downloads *asynchronous* — in other words, setting things up so that the downloads can keep chugging along while the user continues to use the application.

To do that, I show you how to use the `NSURLConnection` class to make the connection to the server needed by an `NSURLRequest` object and download the contents.

NSURLDownload

Although the `NSURLConnection` (the class you'll be using to add asynchronicity to the mix) provides data to the delegate as the data is downloaded, another class is also part of the URL loading system — `NSURLDownload`, which writes the request data directly to disk. I leave you to explore `NSURLDownload` on your own. There are some significant differences between the two classes. For example, the `NSURLConnection` class provides a delegate method that allows an application to control the caching — although you won't be doing that here — whereas `NSURLDownload` downloads aren't cached.

Authentication and credentials

When I first started programming on the iPhone, I was concerned about how to access them — how the heck do you get your app to jump through all those hoops? Although I don't use it in the example, working with servers or websites that require a password is available to you in the URL loading system as well.

The URL loading system provides classes that you can use for credentials as well as providing secure *credential persistence* — storage of the credentials, in other words. Credentials can be specified to persist for a single request, for the duration of an application's launch, or permanently in the user's keychain.

Cookie storage

Cookies — those ubiquitous pieces of data that websites have browsers store for them as a way of keeping track of you, the user — are often used to provide storage of data across URL requests. The URL loading system provides interfaces to create and manage cookies as well as sending and receiving cookies from web servers.

Protocol support

A *protocol* is a convention that defines a set of rules that computers follow to communicate with each other across a network. It includes rules for connection, communication, and data transfer between two computers. The URL loading system natively supports `http://`, `https://`, `file://`, and `ftp://` protocols, and it also allows you to extend the protocols that are supported for transferring data.

Downloading data synchronously revisited

Many of the methods used in RoadTrip (and many other apps) to load files are blocking (synchronous) calls — `arrayWithContentsOfURL:` is one obvious example. When working with data over networks, it's (sometimes) best to do things asynchronously, as I've made clear a number of times already.

Although this is true, synchronous downloading is not an evil to be avoided at all costs — it does have its uses. Luckily for you and me, it turns out that the URL loading system is accommodating in that respect. As you saw in Chapter 8, it provides simple and convenient support for the synchronous downloading of the contents of a URL (which you have been doing) using the class method `sendSynchronousRequest:returningResponse:error:`.

Even though using this method is simple and convenient, it does have some limitations, including the following:

- Your application is blocked until the data has been completely downloaded, an error occurs, or the request times out. (Sorry to sound like a broken record on this point, but it really needs to be said.)
- There isn't much support for authentication. If the request requires authentication in order to make the connection, valid credentials must already be available in the `NSURLCredentialStorage` or must be provided as part of the requested URL.
- There is no means of modifying the default behavior of response caching or accepting server redirects.

Using NSURLConnection — Downloading data asynchronously

`NSURLConnection` provides the most flexible method of downloading the contents of a URL, so of course you'll be using it. (Only the best for my readers.) It provides a simple interface for creating and canceling a connection, and it does that by using delegate methods to control what happens during the process.

Although working with `NSURLConnection` may appear daunting at first, it actually is very similar to what you did to parse the XML data in Chapter 8. In fact, all you need to do is create the connection and then implement a few delegate methods, such as

- `connection:didReceiveResponse:`
- `connection:didReceiveData:`
- `connection:didFailWithError:`
- `connectionDidFinishLoading:`

Figure 9-1 gives you a sense of how these methods work with `NSURLConnection` to get the job done.

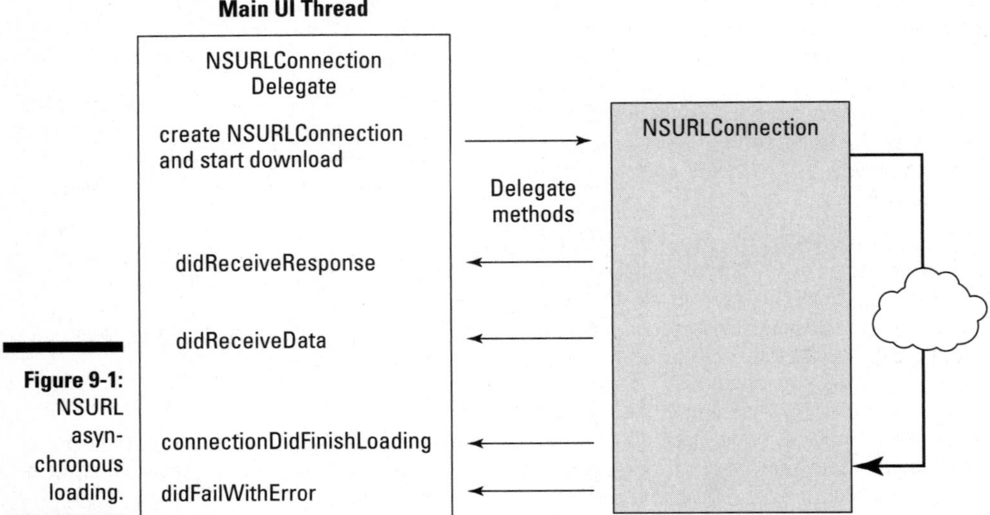

Figure 9-1: NSURL asynchronous loading.

There are also some additional methods you can choose (on your own) to implement:

- `connection:willCacheResponse:`
- `connection:willSendRequest:redirectResponse:`
- `connection:didReceiveAuthenticationChallenge:`
- `connection:didCancelAuthenticationChallenge:`

Using Web Services Asynchronously

In Chapter 7, you added code to `WSManager` to create the synchronous `NSURLConnection`.

Although this technique is acceptable for that limited functionality, a full-blown implementation of the asynchronous URL loading system deserves a class of its own — the `WSLoader`. In the following sections, I have you start by adding the `WSLoader` class to RoadTrip.

The WSLoader class is yet another example of code that is reusable in your own applications. (Hey, I use one very similar to it all the time in my own apps.) If you were starting an app from scratch, you'd simply add this class (and the WSManager class you added in Chapter 7) and you'd be ready to use web services in your app.

Adding the WSLoaderClass

Ready? Go!

1. **In the Project navigator, select the Web Service Classes group, right-click the selection, and then choose New File from the menu that appears to open the New File dialog.**

   Alternatively, you can select the Model Classes group and choose File⇨New⇨New File from the main menu (or press ⌘+N).

   You see a dialog that enables you to select a file type.

2. **In the left column of the dialog, select Cocoa Touch under the iOS heading; next, select the Objective-C class template in the top-right pane; then click Next.**

3. **In the Class field, enter** WSLoader, **select NSOBject from the Subclass Of drop-down menu, and Then click Next.**

   A save sheet appears.

4. **In the Save sheet, click Create.**

Add the bolded code in Listing 9-1 to WSLoader.h to have WSLoader adopt the NSURLConnectionDelegate protocol as well as declare its two methods — initWithRequest:successBlock:failureBlock: and startLoading.

Listing 9-1: Updating the WSLoader.h Interface

```
@interface WSLoader : NSObject <NSURLConnectionDelegate>

- (id)initWithRequest:(NSURLRequest *)aRequest
          successBlock:(void (^)(NSDictionary *))success
          failureBlock:(void (^)(NSDictionary *))failure;
- (BOOL)startLoading;

@end
```

Add the bolded code in Listing 9-2 to `WSLoader.m` to add the instance variables you'll use.

Listing 9-2: Adding a WSLoader Class Extension to WSLoader.m

```
#import "WSLoader.h"

@interface WSLoader () {

  NSURL *url;
  NSURLRequest *request;
  NSURLConnection *nsurlConnection;
  void (^didFinish)(NSDictionary *);
  void (^didFail)(NSDictionary *);
  NSMutableData *data;
}
@end

@implementation WSLoader
```

In the initialization method, you initialize the instance variables, save a reference to the success and failure blocks, and create the mutable `data` object. (Just as with the XML parser, all the data may not come in at once, so you set it up so that you'll add to the data as it arrives.) Add the code in Listing 9-3 to `WSLoader.m` to add the `initWithRequest:successBlock:failureBlock:` method.

Listing 9-3: Adding initWithRequest:successBlock:failureBlock: to WSLoader.m

```
- (id)initWithRequest:(NSURLRequest *)aRequest
          successBlock:(void (^)(NSDictionary *))success
          failureBlock:(void (^)(NSDictionary *))failure {

  if ((self = [super init])) {
    didFinish = success;
    didFail = failure;
    request = aRequest;
    url = request.URL;
    data = [NSMutableData dataWithLength:0];
  }
  return self;
}
```

After the `WSLoader` is initialized, it will be sent the `startLoading` message. To set that up, add the code in Listing 9-4 to `WSLoader.m`.

Listing 9-4: Adding startLoading to WSLoader.m

```
- (BOOL)startLoading {

  nsurlConnection = [[NSURLConnection alloc]
           initWithRequest:request delegate:self
           startImmediately:YES];
  if (nsurlConnection == nil) {
    return NO;
  }
  return YES;
}
```

This creates and the initiates a connection for a URL, the first step in the downloading process. This connection links you to the web service (or website you want to download data from).

You create an `NSURLConnection` instance by using the `NSURLRequest` and specifying the delegate.

```
NSURLConnection * connection = [[NSURLConnection alloc]
    initWithRequest:request delegate:self
                            startImmediately:YES];
```

Because you specified `startImmediately:YES` the connection should begin loading data immediately. If you specified `NO`, you must schedule the connection in a run loop before starting it. (You're on your own there, buddy.)

You should be aware that after you send this message, the request will have been copied, and any changes you make to it won't affect this download.

Well, that's that. You've finished the setup — not very exciting, I know, but necessary. At this point, you'll add the following `NSURLConnectionDelegate` methods to `WSLoader`:

* `connection:didReceiveResponse:`
* `connection:didReceiveData:`
* `connectionDidFinishLoading:`
* `connection:didFailWithError:`

connection:didReceiveResponse:

After the connection has been established and the server has determined that it has enough information to create response, the delegate receives the connection:didReceiveResponse: message. This message lets you know that the server is out there and that it is *ready to roll!*

You need to know that your delegate may receive the connection:didReceiveResponse: message more than once for a connection. This could happen as a result of a server redirect or for a couple other obscure reasons. This means that each time a delegate receives the connection:didReceiveResponse: message, it will need to reset any progress indication and discard all previously received data. To have the delegate do that, add the code in Listing 9-5 to WSLoader.m.

Listing 9-5: Adding connection:didReceiveResponse: to WSLoader.m

```
- (void)connection:(NSURLConnection *)connection didReceiv
          eResponse:(NSURLResponse *)response {

  [data setLength:0];
}
```

The code simply resets the length of the received data to 0 each time it's called.

connection:didReceiveData:

When the connection is established (and you've been informed that the remote computer has made the connection via connection:didReceiveResponse:), the delegate is sent the connection:didReceiveData: message as the data is received. (This whole process is similar to the XML parser process I discuss in Chapter 8.)

Because you may not get all the data at once, you need to append the data as you receive it to any already received data in the NSMutableData object (conveniently labeled data) you created back in Listing 9-3.

This appending business is handled by the code in Listing 9-6, which you should add to URLLoader.m.

Listing 9-6: Adding connection:didReceiveData: to WSLoader.m

```
- (void)connection:(NSURLConnection *)connection
                didReceiveData:(NSData *)receivedData {

  [data appendData:receivedData];
}
```

You just continue to add the data to the data object as you get it. (You can also use the connection:didReceiveData: method to provide an indication of the connection's progress to the user.)

Unless an NSURLConnection receives a cancel message, the delegate will receive either the connectionDidFinishLoading: or the connection:didFailWithError: message, but never both.

connectionDidFinishLoading:

When the connection succeeds in downloading the request, the delegate receives the connectionDidFinishLoading: message, and it's all over. Your delegate will receive no further messages from the connection, and you can release the NSURLConnection object.

Enter the code in Listing 9-7 to URLLoader.m to take the cake out of the oven and put the icing on it.

Listing 9-7: Adding connectionDidFinishLoading: to WSLoader.m

```
- (void)connectionDidFinishLoading:
                              (NSURLConnection *)connection {

  NSDictionary *response = [NSDictionary
            dictionaryWithObject:data forKey:@"response"];

  didFinish(response);
  nsurlConnection = nil;
}
```

This method takes the data that has been downloaded, packages it up nicely in a dictionary with a key of response, and sends it back to the success block that was passed in when the WSLoader was initialized. You also set the connection (nsurlConnection) to nil to release it.

connection:didFailWithError:

If an error crops up during the download, your delegate receives a connection:didFailWithError: message. You get an NSError object passed in as a parameter that specifies the details of the error. It also provides the URL of the request that failed in the user info dictionary with the key of NSErrorFailingURLStringKey.

After your delegate receives a message connection:didFailWithError:, it's all over, and your delegate won't get any more messages for that connection.

Enter the code in Listing 9-8 into URLLoader.m to get this bit to work for you.

Listing 9-8: Adding connection:didFailWithError: to WSLoader.m

```
- (void)connection:(NSURLConnection *)connection
                          didFailWithError:(NSError *)err {

  NSDictionary *responseError = [NSDictionary
                  dictionaryWithObject:err forKey:@"error"];
  didFail(responseError);
  nsurlConnection = nil;
}
```

If you fail, you wrap up your failure all nice and tidy in a dictionary with a key of `error` and call the failure block and let the caller deal with it. (You can find more on that in the next section.) You also set the connection to `nil` to release it.

That's a lot of listings to deal with, but the bottom line here isn't that big a deal. To make an asynchronous request, you have to do only three things:

- Create a `WSLoader` object with an `NSURLRequest` and send it a message to `startLoading`.
- If the connection is successful, you'll receive the `connectionDidFinish:` message, you'll return the data by calling the success block, and the `WSManager` will then process it.
- If the connection failed, you'll get a `connectionDidFail:` message, you'll return the error by calling the failure block, and the `WSManager` will then handle it.

Using the WSLoader

With the `WSLoader` in place, you now need to modify the `WSManager` to use it to make a request for an asynchronous load.

Add the bolded code in Listing 9-9 to `WSManager.h` to add the `geocodeAsynchronouslyXML: successBlock:failureBlock:` method to (surprise, surprise) make an asynchronous request for XML data of the Geocoder web service.

Listing 9-9: Updating the WSManager.h Interface

```
#import <Foundation/Foundation.h>
@interface WSManager : NSObject

- (void)geocodeSynchronouslyXML:
         (NSMutableDictionary *)userParams
         successBlock:(void (^)(NSDictionary *))success
         failureBlock:(void (^)())failure;
- (void)geocodeAsynchronouslyXML:
         (NSMutableDictionary *)userParams
         successBlock:(void (^)(NSDictionary *))success
         failureBlock:(void (^)())failure;

@end
```

The `geocodeAsynchronouslyXML: successBlock:failureBlock` method will send the `requestAsynchronousWebService:` message declaration to do the asynchronous load of the Geocoder web service's XML data. Add the bolded code in Listing 9-10 to `WSManager.m` to declare `geocodeAsynchronouslyXML: successBlock:failureBlock`.

Listing 9-10: Updating the WSManager Class Extension in WSManager.m

```
#import "WSManager.h"
#import "WSLoader.h"

@interface WSManager () {

  void (^returnSuccess)(NSDictionary *);
  void (^returnFail)();
  NSString *webService;
  NSMutableDictionary *params;
}
- (void)setupGeocodingWebService;
- (NSMutableURLRequest *)createGETRequest:
     (NSString *)baseURL
                  withParams:(NSDictionary *)userParams;
- (void)requestSynchronousWebService:
                        (NSMutableURLRequest *)request;
- (void)requestAsynchronousWebService:
                        (NSMutableURLRequest *)request;
@end
```

To put the `geocodeAsynchronouslyXML: successBlock:failureBlock` method in place, add the code in Listing 9-11 to `WSManager.m`.

Listing 9-11: Add geocodeAsynchronouslyXML:successBlock:failureBlock: to WSManager.m

```
- (void)geocodeAsynchronouslyXML:(NSMutableDictionary *)
                                                    userParams
        successBlock:(void (^)(NSDictionary *))success
        failureBlock:(void (^)())failure {

  [self setupGeocodingWebService];
  returnSuccess = success;
  returnFail = failure;
  webService =
      @"http://maps.googleapis.com/maps/api/geocode/xml?";
  [params addEntriesFromDictionary:userParams];
  NSMutableURLRequest *request = [self
         createGETRequest:webService withParams:params];
  [request setCachePolicy:
                NSURLRequestReloadIgnoringLocalCacheData];
  [request setTimeoutInterval:60];
  [self requestAsynchronousWebService:request];
}
```

The `geocodeAsynchronouslyXML: successBlock:failureBlock` method illustrates the general form for adding a new web service request to the `WSManager`. You'll be adding a method like this again in Chapter 10 when you want the response to be in JSON format, and then again in Part IV when you add the code necessary to use your own web services to RoadTrip.

The `geocodeAsynchronouslyXML:successBlock:failureBlock:` message is similar to the `geocodeSynchronouslyXMLsuccessBlock:failureBlock:` message you implemented in Chapter 7. A few differences do exist, however.

First, `geocodeAsynchronouslyXML:successBlock:failureBlock:` sets a cache policy:

```
[request setCachePolicy:
              NSURLRequestReloadIgnoringLocalCacheData];
```

You'll use `NSURLRequestReloadIgnoringLocalAndRemoteCacheData`, which specifies that not only should the local cache data be ignored, but that everyone else who might have been doing any data caching (proxies and other intermediates) should ignore their caches so far as the protocol allows. You do have a few other choices:

```
NSURLRequestUseProtocolCachePolicy
NSURLRequestReloadIgnoringLocalCacheData
NSURLRequestReturnCacheDataElseLoad
NSURLRequestReturnCacheDataDontLoad
NSURLRequestReloadRevalidatingCacheData
```

I leave you to explore these choices on your own.

Second, `geocodeAsynchronouslyXML:successBlock:failureBlock:` sets a timeout interval for the connection — in this case, a timeout of 60 seconds.

Finally, it sends the `requestAsynchronousWebService:` message.

Take a closer look at `requestAsynchronousWebService:` — the method that will do the heavy lifting for you when it comes to asynchronous loading. Adding `requestAsynchronousWebService:` message effectively finishes your prep work with the `WSManager` so that it will be in a position to use the URL loading system to do an asynchronous load.

Start by implementing `requestAsynchronousWebService:`. To do that, add the code in Listing 9-12 to `WSManager.m`.

Listing 9-12: Adding requestAsynchronousWebService: to WSManager.m

```
- (void)requestAsynchronousWebService:(NSURLRequest *)
                                                request {

  void (^success) (NSDictionary *) =
                             ^(NSDictionary *response ){
    NSData *data = [response objectForKey:@"response"];

    NSString *responseStr =
      [[NSString alloc] initWithData:data encoding:
                                  NSUTF8StringEncoding];
    NSLog(@"XML response:\n%@\n", responseStr);

    if (!data) {
      UIAlertView *alert = [[UIAlertView alloc]
        initWithTitle:
                 @"Your request could not be carried out"
        message:@"There is a problem on the cloud server"
        delegate:nil
        cancelButtonTitle:@"OK" otherButtonTitles:nil];
      [alert show];
      returnFail (nil);
    }
    else {
```

(continued)

Listing 9-12 *(continued)*

```
      returnSuccess (response);
    }
  };

  void (^failure) (NSDictionary * ) =
                             ^(NSDictionary *response ){
    NSError *error = [response objectForKey:@"error"];

    UIAlertView *alert = [[UIAlertView alloc]
      initWithTitle:
                  @"Your request could not be carried out"
      message:[error localizedDescription]
      delegate:nil
      cancelButtonTitle:@"OK" otherButtonTitles:nil];
    [alert show];
    returnFail (nil);
  };

  WSLoader *wsLoader = [[WSLoader alloc]
          initWithRequest:request successBlock:success
          failureBlock:failure];
  if (![wsLoader startLoading]) {
    UIAlertView *alert = [[UIAlertView alloc]
      initWithTitle:
                  @"Your request could not be carried out"
      message:
            @"The nsurlConnection could not be initialized"
      delegate:nil
      cancelButtonTitle:@"OK" otherButtonTitles:nil];
    [alert show];
    returnFail (nil);
  }
}
```

`requestAsynchronousWebService:` is similar to a method you implemented previously in Chapter 7, `requestSynchronousWebService:`. This time, however, instead of sending the `sendSynchronousRequest:returningResponse:error:` message (the message the `requestSynchronousWebService:` method sends to the `NSURLConnection`), the `requestAsynchronousWebService:` method sends the `initWithRequest:successBlock:failureBlock:` message to the `WSLoader`.

In addition, `requestAsynchronousWebService:` implements two blocks, but the code in each is virtually identical to the code in `requestSynchronousWebService:`.

As you can see in `requestAsynchronousWebService:` the code in the success block gets the response in the form of a dictionary from the `WSLoader` (I've bolded that bit), and either posts an alert if there is no data and calls `returnFail` or, if there is data, calls `returnSucess` returning the response dictionary.

```
void (^success) (NSDictionary *) =
                                    ^(NSDictionary *response){
  NSData *data = [response objectForKey:@"response"];

  NSString *responseStr =
  [[NSString alloc] initWithData:data encoding:
                                    NSUTF8StringEncoding];
  NSLog(@"XML response:\n%@\n", responseStr);

  if (!data) {
    UIAlertView *alert = [[UIAlertView alloc]
      initWithTitle:@"Your request could not be carried
                                                          out"
      message:@"There is a problem on the cloud server"
      delegate:nil
      cancelButtonTitle:@"OK" otherButtonTitles:nil];
    [alert show];
    returnFail (nil);
  }
  else {
    returnSuccess (response);
  }
};
```

In `requestSynchronousWebService:` you do the same thing, but since you don't get the response in a dictionary, you create one (I've bolded that):

```
NSData *synchronousData =
    [NSURLConnection sendSynchronousRequest:request
               returningResponse:&response error:&error];

if (!synchronousData) {
  UIAlertView *alert = [[UIAlertView alloc]
    initWithTitle:@"Your request could not be carried out"
    message: @"There is a problem on the cloud server"
    delegate:nil
    cancelButtonTitle:@"OK" otherButtonTitles:nil];
    [alert show];
    returnFail (nil);
}
else {
  NSDictionary *responseDict =
```

```
    [NSDictionary dictionaryWithObject:synchronousData

            forKey:@"response"];
  returnSuccess (responseDict);
}
```

The code used in the case of a failure is also virtually the same. (You can examine that on your own.)

You're in the home stretch now. To cross the finish line, you first need to add a new method to request the asynchronous load. To do that, add the bolded declaration in Listing 9-13 for `geocodeAsynchronouslyXML:` to `RTModel.m`.

Listing 9-13: Updating the RTModel Interface in the RTModel.m Implementation

```
@interface RTModel () {
…
}
@property (readonly, strong, nonatomic)
        NSFetchRequest *sharedPointOfInterestFetchRequest;
- (void)geocodeSynchronouslyXML:(NSString *)findLocation;
- (void)geocodeAsynchronouslyXML:(NSString *)findLocation;
@end
```

With that out of the way, add the new `geocodeAsynchronouslyXM:findLocation:` method in Listing 9-14 to `RTModel.m`.

The `geocodeAsynchronouslyXM:findLocation:` method is another (highly reusable) general form that you could plug in to any app you came up with that needed to have a model class send a message to the `WSManager` to make a web service request and then process the result. As you'll see in Part IV, this is the way you'll make requests of the web services you'll implement to return the latest points of interest.

Speaking of reusing code, in order to add `geocodeAsynchronouslyXM:findLocation:`, all you really need to do is take these steps:

1. **Copy and paste the old `geocodeSynchronouslyXML:findLocation:` method into `RTModel.m`.**
2. **Change the name.**
3. **Delete the bolded-underlined-italicized code in Listing 9-14.**
4. **Add the code in bold in Listing 9-14.**

Listing 9-14: Adding geocodeAsynchronouslyXML: in RTModel.m

```
- (void)geocodeAsynchronouslyXML:
                                (NSString *)findLocation {

  void (^success) (NSDictionary *) =
                                ^(NSDictionary *response) {

    data = [response objectForKey:@"response"];
    responseStr = [[NSString alloc] initWithData:data
                        encoding: NSUTF8StringEncoding];
    NSLog(@"XML response:\n%@\n", responseStr);

    CLLocationCoordinate2D coordinate;
    coordinate.latitude = [latitude doubleValue];
    coordinate.longitude = [longitude doubleValue];

    Annotation *foundAnnotation =
                                [[Annotation alloc] init];
    foundAnnotation.coordinate = coordinate;
    foundAnnotation.subtitle =
      [NSString stringWithFormat:@"Lat:%f Lon:%f",
         [latitude doubleValue], [longitude doubleValue]];
    foundAnnotation.title = findLocation;

    foundLocation = [[CLLocation alloc]
      initWithLatitude:foundAnnotation.coordinate.latitude
          longitude:foundAnnotation.coordinate.longitude];
    responseStr = [[NSString alloc]
        initWithData:data encoding:NSUTF8StringEncoding];
    addFindLocationCompletionHandler
                                (foundAnnotation, nil);
  };

  void (^failure) (NSError *) = ^(NSError *error ){
    NSString *errorMessage = [error localizedDescription];
    UIAlertView *alertView = [[UIAlertView alloc]
      initWithTitle:@"Error getting response from server"
         message:errorMessage delegate:nil
         cancelButtonTitle:@"OK" otherButtonTitles:nil];
    [alertView show];
    return;
  };

  latitude = @"n/a";
  longitude = @"n/a";
  errorCode = 0;
  responseErrorMessage = @"";
  NSMutableDictionary *params =
```

(continued)

Listing 9-14 *(continued)*

```
                        [[NSMutableDictionary alloc] init];
  [params setObject:findLocation forKey:@"address"];
  WSManager *wsManager = [[WSManager alloc] init];
  [wsManager geocodeSynchronouslyXML:params
             successBlock:success failureBlock:failure];
  [wsManager geocodeAsynchronouslyXML:params
             successBlock:success failureBlock:failure];

}
```

Of course, if I were doing all this "for real" and I wanted to actually choose between a synchronous and an asynchronous process, I'd create a third method that implements the overlapping code of `geocodeSynchronouslyXML:findLocation:` and `geocodeAsynchronouslyXML:completionHandler:`. But in this case, you'll go back to using the `CLGeocoder` at the end of this Part of the book, and even if you didn't, there aren't too many reasons why you would want to keep the synchronous method.

Finally, update `addLocation:completionHandler:` in `RTModel.m` by adding the bolded code in Listing 9-15. (Don't forget to comment out the `geocodeSynchronouslyXML:` request.)

Listing 9-15: Update addLocation:completionHandler: in RTModel.m

```
- (void)addLocation:(NSString *)findLocation
    completionHandler:(void (^)(Annotation *annotation,
                              NSError* error)) completion {
  /*
...
   */
  addFindLocationCompletionHandler = completion;
//CLGeocoder* geocoder = [[CLGeocoder alloc] init];
//[geocoder geocodeAddressString:findLocation completionHa
          ndler:clGeocodeCompletionHandler];
//  [self geocodeSynchronouslyXML:findLocation];
    [self geocodeAsynchronouslyXML:findLocation];
}
```

Chapter 10

Adding the JSON Response

In This Chapter

- Seeing how JSON is structured
- Using the JSON deserializer that comes with iOS

JSON is a lot like XML, but different, as you can see in Listings 10-1 and 10-2. Currently, JSON is winning favor over XML when it comes to serializing and transmitting structured data over a network connection (such as from a server and an application). I don't get into which one is better — I know better than to get in the middle of a civil war — but the way JSON is structured makes it more desirable for the kinds of web services you'll be working on. I could, of course, be all even-handed and point out that many folks believe you should use XML, but I won't get into that here because, frankly, I have trouble being so darned even-handed all the time. Pick the one you like and go with it, but it seems to me that JSON is the freight train these days, and XML has been regulated to the milk run.

Working with JSON

JSON (an acronym for *J*ava*S*cript *O*bject *N*otation; often — but not always — pronounced like the name Jason) is derived from the JavaScript programming language and does a great job of representing simple data structures and associative arrays, called *objects.* Even though it has JavaScript in its name, it is language-independent, and there are parsers available for most programming languages. It uses conventions that are familiar to developers that use, among many others, Objective-C and Python, as well as the other C based languages.

Most folks agree that JSON is faster to process and — what's better — that it's easier to write programs that process JSON. It has few optional features, it's human-legible and reasonably clear, its design is formal and concise, JSON documents are easy to create, and (for good measure) it uses Unicode. And because it's more concise, it takes less time to download when it's doing its thing (possibly improving the user experience) and is happy with less bandwidth (similarly improving the developer experience).

After all that, it's probably a bit clearer why I'm firmly in the JSON camp. But if you need more convincing, take a few moments and compare the XML output in Listing 10-1 with the JSON output in Listing 10-2.

Listing 10-1: The XML Output


```
<?xml version="1.0" encoding="UTF-8"?>
<GeocodeResponse>
 <status>OK</status>
 <result>
  <type>point_of_interest</type>
  <type>courthouse</type>
  <type>establishment</type>
  <formatted_address>Empire State, 350 5th Avenue Suite
          300, New York, NY 10118, USA</formatted_
          address>
  <address_component>
   <long_name>Empire State</long_name>
   <short_name>Empire State</short_name>
   <type>point_of_interest</type>
   <type>establishment</type>
  </address_component>
  <address_component>
   <long_name>350</long_name>
   <short_name>350</short_name>
   <type>street_number</type>
  </address_component>
  <address_component>
   <long_name>5th Avenue Suite 300</long_name>
   <short_name>5th Avenue Suite 300</short_name>
   <type>route</type>
  </address_component>
  <address_component>
   <long_name>Midtown</long_name>
   <short_name>Midtown</short_name>
   <type>neighborhood</type>
   <type>political</type>
  </address_component>
  <address_component>
   <long_name>Manhattan</long_name>
   <short_name>Manhattan</short_name>
   <type>sublocality</type>
   <type>political</type>
  </address_component>
  <address_component>
   <long_name>New York</long_name>
   <short_name>New York</short_name>
   <type>locality</type>
   <type>political</type>
  </address_component>
  <address_component>
```

```
    <long_name>New York</long_name>
    <short_name>New York</short_name>
    <type>administrative_area_level_2</type>
    <type>political</type>
   </address_component>
   <address_component>
    <long_name>New York</long_name>
    <short_name>NY</short_name>
    <type>administrative_area_level_1</type>
    <type>political</type>
   </address_component>
   <address_component>
    <long_name>United States</long_name>
    <short_name>US</short_name>
    <type>country</type>
    <type>political</type>
   </address_component>
   <address_component>
    <long_name>10118</long_name>
    <short_name>10118</short_name>
    <type>postal_code</type>
   </address_component>
   <geometry>
    <location>
     <lat>40.7485584</lat>
     <lng>-73.9857465</lng>
    </location>
    <location_type>APPROXIMATE</location_type>
    <viewport>
     <southwest>
      <lat>40.7401048</lat>
      <lng>-74.0017539</lng>
     </southwest>
     <northeast>
      <lat>40.7570109</lat>
      <lng>-73.9697391</lng>
     </northeast>
    </viewport>
   </geometry>
  </result>
 </GeocodeResponse>
```

Listing 10-2: The Same Data Output as JSON

```
{
   "results" : [
      {
         "address_components" : [
            {
```

(continued)

Listing 10-2 *(continued)*

```
            "long_name" : "Empire State",
            "short_name" : "Empire State",
            "types" : [ "point_of_interest",
                                        "establishment" ]
         },
         {
            "long_name" : "350",
            "short_name" : "350",
            "types" : [ "street_number" ]
         },
         {
            "long_name" : "5th Avenue Suite 300",
            "short_name" : "5th Avenue Suite 300",
            "types" : [ "route" ]
         },
         {
            "long_name" : "Midtown",
            "short_name" : "Midtown",
            "types" : [ "neighborhood", "political" ]
         },
         {
            "long_name" : "Manhattan",
            "short_name" : "Manhattan",
            "types" : [ "sublocality", "political" ]
         },
         {
            "long_name" : "New York",
            "short_name" : "New York",
            "types" : [ "locality", "political" ]
         },
         {
            "long_name" : "New York",
            "short_name" : "New York",
            "types" : [ "administrative_area_level_2",
                                              "political"
        ]
         },
         {
            "long_name" : "New York",
            "short_name" : "NY",
            "types" : [ "administrative_area_level_1",
                                            "political" ]
         },
         {
            "long_name" : "United States",
            "short_name" : "US",
            "types" : [ "country", "political" ]
         },
         {
```

```
               "long_name" : "10118",
               "short_name" : "10118",
               "types" : [ "postal_code" ]
            }
         ],
         "formatted_address" : "Empire State, 350 5th
              Avenue Suite 300, New York, NY 10118, USA",
         "geometry" : {
            "location" : {
               "lat" : 40.74855840,
               "lng" : -73.98574649999999
            },
            "location_type" : "APPROXIMATE",
            "viewport" : {
               "northeast" : {
                  "lat" : 40.75701090,
                  "lng" : -73.96973910
               },
               "southwest" : {
                  "lat" : 40.74010480,
                  "lng" : -74.00175390
               }
            }
         },
         "types" : [ "point_of_interest", "courthouse",
                                         "establishment" ]
      }
   ],
   "status" : "OK"
}
```

As I explain in Chapter 9, XML is built up with the help of a series of tags. There is a *start tag* (also called an *opening tag*) and a corresponding *end tag* (or *closing tag*) for each data element in the XML document. In this case, `<latitude>` is the start tag, and `</latitude>` is the end tag. XML is also *self-describing* in the sense that, if you know what the tags are, you can extract the information you want.

JSON, as you can see in Listing 10-2, is a bit different. It's built upon two structures that are, as you might expect given its origins, more in tune with the programming world:

- **A collection of name/value pairs:** In various languages, this is realized as an object, record, struct, dictionary, hash table, keyed list, or associative array.
- **An ordered list of values:** In most languages, this is realized as an array, vector, list, or sequence.

JSON uses key-value pairs to represent data. The key and value are separated by a colon (`:`), whereas pairs are separated by a comma (`,`). In the following JSON snippet, for example, the pair latitude/longitude (`"lat"` and `"lng"`) is separated by a comma, and the latitude key (`"lat"`) is separated from its associated value (`40.75701090`) by a colon:

```
"lat" : 40.75701090,
"lng" : -73.96973910
```

You can use several different data types to represent the value in the key-value pair:

- **Number (double precision floating-point format):**

  ```
  "lat" : 40.75701090,
  "lng" : -73.96973910
  ```

- **String (double-quoted Unicode with backslash escaping):**

  ```
  "long_name" : "Empire State",
  ```

- **Boolean (true or false):**

  Sorry, but there's no neat example in the Google Geocoder output, but you can imagine something appropriate, I'm sure.

- **Array (an ordered sequence of values, comma-separated and enclosed in square brackets):**

  ```
  "address_components" : [
    {
        "long_name" : "Empire State",
        "short_name" : "Empire State",
         "types" : [ "point_of_interest",
                                       "establishment" ]
    },
   ...
  ],
  ```

- **Object (a collection of key-value pairs, comma-separated and enclosed in curly braces):**

  ```
    {
        "long_name" : "Empire State",
        "short_name" : "Empire State",
         "types" : [ "point_of_interest",
                                       "establishment" ]
    },
  ```

  The keys must be strings, and each key/string (as well as the associated string values) must be enclosed in double quotes.

  ```
  "long_name" : "Empire State",
  ```

- **null:**

  Can be set on any type of data, including arrays, objects, number and Boolean types

As you can see, these key-value pairs are in fact what you may know as property list objects — a *serializable object* that can convert itself into a stream of bits so that it can be stored in a file, and which can then reconstitute itself into the object it once was in an earlier life when it is read back in.

Parsing the JSON Response

Within the context of the RoadTrip app, you're going to be using JSON to handle requests made of the Google Geocoding API web service. Google, in its infinite wisdom, has its own little tutorial about the ins and outs of geocoding requests — including a section on JSON formatting — which you can access by going to `http://code.google.com/apis/maps/documentation/geocoding`. (Figure 10-1 shows the opening sections of that tutorial.)

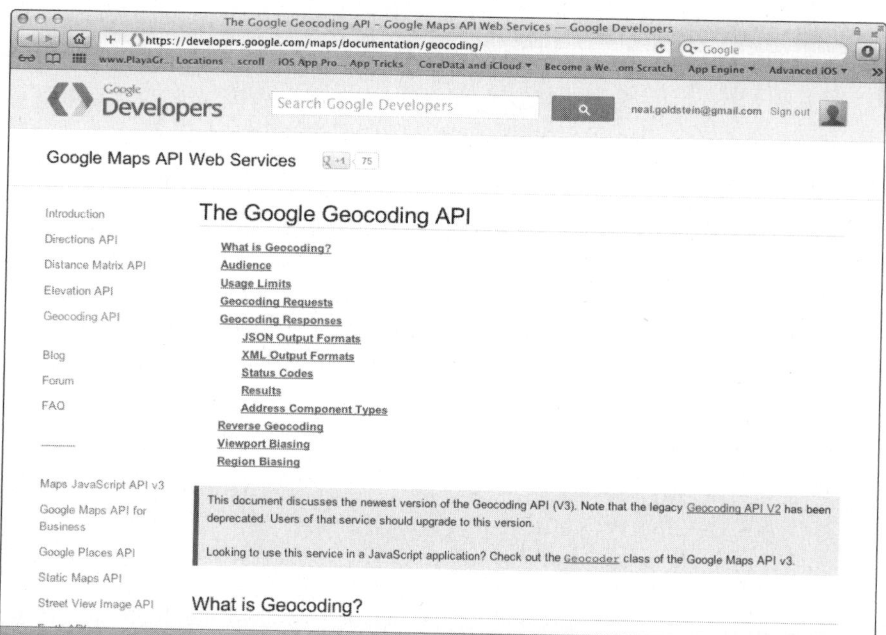

Figure 10-1: The Google Geocoding API.

If you were to follow the JSON Output Formats link, you'd find another example of how to get the JSON output as well as an example of the output itself.

Taking a closer look at Google's sample JSON output, you can see that there's an output flag within the URL request's path:

```
http://maps.googleapis.com/maps/api/geocode/json?
   address=1600+Amphitheatre+Parkway,+Mountain+View,+CA
                                       &sensor=true_or_false
```

(You'll need to replace `true_or_false` with `true` or `false`)

The following is the response to a json (the request is case sensitive) response on a Geocoder request to forward geocode "1600 Amphitheatre Parkway, Mountain View, CA," as detailed here:


```
{
  "status": "OK",
  "results": [ {
    "types": street_address,
    "formatted_address": "1600 Amphitheatre Pkwy, Mountain
                                       View, CA 94043, USA",
    "address_components": [ {
      "long_name": "1600",
      "short_name": "1600",
      "types": street_number
    }, {
      "long_name": "Amphitheatre Pkwy",
      "short_name": "Amphitheatre Pkwy",
      "types": route
    }, {
      "long_name": "Mountain View",
      "short_name": "Mountain View",
      "types": [ "locality", "political" ]
    }, {
      "long_name": "California",
      "short_name": "CA",
      "types": [ "administrative_area_level_1",
                                       "political" ]
    }, {
      "long_name": "United States",
      "short_name": "US",
      "types": [ "country", "political" ]
    }, {
      "long_name": "94043",
      "short_name": "94043",
      "types": postal_code
    } ],
    "geometry": {
      "location": {
        "lat": 37.4219720,
        "lng": -122.0841430
      },
```

```
      "location_type": "ROOFTOP",
      "viewport": {
        "southwest": {
          "lat": 37.4188244,
          "lng": -122.0872906
        },
        "northeast": {
          "lat": 37.4251196,
          "lng": -122.0809954
        }
      }
    }
  } ]
}
```

As you can see, the JSON response has two root elements:

```
{
  "status": "OK",
  "results": [ {
  } ]
}
```

The "status" part contains metadata on the request — the status codes that I explain in Chapter 7. They are the same for both XML and JSON.

The "results" part contains an array of geocoded address information.

To be honest, it's not *that* different from the XML response, but it's different enough to require some work to get it right. Google notes that the output is much smaller (which is helpful when downloading across a network) and is now the preferred output format. (Putting its code where its mouth is, the Google documentation — except for the XML output explanation — uses the JSON syntax.)

There are a few differences in the response that the documentation also notes:

- XML results are wrapped in a root <GeocodeResponse> element.

```
<?xml version="1.0" encoding="UTF-8"?>
<GeocodeResponse>
 <status>OK</status>
 <result>
...
 </result>
</GeocodeResponse>
```

- JSON denotes entries with multiple elements by plural arrays (`types`).

```
"address_components": [ {
        "long_name": "1600",
        "short_name": "1600",
        "types": street_number
    }, {
        "long_name": "Amphitheatre Pkwy",
        "short_name": "Amphitheatre Pkwy",
        "types": route
    }, {
...
} ],
```

- XML denotes such entries using multiple singular elements (`<type>`).

```
  <type>street_address</type>
  <formatted_address>1600 Amphitheatre Pkwy, Mountain
        View, CA 94043, USA</formatted_address>
  <address_component>
   <long_name>1600</long_name>
   <short_name>1600</short_name>
   <type>street_number</type>
  </address_component>
  <address_component>
   <long_name>Amphitheatre Pkwy</long_name>
   <short_name>Amphitheatre Pkwy</short_name>
   <type>route</type>
```

- If an element is blank, it represented by an empty array in JSON; in XML, it is simply not there.

Processing a JSON Response

Just as with the XML response, you are going to have to parse the JSON response

Start by adding the JSON version of the `geocodeAsynchronously...` method. You'll also need to use the `RTDefines` file and I have you import that as well. To do that, add the bolded code in Listing 10-3 to `RTModel.m`.

Listing 10-3: Updating the RTModel Class Extension in RTModel.m

```
#import "RTModel.h"
#import "RTAppDelegate.h"
#import "Destination.h"
#import "PointOfInterest.h"
#import "Annotation.h"
#import "SharedPointOfInterest.h"
```

```
#import "WSManager.h"
#import "RTDefines.h"

typedef void (^addLocationCompletionHandler)(Annotation
          *annotation, NSError* error);

@interface RTModel () {
  NSDictionary *destinationData;
  Destination* destination;
  NSMutableArray *events;
  NSMutableArray *pointsOfInterest;
  NSMutableArray *itinerary;
  NSMutableArray *pointsOfInterestData;
  addLocationCompletionHandler
                      addFindLocationCompletionHandler;
  CLLocation *foundLocation;
  NSMutableData *data;
  NSString *latitude;
  NSString *longitude;
  NSString *responseStr;
  NSUInteger errorCode;
  NSString *responseErrorMessage;
  NSString *address;

  BOOL inLocation;
  BOOL foundFirstLocation;

  BOOL accumulatingParsedCharacterData;
  NSMutableString *currentParsedCharacterData;

}
@property (readonly, strong, nonatomic)
       NSFetchRequest *sharedPointOfInterestFetchRequest;
- (void)geocodeSynchronouslyXML:(NSString *)findLocation;
- (void)geocodeAsynchronouslyXML:(NSString *)findLocation;
- (void)geocodeAsynchronouslyJSON:
                              (NSString *)findLocation;
@end
```

Next, you update the `addLocation:completionHandler:` method so that it knows now to send the message to Geocode with a JSON response. You comment out the

```
[self geocodeAsynchronouslyXML:findLocation];
```

statement and add the

```
[self geocodeAsynchronouslyJSON:findLocation]; statement
```

in bold in Listing 10-4 in `RTModel.m`.

Listing 10-4: Updating addLocation:completionHandler: in RTModel.m

```
- (void)addLocation: (NSString *)findLocation
    completionHandler:(void (^)(
     Annotation *annotation, NSError* error)) completion {
  /*
...
   */
  addFindLocationCompletionHandler = completion;
//CLGeocoder* geocoder = [[CLGeocoder alloc] init];
//[geocoder geocodeAddressString:findLocation completionHa
          ndler:clGeocodeCompletionHandler];
//[self geocodeSynchronouslyXML:findLocation];
//[self geocodeAsynchronouslyXML:findLocation];
  [self geocodeAsynchronouslyJSON:findLocation];
}
```

Next, you declare a `WSManager` method to construct a Geocoder web service request with a JSON response by adding the bolded code in Listing 10-5 to `WSManager.h`.

Listing 10-5: Updating the WSManager.h Interface

```
@interface WSManager : NSObject

- (void)geocodeSynchronouslyXML:(NSMutableDictionary *)
          userParams successBlock:(void (^)(NSDictionary
          *))success failureBlock:(void (^)())failure;
- (void)geocodeAsynchronouslyXML:(NSMutableDictionary *)
          userParams successBlock:(void (^)(NSDictionary
          *))success failureBlock:(void (^)())failure;
- (void)geocodeAsynchronouslyJSON:
                         (NSMutableDictionary *)userParams
          successBlock:(void (^)(NSDictionary *))success
          failureBlock:(void (^)())failure;

@end
```

With all the prep work out of the way, you can now add the `geocodeAsynchronouslyJSON: successBlock:failureBlock` method itself by adding the code in Listing 10-6. Much of this is identical to the `geocodeAsynchronouslyXML:successBlock:failureBlock:` method you added in Chapter 9, and as I said then, this method illustrates the general form for adding a new web service request to the `WSManager`.

If you'd like, here's an opportunity to use copy and paste. You can copy `geocodeAsynchronouslyXML:successBlock:failureBlock:` and then take the name, the `webService` bit, and the message to request the web service and change it to what I have bolded in Listing 10-6.

I leave it up to you to generalize it at your leisure.

The `geocodeAsynchronouslyJSON: successBlock:failureBlock` method will also send the `requestAsynchronousWebService:request` message declaration to do the asynchronous load of the Geocoder web service's JSON data. But you already added that in Chapter 9, which all goes to show how easy it is to add a new web service request to the `WSManager` class. (See, I told you so.)

Listing 10-6: Adding geocodeAsynchronouslyJSON:successBlock:failureBlock: to WSManager.m

```
- (void)geocodeAsynchronouslyJSON:(NSMutableDictionary *)
                                              userParams
        successBlock:(void (^)(NSDictionary *))success
        failureBlock:(void (^)())failure {

  [self setupGeocodingWebService];
  returnSuccess = success;
  returnFail = failure;
  webService =
    @"http://maps.googleapis.com/maps/api/geocode/json?";
  [params addEntriesFromDictionary:userParams];
  NSMutableURLRequest *request = [self
        createGETRequest:webService withParams:params];
  [request setCachePolicy:
   NSURLRequestReloadIgnoringLocalCacheData];
  [request setTimeoutInterval:60];
  [self requestAsynchronousWebService:request];
}
```

Next, you need to add the method to `RTModel.m` that actually makes the web service request to the `WSManager` — `geocodeAsynchronouslyJSON:`.

To do that, add the bolded declaration for this method, `geocodeAsynchronouslyXML:` in Listing 10-7 to `RTModel.m`.

Listing 10-7: Updating the RTModel Interface in the RTModel.m Implementation

```
#import "RTModel.h"
#import "RTAppDelegate.h"
#import "Destination.h"
#import "PointOfInterest.h"
#import "Annotation.h"
#import "SharedPointOfInterest.h"
```

(continued)

Listing 10-7 *(continued)*

```
#import "WSManager.h"

typedef void (^addLocationCompletionHandler)(Annotation
          *annotation, NSError* error);

@interface RTModel () {
  NSDictionary *destinationData;
  Destination* destination;
  NSMutableArray *events;
  NSMutableArray *pointsOfInterest;
  NSMutableArray *itinerary;
  NSMutableArray *pointsOfInterestData;
  addLocationCompletionHandler
                      addFindLocationCompletionHandler;
  CLLocation *foundLocation;
  NSMutableData *data;
  NSString *latitude;
  NSString *longitude;
  NSString *responseStr;
  NSUInteger errorCode;
  NSString *responseErrorMessage;
  NSString *address;

  BOOL inLocation;
  BOOL foundFirstLocation;

  BOOL accumulatingParsedCharacterData;
  NSMutableString *currentParsedCharacterData;

}
@property (readonly, strong, nonatomic) NSFetchRequest
          *sharedPointOfInterestFetchRequest;
- (void)geocodeSynchronouslyXML:(NSString *)findLocation;
- (void)geocodeAsynchronouslyXML:(NSString *)findLocation;
- (void)geocodeAsynchronouslyJSON:
                              (NSString *)findLocation;
@end
```

To keep things rolling along, you need to add some new constants to `RTDefines.h` — the bolded code in Listing 10-8, to be more precise. You'll be using these constants to process the JSON response.

Listing: 10-8: Adding Some New Constants

```
#define kDestinationPreferenceKey
                              @"DestinationPreferenceKey"
#define kTrackLocationPreference
                               @"trackLocationPreference"
#define kDestinationCell @"DestinationCell"
#define kItineraryCell @"ItineraryCell"
#define kPointOfInterestCell @"PointOfInterestCell"

#define kAccelerometerFrequency 25
#define kFilteringFactor .1
#define kAccelerationThreshold 2.0
#define kMetersToMiles 1609.344

#define kMetersToMiles 1609.344

#define RESPONSE_STATUS  @"status"
#define RESPONSE_STATUS_TEXT  @"status_text"
#define RESPONSE_STATUS_OK  @"ok"
```

These may look a little different from the constants you're used to because I'm thinking ahead here and trying to save you some work; you'll use them in Part IV, where you'll use Python to create your own web services. The naming convention for a Python constant is all capital letters with underscores separating words.

Time now to add the new `geocodeAsynchronouslyJSON:` method in Listing 10-9 to `RTModel.m`.

This method is identical in form — and even has some of the same code — as the `geocodeAsynchronouslyXML:` you added in Chapter 9.

As I explain Chapter 9, this is an example of a general form that you would use in your app — how to have a model class send a message to the `WSManager`, have the `WSManager` then make a web service request, and then process the result. In this case, the only difference is in how you process the response — JSON as opposed to XML.

And, because the differences are so slight, this is a great opportunity to save yourself some work by doing the ol' copy-and-paste thing one more time. To make the modifications, you need to follow these steps:

1. **Copy** geocodeAsynchronouslyXML: **in** RTModel.m **and paste it back into** RTModel.m.
2. **Change the method name from** geocodeAsynchronouslyXML **to** `geocodeAsynchronouslyJSON`.
3. **Delete the** success **block:**

```
void (^success) (NSDictionary *) =
                             ^(NSDictionary *response) {
...

addFindLocationCompletionHandler
                                 (foundAnnotation, nil);
};
```

4. **Add the new** success **block in Listing 10-9 to the** geocodeAsyn chronouslyJSON: **method — put it where the old** success **block was.**

   I'll explain this code after the next step

5. **Delete the** geocodeAsynchronouslyXML:successBlock:failureBlock: **message to** WSManager **and replace it with the** geocodeAsynchronously JSON:successBlock:failureBlock: **message in the** geocodeAsynchronously JSON: **method you just added to** RTModel.m **by deleting the bolded-underlined-italicized code in Listing 10-10, and replacing it with the bolded code in Listing 10-10.**

Listing 10-9: The success block for `geocodeAsynchronouslyJSON:`

```
void (^success) (NSDictionary *) =
                             ^(NSDictionary *response) {


  data = [response objectForKey:@"response"];
  responseStr = [[NSString alloc] initWithData:data
                          encoding: NSUTF8StringEncoding];
  NSLog(@"JSON response:\n%@\n", responseStr);

  NSError *error = nil;
  NSDictionary *responseDict =
       [NSJSONSerialization JSONObjectWithData:data
                                options:0 error:&error];

  if (error != nil) {
    UIAlertView *alert = [[UIAlertView alloc]
      initWithTitle:
                @"Your request could not be carried out"
      message:@"There is a problem with the data returned
                                          from the server"
      delegate:nil
      cancelButtonTitle:@"OK" otherButtonTitles:nil];
    [alert show];
```

```
  return;
}
else {
  NSString *statusCode =
            [responseDict valueForKey:RESPONSE_STATUS];
  if (![RESPONSE_STATUS_OK caseInsensitiveCompare:status
        Code] ==
                                        NSOrderedSame) {
    NSString* errorMessage;
    NSString *error =
       [responseDict valueForKey:RESPONSE_STATUS_TEXT];
    NSString *trimmedError =
      [error stringByTrimmingCharactersInSet:
          [NSCharacterSet
                whitespaceAndNewlineCharacterSet]];
    if ((error == nil) ||
         ((id) error == [NSNull null]) ||
         ([error length] == 0) || (trimmedError == 0))

      errorMessage =  @"An error occurred while
        communicating with the server.  We will look
                                          into this";
    else
      errorMessage = error;
      UIAlertView *alert = [[UIAlertView alloc]
        initWithTitle:@"Your request could not be
        carried out - the server responded
                                       with an error"
         message:errorMessage
         delegate:nil
         cancelButtonTitle:@"OK" otherButtonTitles:nil];
      [alert show];
      return;
    }
  }

NSArray *results =
                [responseDict objectForKey:@"results"];
if ([results count]  > 0) {
  Annotation *foundAnnotation =
                          [[Annotation alloc] init];
  NSDictionary *result = [results objectAtIndex:0];
  NSDictionary *geometry =
                   [result objectForKey:@"geometry"];
  NSDictionary *location =
                 [geometry objectForKey:@"location"];
  latitude = [location valueForKey:@"lat"];
  longitude  = [location valueForKey:@"lng"];

  CLLocationCoordinate2D coordinate;
  coordinate.latitude = [latitude doubleValue];
  coordinate.longitude = [longitude doubleValue];
```

(continued)

Listing 10-9 *(continued)*

```
      foundAnnotation.coordinate = coordinate;
      foundAnnotation.subtitle =
      [NSString stringWithFormat:@"Lat:%f Lon:%f",
          [latitude doubleValue], [longitude doubleValue]];
      foundAnnotation.title = findLocation;

      addFindLocationCompletionHandler(foundAnnotation,
                                                     nil);
   }
};
```

Listing 10-10: Send the `geocodeAsynchronouslyJSON:successBlock:failureBlock:` message instead

```
- (void)geocodeAsynchronouslyJSON:
                                (NSString *)findLocation {
void (^success) (NSDictionary *) =
                               ^(NSDictionary *response) {

    …
   };

   void (^failure) (NSError *) = ^(NSError *error ){
    …
   };

   latitude = @"n/a";
   longitude = @"n/a";
   errorCode = 0;
   responseErrorMessage = @"";
   NSMutableDictionary *params =
                       [[NSMutableDictionary alloc] init];
   [params setObject:findLocation forKey:@"address"];
   WSManager *wsManager = [[WSManager alloc] init];
   [wsManager geocodeAsynchronouslyXML:params
               successBlock:success failureBlock:failure];

   [wsManager geocodeAsynchronouslyJSON:params
               successBlock:success failureBlock:failure];
   }
```

When you're done, `geocodeAsynchronouslyJSON:` should look like Listing 10-11.

Listing 10-11: Adding geocodeAsynchronouslyJSON: to RTModel.m

```
- (void)geocodeAsynchronouslyJSON:
                                (NSString *)findLocation {
  void (^success) (NSDictionary *) =
                               ^(NSDictionary *response) {


    data = [response objectForKey:@"response"];
    responseStr = [[NSString alloc] initWithData:data
                      encoding: NSUTF8StringEncoding];
    NSLog(@"JSON response:\n%@\n", responseStr);

    NSError *error = nil;
    NSDictionary *responseDict =
       [NSJSONSerialization JSONObjectWithData:data
                                  options:0 error:&error];

    if (error != nil) {
      UIAlertView *alert = [[UIAlertView alloc]
        initWithTitle:@"Your request could not be carried
          out"
        message:@"There is a problem with the data
          returned from the server"
        delegate:nil
        cancelButtonTitle:@"OK" otherButtonTitles:nil];
      [alert show];
      return;
    }
    else {
      NSString *statusCode =
               [responseDict valueForKey:RESPONSE_STATUS];
      if (![RESPONSE_STATUS_OK caseInsensitiveCompare:stat
           usCode] ==
                                         NSOrderedSame) {
        NSString* errorMessage;
        NSString *error =
          [responseDict valueForKey:RESPONSE_STATUS_TEXT];
        NSString *trimmedError =
          [error stringByTrimmingCharactersInSet:
            [NSCharacterSet
                  whitespaceAndNewlineCharacterSet]];
        if ((error == nil) ||
          ((id) error == [NSNull null]) ||
          ([error length] == 0) || (trimmedError == 0))

          errorMessage =  @"An error occurred while
          communicating with the server.  We will look
          into this";
```

(continued)

Listing 10-11 ***(continued)***

```
      else
        errorMessage = error;
        UIAlertView *alert = [[UIAlertView alloc]
          initWithTitle:@"Your request could not be
                  carried out - the server responded
                  with an error"
          message:errorMessage
          delegate:nil
          cancelButtonTitle:@"OK"
         otherButtonTitles:nil];
      [alert show];
      return;
    }
  }

  NSArray *results =
               [responseDict objectForKey:@"results"];
  if ([results count]  > 0) {
    Annotation *foundAnnotation =
                            [[Annotation alloc] init];
    NSDictionary *result = [results objectAtIndex:0];
    NSDictionary *geometry =
                    [result objectForKey:@"geometry"];
    NSDictionary *location =
                  [geometry objectForKey:@"location"];
    latitude = [location valueForKey:@"lat"];
    longitude  = [location valueForKey:@"lng"];

    CLLocationCoordinate2D coordinate;
    coordinate.latitude = [latitude doubleValue];
    coordinate.longitude = [longitude doubleValue];

    foundAnnotation.coordinate = coordinate;
    foundAnnotation.subtitle =
      [NSString stringWithFormat:@"Lat:%f Lon:%f",
      [latitude doubleValue], [longitude doubleValue]];
    foundAnnotation.title = findLocation;

    addFindLocationCompletionHandler(foundAnnotation,
                                               nil);
  }
};

void (^failure) (NSError *) = ^(NSError *error ){
  NSString *errorMessage = [error localizedDescription];
  UIAlertView *alertView = [[UIAlertView alloc]
                           initWithTitle:@"Error
       getting response from server"
       message:errorMessage delegate:nil
       cancelButtonTitle:@"OK" otherButtonTitles:nil];
  [alertView show];
  return;
```

```
  };

  latitude = @"n/a";
  longitude = @"n/a";
  errorCode = 0;
  responseErrorMessage = @"";
  NSMutableDictionary *params =
                    [[NSMutableDictionary alloc] init];
  [params setObject:findLocation forKey:@"address"];
  WSManager *wsManager = [[WSManager alloc] init];
  [wsManager geocodeAsynchronouslyXML:params
            successBlock:success failureBlock:failure];

  [wsManager geocodeAsynchronouslyJSON:params
            successBlock:success failureBlock:failure];
  }
```

Although this code does the same thing as its XML counterpart as far as creating all the appropriate annotations, the response processing is actually quite different. First and foremost, you have no delegates to deal with; you simply send the `JSONObjectWithData:options:error:` class message to the `NSJSONSerialization`, and it will serialize (notice that because of the property list objects, it's really [de]serialization rather than parsing) the response and return it in a dictionary, with the response keys as the dictionary keys. This technique makes getting the data out of the response much easier than having to figure out the parsing logic. (Although, to be fair, there *are* XML parsers out there that will do similar things — they just aren't found in the iOS SDK.)

```
NSDictionary *responseDict =
       [NSJSONSerialization JSONObjectWithData:data
                             options:0 error:&error];
```

Because you're working over a network *and* using a server to execute your request, there is lots of room for errors. You'll have the `WSLoader` class manage all the out-and-out network errors, but in this particular success block, you'll also handle errors that arise with the actual content of the response.

The first thing you check for is an error from the `NSJSONSerialization` object.

```
if (error != nil) {
  UIAlertView *alert = [[UIAlertView alloc]
    initWithTitle:@"Your request could not be carried out"
    message:@"There is a problem with the data returned
                                         from the server"
    delegate:nil
    cancelButtonTitle:@"OK" otherButtonTitles:nil];
  [alert show];
  return;
}
```

If there's an error, you post an alert. (Okay, that's the least you have to do; at this stage of the game, this is all just really developer-oriented — when you enter the production stage, you'll need to do more than just post a measly alert).

Assuming the deserializer did its job correctly, the next thing you do is check the dictionary for the entry corresponding to the `status` key.

```
if (![RESPONSE_STATUS_OK caseInsensitiveCompare:statusC
         ode] ==
                                          NSOrderedSame) {
```

As I mention earlier, the JSON response has two root elements — `status` and `results` — and they will be the two entries in the dictionary.

Most web services will return some sort of status code to let you know about your request. The Google Geocoding web service is no exception. Its status code can have the following values:

- `"OK"` indicates that no errors occurred; the address was successfully parsed and at least one geocode was returned.
- `"ZERO_RESULTS"` indicates that the geocode was successful but returned no results. This may occur if the geocode was passed a non-existent address or a `lat/lng` in a remote location.
- `"OVER_QUERY_LIMIT"` indicates that you are over your quota.
- `"REQUEST_DENIED"` indicates that your request was denied, generally because of the lack of a sensor parameter.
- `"INVALID_REQUEST"` generally indicates that the query (`address` or `lat/lng`) is missing.

If the status code is not OK, you start checking for various kinds of errors. The first thing you look for is whether the error returned is blank:

```
NSString* errorMessage;
NSString *error =
         [responseDict valueForKey:RESPONSE_STATUS_TEXT];
NSString *trimmedError =
             [error stringByTrimmingCharactersInSet:
     [NSCharacterSet whitespaceAndNewlineCharacterSet]];
if ((error == nil) ||  ((id) error == [NSNull null]) ||
         ([error length] == 0) || (trimmedError == 0))
```

Most of what you see in the above `if` statement is straightforward. You're checking to make sure there is no `error` object in the `RESPONSE_STATUS_`

TEXT, or if there is an error object returned, it is an NSNull object, or the length is 0. (The last two aren't going to happen here, but I did want to show you some responses you might see with other web services.) The trimmed Error is something you may not be familiar with however, so let me explain it.

stringByTrimmingCharactersInSet: removes the characters contained in a given character set. What you're doing here is making sure that if there is an error string returned, it does have something in it. In other words, I want to see if it has more than a space, tab, newline, or nextline character. The whitespaceAndNewlineCharacterSet is a character set containing space, tab, newline, and nextline characters and the stringByTrimming CharactersInSet: method will remove all of those characters and enable you to see if there is any real content there. (This ain't gonna happen in our example, but hey, stringByTrimmingCharactersInSet: is a handy method to know about regardless.)

I'm delving a bit deeper into the weeds here than I did with my explanation of XML processing simply because you'll be doing the same thing you do in geocodeAsynchronouslyJSON: when you create and use your own web service in Part IV. So, I figure that it's better to explain these details now rather than later.

So if the status key is not OK and there is no error entry

```
error == nil
```

or the entry is a null object

```
((id) error == [NSNull null]
```

or if the error length is zero

```
([error length] == 0)
```

or if the error just constrains space, tab, newline, and nextline characters

```
(trimmedError == 0)
```

the alert message will be

```
errorMessage = @"An error occurred while communicating
               with the server.  We will look into this";
```

If you do get back an error object when the status key is not OK, you set the errorMessage to the error and post the alert:

```
errorMessage = error;
UIAlertView *alert = [[UIAlertView alloc]
  initWithTitle:@"Your request could not be
        carried out - the server responded with an error"
  message:errorMessage
  delegate:nil
  cancelButtonTitle:@"OK" otherButtonTitles:nil];
  [alert show];
  return;
  }
}
```

If in fact you don't get any errors at all, you retrieve the array in the `results` key:

```
NSArray *results = [responseDict objectForKey:@"results"];
```

As you saw way back in Listing 10-2, this is an array that has a dictionary consisting of four entries (the one I have bolded below — `geometry` — is the entry you are interest in):

```
"results" : [
      {
         "address_components" : [
            …
         ],
         "formatted_address" : "…",
         "geometry" : {
            …
         },
         "types" : [
            ...
         ]
      }
 ],
```

The braces `[]` indicate the begin and end of an array, and curly braces `{}` indicate the begin and end of a dictionary.

You check to make sure there are values in the results arrays, and if there are, you go ahead and get the values you need to format the annotation.

```
if ([results count]  > 0) {
  Annotation *foundAnnotation = [[Annotation alloc] init];
```

You're looking for the latitude and longitude. To do that, you get the single array entry — the dictionary:

```
NSDictionary *result = [results objectAtIndex:0];
```

In the result dictionary you get the value for the `geometry` key, which is also a dictionary:

```
NSDictionary *geometry =
                         [result objectForKey:@"geometry"];
```

If you take another look at Listing 10-2, you can see that the `geometry` dictionary has three entries

```
"geometry" : {
   "location" : {
      "lat" : 40.74855840,
      "lng" : -73.98574649999999
   },
   "location_type" : "APPROXIMATE",
   "viewport" : {
      "northeast" : {
         "lat" : 40.75701090,
         "lng" : -73.96973910
      },
      "southwest" : {
         "lat" : 40.74010480,
         "lng" : -74.00175390
      }
   }
```

`Location_type` gives some additional data about the location and `viewport` is a bounding box used to frame a result when displaying it — interesting perhaps, but not what you're looking for. (For our purposes, neither of these entries is important.) You need to zero in on `location`. The value of the `location` key is also a dictionary:

```
NSDictionary *location =
                         [geometry objectForKey:@"location"];
```

The `location` dictionary has two entries — the latitude and longitude you're looking for:

```
"location" : {
   "lat" : 40.74855840,
   "lng" : -73.98574649999999
},
```

You then grab those values and format the annotation:

```
latitude = [location valueForKey:@"lat"];
longitude  = [location valueForKey:@"lng"];
CLLocationCoordinate2D coordinate;
coordinate.latitude = [latitude doubleValue];
coordinate.longitude = [longitude doubleValue];

foundAnnotation.coordinate = coordinate;
foundAnnotation.subtitle =
  [NSString stringWithFormat:@"Lat:%f Lon:%f",
        [latitude doubleValue], [longitude doubleValue]];
foundAnnotation.title = findLocation;

addFindLocationCompletionHandler(foundAnnotation, nil);
```

After all this work you'll see the annotation (the red pin with the callout) that you see in Chapter 8, Figure 1.

There's a Pattern to Using Web Services

One of my goals for this book is to give you some patterns that you can reuse in your own apps. In that regard, `WSLoader` and `WSManager` can function as a framework for making web service requests and processing the response. To support a set of web services using a given resource, you would do the following:

1. Add a method to `WSManager` that makes the request for a given HTTP method (`GET`, `DELETE`, `POST`, etc.)
2. Add a method to `WSManager` to set up the request if there are parameters common to a set of web services.
3. Add a method to `WSManager` to create the `NSURLRequest` for a given HTTP method (`GET`, `DELETE`, `POST`, etc)
4. Add a method to `YourModel` to make the request to the `WSManager` for the web service.
5. Add a method to `YourModel` that processes the JSON response (returning it in a dictionary) and checks for errors.

In the next few sections I'll explain each one of these steps and — when I can — give you a template for the method. In the remainder of this book, you'll be using these templates as you enhance RoadTrip to use the web services you'll be creating.

Add a method to WSManager that makes the request

For a new web service, start by adding a method to `WSManager` that makes the web service request. You'll need a version of this method for each type of HTTP request (`GET`, `DELETE`, `POST`, and so on). You can see a template for the method in Listing 10-12.

Listing 10-12: The WSManager Request

```
- (void) webServiceHTTPMethodWebService:(NSString*)service
          userParams:(NSMutableDictionary *)userParams
          successBlock:(void (^)(NSDictionary *))success
          failureBlock:(void (^)())failure {


  [self setupWebServiceWebService];
  returnSuccess = success;
  returnFail = failure;
  webService = [NSString stringWithFormat:@"%@%@?",
                                   BASE_URL, service];
  [params addEntriesFromDictionary:userParams];
  NSMutableURLRequest *request = [self
      createHTTPMethodRequest:webService
                                   withParams:params];
  [request setCachePolicy:
              NSURLRequestReloadIgnoringLocalCacheData];
  [request setTimeoutInterval:60];
  [self requestAsynchronousWebService:request];
}
```

This a generic web service request — the `service` parameter allows you to specify which web service you want.

You'll create a request using the appropriate HTTP method (`GET`, `PUT`, `DELETE`, and so on) based on what you want to do.

Add a method to WSManager to set up the request

You'll want to add a method to set up the web service if there are parameters common to the set of web services. (In Part IV, I explain about `key`, which is one of those kinds of parameters.) A template for that kind of method is shown in Listing 10-13

Listing 10-13: Doing Your Web Service Setup

```
- (void)setupWebServiceWebService {

params = [[NSMutableDictionary alloc] init];
//add your parameters here
}
```

Add a method to WSManager to create the NSURLRequest

You actually already created a method that will create a `NSURLRequest` for a web service that uses a `GET` method and the necessary parameters needed by the web service back in Chapter 7 — `createGETRequest:withParams:`. You'll be able to use that method for any web service that use the `GET` method, but you'll have to add new methods to support other HTTP methods such as `POST` and `DELETE`, which you will do in the Bonus Chapter, "Adding and Deleting Points of Interest," available for download from this book's website

A template for that kind of method is shown in Listing 10-14.

Listing 10-14: Creating the NSURL Request

```
- (NSMutableURLRequest *)createHTTPMethodRequest:
      (NSString *)baseURL
                  withParams:(NSDictionary *)userParams {

  NSMutableString *queryString = [NSMutableString string];
  if (userParams != nil) {
    for (id key in userParams) {
      id value = [userParams valueForKey:key];
      NSString *paramString =
        [NSString stringWithFormat:@"%@=%@&", key, value];
      paramString = [paramString
           stringByAddingPercentEscapesUsingEncoding:
                                NSASCIIStringEncoding];
      [queryString appendString:paramString];
    }
  }
//add method specific code here
  return request;
}
```

Add a method to YourModel to make the request to the WSManager

Turning to your model class, you'll need to add a method there to make the request and process the result. You'll (probably) need one of these methods for each web service request

A template for that kind of method is shown in Listing 10-15.

Listing 10-15: Requesting a Web Service

```
- (void)requestWebService {

void (^success) (NSDictionary *) =
                              ^(NSDictionary *response) {


  NSDictionary *responseDict =
       [self createWebServiceResponseDictionary:response];
    if (!responseDict)
      return;
  //Your unique processing here
  };

  void (^failure) (NSError *) = ^(NSError *error ){
    NSString *errorMessage = [error localizedDescription];
    UIAlertView *alertView = [[UIAlertView alloc]
       initWithTitle:@"Error getting response from server"
       message:errorMessage delegate:nil
       cancelButtonTitle:@"OK" otherButtonTitles:nil];
    [alertView show];
    return;
  };

  NSMutableDictionary *params =
                      [[NSMutableDictionary alloc] init];
  [params requiredObjectsAndKeys];
  WSManager *wsManager = [[WSManager alloc] init];

  [wsManager webServiceHTTPMethodWebService:@"webservice"
          userParams:params successBlock:success
                                 failureBlock:failure];

  }
```

`createWebServiceResponseDictionary:` is a method that takes advantage of the code that will stay the same across any model method — the code that processes the response and checks for errors.

Adding a method to `YourModel` *that processes the JSON response*

Finally, still in your model class, add the method that processes a JSON response and checks for errors.

A template for that kind of method is shown in Listing 10-16.

Listing 10-16: Process JSON response

```
- (NSDictionary *)
    createWebServiceResponseDictionary:
                                    (NSDictionary *)response {

  data = [response objectForKey:@"response"];

  NSError *error = nil;
  NSDictionary *responseDict =
    [NSJSONSerialization JSONObjectWithData:data options:
            NSJSONReadingMutableContainers error:&error];

  if (error != nil) {
    UIAlertView *alert = [[UIAlertView alloc]
    initWithTitle:@"Your request could not be carried
                                                      out"
      message:@"There is a problem with the data returned
                                         from the server"
      delegate:nil cancelButtonTitle:@"OK"
      otherButtonTitles:nil];
    [alert show];
    return nil;
  }
  else {
    NSString *statusCode =
               [responseDict valueForKey:RESPONSE_STATUS];
    if (![RESPONSE_STATUS_OK caseInsensitiveCompare:status
          Code] ==
                                         NSOrderedSame) {
      NSString* errorMessage;
      NSString *error =
          [responseDict valueForKey:RESPONSE_STATUS_TEXT];
      NSString *trimmedError =
        [error stringByTrimmingCharactersInSet:
           [NSCharacterSet
                      whitespaceAndNewlineCharacterSet]];
      if ((error == nil) ||
          ((id) error == [NSNull null]) ||
          ([error length] == 0) || (trimmedError == 0))

        errorMessage =  @"An error occurred while
          communicating with the server.  We will look
```

```
                                          into this";
      else
        errorMessage = error;
      UIAlertView *alert = [[UIAlertView alloc]
         initWithTitle:@"Your request could not be
         carried out - the server responded with an error"
        message:errorMessage delegate:nil
        cancelButtonTitle:@"OK" otherButtonTitles:nil];
      [alert show];
      return nil;
    }
  }
  return responseDict;
```

You implemented a similar logic in the success block of the `geocodeAsynchronouslyJSON:` method in Listing 10-9. The difference there was that instead of

```
NSDictionary *responseDict =
       [NSJSONSerialization JSONObjectWithData:data
                                   options:0 error:&error];
```

I am using

```
    NSDictionary *responseDict =
       [NSJSONSerialization JSONObjectWithData:data option
          s:NSJSONReadingMutableContainers error:&error];
```

(I bolded the differences to make them more obvious)

`options:0` serialized the JSON response into non-mutable arrays and dictionaries. `options: NSJSONReadingMutableContainers` serializes the response into mutable arrays and dictionaries that you can later add and remove entries from.

And you're done — at least in terms of the broad strokes. In Part IV, you'll use these prototypes to make calls to the web services you'll develop and get a chance to fill in the details.

Putting It All Back Together

Now that I've put you through your paces in terms of the mechanics of web services consumption, in preparation for Part IV I'd like you to roll back to how you did geocoding before. You'll continue using `WSManager` and `WSLoader`, but I'll have you return to using the `CLGeocoder` in the iOS SDK. Don't worry; you can leave all the code you've added. To return to using the `CLGeocoder`, just uncomment out the code in the `addLocation:completionHandler:` method by deleting the bolded-underlined-italicized comment identifier (`//`)

and the comment start (/*) and end (*/) sequence identifiers, and then comment out the bolded code in Listing 10-17.

Listing 10-17: Back to Where You Were

```
- (void)addLocation: (NSString *)findLocation
          completionHandler:(void (^)
    (Annotation *annotation, NSError* error)) completion {
/*
  void (^clGeocodeCompletionHandler)(NSArray *, NSError *)
          = ^(NSArray *placemarks, NSError *error){
    CLPlacemark *placemark = [placemarks objectAtIndex:0];
    Annotation *foundAnnotation;
    if (error!= nil || placemark == nil) {
      NSLog(@"Geocoder Failure! Error code: %u,
          description: %@, and reason: %@", error.
          code, [error localizedDescription], [error
          localizedFailureReason]);
    }
    else {
      foundAnnotation = [[Annotation alloc]init];
      foundAnnotation.coordinate =
                          placemark.location.coordinate;
      foundAnnotation.subtitle =
        [NSString stringWithFormat:@"Lat:%f Lon:%f",
          placemark.location.coordinate.latitude,
          placemark.location.coordinate.longitude];
      foundAnnotation.title = findLocation;
    }
    foundLocation = [[CLLocation alloc]
      initWithLatitude:foundAnnotation.coordinate.latitude
         longitude:foundAnnotation.coordinate.longitude];
    addFindLocationCompletionHandler
                            (foundAnnotation, error);
  };
*/
  addFindLocationCompletionHandler = completion;
//CLGeocoder* geocoder = [[CLGeocoder alloc] init];
//[geocoder geocodeAddressString:findLocation completionHa
          ndler:clGeocodeCompletionHandler];
//[self geocodeSynchronouslyXML:findLocation];
//[self geocodeAsynchronouslyXML:findLocation];
//[self geocodeAsynchronouslyJSON:findLocation];
}
```

Part IV
Building Your Own Web Service

"These are the parts of your life that aren't stored in the cloud."

In this part . . .

Here's where you use Python (I show you how) to create your own web services and upload them to Google App Engine, where they'll be available to anyone with an Internet connection (and your super-special secret API key).

After that, it's "Up In The Air, Junior Birdman" — doing the whole thing again, but this time for your own app.

Chapter 11

The RoadTrip Web Services

In This Chapter

- Designing a web service
- Understanding the web service specifications

As things now stand in the RoadTrip app, the points of interest available to a user to add to his or her itinerary come bundled with the app in the `Destinations.plist`. This, of course, does tend to make updating the points of interest a bit cumbersome because to do so you would have to send out a new version of the app.

In this part, you get to change that.

First, you'll have the app download the points of interest using a web service. In broad terms, this ends up being very similar to how you used the Google Geocoding API, as spelled out in Chapter 7. In this case, however, you actually use your own web services — ones that you create — instead of ones commonly available. What's more, because you want to save network bandwidth and create the best possible user experience, you'll create a web service that the RoadTrip app can use to determine whether it has the latest set of points of interest and then download only the latest set if an update is actually required.

You'll also, as the developer, need to be able to add and delete points of interest from the web service's database.

Over the next few chapters, you'll be implementing these various web services using Google's App Engine as the host.

Designing Web Services

Although a web service is a web service is a web service, you could be designing them in two very different contexts.

The first context is application-oriented. In this case, you have an application and you want to use web services to create an Application Ecosystem and reap the benefits that they provide, such as the ability to do the following:

- **Offload processing** and data to a larger more powerful computer, allowing you to create applications that would normally tax the device's capability.
- **Deliver the most up-to-date information.**
- Allow multiple applications, even multiple instances of the same application, to **share data.**
- Have a greater control over data and business rules, enabling a way to create *authoritative* data and business rules.
- **Deliver a seamless and consistent user experience** across multiple applications that share data and business rules.

The second context in which you can design web services is resource-oriented. You have access to a number of existing resources that you want to be able to exploit in applications to deliver the same kind of benefits in the preceding list. In this case, you'll need to design the web services to be sure that you don't create a hodgepodge of one-off web services that are difficult and expensive to maintain and develop. Instead, you'll want to create a (web) service-oriented architecture driven by both the available resources and enterprise level requirements.

Although a resource-oriented approach is interesting and capable of providing a very high return on time and effort invested, I'm showing you the application-oriented approach in this chapter.

Regardless of which direction you take, you need to follow some fundamental principles when designing your web services. I explain them next. (Admittedly, the web services needed to support RoadTrip are pretty simple, but the fundamental principles of web services design apply to them nonetheless.)

The Point of a Web Services Architecture

When you're designing the web services you need, you need think in terms of a *service-oriented architecture.* And just as I explain in Chapter 6 that the REST (Representational State Transfer) architecture was developed to meet certain requirements, a service-oriented architecture also needs to meet certain requirements. Although there are lots of variations and extensions on the theme, at the end of the day your design really comes down to two requirements:

- Services have to be extensible and easy to change.
- Services have to optimize network performance.

Design for extensibility (and change)

Extensibility is really the whole point behind not only web service design, but object-oriented programming as well — the "and change" part of this section's title is, honestly speaking, pretty redundant. What you want is an application that you can extend as requirements broaden, enhance, as requirements deepen, and modify as requirements change.

It would also be nice to be able to reuse web services in other contexts, but with the exception of frameworks, re-usability has been an elusive goal for object-oriented programming and web services.

But what does work is taking advantage of a set of common services when you're developing an application in either an Application Ecosystem or a Multi-Application Ecosystem. For example, you may have several applications that need to have access to customer information, as illustrated in Figure 11-1. There you can see several applications accessing the same web services.

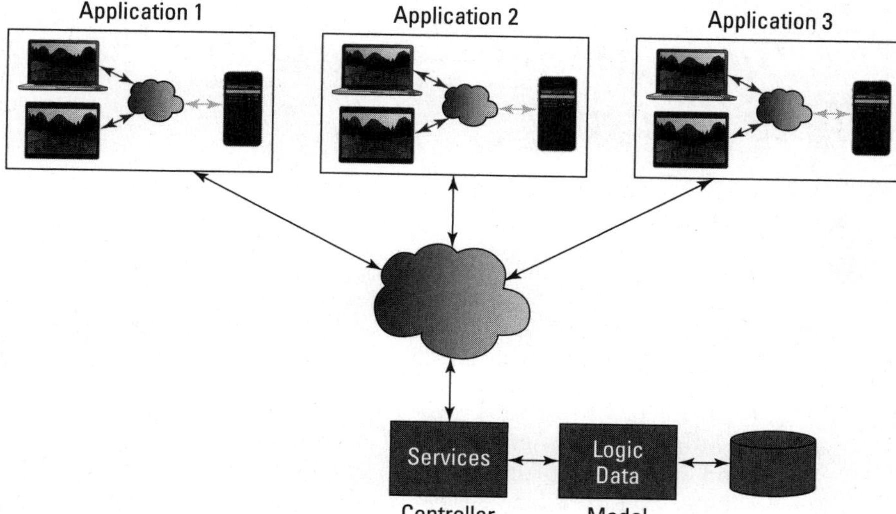

Figure 11-1: The Multi-Application Ecosystem.

Optimizing network performance

The overall design goals for a service-oriented architecture are generally similar to what you'd put together for an object-oriented one. There *is,* however, one added wrinkle in designing a service-oriented architecture that is not normally taken into account when designing an object-oriented architecture — network performance.

Whenever services are provided over a network, *time* gets introduced as an important factor. The simple fact of the matter is that the connection setup as well as the routing of both the request and response take time. That means you'll need to design services that try to reduce the total time spent in network setup and routing.

Optimizing network performance is important to do right from the start. If your web service application takes 5 seconds to process a request because of network latency, you'll have unhappy users (and pretty soon no users).

There's another issue here as well.

The less time you spend in network overhead processing, authentication/authorization, and serialization, the more your existing hardware can handle, But you need to be sure that additional processing power can be added transparently when necessary. This is what the term *scalable* means. That is, as demands on your servers increase, you need to be able to simply add more hardware that does more of the same thing.

The Basic Model — Stateless Client Server

I'm not saying anything drastically new when I tell you that web services are really all about client-server.

The *client-server* model of computing distributes the tasks of an application between the providers of a resource or service (called *servers*) and service requesters (called *clients*). The client-server model has been around for quite a while — since the 1980s, which of course is ancient history. Back in the day, it was used in reference to personal computers on a network (usually a LAN). It has evolved over time and is recognized now as the one of the central ideas of network computing. As I explain back in Chapter 6, the Internet's main application protocols, such as HTTP, SMTP, Telnet, and DNS, use client-server. Web browsers and web servers have a client-server relationship as well.

Although in the case of web services, clients and servers communicate over a network and run on separate hardware, the approach actually includes the possibility that the client and server may reside in the same system (as it does when you are testing using `localhost`). A server has one or more "programs" (web services) which share their resources with clients. A client doesn't share any of its resources, but it gets most of its resources — and often much of its functionality — from the server.

In short, *client-server* is about the relationship of cooperating programs in an application with the server proving a service to one or many clients, which make requests for such services.

I pointed out some of the advantages to this approach in the "Designing Web Services" section, earlier in the chapter, but I want to stress another advantage as well: Because clients are consumers that request representations using a well-defined interface, they aren't concerned with the mechanics of how something actually gets done or how it gets stored. (For more on my use of the term *representations* here, see Chapter 6.) This lack of interest means that it's much easier to isolate the client code from those kinds of changes. Servers, on the other hand, aren't concerned with the user interface or user state, so servers can be simpler and less concerned with changes in implementation side effects. Servers and clients may also be replaced and developed independently, as long as the interface is not altered.

Score 1 point for extensibility.

But client server is not always the same client server. In the case of service-oriented architectures, the clients need to be stateless. That means no client context is stored on the server between requests. (That doesn't mean that clients can't send data to update the server.) Each request from any client contains all the information necessary to service the request, and any session state is held in the client. As I explain in Chapter 6 in my coverage of REST, this allows for scalability of servers, since a request can always be routed to any available server.

And so score 1 point for scalability.

Making Services Extensible

Although you can apply many, many principles of software engineering when creating extensible software, there are two principles that seem fundamental to both object-oriented programming and service-oriented architectures: encapsulation (at the individual service level) and loose coupling (at the architectural level).The next two sections take a stab at explaining these principles.

Keep things private with encapsulation

A good object-oriented program limits its exposure to the outside world, and a good web service should do the same. Implementation details shouldn't be visible outside of a service boundary. If they are, you run the risk of creating a dependency on the service implementation by the service's clients and limits your options in changing or modifying the service.

When it comes to data, the REST architecture that I explain in Chapter 6 provides real guidance here. Thinking in terms of resource representations keeps the implementation details of the data well hidden from the client.

In addition, you need to limit the services you make public because there will be services you create that will be used within a web service, but not meant to be used by clients.

Loose coupling

Although there have been millions of words spoken about how to design services, the two most important words are

Loose coupling

Loose coupling allows you to make changes without breaking clients (including other services) that use the service under consideration.

So what exactly is loose coupling?

A *loosely coupled* system is one where each of its components has little or no knowledge (or makes no use of the knowledge it may have) of other components. It had its start in object-oriented programming, where it referred to the degree of direct knowledge that one class has of another. Loose coupling was not about encapsulation or about one class's knowledge (or lack thereof) of another class's attributes or implementation, but rather it was about knowledge (or lack thereof) of that other class *itself.*

Applying loose coupling to services in the aggregate means presenting a minimum interface to the clients. The client deals with as few services as possible. So, even though you may want to break down a service into smaller pieces (for example, using a technique known as composition), you never want the client to know that fact. The client is happy dealing with one service, even if that service then turns around and redistributes that work to other services.

Making services cohesive, complete, and non-overlapping

When you first start working with services, you might have a tendency to develop a service for every occasion. This tendency can create a real mess at the enterprise level if you're exposing resources to be used by mobile devices that replicate (or even extend) existing functionality available on other platforms (as web applications, for example).

Without a well-planned architecture, you'll risk finding yourself with a mess of services that become a maintenance and evolvability nightmare.

Your service-oriented architecture needs to be *complete* (meet all the requirements) in specifying the required services at the enterprise level. For example, a trade service allows you to create, modify, cancel, and track a trade. Services are then linked together — say, a service that creates a trade request together with another that reports the results — to support the business process.

Finally, services need to be functionally cohesive, a set of operations that belong together because of their function. A trade service does not also make coffee for you, as nice as that would be.

Well-Formed Services

Before I let you loose so you can tackle all the services you'll need to support RoadTrip, I want you to understand what services are not. If you have any programming experience at all, you probably have some ideas about how to do program design, and I want to make sure you don't let those notions — as admirable as they may be in another context — get in your way.

Services are not functions

In the early days of service-oriented architectures, there was a tendency to implement services as something called Remote Procedure Calls — RPC, for short. RPC web services presented a distributed function (or method) call interface to users. If you've done any development work, you're sure to have stumbled across an RPC web service at some point in your professional life. The trouble with the whole RPC concept, though, is that it insists on micromanaging every step in the process. Putting it succinctly, services should be about teleportation to your destination, not turn-by-turn navigation. You want to tell services what you need, not be required to send detailed instructions in the form of method calls to a service on how to do that. Services should not be recipes that need to be slaved over; rather, they should be finished products served to the user on a silver platter.

Not that I'm piling on or anything, but aside from the tight coupling between the client and the server (bad dog!) and the lack of encapsulation (very bad dog!), RPC-type services could, under certain circumstances leave the underlying data in an inconsistent state (truly evil dog!). So, my advice to you: Banish all thought of RPCs.

Services are not methods

Although anyone with object-oriented programming experience is hip to the Services-Are-Not-Functions manifesto, there's a risk that budding developers could still think about services in terms of remote objects.

In Chapter 6, I explain that even though REST is not the appropriate architecture for our services, the REST architecture nevertheless embodies a set of basic principles that you can use.

The two principles I want to examine here are a) identification of resources and b) manipulation of resources through representations.

Let's start with resources. The *resource* is the key abstraction of information in REST, where any information that can be named can be a resource. As far as RoadTrip is concerned, points of interest are a resource.

Now let's look at manipulation of resources through representation.

A resource has one or more representations that are conceptually separate from the resource itself. As you will soon discover, there are several representations of the points of interest resource you'll be needing.

One of these representations can be thought of as all the points of interest for a destination. Another representation would illustrate the last time the resource was updated to let you know if you should download a new set, There are also a few more you'll discover later in this chapter. These representations correspond to the web services you will be creating.

So what does this have to do with object-oriented programming?

There is a temptation to think about resources as objects (not a problem) and web services as methods (a potential problem).

The real problem with thinking about services as methods is that methods may be at a level of granularity that is too detailed for services.

Think about a service as a bakery. As a customer, you don't enter the bakery and provide the recipe for the lemon meringue pie and tell the people involved what to do to turn out that pie. (That would be the RPC route, and we're *not* going there.) You don't even tell each participant in the scenario what to do. (Delivery person, you deliver those ingredients; baker, you make and bake the pie; floor person, you carry the finished pie out to the front — the object-oriented approach, in other words). Instead, you walk in and get the pie; it's as simple as that.

Both the RPC and Services-as-Objects approaches produce what is known as *chatty* interfaces, where you send lots of messages with (relatively) small amounts of data transferred. Although sometimes that is appropriate (sending the date and time a resource was last updated for example) often it's not. Network round trips to and from a web service are costly enough, and the cost goes up when clients need to issue multiple requests to a web service to complete a single logical operation. The more trips you make to the server, the more overhead you get in processing, authentication and authorization, and serialization, which of course means more network latency.

Face it: When you want that pie, you want to be able to just get it and not get involved in issuing any other instructions. Yet even though your interface to a service should offer data in Big Gulp dimensions, that doesn't mean that the service implementation itself is not made up of objects; in fact, it *should* be, with the service acting as a wrapper for those objects (just as Trip does for the other model objects in RoadTrip). *A service should encapsulate all the complexity of the business logic* (which is now in the service and not the client) and expose a simple "method" that allow clients to perform single logical operations and that is designed to minimize round trips.

The Resource

As I explain, a web service is all about accessing a resource. In the case of the RoadTrip application, the resource will be the points of interest. The resource you come up with will be implemented as an application hosted on the trusty Google App Engine and will be named (drumroll, please) `rtpointsofinterest`.

Although `rtpointsofinterest` is the name of my resource as it applies to RoadTrip, you'll have to come up with your own name for the resource you create in your own app (Google won't let you use the same name). In the next chapter, you'll have the opportunity to create a name for your resource, and you'll have to substitute your name for `rtpointsofinterest`. The web services that you'll define here can (and should) be named the same, however, so keep that in mind as you go through this chapter.

In this chapter, you specify the web services that will be used by your application. Now, the Google Geocoding web service starts this process off by specifying the base URL, as follows:

```
https://maps.googleapis.com/maps/api/geocode
```

For the points-of-interest resource, you'll need to specify a base URL as well. In fact you'll specify two. When you deploy `rtpointsofinterest` to the cloud it will look like:

```
https://rtpointsofinterest.appspot.com/
```

During the development process however, you'll use a simulator, and that base URL will be slightly different, and I explain that in Chapter 12.

The Response

Ask and ye shall receive. In the world of web services, a request for a representation of a resource is meant to elicit a response. For RoadTrip, it makes sense to have this response be a dictionary in JSON format. (For the whole JSON versus XML discussion, see Chapter 7.)

To be more precise, the response will be a dictionary with a single entry with a key of `response` (this is created for you automatically in your App Engine Python application) which will contain the response itself. Since responses need to let the caller know about the success of the request, you'll always include an entry with the key of `status` in the `response` dictionary. The value here will be either

```
ok
```

or

```
error
```

For a successful `GET` request, you'll create a dictionary entry in the `response` dictionary with the key of `results`, which will contain an array of dictionaries of Point of Interest data, much like the current Destination plist. (I'll specify the keys for the dictionary in each of the applicable web service descriptions.) For all other successful requests, instead of a `results` key whose value is a dictionary, you'll return a `status_text` key whose value is text that indicates the success of the request.(Again, I'll specify the specific string when I specify the web services that will create that response.)

For unsuccessful requests (the value of the status key is `error`), a `status_text` entry will contain the information about the error. (I explain those as they come up.)

Limiting Unauthorized Web Service Use

When you create web services and make them available on the Internet, you want to make sure only clients that are authorized to use the service can do so.

You can easily make sure of that by implementing a simple API key. The idea is that all clients would need to send their secret key to the server for each web service call. On the server side, you check to make sure that this key is valid and allows access to the API.

An API key can also be used for access control: You can limit the number of accesses per day for a particular API key.

The API key will be a required parameter for all the `rtpointsofinterest` web services (If you recall the Geocoding web service also had a required parameter, albeit for a different reason). When you actually dig down into the code needed to create your web service — see the next section — I'll point out where you'll be adding the API key parameter.

Designing a Web Service

As I explained, you have two paths you can choose from when it comes to designing web services: You can either base them on existing resources or design the web service from scratch to meet the requirements of your application. Right now, you're going to take a look at how to design a web service from scratch.

First things first: What services exactly do you need to enable in order to have RoadTrip manage its points of interest?

Obviously, the first one that comes to mind is a service capable of returning all points of interest for a destination — which is what the `RTModel` method `loadPointsOfInterest` does now.

```
- (void) loadPointsOfInterest {

  RTAppDelegate *appDelegate =
           [[UIApplication sharedApplication] delegate];
  NSString *fileComponent =
    [NSString stringWithFormat:@"%@%@%@", @"POI",
            appDelegate.destinationPreference, @".poi"];
  NSString *filePath = [RTModel filePath:fileComponent];
```

```
  NSURL *pointsOfInterestDataURL =
                            [NSURL fileURLWithPath:filePath];
  pointsOfInterestData = [NSMutableArray
        arrayWithContentsOfURL:pointsOfInterestDataURL];
...
}
```

Start by figuring out what data the resource requires in order to be able to return the representation required by the client — the *representation of the resource,* to use the terminology from Chapter 6.

The obvious place to start is the data requirements for the `SharedPointOfInterest` class. The following lines of code show the properties that manifest those data requirements:

```
@property (nonatomic, retain) NSString * name;
@property (nonatomic, retain) NSString * address;
@property (nonatomic, retain) NSString * comment;
@property (nonatomic, retain) NSNumber * displayOrder;
@property (nonatomic, retain) NSString * latitude;
@property (nonatomic, retain) NSString * location;
@property (nonatomic, retain) NSString * longitude;
@property (nonatomic, retain) NSString * subtitle;
@property (nonatomic, retain) NSString * title;
```

That was fine for Chapter 3, but you don't need to include all that data in the resource. The `title` and `subtitle`, for example, are used when the `PointOfInterest` object is playing its role as a map annotation, so I don't need them in the resource. I also don't need to bother with `displayOrder`, because that's there only for the sake of the view controller.

Keep in mind, though, that because the data comes from a web resource, you have to deal with some additional pieces of the puzzle. When your app owns all the data — meaning it doesn't have to venture out on the web to track something down — it's pretty easy to identify a point of interest. In RoadTrip, for example, the itinerary is set up in such a way that you have an object associated with each point of interest that you can then use to track that point of interest.

When the data is on a web server, however, you need a mechanism in place that allows you to connect that downloaded data with the data in the web service, and to do that you need to add `id` as a data element.

Finally, you may be interested in the freshness of a point of interest, or you may want to determine the last time it was updated. Although you won't need it in this book, you'll definitely want to include an `updated` field for future enhancements.

So, with all the puzzle pieces in place, the data that makes up the resource should look like the following:

```
class PointOfInterest(db.Model):
    name = db.StringProperty(required=True)
    description = db.StringProperty()
    location = db.StringProperty()
    address = db.StringProperty()
    destination = db.StringProperty(required=True)
    coordinate = db.GeoPtProperty(required=True)
    updated = db.DateTimeProperty(required=True,
                                  auto_now_add = True)
```

Of course, other than the names listed, you're probably not familiar with what all of that code means. Don't worry; I explain it all in Chapter 13. For now, all you'll need to concentrate on is the data itself.

Now let's look at the representations needed by RoadTrip. You need the following web services to start with:

- `pointsofinterest`: Returns the points of interest for a destination. This is what the application currently constructs from the Point of Interest data in the `plist` and what the user can also add to.
- `lastupdate`: Returns the date and time the resource itself last updated. You'll check that before you download the Points of Interest representation using the `pointsofinterest` web service. If it hasn't updated since the last time you downloaded it, you'll continue to use the current (cached) data.

Of course, you also want to be able to add and delete points of interest from the resource, so you need some web services to do that:

- `allpointsofinterest`: Returns a representation of all the points of interest, regardless of destination.
- `addpointofinterest`: Adds a point of interest.
- `deletepointofinterest`: Deletes a point of interest with a record id.

To define each of these web services, you need to specify

- The request and its parameters
- The response and its format

Now I take you through specifying a request message and the response for each of those services, based on RoadTrip's requirements for points of interest. I'm not going to take you through the logic of how I derived these — that would take an entire book on its own. Instead, I'll have you learn by example.

I start with `pointsofinterest` because that is the *raison d'être* for the web service.

The pointsofinterest Web Service

Here's what you need to return the points of interest for a destination.

The request

To access the `pointsofinterest` service over HTTP, use the following:

```
http://rtpointsofinterest.appspot.com/pointsofinterest?
                         key=yourKey&destination=destination
```

Parameters

All parameters are required.

- `key` (required): the API key. (See the "Limiting Unauthorized Web Service Use" section, earlier in the chapter, for more on the API key.)
- `destination` (required)

The response

Successful response

The value for the `results` key will contain an array of dictionaries each of which has the following keys and value types:

```
Key                 Value
updated             string
description         string or null
destination         string
longitude           string
location            string or null
address:            string or null
latitude            string
id                  string
```

The `updated` (date) format is `yyyy-MM-dd HH:mm:ss.SSSSSS` and follows the Unicode Technical Standard #35 as specified at `http://unicode.org/reports/tr35/`.

Error Response

The status_text key value can contain the following:

```
exception: missing key
exception: invalid key: key
exception: missing destination
```

The lastupdate Web Service

Here's how you return the last time the resource was updated.

The request

To access the lastupdate service over HTTP, use the following:

```
http://rtpointsofinterest.appspot.com /lastupdate?
                              key=yourKey&destination=destination
```

Parameters

All parameters are required.

- key (required): The API key. (See the "Limiting Unauthorized Web Service Use" section, earlier in the chapter, for more on the API key.)
- destination (required)

The response

Successful Response

The value for the results key will contain an array of dictionaries each of which has the following keys and value types:

```
Key                Value
datetime           string
```

The datetime format is yyyy-MM-dd HH:mm:ss.SSSSSS and follows the Unicode Technical Standard #35 as specified at http://unicode.org/reports/tr35/.

Error Response

The `status_text` key value can contain the following:

```
exception: missing key
exception: invalid key: key
exception: missing destination
exception: no points of interest
```

The allpointsofinterest Web Service

Here's how you return all the points of interest.

The request

To access the `allpointsofinterest` service over HTTP, use the following:

```
http://rtpointsofinterest.appspot.com/allpointsofinterest?
                                                key=yourKey
```

Parameters

All parameters are required.

- `key` (required): the API key. (See the "Limiting Unauthorized Web Service Use" section, earlier in the chapter, for more on the API key.)

The response

Successful response

The value for the `results` key will contain an array of dictionaries each of which has the following keys and value types:

```
Key                 Value
updated             string
description         string or null
destination         string
longitude           string
location            string or null
address:            string or null
latitude            string
id                  string
```

The date format is `yyyy-MM-dd HH:mm:ss.SSSSSS` and follows the Unicode Technical Standard #35 as specified at `http://unicode.org/reports/tr35/`.

Error Response

The `status_text key` value can contain the following:

```
exception: missing key
exception: invalid key: key
```

The addpointofinterest Web Service

Here's how you add a point of interest to the resource.

The request

This is a `POST` request.

To access the `allpointsofinterest` service over HTTP, use the following:

```
http://rtpointsofinterest.appspot.com/addpointofinterest?
                                              key=yourKey
```

Parameters

- `key` (required): the API key. (See the "Limiting Unauthorized Web Service Use" section, earlier in the chapter, for more on the API key.)

The message body should include the following keys with string values:

```
Key
name (required)
description (optional)
destination (required)
longitude (required)
latitude(required)
location  (optional)
address (optional)
```

The response

Successful response

The value for the status_text key will be

```
added
```

Error response

The status_text key value can contain the following:

```
exception: missing key
exception: invalid key: key
exception: Property name is required
exception: Property destination is required
```

The deletepointofinterest Web Service

Here's how you delete a point of interest from the resource.

The request

This is a DELETE request.

To access the deletepointofinterest service over HTTP, use the following:

Example

```
http://rtpointsofinterest.appspot.com/
        deletepointofinterest?key=yourKey&id=recordid
```

Parameters

- key (required): The API. (See the "Limiting Unauthorized Web Service Use" section, earlier in the chapter, for more on the API key.)
- id (required): The record id of the point of interest to be deleted.

The response

Successful Response

The value for the `status_text` key will be

```
deleted
```

Error Response

The `status_text` key value can contain the following:

```
exception: missing key
exception: invalid key: key
exception: invalid id: id
exception: missing id
```

Additional Error Considerations

Although I've had you specify the possible error responses originating from your web service, server errors can occur as well. For example, omitting longitude or latitude — or inputting an invalid longitude or latitude — result in a `BadValueError:` on the server and an empty response array. You'll deal with such errors in the same way you did with the possibility of server errors when you used the Geocoder web service. (More on that in later chapters.)

Chapter 12

The App Engine Implementation

In This Chapter

- Figuring out what Google App Engine actually is
- Seeing how App Engine works
- Creating your App Engine application

I'm going to make it easy for you: Go ahead and use Google App Engine to implement the web services required by RoadTrip. Just trust me on this one. With Google App Engine, you have a stress-free way of building an application (what they call a group of related web services) that will run in the cloud. And by "stress-free," I have to say, yes, this strategy is really stress-free in terms of both building your web service as well as maintaining it.

Google App Engine

Google App Engine lets you run your web applications on Google's infrastructure. It's actually pretty easy to build and deploy applications using App Engine. What's more, you don't have to worry at all about servers, databases, database size, load, or scalability. App Engine does all of that for you. Admittedly, you do pay a small price for such convenience — you have limited control over the software that runs on the server, other than your application — but I'm here to tell you that the price is worth it.

You *can* serve your application using your own domain name (such as `www.rtpointsofinterest.com`), but that method has a few limitations, so I'm going to have you serve your application using a free name on the `http://appspot.com` domain.

The application environment

Except for the obvious stuff you'll be doing with your own application (remember an App Engine application is a bundle of web services), you'll work with the software (features) that App Engine has to offer, which are considerable. They include the following:

- Web serving
- Data storage with queries, sorting, and transactions
- Automatic scaling and load balancing
- APIs for authenticating users and sending e-mail using Google Accounts
- A fully featured local development environment that simulates Google App Engine on your computer
- Access to web services or other data on the Internet, using App Engine's URL fetch service
- Several others that I leave you to explore as you need them

An App Engine account is free with up to 1GB of storage and up to 5 million page views a month. You'll have to pay for anything above that.

You can register up to ten applications per developer account.

App Engine provides three runtime environments for you to develop for — Python, Java, and Go. For the purposes of this book, you'll be using the Python environment. Don't worry if you don't know Python. (I didn't know it until I started working with App Engine.) Although you won't be a certified Python rock star when you're done, I talk you through the Python code, and who knows, maybe you'll fall in love with Python and explore it on your own.

How App Engine works

As I explain in Chapter 6 — and as you saw in action in Chapters 7–9 — a Resource-Based (HTTP API) Web Service is a defined set of HTTP request messages coupled with well-defined structure for all response messages. Here, the request is defined in a URI (Universal Resource Identifier), which most people refer to as a URL (Universal Resource Locator).

In Chapter 7, you put the Google Geocoding web service to use by creating a geocoding request that looked like the following:

```
http://maps.googleapis.com/maps/api/geocode/xml?
address=1600+Amphitheatre+Parkway,+Mountain+View,+CA&
sensor=true_or_false
```

When you sent that request, a Google Maps web server processed the request and sent it to the right program. The whole process is shown in Figure 12-1.

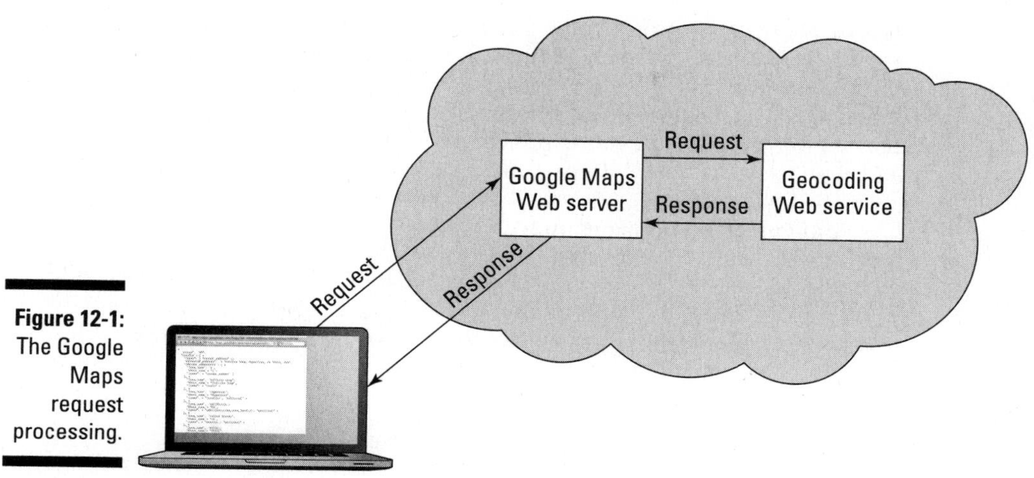

Figure 12-1: The Google Maps request processing.

You're going to take over this process whole cloth from the Google Geocoding web service and put it to use for your own web service, as shown in Figure 12-2.

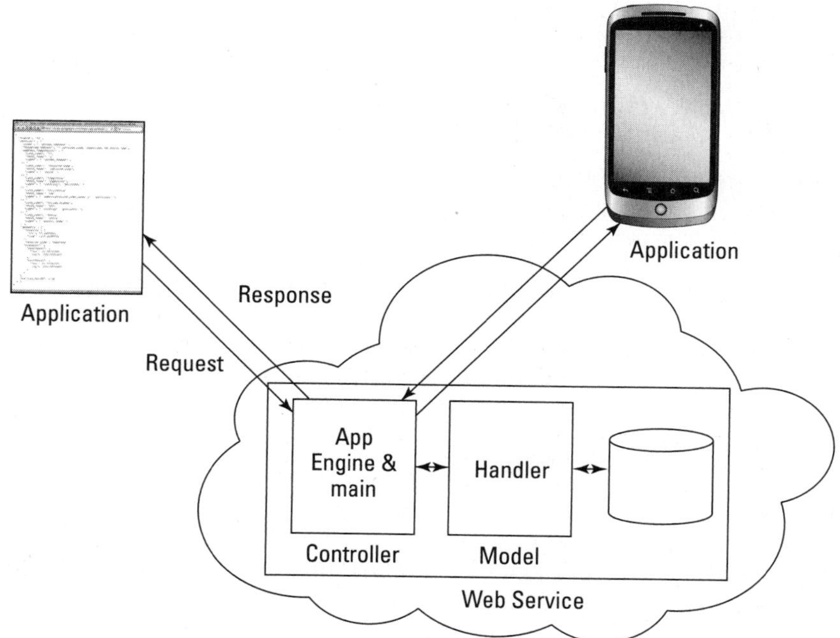

Figure 12-2: How it all works.

The beauty of it all is that when you're running your web service on App Engine, App Engine handles all the stuff you see in Figure 12-2 for you.

When a user makes a request, the request is routed to the frontend servers. The frontend determines the application for which the request is intended and then uses the applications configuration to determine the next step.

The configuration you came up with for your application and hardwired into it describes how requests should be routed based on their URL paths. For example, in Listing 12-1, you see the `app.yaml` (configuration) file for the `rtpointsofinterest` application. If you look at what I've set in bolded text, you can guess that all requests to `rtpointsofinterest` should be routed to a script called `main`.

Listing 12-1: An App-Routing Specification

```
application: rtpointsofinterest
version: 1
runtime: python27
api_version: 1
threadsafe: yes

handlers:
- url: /favicon\.ico
  static_files: favicon.ico
  upload: favicon\.ico

- url: .*
  script: main.app

libraries:
- name: webapp2
  version: "2.5.1"
```

As you'll soon see, you'll also specify the routing in your main script — that is, you'll answer the question, "What script should handle the web services I specified in Chapter 11?" Eventually, a URL path will map to a *request handler* — and, yes, you will eventually have to create a request handler for each of your web services that you have mapped to a URL. (You can also map URLs to a static file such as an image or a file of JavaScript code — but you won't be doing that here.)

In your case, because the URL path of the request gets mapped to one of the application's request handlers, the application server pool is either going to start up an instance of your application or reuse an existing instance if one is already running from a previous request. The server invokes the application by calling the request handler that corresponds with the URL path of the request and waits for its response.

The request handler prepares the response, then returns it and terminates. Be aware that the app server won't send any data to the client until the request handler has terminated, so you cannot stream data or keep a connection open for a long time. When the handler terminates, the app server returns the response, and the request is complete.

The server manages the local resources available to the application, including CPU cycles, memory, and execution time, and ensures that apps do not consume system resources in a way that interferes with other apps.

You can also configure the frontend to authenticate the user with Google Accounts, which will handle user account creation and sign-in. Using Google Accounts lets the user start using your application faster because the user may not need to create a new account. It also saves you the effort of implementing a user account system just for your application.

The frontend can restrict access to URL paths with several levels of authorization: All users, users who have signed in, and users who are application administrators. With a Google Apps domain, you can also set your application to allow only users on the domain to access URLs.

Now, in terms of your own application code, remember that it executes in its own little *sandbox,* like in iOS, that isolates your application in a secure, reliable environment that is independent of the hardware, operating system, and even the physical location of the server.

Just as with the iOS sandboxed environment, your application can't write data to the local file system or make arbitrary network connections. Instead, apps must use the services provided by App Engine to store data and communicate over the Internet — the URL fetch service, for example, or e-mail service. In addition, other computers can connect to your application only by making HTTP (or HTTPS) requests on the standard ports — not a problem in this case, but something you need to be aware of.

On the other hand, the sandbox does make it possible for App Engine to distribute web requests for your application across multiple servers, and to start and stop servers to meet traffic demands. Of course, for your application to be able to run across multiple servers, there needs to be a datastore capable of supporting that.

Apps can use the App Engine datastore for reliable, scalable persistent storage of data that is replicable across datacenters. App Engine offers a bunch of data modeling tools, and the API supports two interfaces for performing datastore queries. The first is GQL, a SQL-like query language, which won't concern us here.

The second is Google Cloud SQL, which provides a relational SQL database service for your App Engine application. Google Cloud Storage provides storage for objects and files up to terabytes in size.

Keep in mind that you're responsible for deploying new versions of your application software, configuration as well as for updating the version served on App Engine. Updates to an application propagate quickly, but be aware that if you update your application, all requests that started *before* the switch are allowed to complete using *their* version of the application. (An application that makes an HTTP request to itself might find itself in a pickle, but you can manage that situation in your own code if you really need to.)

App Engine SDKs

App Engine comes with software development kits (SDKs) for its three supported runtime environments: Java, Python, and Go. Each SDK includes a web server application that emulates all the App Engine services on your local computer. What the Xcode Simulator does for the iPhone and iPad, GoogleAppEngineLauncher does for App Engine.

Each SDK includes all the APIs and libraries available on App Engine. The web server also simulates the secure sandbox environment, including checks for attempts to access system resources disallowed in the App Engine runtime environment.

The Administration Console is the web-based interface for managing your applications running on App Engine. You can use it to create new applications, configure domain names, change which version of your application is live, examine access and error logs, and even browse an application's datastore. I show you how to do all that in Chapter 13.

To make it easy to get started, App Engine includes a simple web framework — similar in spirit to the iOS frameworks — that goes by the name of webapp2. It's a lightweight Python web framework compatible with Google App Engine's webapp framework. The Python environment supports a number of other frameworks — Django, for example — but for what I'm showing you, it's best to just stick with webapp2.

Not every Python web application framework works completely with the App Engine Python runtime environment. Constraints imposed by App Engine's sandboxing logic, especially the restriction on modules that use compiled C code, limit which frameworks work out of the box. Django (`www.djangoproject.com`) is known to work well, and others have been adapted with additional software.

Using Python with App Engine

The dedicated Python runtime environment you'll be using for your web service includes an optimized Python interpreter and the Python standard library. As I explained earlier in the chapter, the runtime environment is sandboxed to make sure your application is secure and isolated from other apps on the system.

"Why Python?" you may ask. Part of Python's appeal as a programming language is that it allows you to program in any style you want, from object-oriented programming and structured programming to functional programming and aspect-oriented programming. It's also quite similar to languages such as Objective C, C, and Java, so if you've done any programming in those languages, you should be able to pick it up rather quickly. In any event, I explain the language and its libraries as I go along.

The Python SDK you'll be using includes GoogleAppEngineLauncher, a tool you can use to simulate the App Engine environment, including a local version of the datastore, Google Accounts, and the ability to fetch URLs and send e-mail directly from your computer using the App Engine APIs. The SDK also features a data modeling API and the webapp2 application framework, as well as tools for testing your application, uploading your application files, managing datastore indexes, downloading log data, and uploading large amounts of data to the datastore.

GoogleAppEngineLauncher runs on your computer (similar to the Xcode simulator) and provides a graphical interface for many common App Engine development tasks. This makes it much easier to develop Python applications that run on App Engine.

Application code written for the Python environment must be written exclusively in Python. The Python environment includes the Python standard library, and because not all of the library's features can run in the sandbox environment, several modules in the standard library whose core features are not supported by the runtime environment have been disabled. That means any code that tries to import them will raise an error.

Extensions written in the C language are not supported. You can upload other third-party libraries with your application, as long as they are implemented in pure Python.

The Python runtime environment uses Python version 2.7.

What You Need to Develop for App Engine

Ready for the Great Adventure? Follow these steps to create your application:

1. **Point your browser to** `http://developers.google.com/appengine`**.**

   You're greeted by what you see in Figure 12-3.

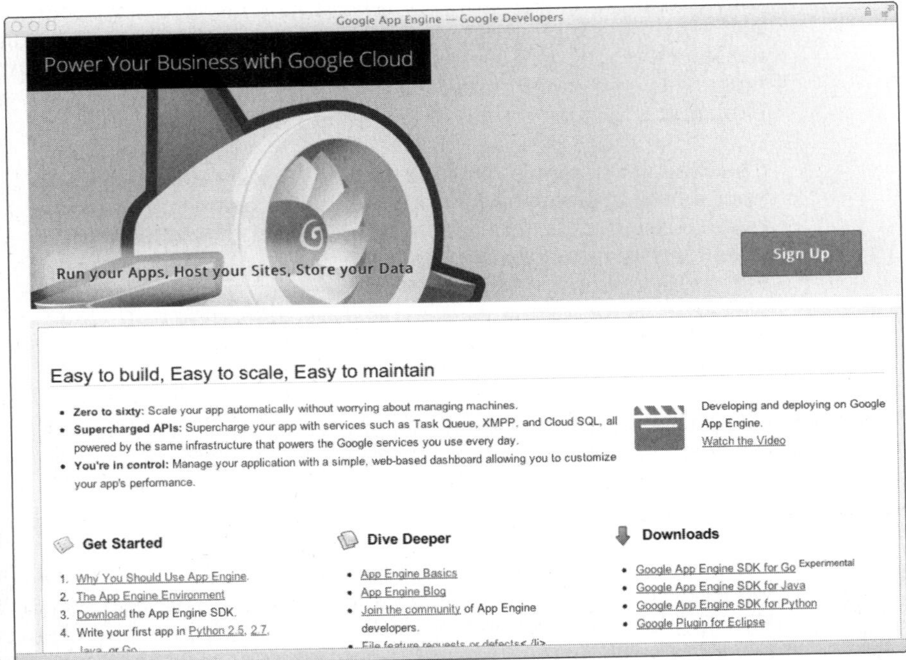

Figure 12-3: App Engine home.

2. **Click the big red Sign Up button shown in Figure 12-3.**

   Hard to miss, isn't it?

3. **In the new page that appears (see Figure 12-4), enter your Google account information — or create a Google account if you don't already have one.**

   Doing so brings you to the Welcome to Google App Engine page, as shown in Figure 12-5.

4. **Click the page's Create Application button.**

   You're brought to a page (see Figure 12-6) where you're asked to verify your account using SMS.

5. **Give Google your mobile phone number and then click Send.**

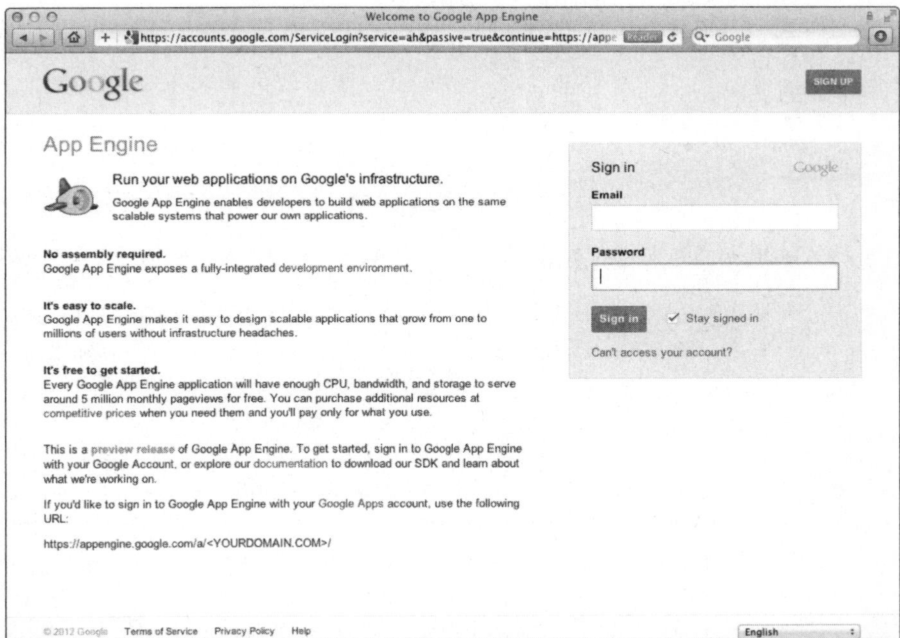

Figure 12-4: Sign up.

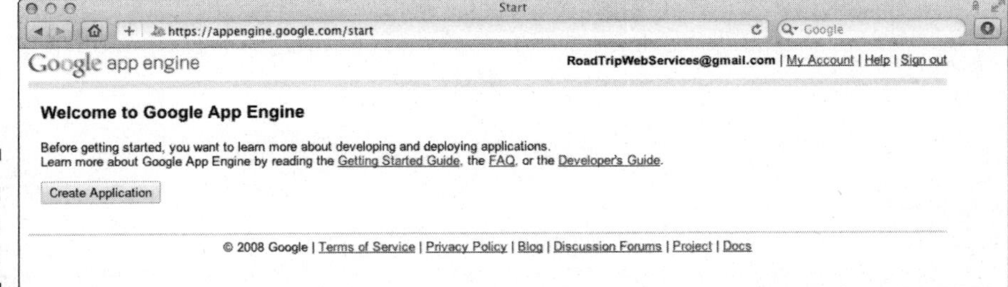

Figure 12-5: Create an application.

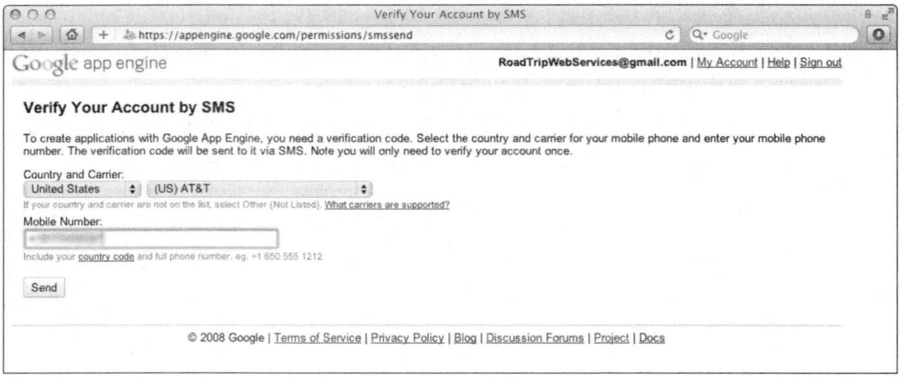

Figure 12-6: Enter your mobile number.

Clicking Send brings up the page you see in Figure 12-7, which informs you that an authorization code has been sent to your mobile number. In no time, you'll get a text message with an authentication code.

6. **After receiving your authentication code, enter it into the field labeled Enter Account Code and click the Send button.**

   If everything works as it should, Figure 12-8 magically appears, and you're then asked to create your application identifier.

7. **Feel free to enter whatever name strikes your fancy into the Application Identifier field.**

   I'm naming mine `rtpointsofinterest` (which means you can't use that one because it's already taken), and that's what I'll be referring to in this book. You'll have to substitute your own application name when necessary. *Lowercase* letters, digits, and hyphens are acceptable characters.

8. **Enter an appropriate name into the Application Title field.**

   This is the name that users will see when they access the application.

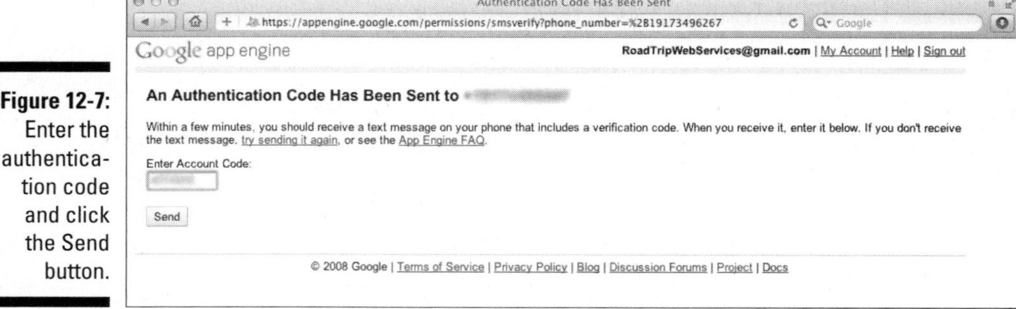

Figure 12-7: Enter the authentication code and click the Send button.

9. **Read through the Terms of Service, select the I Accept These Terms check box, and then click the Create Application button.**

   The Terms of Service are pretty boilerplate. Keep in mind that you can have only ten applications per account in this free version. (Naturally, you have the option of a paid version with more flexibility, but if you're careful you can get by with the freebie version.) And, oh yes, you can't sign up for multiple accounts because Google will send an account verification code to a given cellphone number only once.

   Again, if everything goes right (and there's no reason it shouldn't as long as you follow the directions — something I personally have a problem with on occasion), you see the Application Registered Successfully page, as shown in Figure 12-9. Here you can find a few links to pages that are chock-full of information about how you can put Google App Engine to work.

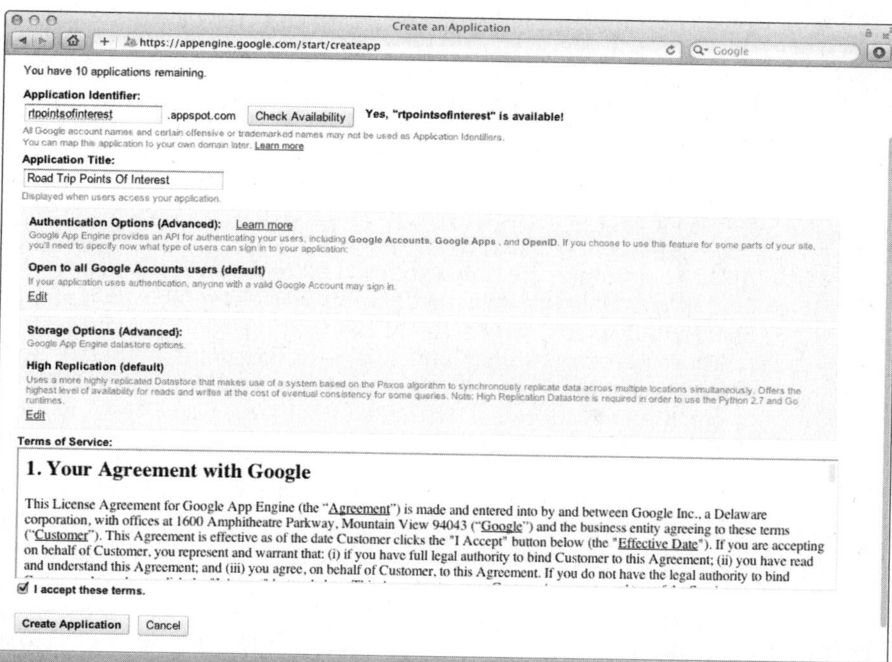

Figure 12-8: Create your application.

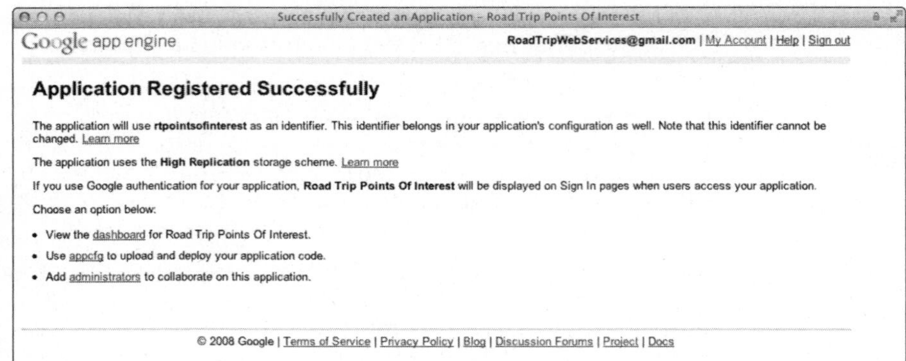

Figure 12-9: Application created successfully!

Although you don't need to create your App Engine application first in order to get started on your own (real) application, I suggest you do so. When you create your application using the SDK on your computer, you'll need to name it, and this will be the name you'll need to use to upload it. If it turns out that that name isn't available when you create your App Engine application, you'll have to change your application's name. This is not a big deal unless you, like I did, wrote a few chapters of a book with screenshots using a name that was not available and had to go back and change the application name and all the screenshots.

At this point, take the time explore a bit more and get a feel of the lay of the land. If you click the View the Dashboard link on the Application Registered Successfully page, you end up at the Dashboard page, where you find a plethora of informational links that — at this point, at least — won't make much sense. (See Figure 12-10.) I explain some of it as you build your application, but because this isn't a book on Google App Engine, I give you the Goldilocks tour — not too big, not too little, but just enough so that you can understand what you need to do to create a web service.

After successfully registering your application, your next step is to go ahead and download GoogleAppEngineLauncher to your desktop:

1. **On the Dashboard page, scroll down until you see the Downloads link on the left side of the page under Resources, then click that link.**

   You can also go back to the Google App Engine home page at `https://developers.google.com/appengine`, scroll down the page to the Getting Started steps, and click the link in Step 3, Download the App Engine SDK.

   Either path takes you to the Downloads page you see in Figure 12-11.

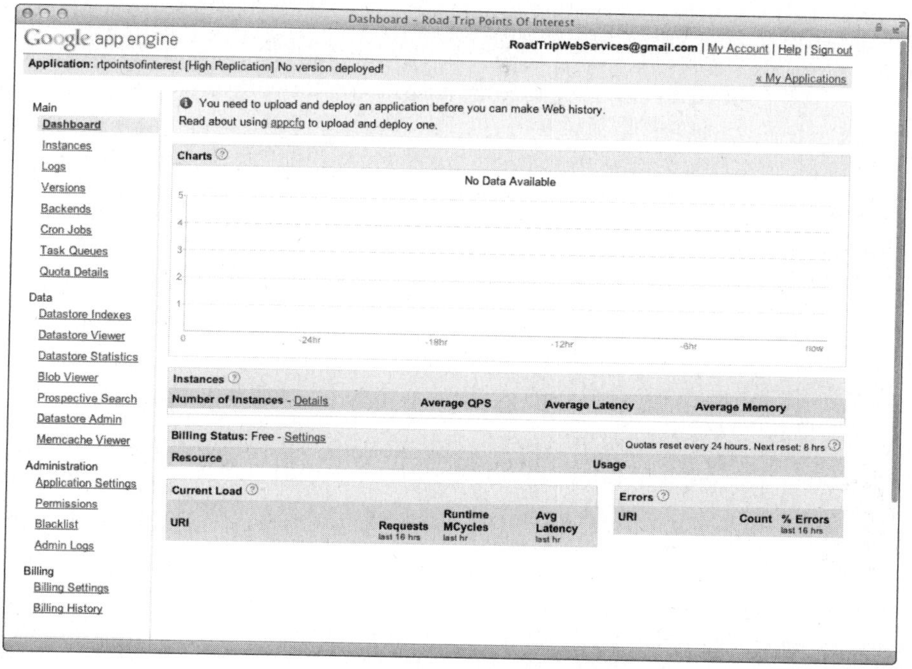

Figure 12-10: The app engine dashboard.

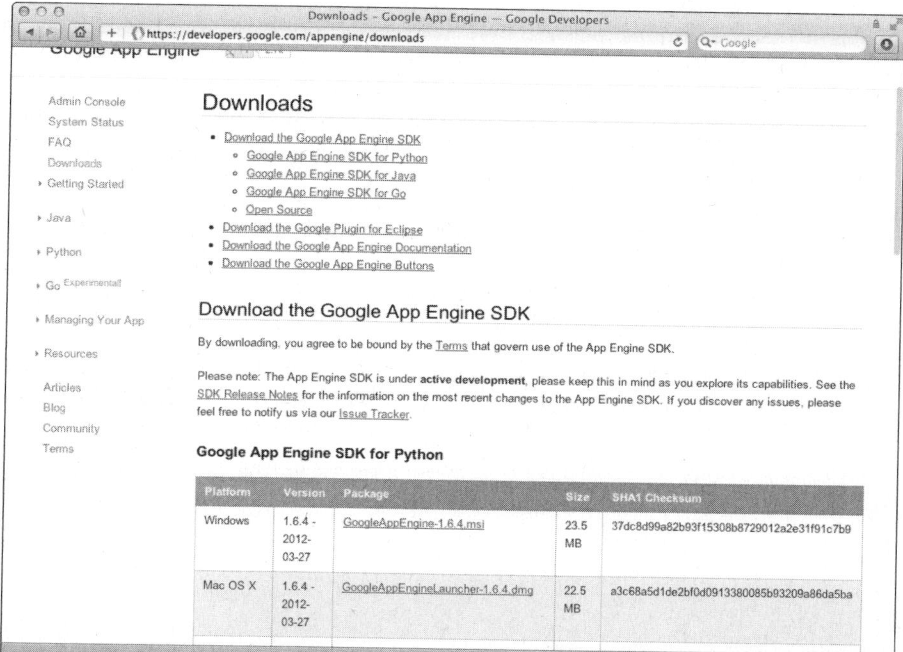

Figure 12-11: Download the Google AppEngine Launcher.

2. **Click the GoogleAppEngineLauncher-1.6.4.dmg link (or the latest non-beta OS X version) to download it.**

3. **After the file package downloads to your machine, drag it to your desktop, and double-click it to open it.**

   You'll see the GoogleAppEngineLauncher. You may be tempted to double-click it. If you do (as I have more than once), you get a message that says `GoogleAppEngineLauncher is an application downloaded from the Internet. Are you sure you want to open it?` If you click Open, you get another message (see Figure 12-12) that explains that what you *really* need to do is drag GoogleAppEngineLauncher to your desktop (or Applications folder), and that if you don't, dire things could happen.

   Here's another case of needing to follow the directions.

4. **Drag GoogleAppEngineLauncher into your Applications folder, launch it, and then pin it to the Dock.**

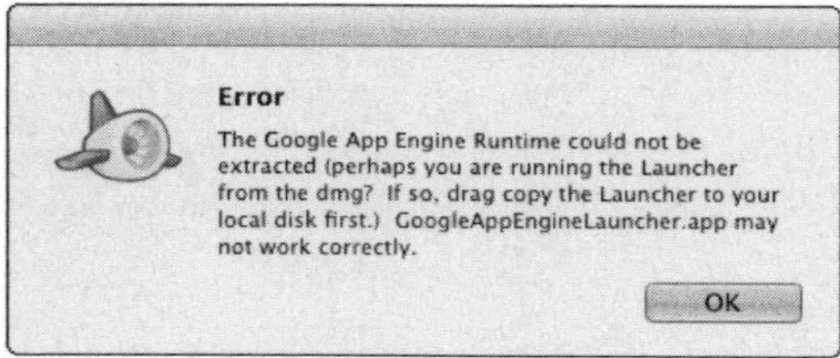

Figure 12-12: Do what it says.

5. **When you do launch GoogleAppEngineLauncher, you see a few messages about Command Symlinks — if you're okay with creating the links (or have no idea what they are) click OK and enter your password when asked.**

   At long last, GoogleAppEngineLauncher makes its appearance, as shown in Figure 12-13.

As I mention in the "App Engine SDKs" section, earlier in this chapter, App Engine includes a simple web application framework known as webapp2. The whole idea behind such a framework is to make it easy to get started — a concept I fully support, which is why I have you use it. For larger applications, third-party frameworks such as Django work well with App Engine.

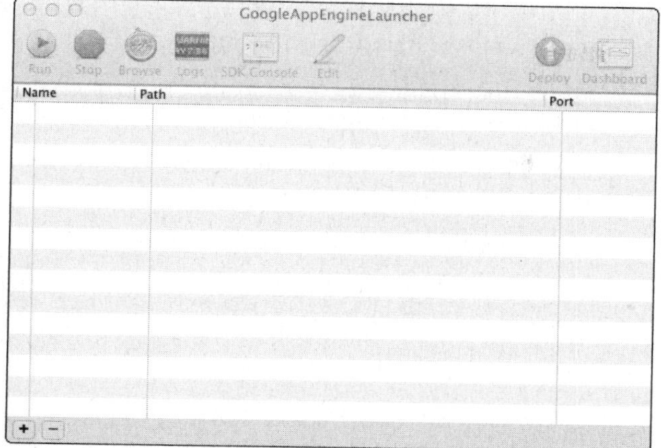

Figure 12-13: The Google AppEngine Launcher.

To create an application that includes the webapp2 framework, do the following:

1. **In GoogleAppEngineLauncher, choose File➪New Application, or press ⌘+N, or simply click the plus sign at the bottom of the GoogleAppEngineLauncher window.**

   Doing so brings up the New Application Settings dialog box, as shown in Figure 12-14.

2. **Using the appropriate fields in the New Application Settings dialog box, name your new application whatever you named it — the application identifier — when you created your App Engine application. Then select the directory where you want to place your application folder.**

   As you can see from Figure 12-14, I have placed the application folder on my desktop.

   Notice the Port field. GoogleAppEngineLauncher assigns your application a port number when you add it to the launcher, starting with 8080. As you add more applications, the number is increased so your number may not be 8080.

   The idea here is that a URL request gets routed to a web server running in the cloud. A web server processes the request by sending it to the right program. When you're running your application out there in the real world, App Engine handles all of that for you. But when you're using GoogleAppEngineLauncher in order to launch a trial run of your application, you'll be using something called localhost — IP address 127.0.0.1, to be precise — and every computer has one.

Localhost (meaning this computer) is the standard hostname given to the address of the loopback network interface — which is simply a way to route requests directly back to the source (your computer) so you can test stuff without having to go out on to a network.

Figure 12-14: Create your application.

3. **Click the Create button.**

   Your application gets added to the GoogleAppEngineLauncher, as shown in Figure 12-15.

Figure 12-15: Ready to run.

If you need to reload your application into GoogleAppEngineLauncher for any reason, you *don't* want to click the + button. That creates a new application. Instead, choose File➪Add Existing Application or press ⌘+Shift+N.

Time to let GoogleAppEngineLauncher put the `rtpointsofinterest` application (or whatever your application name is) through its paces:

1. **In GoogleAppEngineLauncher, click the green Run button on the far-left side of the toolbar.**

   After a short pause, the icon to the left of your application in the listing turns a nice shade of green as well, as you can see in Figure 12-16. (Okay, I know this book is in black and white, but trust me — it really is green.)

2. **Click the Stop button.**

   As you might expect, clicking Stop stops the application execution.

3. **Click the Red button again to restart your application.**

4. **Click the Browse button (you have to click in the toolbar first to enable the button).**

   Not what you expected, right? Click the Browse button, and you're connected to the current project in the browser, as you can see in Figure 12-17.

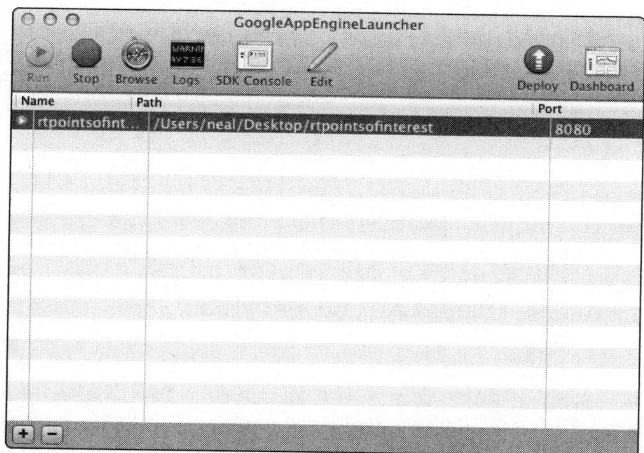

Figure 12-16: It really is running!

This is the equivalent of entering

```
http://localhost:8080/
```

in your browser.

Long story short: If you click the Browse button, you see the results in the browser — a real Hello World application, as shown in Figure 12-17. (Be still my beating heart.) The only thing the default application you just created can do at this point is display something in a browser window.

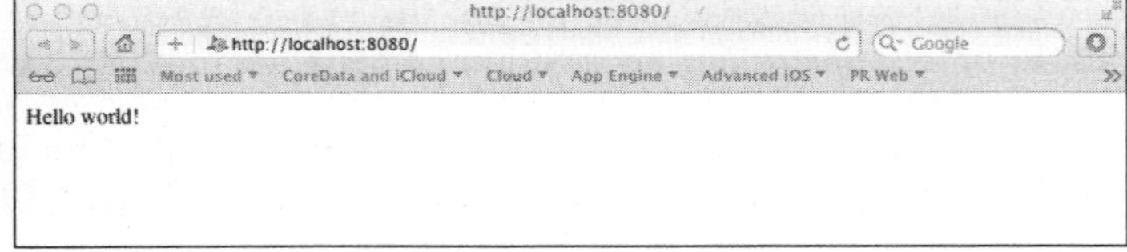

Figure 12-17: Running in the browser.

5. **Click the Logs button.**

   You get what you see in Figure 12-18. At this stage of the game, none of the warnings you see here are particularly pertinent (thank goodness), but as your work progresses, the info found in the Log Console could become more helpful.

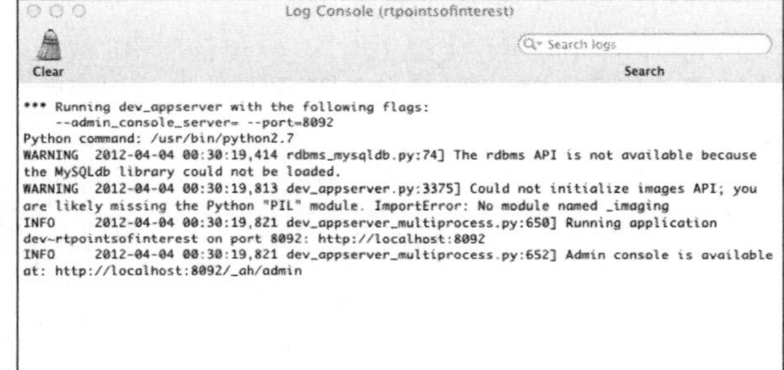

Figure 12-18: The Log Console.

Now, of course you may be asking yourself, how can I change Hello World into something cleverer, like "Welcome to the Wild Wacky World of Web Services"? In order to do that, you're going to need a text editor that includes syntax coloring and function navigation for Python.

You can actually use any text editor you want, including TextEdit. (You can even be quite clever and use Xcode, but that would involve quite a bit of work — I let you figure that one out on your own.) But because TextWrangler includes syntax-coloring and function-navigation for Python, and is free to boot, I say go with TextWrangler.

To grab TextWrangler from the web, just point your browser to `www.textwrangler.com/products` as I have in Figure 12-19. Click the Download link, install it, and then launch it. Now you're ready to rock 'n' roll.

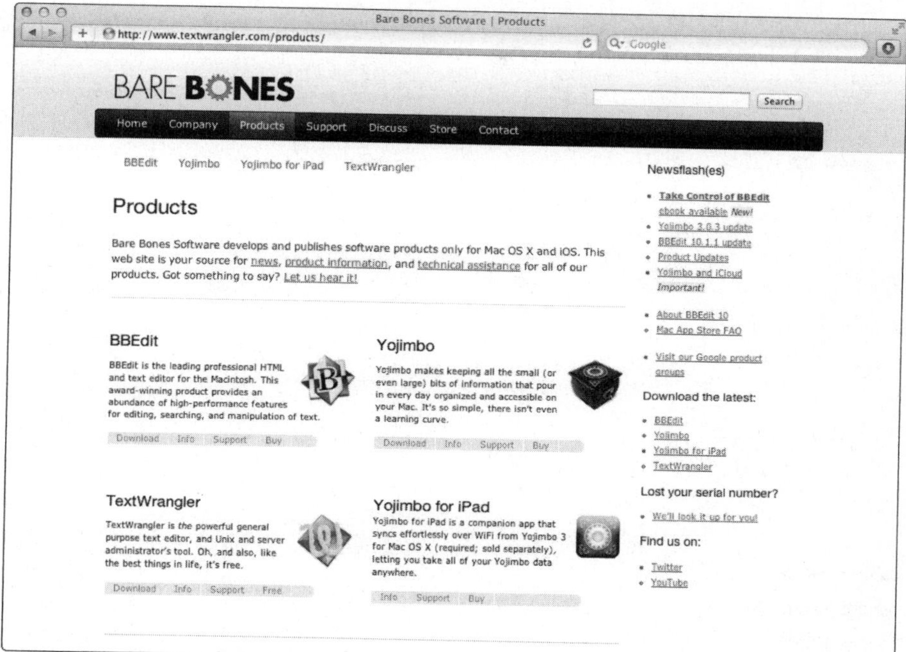

Figure 12-19: Getting Text Wrangler.

The webapp2 Starter Kit

It's time to take look inside the folder GoogleAppEngineLauncher came up with when it first created your application. There you can find three application files (`app.yaml`, `index.yaml`, and `main.py`) as well as one icon file — `favicon.ico`.

Open the three application files. If you're using TextWrangler, as I am, to open the `.yaml` files in the Open dialog you'll first have to select the Everything option from the Enable pop-up menu, as I have in Figure 12-20.

The `app.yaml` is a configuration file required by your Python App Engine application. It specifies request handler and static files URL paths and also includes code information such as the application ID and the version identifier, as you can see in Listing 12-2.

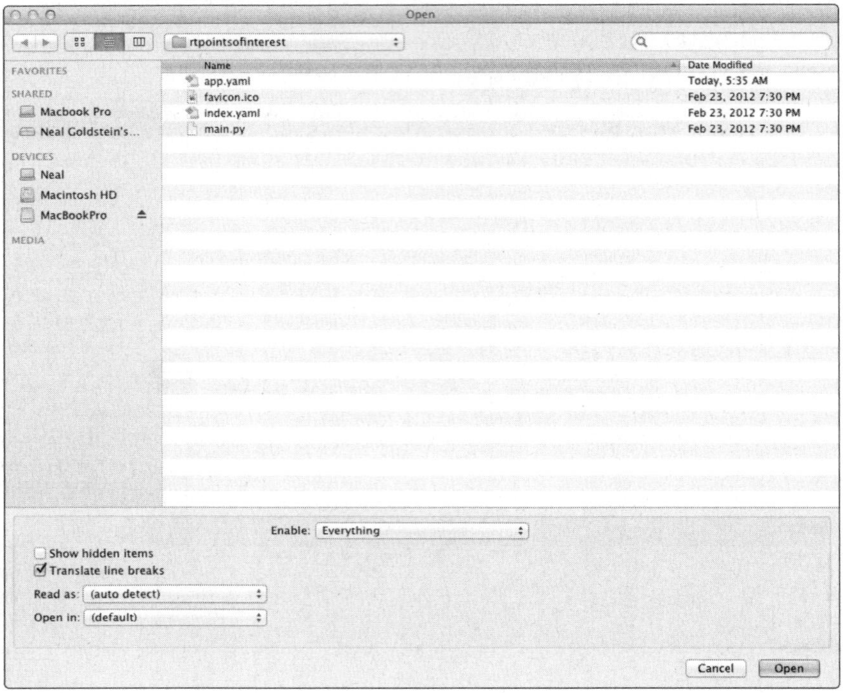

Figure 12-20: Enable everything.

Listing 12-2: app.yaml

```
application: rtpointsofinterest
version: 1
runtime: python27
api_version: 1
threadsafe: yes

handlers:
- url: /favicon\.ico
  static_files: favicon.ico
  upload: favicon\.ico

- url: .*
  script: main.app

libraries:
- name: webapp2
  version: "2.5.1"
```

The app.yaml file is in a format called YAML, an open format for configuration files and network messages. You don't need to know much about the format beyond what you see here.

In this example, the configuration file tells App Engine that this is version 1 of an application called rtpointsofinterest:

```
application: rtpointsofinterest
version: 1
```

App Engine keeps a copy of your application for each version used, and an administrator can change the version in the Administration Console, test versions, and so on.

The configuration file also tells App Engine that this application uses version 1 of the Python runtime environment (the API version) using Python 2.7 and that it is *threadsafe,* which means that App Engine will send requests concurrently:

```
runtime: python27
api_version: 1
threadsafe: yes
```

If Google releases a new version of your runtime environment's API, your application will continue to use the one specified here. To use a new environment, you'll need to change this value and upload the changed code.

Currently there is only one version of the Python runtime environment.

There are two kinds of handlers: static file handlers and script handlers. A static file handler returns the contents of a file — an image, for example — as the response.

```
- url: /favicon\.ico
  static_files: favicon.ico
  upload: favicon\.ico
```

I'm not going to spend time on static file handlers, but for your information, a user's browser requests a favicon.ico file when it loads the page — it's your website's icon that is typically displayed in the user's browser URL bar, next to the web address of your site.

A script handler runs a Python script in your application to determine the response for the given URL.

```
- url: .*
  script: main.app
```

App Engine uses this specification to route requests for your application; it informs App Engine that every request for this application (every URL that matches the regular expression `/.*`) is to be handled by a Python script named `main.app`.

You always code a handler to handle a request that matches a URL pattern. The mapping defines a URL pattern to match as well as the script to be executed. You're going to map web service requests to *handlers,* to use Python terminology. (Handlers here correspond to the controllers you'd see in the Model Application Controller architecture.)

In this case, all URls use the `main.app` script, where you'll then map the URL on to the right handler.

Finally, you specify the webapp2 framework:

```
libraries:
- name: webapp2
  version: "2.5.1"
```

And that's it for the `app.yaml` file. Next on the list: the `index.yaml` file, as shown in Listing 12-3.

Listing 12-3: index.yaml

```
indexes:

# AUTOGENERATED

# This index.yaml is automatically updated whenever the
         dev_appserver
# detects that a new type of query is run.  If you want to
         manage the
# index.yaml file manually, remove the above marker line
         (the line
# saying "# AUTOGENERATED").  If you want to manage some
         indexes
# manually, move them above the marker line.  The index.
         yaml file is
# automatically uploaded to the admin console when you
         next deploy
# your application using appcfg.py.
```

The App Engine datastore uses indexes for every query your application makes; the indexes are specified in this file. Fortunately, you don't have to do much in terms of your `index.yaml` file since the development system will take care of it for you. When your application tries to do a query that needs an index not found in this file, the development server will create the index and add it to the file.

So, if during testing the application does every possible query it could ever make (as one would expect, right?), then this file should be complete. You'll need to work with this file only to delete indexes that you're no longer using or to define ones that were not created during development.

Right now, this file is empty, and since you won't be generating any indexes here it will continue to look the same. But if you did do a query — for example, filtering the points of interest by destination and ordering them by the last time they were updated with the last update first — you'd see the following:

```
- kind: PointOfInterest
  properties:
  - name: destination
  - name: updated
    direction: desc
```

`properties` is a list, one element per column in the index, where each column has a name and an optional direction that is either `asc` (ascending order, the default) or `desc` (descending order). The order of the Properties list is significant: The index is sorted by the first column first, then by the second column, and so on.

The webapp Framework

The great thing about frameworks is that they make web application development easier, faster, and less error prone. To get a sense of how easy it can be, this section looks at how the `webapp` framework deals with the four major pieces of the puzzle involved in getting a request, handling it, and sending back the response — done by the `WSGIApplication`, the `RequestHandler`, and the `Request` and `Response` classes used by a request handler, respectively.

To start, take a look at `main.py`, the default handler for all URLs. (You can see `main.py` in all its glory in Listing 12-4.)

I want you to pay attention to two particular pieces in `main.py` — the two components that make up the application.

- `WSGIApplication`: An instance that routes incoming requests to handlers based on the URL (this implements the `main.app` script specified in `app.yaml`).
- `MainHandler`: A `RequestHandler` class that processes requests and builds responses. You'll create several of these in your application, including one to handle each web service request.

Listing 12-4: main.py

```
import webapp2

class MainHandler(webapp2.RequestHandler):
    def get(self):
        self.response.out.write('Hello world!')

app = webapp2.WSGIApplication([('/', MainHandler)],
                              debug=True)
```

The first statement you see here is

```
import webapp2
```

`import webapp2` imports the webapp2 module and creates a reference to the module in the current namespace. Or, in other words, after you've run this statement, you can use `webapp2.`*`name`* to refer to things defined in webapp2 — `webapp2.WSGIApplication`, for example.

Now skip to this line:

```
app = webapp2.WSGIApplication([('/', MainHandler)],
                              debug=True)
```

Here you start things off by creating an instance of the application. (`webapp2.WSGIApplication` is a class — in Python, class instantiation uses function notation.)

```
app = webapp2.WSGIApplication(...)
```

You then assign the instance to the variable `app`.

The first parameter

```
[('/', MainHandler)],
```

defines a *route* — the request handler, `MainHandler`, gets mapped to the root URL (/). The `[]` is a Python array or list, which means there can be more than one specified. (In fact, you'll create routes for each service you implement; I explain more about that shortly.)

This is similar to what you'd do to create an iOS app. `main.m` in RoadTrip, for example, has a similar structure, as shown below:

```
int main(int argc, char *argv[])
{
  @autoreleasepool {
      return UIApplicationMain(argc, argv, nil, NSStringFr
           omClass([RTAppDelegate class]));
  }
}
```

The application itself is represented by an instance of the class `webapp2.WSGIApplication`. The `WSGIApplication` class implements the WSGI interface, a standard interface between web application frameworks and web servers. (WSGI is short for *W*eb *S*erver *G*ateway *I*nterface, if you're interested.)

Much like `UIApplication` in the iOS framework, the `WSGI` application provides the plumbing for your application. All you need to do is provide the code to deliver the application content.

`WSGIApplication` receives a request and dispatches the appropriate handler, just as the `UIApplication` object does for an event in its main event loop. It also returns the response to the client. It is also responsible for handling uncaught exceptions.

Now a little about Python

If you look very closely at Listing 12-5, you'll notice that the variable name `app` is not declared and has no type associated with it. You may ask yourself "What's up with that?"

Python has local and global variables like most other languages, but it has no explicit variable declarations. Variables spring into existence by being assigned a value, and they're automatically destroyed when they go out of scope.

Python has typed objects but untyped variable names. *Untyped* means that the type is not checked at compile time. Instead, a method call may fail. This provides polymorphism without inheritance.

In Objective-C, for example, the compiler will give you an error if you try to send a message to an object that doesn't declare those methods. In Python, you can send any message to any object as long as it has those methods. Whether or not a method is actually there is determined at runtime.

Python is object-oriented, and in that sense it looks a lot like Objective-C with its methods and classes. Admittedly, the methods and classes are not *identical,* but they are in most ways *similar.* Where there are major differences, I'll walk you through them.

And more on routing

The `WSGIApplication` instance is initialized with a list of mappings of URLs to handler classes. App Engine is all about request handlers; when `webapp` receives a request, it creates an instance of the `RequestHandler` class associated with the URL path in the request.

```
[('/', MainHandler)],
```

This snippet of code, for example, defines one request handler, `MainHandler`, mapped to the root URL (`/`).

`webapp` then calls a method that corresponds with the HTTP action of the request, such as the `get()` method for a HTTP `GET` request. The method processes the request, prepares a response, and then returns. Finally, the application sends the response to the client.

So, when `webapp` receives an HTTP `GET` request to the URL `/`, it instantiates the `MainHandler` class and calls the instance's `get` method, as shown in Figure 12-21. (If it were a `POST`, you'd expect to find a `post` method.)

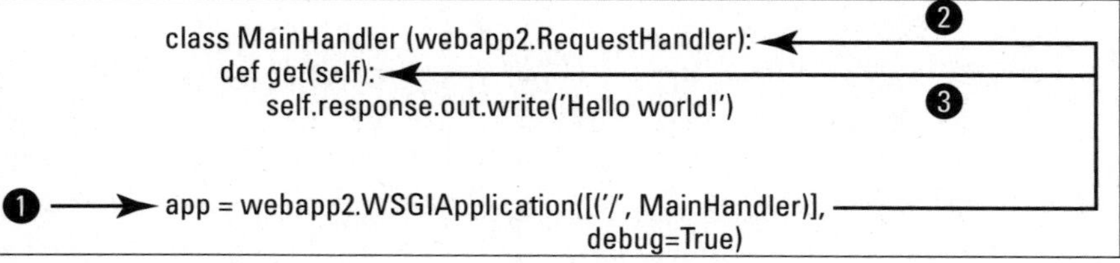

Figure 12-21: How it's all connected.

The way you'd set things up, you'd told App Engine — via the `app.yaml` file — to send all requests to the main script (which is in the `main.py` file as you saw earlier).

```
handlers:
- url: .*
  script: main.app
```

That means the URL you saw in your browser when you clicked the Browse button — `http://localhost:8080/` — was routed to the `MainHandler` class.

Eventually, when the application is all done, you'll see the following in `main.py`:

```
  ('/testdata', TestDataHandler),
('/pointsofinterest', PointsOfInterestHandler),
('/lastupdate', LastUpdateHandler),
('/allpointsofinterest', AllPointsOfInterestHandler),
('/addpointofinterest', AddPointOfInterestHandler),
('/deletepointofinterest', DeletePointOfInterestHandler)],
```

The last five request handers map onto the web services you defined in Chapter 11. You'll use the first one to generate some test data, which means it won't be part of your production application.

Handling handlers

I want you to look a bit more closely at handlers.

When `webapp` receives an HTTP `GET` request to the URL `/`, it instantiates the `MainHandler` class and calls the instance's `get()` method. (Refer to Figure 12-21.)

```
class MainHandler(webapp.RequestHandler):
    def get(self):
```

A class in Python is a lot like an Objective-C class, even down to the `self` variable. It has what you'd call *variables* and *methods* in Objective-C which are accessed by the dot notation. In Python, a method is a function that "belongs to" an object.

So that means that `MainHandler(webapp.RequestHandler):` defines a class, `MainHandler`, that inherits from the `webapp RequestHandler` class.

The class defines methods for each HTTP method supported by the handler — in this case, one method for HTTP `GET` called `get()`. This method name, of course, corresponds to the verb in the HTTP request. For example, in Chapter 7, you created a `GET` request and I had you set the method to `GET`. (If you can't remember, see whether Listing 12-5 refreshes your memory.)

Listing 12-5: createGETRequest:withParams: in WSManager.m

```
- (NSMutableURLRequest *)createGETRequest:(NSString *)
        baseURL withParams:(NSDictionary *)userParams {

  NSMutableString *queryString = [NSMutableString string];
  // add user params
  if (userParams != nil) {
    for (id key in userParams) {
      id value = [userParams valueForKey:key];
      NSString *paramString =
        [NSString stringWithFormat:@"%@=%@&", key, value];
      paramString = [paramString
          stringByAddingPercentEscapesUsingEncoding:
                                     NSASCIIStringEncoding];
      [queryString appendString:paramString];
    }
  }
  NSString *urlString = [NSString stringWithFormat:
                          @"%@%@", baseURL, queryString];
  NSURL *url = [NSURL URLWithString:urlString];
  NSMutableURLRequest *request  =
               [NSMutableURLRequest requestWithURL:url];
  [request setHTTPMethod:@"GET"];
  return request;
```

This GET request will correspond to the `get()` method in the `MainHandler` class (or whatever class is called based on the URL). In Chapter 7, you created the necessary URL. (See whether Listing 12-6 jogs your memory.)

Listing 12-6: Adding geocodeSynchronouslyXML:successBlock:failure Block to WSManager.m

```
- (void)geocodeSynchronouslyXML:(NSMutableDictionary *)
    userParams successBlock:(void (^)(NSDictionary *))
               success failureBlock:(void (^)())failure {


  returnSuccess = success;
  returnFail = failure;
  [self setupGeocodingWebService];
  webService =
      @"http://maps.googleapis.com/maps/api/geocode/xml?";
  [params addEntriesFromDictionary:userParams];
  NSMutableURLRequest *request =
     [self createGETRequest:webService withParams:params];
  [self requestSynchronousWebService:request];
}
```

If App Engine were handling that request instead of, say, Google's Geocoding web service, you would see something like the following:

```
('/maps/api/geocode/xml', XML_Handler),
```

When the handler `get()` method is called, `webapp` makes available `Request` and `Response` objects that are used by a request handler — `self.request` and `self.response`, respectively — that the handler method can in turn access and modify:

```
class MainHandler(webapp2.RequestHandler):
    def get(self):
        self.response.out.write('Hello world!')
```

Inside the method, information about the request is available by accessing `self.request` — the instance of the `Request` class that contains the request.

The `Request` class contains instance methods such as

```
get()
get_all()
arguments()
get_range()
```

and instance variables (also called data attributes) such as

```
body
body_file
remote_addr
url
path
query_string
headers
cookies
```

Although you don't use any of those methods or instance variables here, you'll be using `get()` to extract the parameters for the query string you create with the `GET` (or any other) request. (Don't confuse the response `get()` method with the `GET` request.)

When the webapp2 framework calls a request handler method, the handler instance's `response` variable is also initialized with an empty `Response` instance. The `response` is "filled out" by the handler method — for example, by writing body data to the `out` instance variable or setting headers on the `headers` instance variable.

The Response class contains class methods such as

```
Response.http_status_message()
```

Instance variables such as

```
out
headers
```

and instance methods such as

```
set_status()
clear()
wsgi_write()
```

Typically, the method sets properties on `self.response` to prepare the response, and then it exits.

```
self.response.out.write('Hello world!')
```

And as I said, the response gets sent only when the handler exits.

As I said, a class in Python is a lot like an Objective-C class, although methods and instance variables are accessed by the dot notation

So

```
MainHandler(webapp.RequestHandler):
```

Defines a class `MainHandler` that inherits from the `webapp RequestHandler` class

And

```
self.response.out.write('Hello world!')
```

`self.response` is an instance variable that points to a `Response` class.

The `Response` class has an instance variable `out`, which is an instance of the class that reads and writes a string buffer. The contents of this object are sent as the body of the response when the request handler method returns. `write` is a `StringIO` instance method that actually does the write. As I said, you can think of a method as being a function that "belongs to" an object.

When the handler method exits, the application uses the value of `self.response` as the HTTP response.

A little more Python

Python uses whitespace indentation (known as the *off-side rule*), rather than curly braces or keywords to delimit blocks. An increase in indentation comes after certain statements; a decrease in indentation signifies the end of the current block.

The `def get():` defines the start of a method (function) — the `def` keyword plus the method name and any arguments).

```
def get(self):
```

To include code as part of the function, you indent it as follows:

```
    self.response.out.write('Hello world!')
```

To end the function, you decrease the indentation:

```
app = webapp2.WSGIApplication([('/', MainHandler)],
                                        debug=True)
```

It is important that you pay attention to the indentation. Spaces, not tabs are preferred. In addition, because of the width of this book's printed page, I sometimes have to have functions on two lines. Python does have implicit joining inside parentheses, brackets and braces, as you can see above (there are some style rules you may want to explore on your own). You may also see a string literal (zero or more characters enclosed in matching single ('), double quotes ("), or matching groups of three single or double quotes) on more than one line. While I have to do it because of the width of the printed page, in your code you can't have a string literal on more than one line unless you use an escape sequence (\) as the last character of the line.

The `WSGIApplication` instance is also initialized with a `debug` parameter that tells the application to print error messages to the browser window when a handler returns an exception if the application is running under the development web server.

```
debug=True)
```

`webapp` detects whether it is running under the development server or running as a live App Engine application and will not print errors to the browser when running live — even if debug is `True`. You can set it to `False` to have the development server emulate the live server when errors occur.

Just for fun, change "Hello world" to "Hello Mr. Bill!"

To do that, replace `self.response.out.write('Hello World!')` in `main.py` with the following:

```
#self.response.out.write('Hello World!')
self.response.out.write('<html><body>')
self.response.out.write('<p>Hello Mr Bill!</p>')
self.response.out.write('</body></html>')
```

You can also replace it with any other HTML. (# denotes a comment in Python — here you just commented out the `'Hello World'` response.)

Save the file.

Because Python is a scripted language, when you save the file, the application is updated. That also means that, if you *don't* save the file, the application is *not* updated. Logical, right?

In the GoogleAppEngineLauncher window, click the Browse button.

You now see what's shown in Figure 12-22.

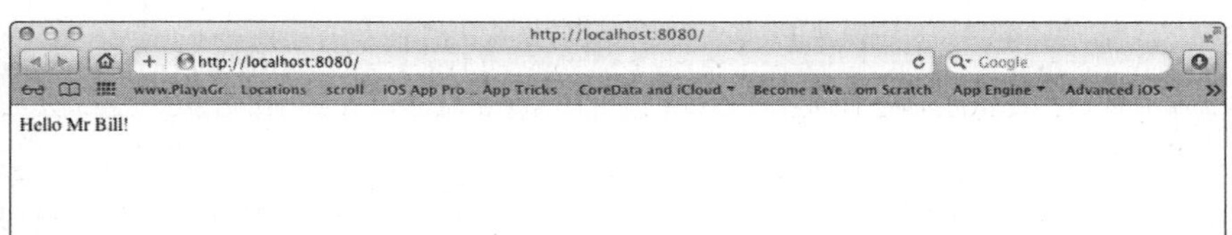

Figure 12-22: Hello Mr. Bill!

Click the Logs button in the GoogleAppEngineLauncher window. You now see the contents of Listing 12-7 in the Logs window.

Listing 12-7: What Should Appear in the Log Window

```
INFO     2012-04-05 14:52:41,362 dev_appserver.py:2884]
                                  "GET / HTTP/1.1" 200 -
```

This describes exactly what just went on — a `GET` request using HTTP 1.1 with a status code of 200 that tells you that request was successfully received, understood, and accepted.

If everything didn't work out as expected (you got no response in your browser window, for example) look in the Logs window. You'll see a lot of stuff, but the most important information is going to be at the bottom.

Imagine, for example, that you formatted your code so it looks something like the following:

```
class MainHandler(webapp2.RequestHandler):
    def get(self):
        #self.response.out.write('Hello World!')
        self.response.out.write('<html><body>')
         self.response.out.write('<p>Hello Mr Bill!</p>')
        self.response.out.write('</body></html>')
```

The Log window would rap you on the knuckles by displaying what you see in Listing 12-8. (I've bolded the important lines.)

Listing 12-8: What May Be on the Log File

```
ERROR     2012-04-13 21:07:29,154 wsgi.py:189]
Traceback (most recent call last):
....
File "/Users/neal/Desktop/rtpointsofinterest/main.py",
                                                line 25
    self.response.out.write("<p>Hello Mr Bill!</p>")
   ^
IndentationError: unexpected indent
INFO      2012-04-13 21:07:29,218 dev_appserver.py:2884]
            "GET / HTTP/1.1" 500 -
```

Python, because it uses indentation to determine scope, is obviously very sensitive about it. You'll need to be careful. Because you're an Objective-C programmer, the lack of curly braces will most likely seem alien to you, but just like the Objective-C's square braces (`[]`) for messages and the colon (`:`) in the method signature may have seemed weird when you first learned Objective-C, after a while you'll get used to it.

Okay, enough fun for now. It's time to do some serious work.

The Model Application Controller Architecture in App Engine

In Chapter 1, I introduce you to the Model Application Controller architecture.

This particular architecture maps well onto webapp2, as you can see in Figure 12-23.

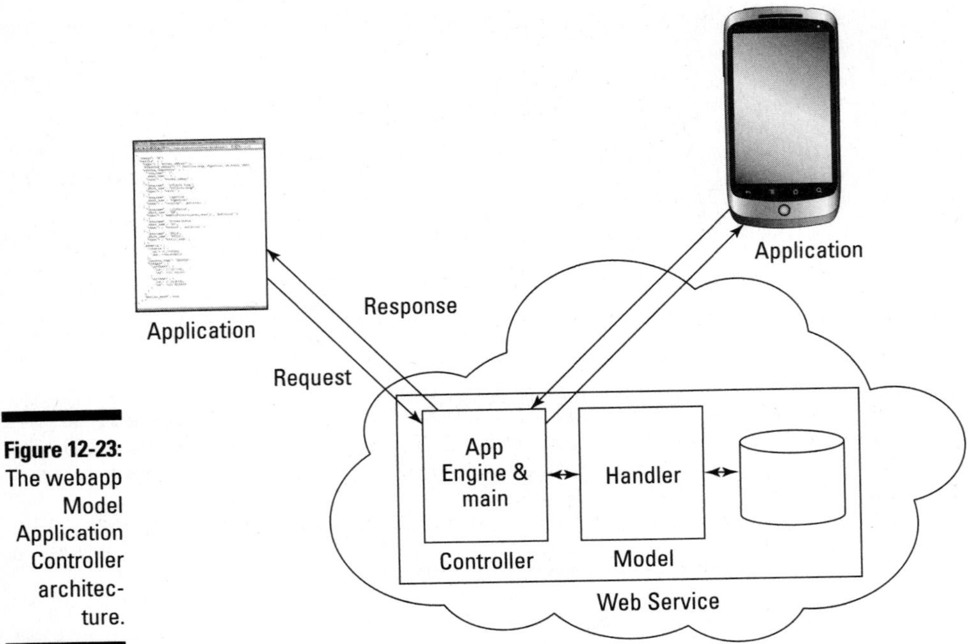

Figure 12-23: The webapp Model Application Controller architecture.

In this implementation of the Model Application Controller architecture, the Google Engine frontend and the main script do the routing to the right web service — a handler, in this case.

You can also see that this implementation works equally well for a website.

The entire process of accessing the application will work something like this:

1. In the case of a web service request from the phone, webapp gets a request from the client (the iPhone app).

   The phone is sending a web service request — `pointsofinterest` — to the webapp for all of the points of interest for the destination of 0 (and with an API key).

   ```
   http://localhost:8080/pointsofinterest?
                                destination=0&key=test123
   ```

2. `webapp` instantiates the right `Handler` class (`pointsofinterest`, for example) and calls the instance's `get` method.

But this also extends to websites, and you can (and should, for the purposes of this book) think of a web browser as actually doing the same thing — making a web service request. When a web browser sends a request to the server for a URL, such as

```
http://localhost:8080/pointsofinterest?
                              destination=0&key=test123
```

you can think of this as a web service request as well. This means the web browser is sending a user web service request for the points of interest for destination `0`.

In both cases, the code that interacts with the model (the data) is virtually identical.

Although I also talk about web and Mac apps in the Model Application Controller architecture, you won't be doing either here. I don't have you implement a Mac application or a website in this book, but just like in a universal app, the code base — in this case handlers rather than view controllers — is the same across mobile, web, and Mac apps.

Chapter 13

The Model's Model

In This Chapter

- Examining the App Engine datastore
- Seeing how models work
- Creating the rtpointsofinterest model
- Generating test data
- Testing web services in a browser

The whole point behind web services is that they allow you to access resources and either return representations of those resources or allow you to operate on them. In the case of `rtpointsofinterest`, that resource is — wait for it — Points of Interest and you'll need a way to create and manage those Points of Interest.

As I explain in Chapter 11, you'll use the App Engine datastore to store your data. The entities are created from Python objects, with the object's attributes becoming properties for the entity.

In the Python API, a (data) *model* is used to describe an entity, and in this chapter, you create the data model for `rtpointsofinterest`.

What's in the Model?

Start by thinking about what kind of data model you need for the `rtpointsofinterest` resource (also known as the Google App Engine application). This model will be derived from the web services you defined in Chapter 11.

Because this is a pretty simple web service and it just happens to focus on points of interest, it should probably come as no surprise that you really only need one model class here — `PointsOfInterest`.

It makes sense to start with the existing `SharedPointOfInterest` class in RoadTrip. I'll use the `SharedPointOfInterest` class rather than the `PointOfInterest` class because it has an associated data model of the kind you'll need to specify in App Engine. You can see the class in Listing 13-1.

Listing 13-1: The SharedPointOfInterest

```
@interface SharedPointOfInterest : NSManagedObject

@property (nonatomic, retain) NSString * name;
@property (nonatomic, retain) NSString * address;
@property (nonatomic, retain) NSString * comment;
@property (nonatomic, retain) NSNumber * displayOrder;
@property (nonatomic, retain) NSString * latitude;
@property (nonatomic, retain) NSString * location;
@property (nonatomic, retain) NSString * longitude;
@property (nonatomic, retain) NSString * subtitle;
@property (nonatomic, retain) NSString * title;
@property (nonatomic, readwrite) CLLocationCoordinate2D
          coordinate;
- (void)loadData:(NSDictionary *)data;
@end
```

Figure 13-1 shows the Core Data model that you created in Chapter 4 to implement `SharedPointOfInterest`.

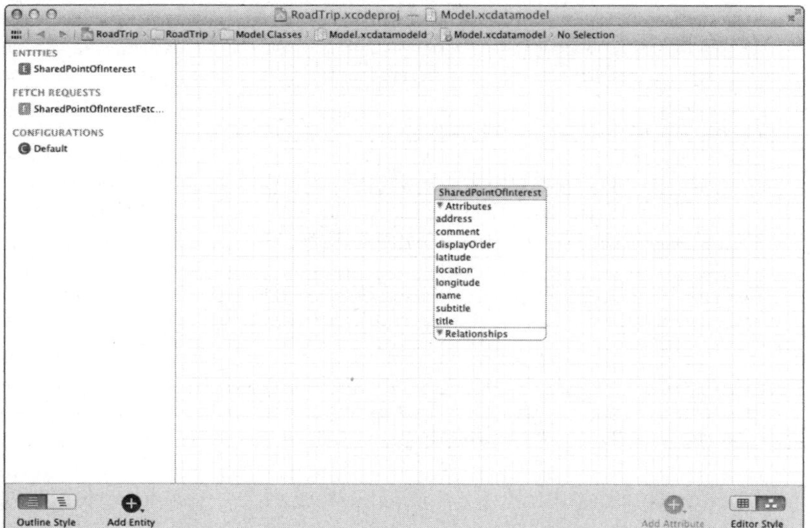

Figure 13-1: The Core Data model.

In this case, you're really interested in only this part:

```
@property (nonatomic, retain) NSString * name;
@property (nonatomic, retain) NSString * address;
@property (nonatomic, retain) NSString * comment;
@property (nonatomic, retain) NSNumber * displayOrder;
@property (nonatomic, retain) NSString * latitude;
@property (nonatomic, retain) NSString * location;
@property (nonatomic, retain) NSString * longitude;
```

`subtitle` and `title` are there in the Core Data model only to meet the requirements of the `MKAnnotation` protocol to display an annotation on a map.

This pared-down version of the model shown in Figure 13-1 contains the data and logic to keep track of all points of interest, so it would make sense to create a similar data model in your web service, and that's what you do next.

But first a little bit more about the App Engine datastore.

The App Engine Datastore

The App Engine datastore was designed to provide the kind of scalable high performance storage required by a web service.

It is in no way, shape, or form a traditional relational database, just as Core Data is not a traditional relational database. The idea here is that an application creates entities (such as the managed object in Core Data) with data values stored as properties of an entity. Each entity in the datastore has a key that uniquely identifies the entity across all entities of the same kind. Property values can be any of the supported property value types. (More on those in a minute.)

Just to make things interesting, there is now a Google Cloud SQL web service — currently in limited preview — that provides the capabilities of a MySQL database. I invite you to explore it on your own.

You use the Datastore API to define data models and create instances of those models to be stored as entities. You can also define rules for validating property values.

In your app, you can perform queries over entities that are filtered and sorted by the values of the properties. The queries are pre-indexed and stored in the `index.yaml` file. (Check out Chapter 12 for more on indexing and the `index.yaml` file.) Whenever the development app server detects that a new type of query is being run, it automatically adds that query to the `index.yaml` file.

Transactions such as creating, updating, or deleting are the basic context for operations on an entity, and a single transaction can include any number of such operations. The transaction takes care of data consistency by ensuring that all of the operations it contains are applied to the datastore as a unit or, if any of the operations fails, that none of them are applied. A single transaction can apply to multiple entities, so long as the entities are descended from a common ancestor, i.e. belong to the same entity group. For example, all points of interest could have an ancestor named *location*. For you database wonks out there, entity groups are not at all like tables in SQL.

Datastore entities are *schema-less.* A *schema* describes the structure of a database system in a formal language supported by the database management system. For example, in a relational database, the schema defines the tables, the fields in each table, and the relationships between fields and tables.

This schema is really your statement of how you think about the data in your application. The problem is that, in a rapidly changing environment, your ideas about the data may change often — and significantly — and a schemaless data model is much easier to adapt to changes than highly structured, rigidly enforced schema.

Core Data, on the other hand, *does* have a schema. But because the Core Data model is so simple, the App Engine and Core Data models will look pretty much the same.

To create the data model, you need to translate the data requirements of your resource into entities and properties. So even though your app will (and RoadTrip currently does) deal with points of interest that have names and locations and so forth, the datastore only knows from entities keys, properties, and indexes.

The model you'll use to describe your data you use is going to be a Python class — one that just happens to inherit from the `Model` class. The `Model` class defines a datastore entity and its properties. Properties are instances of a `Property` class — named values of one of several data types. Supported data types include integers, floating point values, strings, dates, binary data, and others. A `Property` class can have one or more values, and a property with multiple values can have values of mixed types.

You add an entity in Python by calling the constructor of the class and then storing the instance by calling the `put()` method. (In many ways, this is quite similar to how you create an object in Python, even if some aspects of it venture closer to C++ territory.)

An entity is updated by getting the entity's object — by using a query, for example — then modifying its properties, and then finally saving the entity with its new properties.

The webapp Model classes

So now it's time to create the `Model` classes you'll need. You'll start with the `SharedPointOfInterest` managed object class in RoadTrip as a base, in accordance with the reasoning I put forward in the "What's in the Model" section, earlier in the chapter. This task is pretty similar to what you'd do when creating a Core Data model, but you'll have to do all the typing on your own. (Hey, this is Python — no drop-down menus here.)

Start by adding a new file to your application.

In TextWrangler, choose File⇨New⇨Text Document or press ⌘+N.

Save this new file as `datamodel.py` in the `rtpointsofinterest` folder. Saving it as a `.py` file results in TextWrangler knowing it's a Python file. (TextWrangler will also apply text coloring and enable function navigation.)

WARNING!

If you forget the `.py`, App Engine won't see it as a script.

You can find a number of style guides for writing Python code. The PEP 8 — Style Guide for Python Code suggests that you use spaces, not tabs (and I follow that advice), and you should use four spaces for an indentation (and I do that, too). You should limit all lines to a maximum of 79 characters. Python has implied line continuation inside parentheses, brackets, and braces, and that is the preferred way of wrapping long lines — just make sure to indent the continued line.

Ready to wrestle with a Python? Go ahead and add the code in listing 12-2 to `datamodel.py`.

Listing 12-2: The Model Class

```
"""The PointOfInterest class and to_dict method"""
from google.appengine.ext import db

class PointOfInterest(db.Model):
    name = db.StringProperty(required=True)
    description = db.StringProperty()
    location = db.StringProperty()
    address = db.StringProperty()
    destination = db.StringProperty(required=True)
    coordinate = db.GeoPtProperty(required=True)
    updated = db.DateTimeProperty(required=True,
                                  auto_now_add=True)


    def to_dict(self):
        """Return PointOfInterest data in a dictionary"""
        a = {}
        a['id'] = str(self.key().id())
        a['name'] = self.name
        a['description'] = self.description
        a['location'] = self.location
        a['address'] = self.address
        a['destination'] = self.destination
        a['latitude'] = self.coordinate.lat
        a['longitude'] = self.coordinate.lon
        a['updated'] = str(self.updated)

        return a
```

The first line in the module — a string literal enclosed by triple quotes — is known as a `docstring`. A `docstring` is a string literal that occurs as the first statement in a module, function, class, or method definition. This `docstring` simply summarizes the purpose and usage of a Python module. By convention, `docstring`s are enclosed in triple double quotes. (You can also get the object's `docstring` using the `__doc__` attribute.)

You import the `google.appengine.ext.db` module, which will provide you with the `Model` class that you'll use to derive your own model:

```
from google.appengine.ext import db
```

Next you define your model class,

```
class PointOfInterest(db.Model):
```

which, as you can see, is a subclass of the `Model` class.

Be sure to save the files after you make any change or add new code — then and only then will you have updated the `rtpointsofinterest` app.

Model properties are defined by adding class attributes to the model class — kind of like what happens with instance variables in Objective-C. Each class attribute is an instance of a subclass of the `Property` class. A property instance has the *property configuration* — such as whether or not the property is required for the instance to be valid or a default value to use for the instance if none is provided. Listing 13-3 shows the model you just created.

Listing 13-3: The Model

```
class PointOfInterest(db.Model):
    name = db.StringProperty(required=True)
    description = db.StringProperty()
    location = db.StringProperty()
    address = db.StringProperty()
    destination = db.StringProperty(required=True)
    coordinate = db.GeoPtProperty(required=True)
    updated = db.DateTimeProperty(required=True,
                                  auto_now_add=True)
```

`PointOfInterest` inherits from `db.Model`. This defines a `PointOfInterest` model with 7 properties. The `name`, `description`, `location`, `address`, and `destination` are `StringProperty`s, whereas `coordinate` is a `geoPtProperty`, and `updated` is a `DateTimeProperty`.

You declare a property for a model by assigning a property declaration *object* to an attribute of the `Model` class — think property in Objective-C. The name of the attribute — `name` for example — is the name of the datastore property. The `db.StringProperty` object assigned to the `name` attribute says that the `name` property can only be a string. This is more or less equivalent to `@property (nonatomic, retain) NSString *name;` in the `SharedPointOfInterest` managed object.

Some property constructors take parameters to further configure them. For example, `required=True` says that this property is required for a new entity. So, for example, if I tried to create `PointOfInterest` without a name, you would see the following in the browser window if you were testing it there:

```
The server has either erred or is incapable of performing
          the requested operation.

Traceback (most recent call last):

...

BadValueError: Property name is required
```

The last line (the bolded one) is the line that really matters.

Every `PointOfInterest` needs to have at least a `name`, `destination`, `coordinate`, and `updated` (timestamp) property because you've decided that all of those are needed to make a valid `PointOfInterest`. Granted, this is somewhat arbitrary, but without a `coordinate`, for example, you can't display the `PointOfInterest` on the map. Because the datastore is schemaless, you need to enforce this in the code, and the `coordinate` constructor with its `required` parameter enables you to do that.

The datastore properties, though similar, are not exactly the same as Objective-C properties. Datastore properties can ensure that only values that meet certain criteria are assigned to properties (although you could do something similar in a getter). They can assign default values when constructing an object and can even convert values between a data type used by the application and one of the datastore's native value types, or otherwise customize how values are stored.

If someone tries to assign a value of the wrong type to one of these properties, the assignment raises a `db.BadValueError`. For example, if I tried to assign `6` to a name, I'd see the following:

```
BadValueError: Property name must be a str or unicode
                                        instance, not a int
```

As you can see, `coordinate` is a `GeoPtProperty`,

coordinate = db.GeoPtProperty(required=True)

represented by the `GeoPt` class:

```
class GeoPt(lat, lon=None)
```

It's a geographical point represented by floating-point latitude and longitude coordinates, and (fortunately) it validates the input for you. For example, if I tried to use at latitude of `91`, I'd see this:

```
geo = db.GeoPt(lat=91, lon=-179)
BadValueError: Latitude must be between -90 and 90;
                                        received 91.000000
```

Similarly, if I entered a longitude of `-181`, I'd see the following:

```
geo = db.GeoPt(lat=89, lon=-181)
BadValueError: Longitude must be between -180 and 180;
                                        received -181.000000
```

All of the error messages you see here were generated by making changes to some test data that you'll create later in a `TestDataHandler` class. (See "The TestData Class" section, later in this chapter.)

`updated` is a `DateTimeProperty`. I use this field to determine when the last update was made to this point of interest, and although you won't be using it in RoadTrip, I'll have it here for future expansion.

```
  updated = db.DateTimeProperty(required=True,
                                auto_now_add=True)
```

If `auto_now_add` is `True`, the property value is set to the current time the first time the entity is stored in the datastore, unless the property has already been assigned a value. This is useful for storing a "created" date and time for a model instance. (Hey, have you noticed yet that, in Python, variable names are lowercase with underscore, not camel case? Just saying.)

You can also use `auto_now`. If `auto_now` is `True`, the property value is set to the current time whenever the model instance is stored in the datastore, overwriting the property's previous value. This is useful for tracking a last-modified date and time for a model instance. You'll take advantage of this when you create the model to keep track of the last update

Date-time values are stored (and returned) in the UTC time zone.

In your code, you can dynamically add attributes to an entity, ones that are not defined in your model. But when it comes time to save that object, all attributes that aren't declared as properties when it comes time to save the entity to the datastore are ignored.

Adding a method to the model

Listing 13-4 takes things a step further by adding a method to the model. (Notice that, in Python, everything is in a single file — no `.h` and `.m`, in other words.)

Listing 13-4: The to_dict Method

```
def to_dict(self):

    a = {}
    a['id'] = str(self.key().id())
    a['name'] = self.name
    a['description'] = self.description
    a['location'] = self.location
    a['address'] = self.address
    a['destination'] = self.destination
    a['latitude'] = self.coordinate.lat
    a['longitude'] = self.coordinate.lon
    a['updated'] = str(self.updated)

    return a
```

The `to_dict` method returns a point of interest's data as a dictionary. This is similar to a method in `PointOfInterest` in RoadTrip.

```
- (NSDictionary *)returnPointOfInterestData {

  NSDictionary* pointOfInterestData =
    [NSDictionary dictionaryWithObjectsAndKeys:
    self.title, @"Name",
    self.address, @"Address",
    self.location, @"Location",
    self.comment, @"Description",
    [NSNumber numberWithDouble:self.coordinate.latitude],
                                              @"Latitude",
    [NSNumber numberWithDouble:self.coordinate.longitude],
                                             @"Longitude",
    nil];

  return pointOfInterestData;
}
```

In RoadTrip, this method was used to get the data for a `PointOfInterest` (and save it to the file system pre-Core Data) and in fact it serves the same purpose here. When you want to send the `PointOfInterest` data to RoadTrip, you'll use the method for each `PointOfInterest` in the datastore and create an array of these dictionaries.

Using methods such as these means you're creating a representation of the resource (data) to send back to the client.

You start with the method definition:

```
def to_dict(self):
```

Methods are defined using the keyword `def` followed by the *method name.* Method parameters are specified between parentheses following the method name. In Python, you declare `self` as a first parameter of all your methods (there are some nuances here I'm not going to get into) and it works just like `self` in Objective-C — it's a pointer to the object.

The *method body* is enclosed by this method definition on the top. Remember, though, that Python uses whitespace indentation, rather than curly braces or keywords, to delimit blocks (a feature also known as the *off-side rule*). An increase in indentation comes after certain statements; a decrease in indentation signifies the end of the current block.

Methods that are preceded by `@classmethod` are class (rather than instance) methods. This is similar to the class methods you see in Objective-C or static methods in C++.

Class methods are used when a method isn't specific to any particular instance, but still involves the class in some way. A class method receives the class as an implicit first argument.

In Chapter 6, I explain that when you send out data from your web services, you don't want to blindly send out every single attribute of a model to the client — you send out a *representation* of the resource. You want to think of the data you're sending as a response to a service request, not the exposure of a table in a data base that you send to a client and have them do what they want with it. You need to design the service so it delivers the information a client needs — information that may be in the database, or information that you may compute, or even information you compute from aggregated information from other services.

The `to_dict` method is an example of being able to limit the data you return.

Before you start, take a look at an example of the data you'd return if this method were called

```
{
  status: "ok",
  results: [
    {
      updated: "2013-04-09 15:44:32.987245",
      description: "The Grande Dame of museums",
      destination: "0",
      longitude: -73.962383,
      location: "New York City",
      address: "",
      latitude: 40.779012,
      id: "34",
      name: "The Metropolitan Museum of Art"
    }
  ]
}
```

Notice that the address has been left blank — it is not required.

You take this data and create a dictionary that you return with the PointOfInterest data. This dictionary would include the record id (so you can identify a particular point of interest/record and use that id later to update or delete it), name, description, location, address, latitude and longitude (which you get from the coordinate), destination, and the time it was last updated.

This creates an empty dictionary with the identifier of a

```
a = {}
```

You then add the record id (added by App Engine and part of the key), like so:

```
a['id'] = str(self.key().id())
```

This creates dictionary entry with the key of id and a value of key. Each datastore entity has its own key, which uniquely identifies it. The key consists of the entity's type, an identifier (either a key name string or an integer ID), and an optional ancestor path (beyond the scope of this book).

The identifier is assigned when the entity is created. Because it's part of the entity's key, it's associated permanently with the entity and can't be changed. The datastore will automatically assign the entity an integer numeric ID (you'll let that happen here), or you can specify its own key name string for the entity.

You then add the name, description, location, address, and destination by accessing those attributes in the record and using the attribute name as the key.

```
a['name'] = self.name
a['description'] = self.description
a['location'] = self.location
a['address'] = self.address
a['destination'] = self.destination
```

When you add the latitude and longitude, you get those values from the coordinate (which is a GeoPtProperty).

```
a['latitude'] = self.coordinate.lat
a['longitude'] = self.coordinate.lon
```

Finally, you add the following:

```
a['updated'] = str(self.updated)
```

And then you return the dictionary

```
return pointOfInterestData;
```

You defined `updated` as a `DateTimeProperty`. `str()` will convert that value to a string.

Eventually, you're going to return this to a caller (RoadTrip), and because the `NSJSONSerialization` class in the iOS SDK requires everything to be a property list object, you'll be able to include only the following in your response dictionary: dictionaries, arrays, strings, numbers (integer and float), dates, binary data, and Boolean values (with dictionaries and arrays as special types because they are collections and can contain one or multiple data types, including other dictionaries and arrays). Table 13-1 shows the relationship between the Python types and the iOS Foundation framework classes.

Table 13-1 Property List Objects

Abstract Type	*Foundation Framework Class*
Array	NSArray
Dictionary	NSDictionary
String	NSString
Data	NSData
Date	NSDate
Integer	NSNumber (intValue 32-bit), NSNumber (integerValue 64-bit)
Floating-point	NSNumber (floatValue 32-bit), NSNumber (doubleValue 64-bit)
Boolean	NSNumber (boolValue)

Mutable versions of the `Foundation` classes are also supported.

If you're using TextWrangler, you can always check your syntax by choosing #!⇨Check Syntax from the main menu.

Single, double, or triple quotes

In Python, you can use single, double, or triple (triple single or triple double) quotes to identify a string literal. Many Python programmers use double quotes around strings that will be displayed (in a browser for example) and single quotes for program-centric strings, such as a dictionary key. And as I said earlier, triple double quotes are used for `docstrings`.

The TestData Class

Even though I know you can't wait to start adding points of interest to the rtpointsofinterest web service, you'll have to do just that — wait until the Bonus Chapter, available for download from this book's website. But it still would be nice (well, quite necessary, in fact) to be able to have data to test with.

In this section, you create a handler that implements a web service that adds data to the database — one you can use from a browser. This is not the same kind of web service as specified back in Chapter 1 — it's a "developer-only" service that will not only make it possible for you to test your web services, but it also gives me a chance to explain a little more about the datastore and show how web services that use GET methods can be tested in the browser.

Although the Test Hander will implement a GET method, this should not be a GET request at all, because it updates the database. But given what you're using it for and that it's really only a development tool, you can let it slide. It should also be a heads up that you, and only you, decide what a method does, and that I'm leaving it up to you to be disciplined in adopting conventions.

You start by adding a new file to your application.

In TextWrangler, choose File➪New➪Text Document from the main menu or press ⌘+N

Save your new file as testdata_handler.py in the rtpointsofinterest folder. Saving it as a .py file, you'll remember, results in TextWrangler knowing it's a Python file, which means TextWrangler will apply text coloring and enable function navigation. It also means App Engine will recognize the file as a script. Not saving it as a .py file results in the following bit of unpleasantness:

```
ERROR    2013-04-09 21:06:58,202 wsgi.py:189]
Traceback (most recent call last):
...
  File "/Users/neal/Desktop/Cloud Book Final Projects/
           rtpointsofinterest/main.py", line 18, in
           <module>
    from testdata_handler import *
ImportError: No module named testdata_handler
```

Before you add any test data, I want you run your app in GoogleAppEngine-Launcher and then click the SDK Console button in the GoogleAppEngine-Launcher window toolbar. Doing so gives you quite a bit of information, including the fact that there is no data there, as you can see in Figure 13-2.

So next you add some test data, and along the way I show you how to add a new handler, add records to your datastore, and write out to the web page.

Start by adding the code in Listing 13-5 to testdata_handler.py.

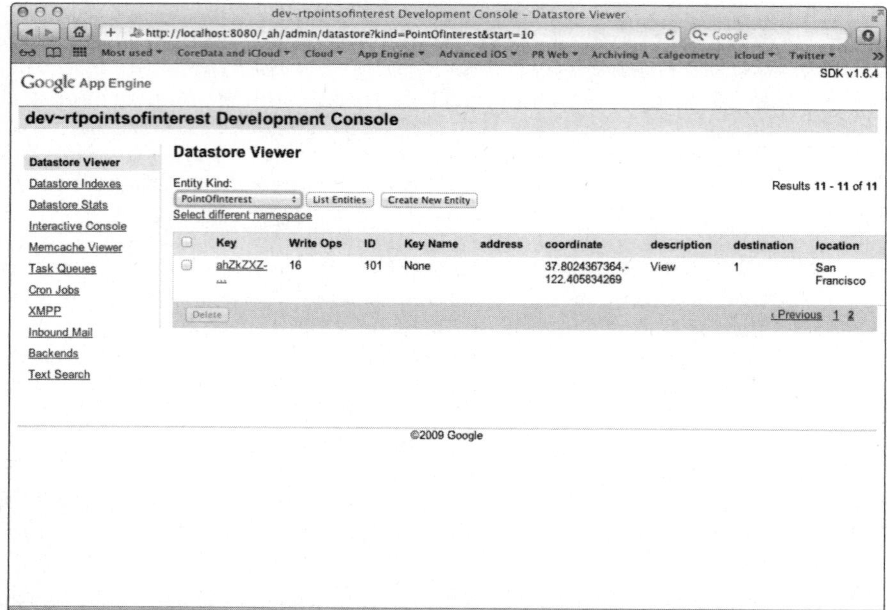

Figure 13-2: Look, Ma, no data!

Listing 13-5: The Test Data Handler

```
"""TestDataHandler class creates test data"""
from google.appengine.ext import webapp
from datamodel import *
import json

class TestDataHandler(webapp.RequestHandler):
    def get(self):
        """Create test data - GET used as a convenience
                                                   for test"""
        db.delete(PointOfInterest.all())

        pointofinterest = PointOfInterest(name='The Statue
                                                  of Liberty',
            description="Pro democracy and anti-monarchy
                                       symbol of freedom",
            location='New York City',
            address='',
            destination='0',
            coordinate=db.GeoPt(lat=40.689244,
                                          lon=-74.044514))
        pointofinterest.put()

        pointofinterest = PointOfInterest(name='Whitney
           Museum of American Art',
            description='American modern and
```

```
                                            contemporary',
        location='New York City',
        address='',
        destination='0',
        coordinate=db.GeoPt(lat=40.773508,
                                    lon=-73.964454))
    pointofinterest.put()

    pointofinterest = PointOfInterest(name='Tenement
                                                Museum',
        description='History comes alive',
        location='New York City',
        address='',
        destination='0',
        coordinate=db.GeoPt(lat=40.719114,
                                    lon=-73.989988))
    pointofinterest.put()


    pointofinterest = PointOfInterest(name='MOMA',
        description='Modern Art',
        location='New York City',
        address='',
        destination='0',
        coordinate=db.GeoPt(lat=40.760669,
                                    lon=-73.976269))
    pointofinterest.put()


    pointofinterest = PointOfInterest(name='Solomon R.
                                  Guggenheim Museum',
        description='A Frank Lloyd Wright building',
        location='New York City',
        address='',
        destination='0',
        coordinate=db.GeoPt(lat=40.782946,
                                    lon=-73.95891))
    pointofinterest.put()


    pointofinterest = PointOfInterest(name='The
                        Metropolitan Museum of Art',
        description='The Grande Dame of museums',
        location='New York City',
        address='',
        destination='0',
        coordinate=db.GeoPt(lat=40.779012,
                                  lon=-73.962383))
    pointofinterest.put()


    pointofinterest = PointOfInterest(name='Golden
```

(continued)

Listing 13-5 ***(continued)***

```
                                                    Gate Bridge',
          description='San Francisco landmark',
          location='San Francisco',
          address='',
          destination='1',
          coordinate=db.GeoPt(lat=37.819722,
                                          lon=-122.478611))
      pointofinterest.put()

      pointofinterest = PointOfInterest(name='San
        Francisco Museum of Modern Art',
          description='Modern Art',
          location='San Francisco',
          address='',
          destination='1',
          coordinate=db.GeoPt(lat=37.785679,
                                           lon=-122.401157))
      pointofinterest.put()

      pointofinterest = PointOfInterest(name='deYoung
                                                   Museum',
          description='Interesting varied collection',
          location='San Francisco',
          address='',
          destination='1',
          coordinate=db.GeoPt(lat=37.771325,
                                            lon=-122.46885))
      pointofinterest.put()

      pointofinterest = PointOfInterest(name='Legion of
                                                    Honor',
          description='Interesting varied collection',
          location='San Francisco',
          address='',
          destination='1',
          coordinate=db.GeoPt(lat=37.784773,
                                           lon=-122.500324))
      pointofinterest.put()

      self.response.out.write('<pre>')
      self.response.out.write("Test data, with %d
          points of interest:" %
                    (PointOfInterest.all().count()))

      self.response.out.write("\n")
      for pointofinterest in PointOfInterest.all():
          self.response.out.write(pointofinterest.name +
             " Added: " + str(pointofinterest.updated) +
             " id = " + str(pointofinterest.key().id())
                                                    +'\n')
      self.response.out.write('</pre>')
```

The `import` statements here are similar in result to the `#import` in Objective-C. `from datamodel import *` imports the `datamodel`, and you can then refer to things defined in the `datamodel` (such as the `PointOfInterest` class and its attributes).

Moving a bit further down Listing 13-5, you see the following:

```
db.delete(PointOfInterest.all())
```

`db.delete` is a `Model` class *instance* method that deletes an entity from the datastore. `all()` is a `Model` class *class* method that returns a `Query` object that represents all of the entities for this model in the datastore — all the points of interest, in other words. (You want to start out with a clean slate here.)

Next, you create a `PointOfInterest` instance by using a `Model` class constructor specifying the initial values for the instance's properties as keyword arguments.

```
pointofinterest = PointOfInterest(name=
                  'The Statue of Liberty',
                  description='Pro democracy and anti-
                               monarchy symbol of freedom',
                  location='New York City',
                  address='',
                  destination='0',
                  coordinate=db.GeoPt(
                    lat=40.689244, lon=-74.044514))
```

Each keyword corresponds to an attribute defined in the `Model` class. If the value is required (`name`, for example), and you don't supply it, you'll get an error like the one you saw in "The webapp model classes" section, earlier in the chapter.

Be aware that, because indentation is so important in Python, I do my best within the confines of the book page width to make things clear. Just be aware that if a string literal spreads out over to two lines, for example:

```
description='Pro democracy and anti-
                              monarchy symbol of freedom',
```

you should keep them on one line.

Next you add the instance to the datastore:

```
pointofinterest.put()
```

`put()` is a `Model` instance method that adds the `Model` instance to the datastore as an entity. If you're creating the instance (as you are here), this method creates a new data entity in the datastore. Otherwise, it updates the data entity with the current property values.

Finally, you write out the response:

```
self.response.out.write('<pre>')
self.response.out.write("Test data, with %d points of \
  interest:" % (PointOfInterest.all().count()))
self.response.out.write("\n")
for pointofinterest in PointOfInterest.all():
    self.response.out.write(pointofinterest.name +
              " Added: " + str(pointofinterest.updated) +
              " id = " + str(pointofinterest.key().id())
              +'\n')
```

`<pre>` is an HTML opening tag of the `pre` element that defines preformatted text — text which is usually displayed in fixed-width font (Courier is the standard) and preserves both spaces and line breaks. It's generally used for computer code.

As I say in Chapter 12, the handler is initialized with both a `Request` and a `Response` object. The `Response` class object has an instance variable `out` which is an instance of the `StringIO` class that that reads and writes a string buffer. The following lines of code allow you to write to a browser:

```
self.response.out.write("Test data, with %d points of \
  interest:" % (PointOfInterest.all().count()))
```

`String` objects have one unique built-in operation: The `%` operator (modulo), which is also known as the string formatting or interpolation operator. The *conversion specifier* — in this case, `%d` for *signed integer decimal* — is replaced with the value(s) that follow the string formatting operator. It works similarly to the way string formatting in `NSString` and `NSLog` does in iOS.

Remember that `all()` is a Model *class* class method and that it returns a `Query` object that represents *all* of the entities for this model in the datastore — every stinking one. The contents of this object are sent as the body of the response when the request handler method returns. `write` is an instance method that actually does the write.

When the handler method exits, the application uses the value of `self.response` as the HTTP response.

`count()` is a `Query` method that returns the number of results in this query. It is somewhat faster than retrieving all of the data, but the amount of time still grows with the size of the result set.

The `for-in` statement in Python iterates over the items of any sequence (a list or a string) in the order that they appear in the sequence.

It is not safe to modify the sequence being iterated over in the loop. If you need to modify the list, you must iterate over a copy.

Finally, to be able to request this service from `rtpointsofinterest`, add the bolded code in Listing 13-6 to `main.py`.

Listing 13-6: Updating main.py

```
import webapp2
from testdata_handler import *

class MainHandler(webapp2.RequestHandler):
  def get(self):
    #self.response.out.write('Hello world!')
    self.response.out.write("<html><body>")
    self.response.out.write("<p>Hello Mr Bill!</p>")
    self.response.out.write("</body></html>")


app = webapp2.WSGIApplication([('/', MainHandler),
           ('/testdata', TestDataHandler)],
           debug=True)
```

As I explain in Chapter 11, when your webapp application receives a request, it creates an instance of the `RequestHandler` class associated with the URL path in the request. To ensure that the right class gets called, you need to add the request handler to `main.py` and map it to the URL. webapp then calls a method that corresponds with the HTTP action of the request, such as the `get()` method for a HTTP `GET` request.

The statement `from testdata_handler import *` imports the module in the `test_handler` file you just created.

The addition to the webapp2WSGIApplication constructor — `('/test-data', TestDataHandler)` — tells App Engine that if you ever get a request that ends in `testdata`, you need to run the `TestDataHandler` script (which is now accessible because you imported the `testdata_han-dler` file in which the script resides).

Testing in Your Browser

Now that you have your stuff together, you can make the request in your browser. Back in Chapter 6, when I demonstrated the Geocode web service, I had you enter the following:

```
http://maps.googleapis.com/maps/api/geocode/json
   ?sensor=false&address=1 Infinite Drive, Cupertino, CA&
```

To add the test data, enter this URL in your browser:

```
http://localhost:8080/testdata
```

Doing so brings up what you see Figure 13-3.

Now click the SDK Console button in the GoogleAppEngineLauncher window toolbar again, and you can see lots of nice data, as demonstrated in Figure 13-4.

Now that you have some data to work with, you can start implementing the web services you specified in Chapter 10 in `rtpointsofinterest` and make those requests in RoadTrip. And you'll do that in the next chapter.

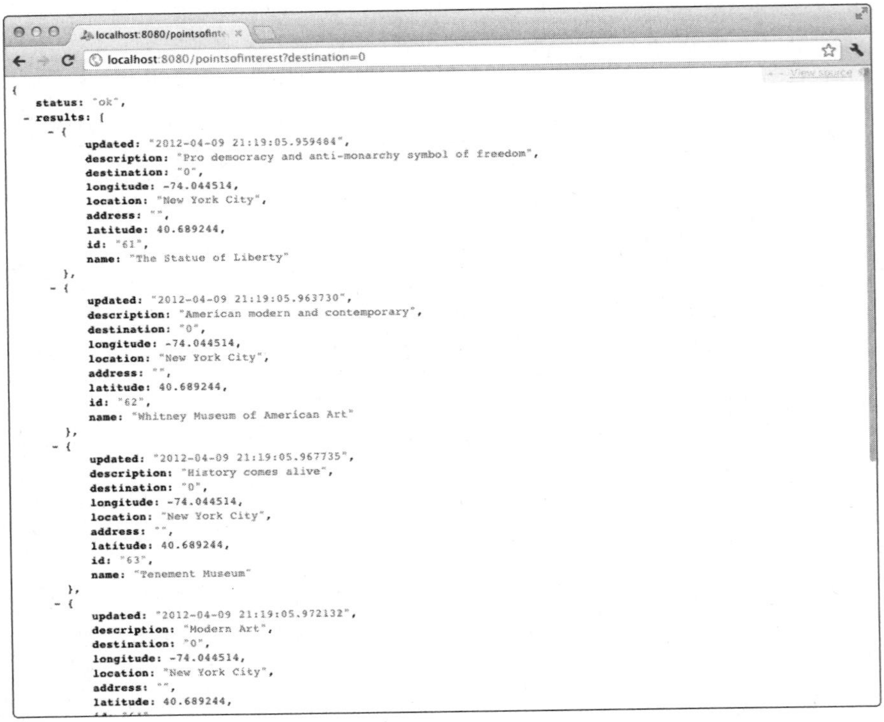

localhost:8080/pointsofinte

localhost:8080/pointsofinterest?destination=0

{
  status: "ok",
 - results: [
   - {
       updated: "2012-04-09 21:19:05.959484",
       description: "Pro democracy and anti-monarchy symbol of freedom",
       destination: "0",
       longitude: -74.044514,
       location: "New York City",
       address: "",
       latitude: 40.689244,
       id: "61",
       name: "The Statue of Liberty"
     },
   - {
       updated: "2012-04-09 21:19:05.963730",
       description: "American modern and contemporary",
       destination: "0",
       longitude: -74.044514,
       location: "New York City",
       address: "",
       latitude: 40.689244,
       id: "62",
       name: "Whitney Museum of American Art"
     },
   - {
       updated: "2012-04-09 21:19:05.967735",
       description: "History comes alive",
       destination: "0",
       longitude: -74.044514,
       location: "New York City",
       address: "",
       latitude: 40.689244,
       id: "63",
       name: "Tenement Museum"
     },
   - {
       updated: "2012-04-09 21:19:05.972132",
       description: "Modern Art",
       destination: "0",
       longitude: -74.044514,
       location: "New York City",
       address: "",
       latitude: 40.689244,

Figure 13-3: Executing the web service request in the browser.

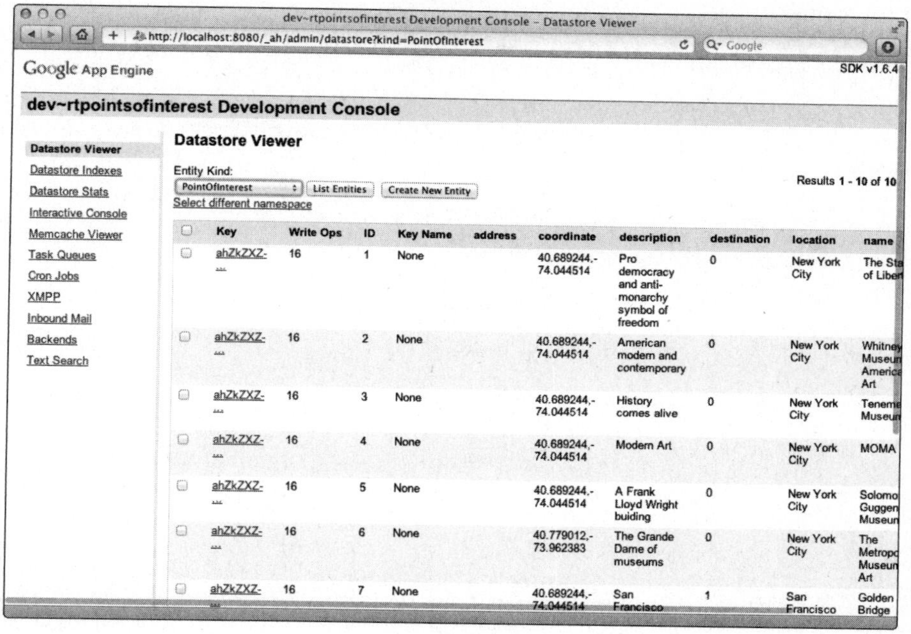

Figure 13-4: Lots of places to see.

Chapter 14

Creating and Using the pointsofinterest Web Service

In This Chapter

- Creating the pointsofinterest web service
- Modifying RoadTrip to use the pointsofinterest web service
- Downloading points of interest only when necessary
- Making sure the points of interest are current

Chapter 13 is all about getting your data model ready to go. In this chapter, you tackle one of the main `rtpointsofinterest` web services — `pointsofinterest` — and then go on to develop the `lastupdate` web service, which will keep RoadTrip from having to do unnecessary downloads.

Oh, and by the way, you'll modify RoadTrip to use both of these web services as well.

The pointsofinterest Web Service

You're finally going to get to return some data to the app, and as you might expect, you're going to add a new handler to the app you created using App Engine.

To do that, first add a new file to your application. In TextWrangler, choose File⇨New⇨Text Document from the main menu or press ⌘+N.

Save the new file as `pointsofinterest_handler.py` in the `rtpointsofinterest` (or your app's) folder.

You're going to see some strange line breaks in my upcoming listings because an entire line of code won't always fit on the page. In your listings, you should always place string literals on one line. Remember that Python is sensitive to indents, so be careful about breaking statements.

As I explain in Chapter 11, when your webapp application receives a request, it creates an instance of the RequestHandler class associated with the URL path in the request. To get the right class called, you add the request handler to main and map it to the URL, as you did with TestHandler in Chapter 13. webapp then calls a method that corresponds with the HTTP action of the request — the get() method for a HTTP GET request, for example. The method processes the request, prepares a response, and then returns. Finally, the application sends the response to the client.

It's time now to start adding the necessary code to main.py so your web service will be able to do all that.

First step: Add the bolded code in Listing 14-1 to main.py.

Listing 14-1: Updating main.py

```
import webapp2
from testdata_handler import *
from pointsofinterest_handler import *


class MainHandler(webapp2.RequestHandler):
    def get(self):
            # self.response.out.write('Hello world!')
        self.response.out.write("<html><body>")
        self.response.out.write("<p>Hello Mr Bill!</p>")
        self.response.out.write("</body></html>")

app = webapp2.WSGIApplication([('/', MainHandler),
        ('/testdata', TestDataHandler),
        ('/pointsofinterest', PointsOfInterestHandler)],
          debug=True)
```

TestHandler gets treated the exact same way in Chapter 12.

But before you add the PointsOfInterestHandler class to your rtpointsofinterest, you have to do some prep work.

One of the requirements you have for clients of your web services is that they have an API key and include a (required) parameter in the query string. Because that is required for all web service requests, you don't want to have to duplicate the code to check it in every handler. Instead, you'll create a new class — AccessHandler (derived from RequestHandler). That new class will include a method — the validate() method — that will validate the API key. Then you'll derive all of your classes for AccessHandler and simply call the validate() method to do the key validation.

As usual, start by adding a new file to your application. In TextWrangler, choose File⇨New⇨Text Document from the main menu or press ⌘+N.

Save the new file as `access_handler.py` in the `rtpointsofinterest` (or your app's) folder.

Now add the code in Listing 14-2 to `access_handler.py`.

Listing 14-2: The AccessHandler

```
"""Check for an api key to allow access"""
from google.appengine.ext import webapp
from datamodel import *

class AccessHandler(webapp.RequestHandler):

    keys = ['test123', 'test456']

    def validate(self):
            key = self.request.get('key')

            if (not key):
                raise Exception ("missing key")
            try:
                i = AccessHandler.keys.index(key)
            except Exception, ex:
                raise Exception ("invalid key: " + key)
```

Going through the listing, you can see that you first define the class:

```
AccessHandler(webapp.RequestHandler):
```

and then define an instance variable `keys`:

```
keys = ['test123', 'test456']
```

The line of code above defines what is known in Python as a list — an *array*, in Objective-C terms — with two string elements, `test123` and `test456`.

Of course, in a production app you might have this list in the datastore or even access it using a web service.

Then you define your first method:

```
def validate(self):
```

The first thing you do here is get the `key` parameter from the request.

As you recall, the request is passed on to the request handler to process. An instance of the `Request` class contains information about an incoming web request. You can access all the information in the request using the `request` object.

key = self.request.get('key')

This returns the value of the query (URL) or `POST` argument with the given name — `key`. If multiple arguments have the same name, the first argument's value is returned.

If the value's not there, you raise an exception:

```
if (not key):
     raise Exception ("missing key")
```

The `if` statement in Python is similar to those in other languages, differing from the Objective-C version only by the use of a colon (`:`), for example. There can be additional `elif` parts (short for *else if*) with an optional `else` part. An `if...elif...elif...` sequence is used instead of the `switch` or `case` statements found in other languages.

The `raise` statement allows you to force a specified exception to occur, with the only argument to `raise` being an indication of the exception to be raised. This argument must be either an exception instance or an exception class (a class that derives from `Exception`). In this case, you use base exception — `Exception` — by initializing an `Exception` object with the text corresponding to the error (`missing key`).

Raising an exception here will result in a return to the caller, and as you'll soon see, this exception will be handled by its exception handler.

Next you create a `try` block and use the `index` method to see whether the key is in your list of keys:

```
try:
     i = AccessHandler.keys.index(key)
```

Like many other programming languages, Python uses `try...except` blocks to handle exceptions and `raise` to generate them.

The handler continues executing at the beginning of the `try` clause (the statement[s] between the `try` and `except` keywords). If no exception occurs, the `except` clause is skipped, and execution of the `try` statement is finished.

If an exception occurs during execution of the `try` clause, the rest of the clause is skipped. Then, if its type matches the exception named after the `except` keyword, the `except` clause is executed, and execution continues after the `try` statement.

So look at the first (and last) statement in the `try` clause:

```
i = AccessHandler.keys.index(key)
```

The list's `index` method returns the index in the list of the first item whose value is `key`. It will raise an exception if there is no item (that is, if the key passed in cannot be found in the list of keys).

In that case, the `except` clause is executed because the type specified — `Exception` — is the base class for all exceptions:

```
except Exception, ex:
    raise Exception ("invalid key: " + key)
```

In this case, you ignore the exception raised by the `index` method and you raise your own exception — `invalid key` — which will be handled by the caller.

Now you'll add a new file to your application. In TextWrangler, choose File➪New➪Text Document from the main menu or press ⌘+N. Name the new file `pointsofinterest_handler.py` and add the code in Listing 14-3 to it.

Listing 14-3: The PointsOfInterestHandler

```
"""Return all the points of interest for a destination"""
from google.appengine.ext import webapp
from datamodel import *
import json
import logging
from access_handler import *

#class PointsOfInterestHandler(webapp.RequestHandler):
class PointsOfInterestHandler(AccessHandler):

    def get(self):

        data = {}

        try:
            self.validate()
            destination = self.request.get('destination')
            if (destination):
                data['status']="ok"
                pointsofinterest = []
                query = PointOfInterest.all()
                logging.info ("Returning  points of 
           interest for destination: %s" % (destination))
                query.filter('destination = ', 
           destination)
                for pointofinterest in query:
                    pointsofinterest.append(
                                pointofinterest.to_dict())
                data['results'] = pointsofinterest

            else:
```

(continued)

Listing 14-3 *(continued)*

```
            raise Exception("missing destination")
        except Exception,  ex:
            data['status'] = "error"
            data['status_text'] = "exception: %s" % (ex)

        self.response.headers['Content-Type'] =
                                        'application/json'
        self.response.out.write(json.dumps(data))
```

You can see that I've added two new `import` statements here. The first one — `import json` — is used to import a built-in module. (I explain more about JSON as I explain the code.)

As for the second `import` statement — `import logging` — this lets you take advantage of the fact that Google App Engine uses the Python logging module to allow you to log events that take place in your application.

You can see log statements in the GoogleAppEngineLauncher Logging console by clicking the Logs button on the toolbar in the GoogleAppEngineLauncher window. When your app is actually running in App Engine, you can see log statements in the Administration Console. More on that in Chapter 15.

The logging module provides a lot of functionality and flexibility (check it out on your own). This line of code for example,

```
logging.info ("Returning points of interest for
     destination: %s" % destination)
```

simply logs a message (with level INFO) on the Logs window.

Next, you define the `PointsOfInterestHandler` class as well as the first method (`get`):

```
class PointsOfInterestHandler(webapp.RequestHandler):

    def get(self):
```

You start by creating a dictionary to hold the data:

```
data = {}
```

This line creates a dictionary in Python, similar to an iOS `NSDictionary`.

Dictionaries are sometimes found in other languages as *associative memories* or *associative arrays*. Unlike sequences, which are indexed by a range of numbers, dictionaries are indexed by keys, which can be any immutable type; strings and numbers can always be keys.

As in `NSDictionary`, a dictionary in Python is an unordered set of key value pairs, with each key unique within that dictionary. As you saw, a pair of braces creates an empty dictionary: `{}`. Although placing a comma-separated list of `key:value` pairs within the braces adds initial `key:value` pairs to the dictionary, you'll do it by adding the pairs programmatically.

The main operations on a dictionary are storing a value with some key and extracting the value given the key. It's also possible to delete a `key:value` pair with `del`. If you store a new value using a key that is already in use, the old value is overwritten. Unlike in `NSDictionary`, if you try to use a non-existent key, you will get an exception.

Next, you'll see a `try` statement that starts a `try...except` block.

You call the (super class's) `validate()` method:

```
self.validate()
```

If there are any exceptions, the rest of the `try` clause is skipped. I'll explain what happens then after I go through the rest of the `try` clause.

You then get the `destination` from the request:

```
destination = self.request.get('destination')
```

You check to see if there is a `destination` present:

```
if (destination):
```

If the `destination` is not present, you raise an exception:

```
else:
    raise Exception("missing destination")
```

I explain the mechanics of the exception after I go through the rest of the `try` clause.

If there is a `destination`, you add a key to the `data` dictionary (no relation here to metadata in a database management system):

```
data['status']="ok"
```

`"ok"` corresponds to the status you specified that the `pointsofinterest` web service would return in Chapter 10. If you're not successful, you change this later.

You then create an empty array:

```
pointsofinterest = []
```

and get all the PointsOfInterest entities in the datastore:

```
query = PointOfInterest.all()
```

all() is a Model class method that returns a Query object that represents all entities for the kind corresponding to a model — in this case, PointOfInterest. As you'll see, there are Query object methods you can use to filter and specify sort orders to the query before the query is executed.

An application creates a Query object by calling either the Model class's all() class method or the Query constructor (query = db.Query(User)).

If you want to return only a single entity matching your query, you can use the query method get(). This query method will return the first result that matches the query.

```
u = q.get()
```

Next, I log the destination — just to show you how this works.

```
logging.info ("Returning points of interest for
                              destination: %s" % destination)
```

If you were to check out the Logs window, you'd see the following:

```
INFO      2012-04-17 15:06:40,243
                              pointsofinterest_handler.py:18]
Returning points of interest for destination: 0
```

Next, I apply a destination filter to the query:

```
query.filter('destination = ', destination)
```

Here I filter the query according to the destination specified in the web service query string.

Then I add each PointOfInterest in the filtered query to the pointsofinterest array I created:

```
for poi in query:
    pointsofinterest.append(poi.to_dict())
```

append() is an array method that adds to the array. to_dict() is the method you added to the PointOfInterest model in Chapter 13 that returns the point-of-interest data in a dictionary. To refresh your memory,

```
def to_dict(self):
    """Return the PointOfInterest data in a dictionary"""

    a = {}
    a['id'] = str(self.key().id())
    a['name'] = self.name
    a['description'] = self.description
    a['location'] = self.location
    a['address'] = self.address
    a['destination'] = self.destination
    a['latitude'] = self.coordinate.lat
    a['longitude'] = self.coordinate.lon
    a['updated'] = str(self.updated)

    return a
```

With that out of the way, you then add the array of point-of-interest dictionaries to the Results dictionary with a key of `results` (as you specified in Chapter 11).

Now to the `except` clause, as promised.

When you raise an exception, the rest of the `try` clause is skipped and you go immediately to the `except` clause. This would also happen if the exception was raised in the `validate()` method.

There are three exceptions that could have been raised that would lead to you ending up in the `except` clause.

The first two were in the `validate()` method:

```
missing key
invalid key
```

and the third was in the `get()` method:

```
missing destination
```

The `except` clause will be executed if its type matches the exception named after the `except` keyword; here, the type `Exception` is the base class for all exceptions:

```
except Exception,  ex:
   data['status'] = 'error'
   data['status_text'] = 'exception: %s' % ex
```

The code in the `except` clause has access to the exception you raised — `ex`.

You set the `status` key in the `data` dictionary to `error` and add the `status_text` key with whatever the value of the exception is:

```
'exception: %s' % ex'
```

One example of exception text you would have created the exception with is `raise Exception ("missing destination")`.

Execution continues after the `try...except` block.

You set the content type of the response to JSON:

```
self.response.headers['Content-Type'] = "application/json"
```

and then return the response (in JSON format, of course):

```
self.response.out.write(json.dumps(data))
```

This serializes the object as a JSON-formatted stream.

Now if you were to enter the following in Safari, you'd see what you see in Figure 14-1.

```
http://localhost:8080/pointsofinterest?destination=0&
                                                   key=test123
```

In Chrome, you'd be greeted by what you see in Figure 14-2.

If you omitted the `destination` parameter when you called this from your browser, what you would see is

```
{"status": "error", "status_text": "missing destination"}
```

in Safari or

```
{
    status: "error",
    status_text: "exception: missing destination"
}
```

in Chrome.

The Datastore API provides two interfaces for queries: a Query Object interface (which you just used), and a SQL-like query language called GQL, suitable for querying the App Engine datastore. For a complete discussion of the GQL syntax and features, see the GQL Reference in App Engine. In this example, you'll be using the `Query` class.

http://localhost:8080/pointsofinterest?destination=0

{"status": "ok", "results": [{"updated": "2012-04-17 16:19:54.182077", "description": "Pro democracy and anti-monarchy
symbol of freedom", "destination": "0", "longitude": -74.044514, "location": "New York City", "address": "", "latitude":
40.689244, "id": "11", "name": "The Statue of Liberty"}, {"updated": "2012-04-17 16:19:54.184508", "description":
"American modern and contemporary", "destination": "0", "longitude": -73.964454, "location": "New York City", "address":
"", "latitude": 40.773508, "id": "12", "name": "Whitney Museum of American Art"}, {"updated": "2012-04-17
16:19:54.186590", "description": "History comes alive", "destination": "0", "longitude": -73.989988, "location": "New
York City", "address": "", "latitude": 40.719114, "id": "13", "name": "Tenement Museum"}, {"updated": "2012-04-17
16:19:54.188550", "description": "Modern Art", "destination": "0", "longitude": -73.976269, "location": "New York City",
"address": "", "latitude": 40.760669, "id": "14", "name": "MOMA"}, {"updated": "2012-04-17 16:19:54.190723",
"description": "A Frank Lloyd Wright buiding", "destination": "0", "longitude": -73.95891, "location": "New York City",
"address": "", "latitude": 40.782946, "id": "15", "name": "Solomon R. Guggenheim Museum"}, {"updated": "2012-04-17
16:19:54.193703", "description": "The Grande Dame of museums", "destination": "0", "longitude": -73.962383, "location":
"New York City", "address": "", "latitude": 40.779012, "id": "16", "name": "The Metropolitan Museum of Art"}]}

Figure 14-1: Safari output for the allpointsofinterest web service.

localhost:8080/pointsofinterest?destination=0

{
  status: "ok",
- results: [
  - {
      updated: "2012-04-17 16:19:54.182077",
      description: "Pro democracy and anti-monarchy symbol of freedom",
      destination: "0",
      longitude: -74.044514,
      location: "New York City",
      address: "",
      latitude: 40.689244,
      id: "11",
      name: "The Statue of Liberty"
    },
  - {
      updated: "2012-04-17 16:19:54.184508",
      description: "American modern and contemporary",
      destination: "0",
      longitude: -73.964454,
      location: "New York City",
      address: "",
      latitude: 40.773508,
      id: "12",
      name: "Whitney Museum of American Art"
    },
  - {
      updated: "2012-04-17 16:19:54.186590",
      description: "History comes alive",
      destination: "0",
      longitude: -73.989988,
      location: "New York City",
      address: "",
      latitude: 40.719114,
      id: "13",
      name: "Tenement Museum"
    },
  - {
      updated: "2012-04-17 16:19:54.188550",
      description: "Modern Art",
      destination: "0",

Figure 14-2: Chrome formatted output.

As you can see, these requests handlers can be tested by entering a URL in the browser. You can do that for `GET` requests like `pointsofinterest` but unfortunately not for `POST` requests like the ones you'll add in the Bonus Chapter, available for download from this book's website.

Updating RoadTrip

Now that you have an honest-to-goodness callable web service, you can update RoadTrip to use the web service rather than the `Destination.plist` to get the points of interest to display to the user. You'll do this in a method, `loadPointsOfInterestFromWebService`, which will replace the existing `loadPointsOfInterest` method — the one that loads the points of interest from the `Destinations.plist` and makes them available to the `PointsOfInterestController` to display in its view.

Until you upload your app to App Engine, the code you're about to enter will work only in the Simulator. That's one of the reasons I had you surround the iCloud code with `#if` in Chapter 5 — so you could still run RoadTrip in the Simulator.

Go ahead and start with the `WSManager`. I've dropped hints now and then that one of my goals for this book is to give you some patterns that you can reuse in your own apps.

In Chapter 10, I showed you that, with `WSLoader` in your pocket, you had a pattern you could use to enable any app to use a new web service. The process could be summarized as follows:

1. Add a method to `WSManager` that makes the request for a given HTTP method (`GET`, `DELETE`, `POST`, etc.).
2. Add a method to `WSManager` to set up the request if there are parameters common to a set of web services.
3. Add a method to `WSManager` to create the `NSURLRequest` for a given HTTP method (`GET`, `DELETE`, `POST`, etc.).
4. Add a method to `YourModel` to make the request to the `WSManager` for the web service.
5. Add a method to `YourModel` that processes the JSON response (returning it in a dictionary) and checks for errors.

You'll implement that process now using the following specific methods:

1. The `pointsOfInterestGETWebService:userParams:successBlock:failureBlock:` method in `WSManager`
2. The `setupPointsOfInterestWebService` method in `WSManager`
3. The existing `createGETRequest:withParams:` method in `WSManager`
4. The `loadPointsOfInterestFromWebService` method in `RTModel`
5. The `createPointsOfInterestResponseDictionary` method in `RTModel`

Setting up the WSManager methods to make the request and do the setup

Start by updating `WSManager.h` in RoadTrip with the new service request — `pointsOfInterestGETWebService:userParams:successBlock:fail` ureBlock: by adding the bolded code in Listing 14-4. As I explain in Chapter 10, I make this a generic rtpointsofinterest web service request by using the service parameter, which allows me to specify which rtpointsofinterest web service I want.

Listing 14-4: Adding the pointsOfInterestGETWebService Declaration

```
@interface WSManager : NSObject

- (void)geocodeSynchronouslyXML:(NSMutableDictionary *)
          userParams successBlock:(void (^)(NSDictionary
          *))success failureBlock:(void (^)())failure;
- (void)geocodeAsynchronouslyXML:(NSMutableDictionary *)
          userParams successBlock:(void (^)(NSDictionary
          *))success failureBlock:(void (^)())failure;
- (void)geocodeAsynchronouslyJSON:(NSMutableDictionary *)
          userParams successBlock:(void (^)(NSDictionary
          *))success failureBlock:(void (^)())failure;
- (void)pointsOfInterestGETWebService:(NSString*)service
          userParams:(NSMutableDictionary *)userParams
          successBlock:(void (^)(NSDictionary *))success
          failureBlock:(void (^)())failure;
@end
```

Next, you'll add the declaration for the setupPointsOfInterestWebService; by adding the bolded code in Listing 14-5 to WSManager.m.

Listing 14-5: Adding setupPointsOfInterestWebService declaration

```
@interface WSManager () {

  void (^returnSuccess)(NSDictionary *);
  void (^returnFail)();
  NSString *webService;
  NSMutableDictionary *params;
}
- (void)setupGeocodingWebService;
- (NSMutableURLRequest *)createGETRequest:(NSString *)
          baseURL withParams:(NSDictionary *)userParams;
- (void)requestSynchronousWebService:
                    (NSMutableURLRequest *)request;
- (void)requestAsynchronousWebService:
                    (NSMutableURLRequest *)request;
- (void)setupPointsOfInterestWebService;
@end
```

Now add the actual setupPointsOfInterestWebService method in Listing 14-6 to WSManager.m.

Listing 14-6: Setting Up the Web Service Request

```
- (void)setupPointsOfInterestWebService {

  params = [[NSMutableDictionary alloc] init];
  [params setValue:kAppID forKey:@"key"];
}
```

Notice that this particular method allocates the `params` dictionary and adds a `kAppID` (a constant that defines your app ID) with a key of `key` (the required parameter name). Keep in mind that this is a required parameter for *all* `rtpointsofinterest` web services.

You're going to be adding the main method — `pointsOfInterestGETWebService:userParams:successBlock:failureBlock:` — in a second by adding the code in Listing 14-9 to `WSManager.m`.

Before you do that, though, you need to add the `kAppID` constant you use in Listing 14-6 and another constant — `BASE_URL`, which you'll use in the method that the `RTModel` needs to make the web service request — to the `RTDefines.h` file. So, go ahead and add the bolded code in Listing 14-7 to `RTDefines.h`.

Listing 14-7: Updating RTDefines.h

```
#define kDestinationPreferenceKey
          @"DestinationPreferenceKey"
#define kTrackLocationPreference
          @"trackLocationPreference"
#define kDestinationCell @"DestinationCell"
#define kItineraryCell @"ItineraryCell"
#define kPointOfInterestCell @"PointOfInterestCell"

#define kAccelerometerFrequency 25
#define kFilteringFactor .1
#define kAccelerationThreshold 2.0
#define kMetersToMiles 1609.344

#define RESPONSE_STATUS  @"status"
#define RESPONSE_STATUS_TEXT  @"status_text"
#define RESPONSE_STATUS_OK  @"ok"

#define kAppID @"test123"

#if !TARGET_IPHONE_SIMULATOR
#define BASE_URL @"https://rtpointsofinterest.appspot.
          com/"
#else
#define BASE_URL @"http://localhost:8080/"

#endif
```

The kAppID defines an app ID that will allow you to access the web service (an ID that you have in the keys list in the AccessHandler validate() method).

You also add BASE_URL, which provides the base URL to use for the web service request. In fact, you'll specify two. When you deploy rtpointsofinterest to the cloud, it will look like:

```
https://rtpointsofinterest.appspot.com/
```

But as I explain in Chapter 12, you'll need to name your application something other than rtpointsofinterest so you'll replace that rtpointsofinterest with whatever you entered in the Application Identifier field when you created your Application on the Google App Engine website.

During the development process, however, you'll use a simulator, and that base URL will be localhost.

Next, you need to import RTDefines.h into WSManager.m. To do that, add the bolded code in Listing 14-8 to WSManager.m.

Listing 14-8: Adding the Import Statement

```
#import "WSManager.h"
#import "WSLoader.h"
#import "RTDefines.h"

@interface WSManager () {
```

Now you're set to add the new message to WSManager to request the pointsofinterest web service. Add the method in Listing 14-9 to WSManager.m.

Listing 14-9: Calling the pointsofinterest Web Service

```
- (void)pointsOfInterestGETWebService:(NSString*)service
          userParams:(NSMutableDictionary *)userParams
          successBlock:(void (^)(NSDictionary *))success
          failureBlock:(void (^)())failure {

  [self setupPointsOfInterestWebService];
  returnSuccess = success;
  returnFail = failure;
  webService = [NSString stringWithFormat:@"%@%@?",
                                     BASE_URL, service];
  [params addEntriesFromDictionary:userParams];
  NSMutableURLRequest *request = [self
          createGETRequest:webService withParams:params];
  [request setCachePolicy:
   NSURLRequestReloadIgnoringLocalCacheData];
  [request setTimeoutInterval:60];
  [self requestAsynchronousWebService:request];
}
```

Adding the RTModel methods to make the request and process the JSON response

As I mention in Chapter 10, you're going to use a model method to make the request and process the response.

So go ahead and add the bolded code in Listing 14-10 to `RTModel.m` so you can declare my brand-spanking new method `loadPointsOfInterest-FromWebService` that will use the new `pointsofinterest` web service. The added code also declares the `createPointsOfInterestResponse-Dictionary:` method that will do the common work for all the users of a `rtpointofinterest` web service.

Listing 14-10: Adding loadPointsOfInterestFromWebService and createPoint-sOfInterestResponseDictionary: to RTModel.m

```
@interface RTModel () {
…
}
@property (readonly, strong, nonatomic) NSFetchRequest
           *sharedPointOfInterestFetchRequest;
- (void)geocodeSynchronouslyXML:(NSString *)findLocation;
- (void)geocodeAsynchronouslyXML:(NSString *)findLocation;
- (void)geocodeAsynchronouslyJSON:
                                 (NSString *)findLocation;
- (void)loadPointsOfInterestFromWebService;
- (NSDictionary *)
   createPointsOfInterestResponseDictionary:
                                 (NSDictionary *)response;
@end
```

Next, add the code in Listing 14-11 to `RTModel.m` so you can implement `createPointsOfInterestResponseDictionary:`.

Listing 14-11: createPointsOfInterestResponseDictionary

```
- (NSDictionary *)
     createPointsOfInterestResponseDictionary:
                               (NSDictionary *)response {

  data = [response objectForKey:@" response"];
  responseStr = [[NSString alloc] initWithData:data
                        encoding: NSUTF8StringEncoding];

  NSError *error = nil;
  NSDictionary *responseDict =
    [NSJSONSerialization JSONObjectWithData:data options:
           NSJSONReadingMutableContainers error:&error];
```

```
  if (error != nil) {
    UIAlertView *alert = [[UIAlertView alloc]
      initWithTitle:
        @"Your request could not be carried out"
       message:@"There is a problem with the data returned
                                    from the server"
       delegate:nil cancelButtonTitle:@"OK"
       otherButtonTitles:nil];
    [alert show];
    return nil;
  }
  else {
    NSString *statusCode =
               [responseDict valueForKey:RESPONSE_STATUS];
    if (![RESPONSE_STATUS_OK
       caseInsensitiveCompare:statusCode] ==
                                       NSOrderedSame) {
      NSString* errorMessage;
      NSString *error =
          [responseDict valueForKey:RESPONSE_STATUS_TEXT];
      NSString *trimmedError =
         [error stringByTrimmingCharactersInSet:
           [NSCharacterSet
                 whitespaceAndNewlineCharacterSet]];
      if ((error == nil) ||
          ((id) error == [NSNull null]) ||
          ([error length] == 0) || (trimmedError == 0))

        errorMessage =  @"An error occurred while
          communicating with the server.  We will look
                                          into this";
      else
        errorMessage = error;
      UIAlertView *alert = [[UIAlertView alloc]
        initWithTitle:@"Your request could not be carried
                 out - the server responded with an error"
         message:errorMessage delegate:nil
         cancelButtonTitle:@"OK" otherButtonTitles:nil];
      [alert show];
      return nil;
    }
  }
return responseDict;
}
```

As I explain in Chapter 10, this is similar to the `geocodeAsynchronouslyJSON:` method in Listing 10-9 in that chapter, but serializes the response into mutable arrays and dictionaries.

Now you can add the `loadPointsOfInterestFromWebServicc` method shown in Listing 14-12 to `RTModel.m`.

Listing 14-12: The loadPointsOfInterestFromWebService Method

```
- (void)loadPointsOfInterestFromWebService  {

  void (^success) (NSDictionary *) =
                              ^(NSDictionary *response) {

    NSDictionary *responseDict = [self
       createPointsOfInterestResponseDictionary:response];
    if (!responseDict)
      return;

    RTAppDelegate *appDelegate =
             [[UIApplication sharedApplication] delegate];
    NSString *fileComponent =  [NSString
          stringWithFormat:@"%@%@%@", @"Lastdownload",
             appDelegate.destinationPreference, @".poi"];
    NSString *filePath = [RTModel filePath:fileComponent];
    NSURL *lastDownLoadURL =
                        [NSURL fileURLWithPath:filePath];

    NSDateFormatter *dateFormatter =
                         [[NSDateFormatter alloc] init];
    NSTimeZone *timeZone =
                   [NSTimeZone timeZoneWithName:@"UTC"];
    [dateFormatter setTimeZone:timeZone];
        [dateFormatter setDateFormat:
                        @"yyyy-MM-dd HH:mm:ss.SSSSSS"];
    NSString* currentDateTime =
            [dateFormatter stringFromDate: [NSDate date]];
    [currentDateTime writeToURL:lastDownLoadURL
        atomically:YES encoding:NSUTF8StringEncoding
                                             error:NULL];

    NSMutableArray *results =
                  [responseDict objectForKey:@"results"];
    pointsOfInterestData = results;
    fileComponent = [NSString stringWithFormat:@"%@%@%@",
      @"POI", appDelegate.destinationPreference, @".poi"];
    filePath = [RTModel filePath:fileComponent];
    NSURL *pointsOfInterestDataURL =
                        [NSURL fileURLWithPath:filePath];
    [pointsOfInterestData writeToURL:
                 pointsOfInterestDataURL atomically:YES];

    if ([results count]  > 0) {
      pointsOfInterest =
       [NSMutableArray arrayWithCapacity:[results count]];

      BOOL isInItinerary = NO;

      for (NSMutableDictionary *aPointOfIinterest in
                                              results) {
```

```
        for (SharedPointOfInterest *sharedPointOfInterest
                                          in itinerary) {
          if ([sharedPointOfInterest.title
            isEqualToString:[aPointOfIinterest
                                  objectForKey:@"name"]])
            isInItinerary = YES;
        }
        if (!isInItinerary) {
          [pointsOfInterest addObject:
            [[PointOfInterest alloc]
               initWithWebServiceData:aPointOfIinterest]];
        }
        else {
          isInItinerary = NO;
        }
      }
    }
    [[NSNotificationCenter defaultCenter] postNotificati
          onName:@"PointsOfInterestChanged" object:self
          userInfo:nil];
  };

  void (^failure) (NSError *) = ^(NSError *error ){
    NSString *errorMessage = [error localizedDescription];
    UIAlertView *alertView = [[UIAlertView alloc]
         initWithTitle:
                    @"Error getting response from server"
         message:errorMessage delegate:nil
          cancelButtonTitle:@"OK" otherButtonTitles:nil];
    [alertView show];
    return;
  };

  NSMutableDictionary *params =
                      [[NSMutableDictionary alloc] init];
    RTAppDelegate *appDelegate =
             [[UIApplication sharedApplication] delegate];
  [params setObject:appDelegate.destinationPreference
                                 forKey:@"destination"];
  WSManager *wsManager = [[WSManager alloc] init];

  [wsManager
     pointsOfInterestGETWebService:@"pointsofinterest"
          userParams:params successBlock:success
                             failureBlock:failure];
}
```

Be aware that you'll get a compiler error until you add the `initWithWebServiceData:` method.

Here I process the returned data the same way I did in the `loadPointsOf Interest` method. (Chapter 2 has the details on that one.) The only difference is that I use a new `PointOfInterest` method — the `initWithWebService-Data:` method (which you'll add next) instead of `initWithData:` — to create the `PointOfInterest` because dictionary keys returned by the `pointso-finterest` web service are lowercase, whereas the `PointOfInterest` dictionary you get from the `Destinations.plist` has initial caps.

I also create a file where I save the date and time of this download. You use that later to determine whether you need to reload the points-of-interest data.

```
RTAppDelegate *appDelegate = [[UIApplication
            sharedApplication] delegate];
NSString *fileComponent =
  [NSString stringWithFormat:@"%@%@%@", @"Lastdownload",
              appDelegate.destinationPreference, @".poi"];
NSString *filePath = [RTModel filePath:fileComponent];
NSURL *lastDownLoadURL = [NSURL fileURLWithPath:filePath];
```

First you simply set up the file — the string `Lastdownload` — with the current destination as the suffix.

Next you create the string by allocating a date formatter and creating a format that matches the string you get from the date and time stored in App Engine. I don't go into date/time formatting here, but the code is pretty obvious. Date formatting follows the Unicode Technical Standard #35 at `http://unicode.org/reports/tr35`.

```
NSDateFormatter *dateFormatter =
                          [[NSDateFormatter alloc] init];
NSTimeZone *timeZone =
                    [NSTimeZone timeZoneWithName:@"UTC"];
[dateFormatter setTimeZone:timeZone];
[dateFormatter setDateFormat:
                          @"yyyy-MM-dd HH:mm:ss.SSSSSS"];
NSString* currentDateTime =
            [dateFormatter stringFromDate: [NSDate date]];
```

Then I store the current date and time in string format. (Thanks, App Engine!)

I also save the downloaded data to a file.

```
NSMutableArray *results =
                  [responseDict objectForKey:@"results"];
pointsOfInterestData = results;
fileComponent = [NSString stringWithFormat:@"%@%@%@",
      @"POI", appDelegate.destinationPreference, @".poi"];
filePath = [RTModel filePath:fileComponent];
NSURL *pointsOfInterestDataURL =
                       [NSURL fileURLWithPath:filePath];
[pointsOfInterestData writeToURL:
                 pointsOfInterestDataURL atomically:YES];
```

What I'm doing here is caching the data. In Chapter 6, I explain that one of the requirements of a well-designed web service is the ability to use cached data whenever possible. This ability will reduce bandwidth requirements (and, as a side effect, potentially improve the user experience). As you'll soon see in the "Using Cached Data" section, later in this chapter, you'll add a new web service that RoadTrip will be able to use to determine whether it should download all the points of interest or just use the cached data.

Because I tweaked the `WSManager` method to be able to handle any `rtpointsofinterest` web service, I had to include the specific web service — `pointsofinterest`, in this case — that I wanted in the message:

```
[wsManager pointsOfInterestGETWebService:
     @"pointsofinterest" userParams:params
            successBlock:success failureBlock:failure];
```

Adding the required methods to PointOfInterest

Now it's time to take care of the compiler error and add the missing method to the `PointsOfInterest` class. First add the bolded code in Listing 14-13 to `PointOfInterest.h` to declare the method.

Listing 14-13: Updating PointOfInterest.h

```
@interface PointOfInterest : NSObject <MKAnnotation>

@property (nonatomic, readwrite) CLLocationCoordinate2D
            coordinate;
@property (nonatomic, readwrite, copy) NSString *title;
@property (nonatomic, readwrite, copy) NSString *subtitle;
@property (nonatomic, readwrite, copy) NSString *address;
@property (nonatomic, readwrite, copy) NSString *location;
@property (nonatomic, readwrite, copy) NSString *comment;
@property (nonatomic, readwrite, copy) NSString *recordID;

- (id)initWithData:(NSDictionary *)data;
- (id)initWithWebServiceData:(NSDictionary *)data;
- (NSDictionary *)returnPointOfInterestData;
@end
```

With that done, add the code in Listing 14-14 to `PointOfInterest.m` to actually add the method.

Listing 14-14: Adding initWithWebServiceData:

```
- (id)initWithWebServiceData:(NSDictionary *)data {

  self = [super init];
  if (self) {
    CLLocationCoordinate2D coordinate;
    coordinate.latitude =
            [[data objectForKey:@"latitude"] doubleValue];
    coordinate.longitude =
            [[data objectForKey:@"longitude"]doubleValue];
    self.coordinate = coordinate;
    self.title = [data objectForKey:@"name"];
    self.address = [data objectForKey:@"address"];
    self.location = [data objectForKey:@"location"];
    self.comment = [data objectForKey:@"description"];
    self.subtitle = [data objectForKey:@"description"];
    self.recordID = [data objectForKey:@"id"];
  }
  return self;
}
```

You'll notice two things here: First, this method is almost the same as the `initWithData` method that is already there. The main difference is that the keys for the data in the response dictionary returned by the web are in lowercase (in accordance with Python naming conventions), whereas the keys used in the `Destinations.plist` dictionaries have the first letter capitalized. (I used the `info-plist` as a guide where dictionaries have the first letter capitalized.)

You'll also notice that I've added a new property — `recordID`. As I explain in Chapter 12, each entity in the data store has a unique record ID. Until now, I really didn't have to care about things like record IDs because the `RTModel` was managing the objects that contained the data. But now that the data resides in the cloud, you need a way to identify each point of interest in the datastore as well. Although you won't generally need the record ID in RoadTrip — because you download all the points of interest — you might, if you took the application further, have additional data about each point of interest stored in the database (a guide to a point of interest, for example) that the user could download, and you'd need a way to connect the two together.

As it stands, though, the only way you'll use `recordID` is to identify points of interest you want to delete from the datastore. (More on deletions in the Bonus Chapter, available for download from this book's website.)

You have also have to synthesize the getters and setters for the `recordID` property. Add the bolded code in Listing 14-15 to `PointsOfInterest.m`.

Listing 14-15: Synthesize the getters and setters

```
@implementation PointOfInterest

@synthesize coordinate = _coordinate;
@synthesize title = _title;
@synthesize subtitle = _subtitle;
@synthesize address = _address;
@synthesize location = _location;
@synthesize comment= _comment;
@synthesize recordID = _recordID;
```

Send the new message

Finally, you need to change the message in `initWithDestination` from `loadPointsOfInterest` to `loadPointsOfInterestFromWebService`. To do that, delete the bolded-underlined-italicized code and add the bolded code in Listing 14-16 to `initWithDestinationIndex:` in `RTModel.m`. (As a heads up, you'll have to modify two other methods, `persistent-StoreChanged:` and `removeFromItinerary:`, but I'll have you change both after you make some enhancements to the way you use web services later in this chapter.)

Listing 14-16: Updating initWithDestinationIndex:

```
- (id)initWithDestinationIndex:
                        (NSUInteger)destinationIndex {

  if ((self = [super init])) {

    NSURL *destinationsURL = [[NSBundle mainBundle]
          URLForResource:@"Destinations"
          withExtension:@"plist"];
    NSDictionary *destinations = [NSDictionary dictionaryW
          ithContentsOfURL:destinationsURL];
    NSArray *destinationsArray =
          [destinations objectForKey:@"DestinationData"];
    destinationData =
       [destinationsArray objectAtIndex:destinationIndex];
    destination = [[Destination alloc]
             initWithDestinationIndex:destinationIndex];
    [self loadEvents];
    NSManagedObjectContext *context =
                          self.managedObjectContext;
    NSError *error = nil;
    itinerary = [NSMutableArray arrayWithArray:
      [context executeFetchRequest:
             self.sharedPointOfInterestFetchRequest
                                         error:&error]];
```

(continued)

Listing 14-16 ***(continued)***

```
    if (error)
      NSLog(@"Core Data Failure! Error code: %u,
            description: %@, and reason: %@", error.
            code, [error localizedDescription], [error
            localizedFailureReason]);

    __block __weak RTModel *weakSelf = self;

    [[NSNotificationCenter defaultCenter] addObserver
            ForName:@"PersistentStoreAdded" object:self
            queue:nil usingBlock:^(NSNotification *notif) {
      [weakSelf loadItinerary];
      [weakSelf loadPointsOfInterest];
      [weakSelf loadPointsOfInterestFromWebService];

      [[NSNotificationCenter defaultCenter] postNotifica
            tionName:@"DestinationChanged" object:weakSelf
            userInfo:nil];
    }];
#if !TARGET_IPHONE_SIMULATOR

    [[NSNotificationCenter defaultCenter] addObserver:self
            selector:@selector(persistentStoreChanged:)
            name:@"PersistentStoreChanged" object:nil];
#endif
   }
  return self;
}
```

If you were to build and run your app in the Simulator now, you'd see that the points of interest have in fact been downloaded from App Engine. (You could change a word or two in the description in the test data you generate to assure yourself of that fact.) You do however, need to be sure that GoogleAppEngineLauncher is up and running and that you've called the `testdata` web service to be sure there is really data there.

Using Cached Data

As I explain in Chapters 6 and 11, caching data is a way to minimize the amount of network resources you use and may, as a side effect, also improve the user experience.

The way the code in RoadTrip works now, every time you launch the application you download the web services *en masse,* but after that, you never check for updates. What you need to do is check for updates on a regular basis and then download the points of interest only if anything has changed.

The latter technique actually is something you included in your design in Chapter 11, but the former is something I'll explain in the following sections.

Adding the UpdateRecord model

To implement the ability to cache data, you implement the `lastupdate` web service you specified in Chapter 11. But to do that, you need to create a new entity type to store the information about when the last update occurred. To do that, add the bolded code in Listing 14-17 to `datamodel.py`.

Listing 14-17: Updating datamodel.py

```
"""The PointOfInterest class and updateRecord method"""
from google.appengine.ext import db
import logging
import datetime


class PointOfInterest(db.Model):
    name = db.StringProperty(required=True)
    description = db.StringProperty()
    location = db.StringProperty()
    address = db.StringProperty()
    destination = db.StringProperty(required=True)
    coordinate = db.GeoPtProperty(required=True)
    updated = db.DateTimeProperty(required=True, auto_now_
          add = True)

    def to_dict(self):
        """Return the PointOfInterest data in a
                                                dictionary"""

        a = {}
        a['id'] = str(self.key().id())
        a['name'] = self.name
        a['description'] = self.description
        a['location'] = self.location
        a['address'] = self.address
        a['destination'] = self.destination
        a['latitude'] = self.coordinate.lat
        a['longitude'] = self.coordinate.lon
        a['updated'] = str(self.updated)

        return a

class UpdateRecord(db.Model):
    """Return the last update"""

    updated = db.DateTimeProperty(required=True,
```

(continued)

Listing 14-17 *(continued)*

```
                                           auto_now = True)

    @classmethod
    def set_updated(self):

        lastUpdate = UpdateRecord.all()
        lastUpdateRecord = lastUpdate.get()
        if (lastUpdateRecord == None):
            lastUpdateRecord = UpdateRecord()
        lastUpdateRecord.put()

    @classmethod
    def last_updated(self):

        lastUpdate = UpdateRecord.all()
        lastUpdateRecord = lastUpdate.get()
        if (lastUpdateRecord == None):
            raise Exception ("no pointsofinterest")

        a = {}
        a['datetime'] = str(lastUpdateRecord.updated)

        return a
```

Next you define your model class:

```
class UpdateRecord (db.Model):
```

which, as you can see, is a subclass of the `Model` class.

This model class only has one attribute:

```
updated = db.DateTimeProperty(required=True,
                                      auto_now = True)
```

Because `auto_now` is `True`, the `property` value will be set to the current time whenever the model instance is stored in the datastore, doing all the work for you in tracking a last-modified date and time.

You've also defined two methods and made them class methods. Note that class methods in Python are the same as in Objective-C — you don't need an object of that type to call the method.

The first method — `set_updated` — will be called whenever a point of interest is added or deleted.

You first create a query and then get the first and only `UpdateRecord`:

```
lastUpdate = UpdateRecord.all()
lastUpdateRecord = lastUpdate.get()
```

If there is no record yet (the first time through), you create one and save it to the datastore; otherwise. you simply re-store the existing record which will update its `updated` property to the current date and time.

The second method — `last_updated` — uses that record to report the last time it was updated.

You first get the one and only record:

```
lastUpdate = UpdateRecord.all()
lastUpdateRecord = lastUpdate.get()
```

and then you check to see if there is a record there:

```
if (lastUpdateRecord == None):
     raise Exception ("no pointsofinterest")
```

If no record exists, you raise an exception. If there is a record, you add the `datetime` attribute to a dictionary and return it to the method that made the call:

```
a = {}
a['datetime'] = str(lastUpdateRecord.updated)

return a
```

This `last_updated` method will be used by `update_handler`. But before I explain that process, make sure that there is a record to use to test the logic you'll be adding to RoadTrip. You can make sure of that by adding the `set_updated` call to the test handler. To do that, add the bolded code in Listing 14-18 to `testdata_handler.py`.

Listing 14-18: Updating `testdata_handler.py`

```
"""TestDataHandler class creates test data"""
from google.appengine.ext import webapp
from datamodel import *
import json

class TestDataHandler(webapp.RequestHandler):
    def get(self):
        """Create test data - GET used as a convenience
                                                    for test"""
        db.delete(PointOfInterest.all())

...

        pointofinterest = PointOfInterest(name='Legion of
                                                  Honor',
           description='Interesting varied collection',
```

(continued)

Listing 14-18 *(continued)*

```
            location='San Francisco',
            address='',
            destination='1',
            coordinate=db.GeoPt(lat=37.784773,
                                       lon=-122.500324))
        pointofinterest.put()

        UpdateRecord.set_updated()

        self.response.out.write('<pre>')
        self.response.out.write(
            "Test data, with %d points of interest:" %
                          (PointOfInterest.all().count()))

        self.response.out.write("\n")
        for pointofinterest in PointOfInterest.all():
            self.response.out.write(pointofinterest.name +
               " Added: " + str(pointofinterest.updated) +
               " id = " + str(pointofinterest.key().id())
                                                   +'\n')
        self.response.out.write('</pre>')
```

All this does is call the `set_updated()` method whenever it creates test data. With all that spadework done, you can now add the new web service — `lastupdate`.

In TextWrangler, choose File⇨New⇨Text Document from the main menu or press ⌘+N.

Save the new file as `lastupdate_handler.py` in the `rtpointsof interest` folder.

Next, add the bolded code in Listing 14-19 to `main.py` — you should know the drill by now, so I won't beat it to death.

Listing 14-19: Adding to main.py

```
import webapp2
from testdata_handler import *
from pointsofinterest_handler import *
from lastupdate_handler import *

class MainHandler(webapp2.RequestHandler):
  def get(self):
    #self.response.out.write('Hello world!')
    self.response.out.write("<html><body>")
    self.response.out.write("<p>Hello Mr Bill!</p>")
    self.response.out.write("</body></html>")
```

```
app = webapp2.WSGIApplication([('/', MainHandler),
      ('/testdata', TestDataHandler),
      ('/pointsofinterest', PointsOfInterestHandler),
      ('/lastupdate', LastUpdateHandler)],
        debug=True)
```

Next, add the new handler and its `GET` method to `lastupdate_handeler.py` by adding the code in Listing 14-20.

Listing 14-20: The new LastUpdateHandler

```
"""Return the date time of the last PointOfInterest
                                                  transaction"""
from google.appengine.ext import webapp
from datamodel import *
import json
import logging
from access_handler import *

class LastUpdateHandler(AccessHandler):
    def get(self):
        data = {}

        try:
            self.validate()

            destination = self.request.get('destination')
            if (not destination):
                raise Exception ("missing destination")

            data['status']="ok"
            updaterecord = UpdateRecord.last_updated()
            data['results'] = updaterecord

        except Exception,  ex:
            data['status'] = "error"
            data['status_text'] = "exception: %s" % ex
        self.response.headers['Content-Type'] =
                                            'application/json'

        self.response.out.write(json.dumps(data))
```

As you can see, this handler looks a lot like the `PointsOfInterestHandler`. And, as you'll also soon see, adding new web services and using them in your app tends to get pretty repetitive. Oh well, sometimes boring is good.

One important thing to note is that you're also making LastUpdateHandler a subclass of AccessHandler, which means LastUpdateHandler will inherit AccessHandler's ability to validate the API key:

```
class LastUpdateHandler(AccessHandler):
```

Moving further down Listing 14-20, you create an empty dictionary, then make sure the destination parameter is there, and finally check for the key parameter. If it's not present, you raise an exception.

```
data = {}

try:
    self.validate()

    destination = self.request.get('destination')
    if (not destination):
        raise Exception ("missing destination")
```

Otherwise, you add the status key and give it a value of ok.

Now all you need to do is get the last UpdateRecord, add it to the results and return the results as you did in PointsOfInterestHandler.

```
updaterecord = UpdateRecord.last_updated()
data['results'] = updaterecord
```

Now if you enter

```
http://localhost:8080/lastupdate?destination=0&key=test123
```

in Chrome, you'll see something like this:

```
{
    status: "ok",
    results: {
        datetime: "2012-04-17 21:56:05.367248"
    }
}
```

"2012-04-17 21:56:05.367248" indicates the last time I made the tes-tdata request and it loaded the test data. (You will, of course, see a different time and date.)

Updating RoadTrip to use cached data

If you've been a good little developer and have made all the modifications to the code spelled out in the previous sections of this chapter, you can now actually have RoadTrip check to see whether the cached data is current before it goes out and downloads all those points of interest.

Because of what you did in the "Updating RoadTrip" section, earlier in this chapter, you don't have to do anything to `WSManager` to call the `lastupdate` web service. In fact, all you have to do is add the method to `RTModel` tasked with requesting the `lastupdate` web service — the `loadUpdatedPointsOfInterest;` method, to be more precise. In this method, you'll check to see if the date for the last update to the `rtpointsofinterest` database lies after your last download. If it is, you send the `loadPointsOfInterestFromWebService` message and download the latest points of interest.

Start by adding the bolded code in Listing 14-21 to `RTModel.h` to declare the new method.

Listing 14-21: Updating RTModel.h

```
#import <Foundation/Foundation.h>
#import <MapKit/MapKit.h>
#import <CoreData/CoreData.h>
@class Annotation;
@class PointOfInterest;
@class SharedPointOfInterest;

@interface RTModel : NSObject <NSXMLParserDelegate>

+ (RTModel *)model;
- (id)initWithDestinationIndex:
                          (NSUInteger)destinationIndex;
- (void)loadItinerary;
- (void)addToItinerary:(PointOfInterest *)pointOfInterest;
- (void)removeFromItinerary:(SharedPointOfInterest *)
                                        pointOfInterest;
- (void)loadPointsOfInterest;
- (void)loadUpdatedPointsOfInterest;
- (NSArray *)returnPointsOfInterest;
- (void)addPointOfInterest:(NSMutableDictionary *)
                                    pointOfInterestData;
- (UIImage *)destinationImage;
- (NSString *)destinationName;
- (CLLocationCoordinate2D)destinationCoordinate;
- (NSString *)weather;
- (void)loadEvents;
- (NSUInteger)numberOfEvents;
- (NSString *)getEvent:(NSUInteger)index;
- (NSString *)mapTitle;
- (NSArray *)createAnnotations;
- (void)addLocation:(NSString *)findLocation
     completionHandler:(void (^)(Annotation *annotation,
                          NSError* error)) completion;
```

(continued)

Listing 14-21 *(continued)*

```
- (CLLocation *)foundLocation;
+ (NSString *)filePath:(NSString *)fileComponent;
#if !TARGET_IPHONE_SIMULATOR
- (void)persistentStoreChanged:
       (NSNotification*)notification forContext:(NSManaged
          ObjectContext*)context;
#endif

@property (readonly, strong, nonatomic)
           NSManagedObjectContext *managedObjectContext;
@property (readonly, strong, nonatomic)
               NSManagedObjectModel *managedObjectModel;
@property (readonly, strong, nonatomic)
 NSPersistentStoreCoordinator *persistentStoreCoordinator;
@end
```

With that in place, add the `loadUpdatedPointsOfInterest` method shown in Listing 14-22 to `RTModel.m`.

Listing 14-22: Adding loadUpdatedPointsOfInterest

```
- (void)loadUpdatedPointsOfInterest  {

  void (^success) (NSDictionary *) =
                             ^(NSDictionary *response) {

    NSDictionary *responseDict =
      [self createPointsOfInterestResponseDictionary:
                                              response];
    if (!responseDict)
      return;
    RTAppDelegate *appDelegate =
            [[UIApplication sharedApplication] delegate];
    NSString *fileComponent =
      [NSString stringWithFormat:@"%@%@%@",@"Lastdownl
          oad",
             appDelegate.destinationPreference, @".poi"];
    NSString *filePath = [RTModel filePath:fileComponent];
    NSURL *lastDownLoadURL =
                      [NSURL fileURLWithPath:filePath];
    NSString *lastDownLoad =
             [responseDict objectForKey:@"Lastdownload"];
    [lastDownLoad writeToURL:lastDownLoadURL
      atomically:YES encoding:NSUTF8StringEncoding
                                            error:NULL];

    NSDictionary *results =
                 [responseDict objectForKey:@"results"];
```

```
if (results) {
  RTAppDelegate *appDelegate =
        [[UIApplication sharedApplication] delegate];
  NSString *fileComponent =
    [NSString stringWithFormat:@"%@%@%@",
      @"lastdownload", appDelegate.
      destinationPreference, @".poi"];
  NSString *filePath =
                   [RTModel filePath:fileComponent];
  NSURL *lastDownLoadURL =
                   [NSURL fileURLWithPath:filePath];
  NSString *lastSavedDownLoad =
    [NSString stringWithContentsOfURL:lastDownLoadURL
           encoding:NSUTF8StringEncoding error:NULL];

  NSString *lastUpdated =
                 [results objectForKey:@"datetime"];

  if (lastSavedDownLoad) {
    if ([lastSavedDownLoad caseInsensitiveCompare:last
      Updated] ==
                            NSOrderedAscending) {
      [self loadPointsOfInterestFromWebService];
    }
    else {
      pointsOfInterest =
        [NSMutableArray arrayWithCapacity:[results
                                        count]];
      RTAppDelegate *appDelegate =
         [[UIApplication sharedApplication] delegate];
      NSString *fileComponent =
        [NSString stringWithFormat:@"%@%@%@", @"POI",
          appDelegate.destinationPreference, @".poi"];
      NSString *filePath =
                   [RTModel filePath:fileComponent];
      NSURL *pointsOfInterestDataURL =
                   [NSURL fileURLWithPath:filePath];
      pointsOfInterestData =
       [NSMutableArray arrayWithContentsOfURL:
                         pointsOfInterestDataURL];

      BOOL isInItinerary = NO;
      for (NSMutableDictionary *aPointOfIinterest in
                            pointsOfInterestData) {
        for (SharedPointOfInterest
                *sharedPointOfInterest in itinerary) {
          if ([sharedPointOfInterest.title
            isEqualToString:[aPointOfIinterest
                            objectForKey:@"name"]])
```

(continued)

Listing 14-22 *(continued)*

```
                isInItinerary = YES;
              }
              if (!isInItinerary) {
                [pointsOfInterest
                 addObject:[[PointOfInterest alloc]
                 initWithWebServiceData:aPointOfIinterest]];
              }
              else {
                isInItinerary = NO;
              }
            }
        [[NSNotificationCenter defaultCenter] postNotificat
           ionName:@"PointsOfInterestChanged"
                                   object:self userInfo:nil];
        }
      }
      else {
        [self loadPointsOfInterestFromWebService];
      }
    }
  };

  void (^failure) (NSError *) = ^(NSError *error ){
    NSString *errorMessage = [error localizedDescription];
    UIAlertView *alertView = [[UIAlertView alloc]
       initWithTitle:@"Error getting response from server"
       message:errorMessage delegate:nil
       cancelButtonTitle:@"OK" otherButtonTitles:nil];
    [alertView show];
    return;
  };

  NSMutableDictionary *params =
                  [[NSMutableDictionary alloc] init];
  RTAppDelegate *appDelegate =
          [[UIApplication sharedApplication] delegate];
  [params setObject:appDelegate.destinationPreference
                                 forKey:@"destination"];
  WSManager *wsManager = [[WSManager alloc] init];
  [wsManager pointsOfInterestGETWebService:@"lastupdate"
      userParams:params successBlock:success
                                  failureBlock:failure];
}
```

You should already be familiar with much of what this method does because it is similar to the other methods you have added to `RTModel` that make web service requests. Let me focus on a few of its unique aspects.

You first load the file that you saved in `loadPointsOfInterestFromWebService` with these lines:

```
RTAppDelegate *appDelegate =
             [[UIApplication sharedApplication] delegate];
NSString *fileComponent =
     [NSString stringWithFormat:@"%@%@%@",
          @"lastdownload", appDelegate.
          destinationPreference, @".poi"];
NSString *filePath = [RTModel filePath:fileComponent];
NSURL *lastDownLoadURL = [NSURL fileURLWithPath:filePath];
NSString *lastDownLoad =
             [responseDict objectForKey:@"Lastdownload"];
 [lastDownLoad writeToURL:lastDownLoadURL atomically:YES
              encoding:NSUTF8StringEncoding error:NULL];
```

You then get the datetime from the `results` dictionary:

```
NSString *lastUpdated =
                      [results objectForKey:@"datetime"];
```

Finally, you compare the two strings, `lastSavedDownload` and `lastUpdated`.

It's really better practice to leave these as dates and compare the dates since my approach only works if you can guarantee the format of the string. I did it this way because it's a lot simpler:

```
if (lastSavedDownLoad) {
  if ([lastSavedDownLoad
       caseInsensitiveCompare:lastUpdated] ==
                             NSOrderedAscending) {
     [self loadPointsOfInterestFromWebService];
}
else {
```

If the last update is later than the last download, you send the `loadPointsOfInterestFromWebService` message. Otherwise, you load the saved point-of-interest data:

```
pointsOfInterest =
    [NSMutableArray arrayWithCapacity:[results count]];
RTAppDelegate *appDelegate =
         [[UIApplication sharedApplication] delegate];
NSString *fileComponent =
   [NSString stringWithFormat:@"%@%@%@", @"POI",
         appDelegate.destinationPreference, @".poi"];
NSString *filePath = [RTModel filePath:fileComponent];
NSURL *pointsOfInterestDataURL =
                     [NSURL fileURLWithPath:filePath];
pointsOfInterestData = [NSMutableArray
         arrayWithContentsOfURL:pointsOfInterestDataURL];
```

You then construct the pointsOfInterest array:

```
BOOL isInItinerary = NO;
for (NSMutableDictionary *aPointOfIinterest in
                         pointsOfInterestData) {
  for (SharedPointOfInterest *sharedPointOfInterest in
                                          itinerary) {
    if ([sharedPointOfInterest.title isEqualToString:
               [aPointOfIinterest objectForKey:@"name"]])
      isInItinerary = YES;
    }
    if (!isInItinerary) {
      [pointsOfInterest addObject:[[PointOfInterest
       alloc] initWithWebServiceData:aPointOfIinterest]];
    }
    else {
      isInItinerary = NO;
    }
```

You also have to update the RTModel initWithDestination: method to send the loadUpdatedPointsOfInterest message instead of the load-PointsOfInterestFromWebService message. To do that, delete the bolded-underlined-italicized code and add the bolded code in Listing 14-23 to initWithDestinationIndex: in RTModel.m.

Listing 14-23: Update initWithDestination

```
- (id)initWithDestinationIndex:
                                           (NSUInteger)
          destinationIndex {

  if ((self = [super init])) {

    ...

    __block RTModel *weakSelf = self;

    [[NSNotificationCenter defaultCenter] addObserver
          ForName:@"PersistentStoreAdded" object:self
          queue:nil usingBlock:^(NSNotification *notif) {
      [weakSelf loadItinerary];
      [weakSelf loadPointsOfInterestFromWebService];
      [weakSelf loadUpdatedPointsOfInterest];

      [[NSNotificationCenter defaultCenter] postNotifica
           tionName:@"DestinationChanged" object:weakSelf
           userInfo:nil];
      weakSelf = nil;
    }];
```

```
#if !TARGET_IPHONE_SIMULATOR

    [[NSNotificationCenter defaultCenter] addObserver:self
           selector:@selector(persistentStoreChanged:)
           name:@"PersistentStoreChanged" object:nil];
#endif
  }
  return self;
}
```

Keeping the Points Of Interest Current

You have one last thing left to do. When the app is running, you'll never go out and reload the points of interest — the idea here is that the app should generally check to see whether the points of interest should be downloaded only when it is launched or the user selects a new destination. With that being said, though, there are still a few places you might want to periodically check for updates — one being `applicationWillEnterForeground:`. This message is sent every time an app goes from background to foreground but not when the app is first launched.

To make that check, add the bolded code in Listing 14-24 to `application-WillEnterForeground:` in `RTAppDelegate.m`. That way, you can check to see if there are any new points of interest in the cloud when your app is activated from the background.

Listing 14-24: update RTAppDelegate.m

```
- (void)applicationWillEnterForeground:
                                (UIApplication *)application
{
  [[RTModel model] loadUpdatedPointsOfInterest];
}
```

Now is the right time to turn to those other two methods I mentioned earlier that you'll need to change if you want to use web services rather than `RTModel loadPointsOfInterest` — `persistentStoreChanged:` and `removeFromItinerary:`.

Whenever the persistent store changes or you remove a point of interest from the itinerary, you need to update the points-of-interest display to reflect that change. This is also a good time to check whether there are any updates. To make that possible, delete the bolded-underlined-italicized code and add the bolded code in Listing 14-25 to `persistentStoreChanged:`

in `RTModel.m` and then do the same thing in Listing 14-26 to `remove-FromItinerary:`.

Listing 14-25: Modifying the `persistentStoreChanged:` Notification Method

```
- (void)persistentStoreChanged:(NSNotification *)notif {

  …
  [self loadPointsOfInterest];
  [self loadUpdatedPointsOfInterest];

  [[NSNotificationCenter defaultCenter] postNotificatio
          nName:@"PointsOfInterestChanged" object:self
          userInfo:nil];
  [[NSNotificationCenter defaultCenter] postNotific
          ationName:@"ItineraryChanged" object:self
          userInfo:nil];
}
```

Listing 14-26: Modifying the removeFromItinerary: Method

```
- (void)removeFromItinerary:
         (SharedPointOfInterest *)sharedPointOfInterest {

  …
  [self loadPointsOfInterest];
  [self loadPointsOfInterestFromWebService];
  [[NSNotificationCenter defaultCenter]
     postNotificationName:@"ItineraryChanged" object:self
                                              userInfo:nil];
  [[NSNotificationCenter defaultCenter]
     postNotificationName:@"PointsOfInterestChanged"
                                  object:self userInfo:nil];
}
```

When you run this, you need to be sure that App Engine is running and that you have actually run `testdata` to ensure there are points of interest by entering this URL in your browser:

```
http://localhost:8080/testdata
```

Of course, you probably want to go beyond pre-generated test data. So in the next chapter, I'll show you how to use `POST` to add new points of interest and `DELETE` to delete existing ones.

Chapter 15

Deploying Your Web Services

In This Chapter

- Cleaning up your app to deploy it to the cloud
- Tackling security considerations
- Deploying rtpointsofinterest to Google App Engine

So here you are. The Moment of Truth.

RoadTrip can now download points of interest using a web service or two, and Road Trip Editor can add and delete points of interest. All you have left to do is to deploy your resource and its web services (the GoogleAppEngineLauncher application) to Google App Engine, and you'll be officially running in the cloud. At that point, you'll be able to access the points of interest web service and download the points of interest to your device.

Once you've done that, you'll be able to add and delete points of interest from your itinerary and have that synchronized across all your devices courtesy of Core Data and iCloud.

Not a bad day's work.

Interestingly enough, after setting up App Engine, developing the web services, and modifying RoadTrip to use them, actually deploying your app to App Engine is a bit anticlimactic — as in it's really, really easy.

But before you press the button to send your app cloud-wards, there are some things you'll want to do and some things you'll want to consider.

Cleaning Up Your App

The first thing to do is eliminate the web page at `https://rtpointsofinterest.appspot.com/` that displays "Hello Mr. Bill." There really is no need for it in a production environment. You can alternatively expand the web page to display something more useful, but you'll have to do that on your own.

You also don't need to generate test data any longer because you have the Road Trip Editor, so you can eliminate that bit as well.

Then again, you may want to turn TestDataHandler into a bulk loader of points of interest (instead of using Road Trip Editor to do it one at a time) and then delete the handler and redeploy the app after you've done the upload.

When you do want to delete TestDataHandler and the web page, update main.py by deleting the bolded-underlined-italicized code in Listing 15-1.

Listing 15-1: Goodbye, Mr. Bill

```
class MainHandler(webapp2.RequestHandler):
    def get(self):
        #self.response.out.write('Hello world!')
        self.response.out.write("<html><body>")
        self.response.out.write("<p>Hello Mr Bill!</p>")
        self.response.out.write("</body></html>")

app = webapp2.WSGIApplication([('/', MainHandler),
        ('/testdata', TestDataHandler),
        ('/pointsofinterest', PointsOfInterestHandler),
        ('/lastupdate', LastUpdateHandler),
        ('/allpointsofinterest',
          AllPointsOfInterestHandler),
        ('/addpointofinterest',
          AddPointOfInterestHandler),
        ('/deletepointofinterest',
          DeletePointOfInterestHandler)],
         debug=True)
```

You then need to delete the testdata_handler.py file as well.

Lots of possibilities here to modify what you've already done to add new functionality.

Speaking of possibilities, you'll always have some things you want to do, and then again you'll have some things you really want to think about. One of these thinkable things is security.

Transmitting Data Securely Across the Network

Admittedly, the whole security thing isn't much of an issue with RoadTrip, but generally speaking, making sure that data is sent securely from your iOS device to the web service (across the wire) should be a major concern of yours. You should be especially concerned about security when you're sending sensitive information such as passwords or even the user's location.

The easiest and best way to deal with security issues is to use a mechanism that is already in place — one that's been well tested and is well supported. I am of course referring to secure HTTP, or HTTPS for short. Because you're sure to have seen it in your own web interactions, and I give it a brief mention in Chapter 6, I'm going to suggest you explore the finer details of HTTPS on your own. Don't worry, though; I give you the basics here and then show you how to use HTTPS with App Engine.

HTTPS is syntactically identical to the HTTP scheme you've been using so far, but it uses an added encryption layer of the SSL/TLS protocol to protect the data.

That means that, strictly speaking, HTTPS isn't a separate protocol at all; it's simply ordinary HTTP over an encrypted Secure Sockets Layer (SSL) or Transport Layer Security (TLS) connection.

TLS and its predecessor, SSL, are cryptographic protocols that provide communications security over the Internet. TLS and SSL encrypt the segments of network connections above the Transport Layer, using symmetric cryptography — a type of encryption where both the sender and receiver share the same key — for privacy and a keyed message authentication code for message reliability.

Normally, in order to enable a web server to accept HTTPS connections, you would need to create a public key certificate for the web server — a certificate which would then have to be signed by a trusted certificate authority for the web service client (on the iOS device this is the `NSURLConnection` which supports HTTPS) or web browser to accept it. The authority certifies that the certificate holder is indeed the entity it claims to be.

Everything in the HTTPS message is encrypted, including the headers and the request/response data. With some exceptions, an attacker knows only three things: the domain name, the IP addresses, and that there is a connection between the two parties (a fact that's already known).

The main idea of HTTPS is to create a secure channel over an insecure network. This ensures reasonable protection from eavesdroppers and man-in-the-middle attacks (the attacker makes independent connections with the victims and relays messages between them, making them believe that they are talking directly to each other over a private connection, when in fact the entire conversation is controlled by the attacker), provided that adequate cipher suites are used and that the *server certificate is verified and trusted.*

Google App Engine supports secure connections via HTTPS for URLs using the `*.appspot.com` domain. When a request accesses a URL using HTTPS and that URL is configured to use HTTPS in the `app.yaml` file, both the request data and the response data are *encrypted* by the sender before they are transmitted and *decrypted* by the recipient after they are received. Secure connections are useful for protecting customer data, such as contact information, passwords, and private messages.

To configure a URL to accept secure connections, you provide a secure parameter for the handler. To do that for your web service, update `app.yaml` with bolded code in Listing 15-2.

Listing 15-2: Updating app.yaml to Support a Secure Connection

```
application: rtpointsofinterest
version: 1
runtime: python27
api_version: 1
threadsafe: yes

handlers:
- url: /favicon\.ico
  static_files: favicon.ico
  upload: favicon\.ico

- url: .*
  script: main.app
  secure: always


libraries:
- name: webapp2
  version: "2.5.1"
```

With this configuration (`secure`) even a request that does not use HTTPS is automatically redirected (sent) to the HTTPS URL with the same path. When this is done, the message stays intact (the query parameters) — you'll understand why I mention that when I explain the other options.

Another option is `optional`.

```
- url: .*
  script: main.app
  secure: optional
```

`optional` is the default if you don't specify `secure` for a handler. Both HTTP and HTTPS requests are sent to the handler without redirects and the application can examine the request to determine whether HTTP or HTTPS was being used. (`request.url` gives you access to the URL.)

The final option is `never`.

```
- url: .*
  script: main.app
  secure: never
```

In this case, HTTPS requests are automatically redirected to the HTTP equivalent URL. *When this happens, the query parameters are removed from the request.* This is done to ensure that a user doesn't accidentally use a non-secure connection to submit query data that was intended for a secure connection. The first indication of that will be a missing key alert (as you can see in Figure 15-1) when you use RoadTrip — all the query information was stripped off, so of course there is no key.

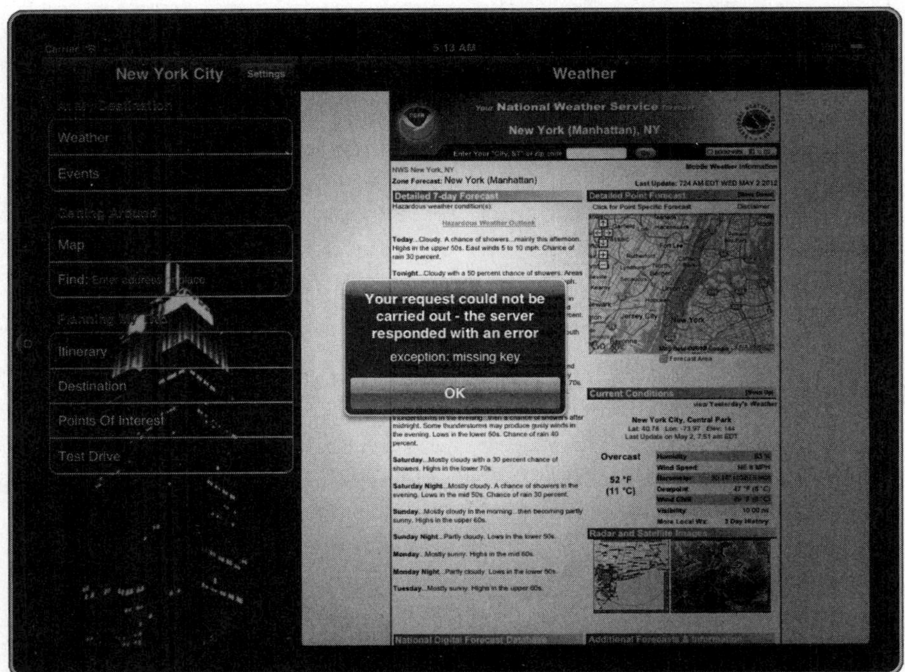

Figure 15-1: The redirect strips out the query string.

To use HTTPS from RoadTrip, all you need to do is specify HTTPS rather than HTTP in your request. All you need to do is replace `http` with `https` (I've bolded the s below) in `RTDefines.h`, as shown in Listing 15-3.

Listing 15-3: Making an HTTPS Request

```
#if !TARGET_IPHONE_SIMULATOR
#define BASE_URL @"https://rtpointsofinterest.appspot.
        com/"
#else
#define BASE_URL @"http://localhost:8080/"
```

HTTPS is also not supported by GoogleAppEngineLauncher, as you can see in Figure 15-2.

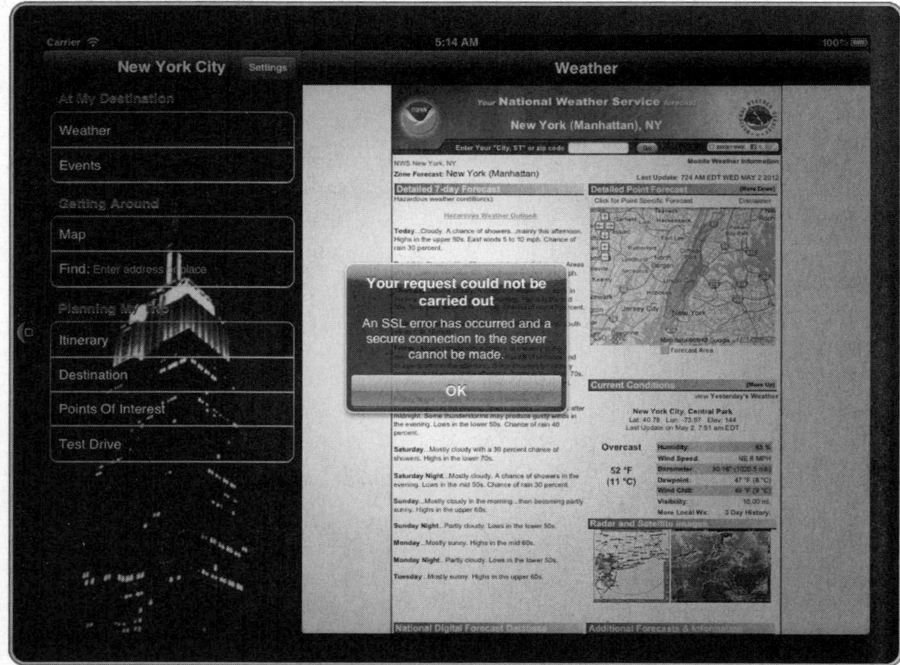

Figure 15-2: There is no SSL support in GoogleApp Engine Launcher.

So don't use HTTPS when you're working on `localhost`.

Storing Data Securely

Right now, you're storing data as a plain text in the App Engine datastore as well as on the device. Security and encryption is a very complex and nuanced subject, and it's out of this book's scope. I do suggest that you explore it on your own. To help with that, Apple has just published a new whitepaper on iOS security that can be found at `http://images.apple.com/ipad/business/docs/iOS_Security_May12.pdf`.

Deploying rtpointsofinterest to Google App Engine

I said it before, and I'll say it again: After all this work, actually deploying `rtpointsofinterest` to Google App Engine is a bit anticlimactic.

In the GoogleAppEngineLauncher (see Figure 15-3), click the Deploy button.

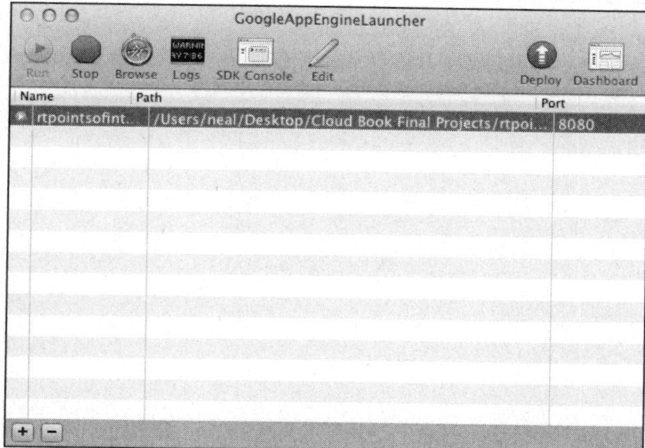

Figure 15-3: Click the Deploy button.

You need to sign in to your Google account, as you can see in Figure 15-4.

You're done.

You can watch all the action in the Logs window. (See Figure 15-5.) You'll be able to keep tabs on your progress — the uploading, the checking for success, and the final checking to see whether the app is serving.

Figure 15-4: Sign in.

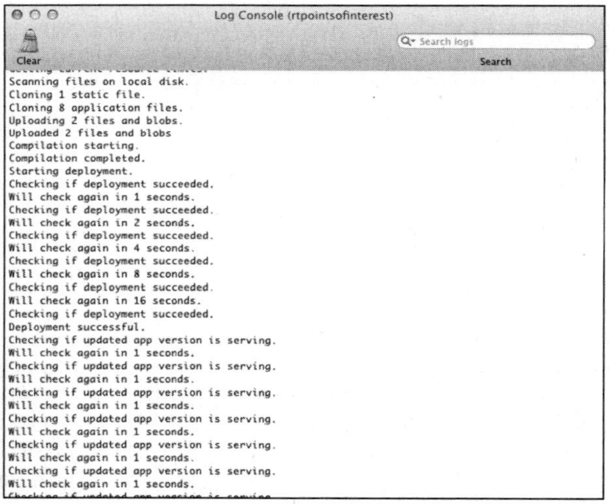

Figure 15-5: The actual deployment.

Then all you need to do is build and run your app on the device, and you'll be off and using the cloud.

You can always monitor your app on App Engine by clicking the Dashboard button. (Refer to Figure 15-3.) Figure 15-6 gives you an idea of the kinds of things you can review.

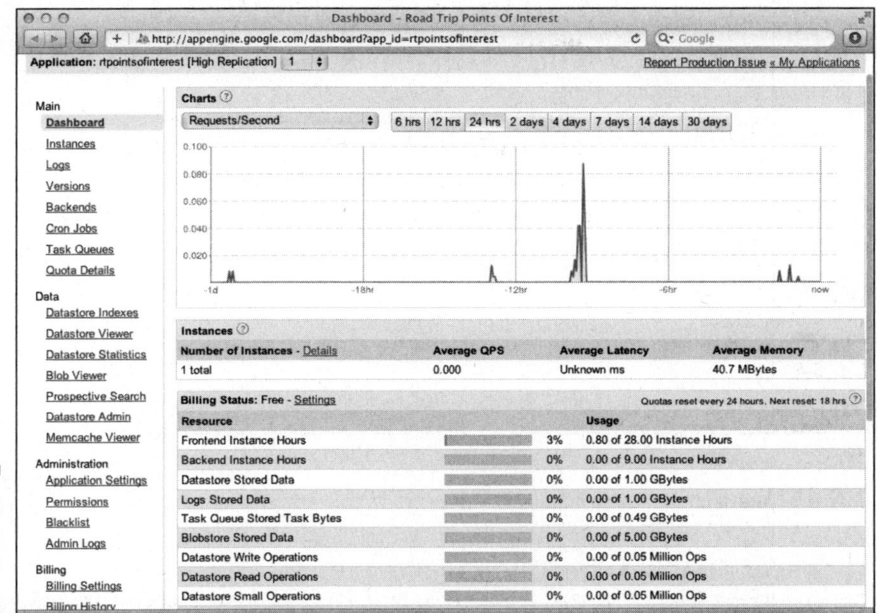

Figure 15-6: Monitoring your app in the cloud.

And with that, you're done!

What's Next

While RoadTrip is not yet a world class application (in the next chapter, I point out some additions that you'd want to make to RoadTrip to kick off the process of making it so), it still is pretty robust and has the basic infrastructure needed to support the Application Ecosystem I explain in Chapter 1.

More importantly for you, you can now easily use `WSManager` and `WSLoader` to implement web services in your own apps, as I explain in Chapter 10. You can also use the Core Data iCloud implementation to enable the user to share data between their devices running RoadTrip. You can also use the Core Data iCloud implementation as a jumping off point to explore the deep and rich functionality that I haven't had the space to cover in this book.

The announcement of iOS 6 has shown us that both iCloud and web services are becoming more and more central to iOS, and with what you have just learned, you are in a good position to take advantage of the new features in iOS 6.

Part V

The Part of Tens

"Shouldn't a cloud app be more transparent than this?"

In this part . . .

Of course, there are always some last-minute words, and here they are in neatly organized lists of ten.

Chapter 16

Ten Ways to Extend the RoadTrip App

In This Chapter

- Discovering some additional features for the RoadTrip app
- Making structural improvements to the app
- Making the Road Trip Editor easier to use

Although the example app developed in this book — the RoadTrip app — has the basic structure and features that you would include in a commercial app of this type, you would have some additional tasks to take care of if you intended to make it a true, viable commercial application.

First and foremost, you'd definitely have to add more content to the app. (Content is king.) You'd also need to add more features, as well as strengthen the basic structure a bit.

In this chapter, I suggest some changes you would need to make to RoadTrip in order to give it a fighting chance at commercial success.

Dealing with Errors

Currently, RoadTrip does a pretty good job of reporting errors, especially when using web services. It can, however, improve that error handling by actually trying to *do* something about the error besides simply reporting it.

Take network connectivity, for example. Currently, if there is no network connection, all RoadTrip does is report that fact. It would be far better if RoadTrip were able to modify the user interface to reflect that (connectionless) state — perhaps by disabling some functionality or even by using cached data. (See the "Cache Data" section, coming up soon in this chapter.) RoadTrip should also notify the user of any change in network connectivity and respond accordingly — again, either disabling some functionality or by using cached data if an Internet connection is no longer available. In this scenario, you'd also have to ensure that RoadTrip can re-enable functionality and use real-time data when the network connection does become available.

Make Events a Web Service

This is an obvious and expected (content) enhancement. Folks definitely want to know what events are planned for a point of interest. If it were me, I would also make events annotations and provide directions to them.

Expand the Point of Interest Data

I would add more data about the point of interest. The user should be able to tap a point of interest on a map and get more detailed information about the point of interest, including directions from her current location.

Crowd Source Points of Interest

Allow users to add their own points of interest that would be shared between devices using iCloud. Allow individual users to upload their points of interest so that that they can be evaluated (by you) and added as an additional place to check out.

Cache Data

If you allow users to turn off Internet access, or if the user is someplace where Internet service isn't available, you need to add the necessary logic to RoadTrip so that it can cache data (such as events). Then, when Internet access isn't available or the user doesn't want to use the Internet, RoadTrip will be able to use the cached data.

Post to Facebook and Twitter

Unless you're living under a rock, you know that social networking apps are all the rage. Twitter support is built into the SDK, but you're on your own when it comes to Facebook.

Send Postcards from the Road

In some of my applications, I have a Postcard feature. It would be nice in RoadTrip to allow the user to take a photo and attach it to an e-mail to make all her friends jealous.

Add Hotels and Reservations

A great feature to include in the RoadTrip app is to allow the user to add hotel reservations. You keep track of them in the app by enabling the user to add a reservation to her calendar, a hotel to the address book, and so on.

It's Never Early Enough to Start Speaking a Foreign Language

With the world growing even flatter and the iPhone and iPad available worldwide, the potential market for your app is considerably larger than just among people who speak English. Localizing an application isn't difficult, just tedious. Although you obviously can't implement all the features in your app all at once (that is, some have to be done later than others), when it comes to localizing the strings you use in your application, you had better build them right — and build them in from the start.

In the Road Trip Editor

Right now, the Road Trip Editor lists all the points of interest. I would allow the user to sort them by destination, location, and so on. This would make it easier to manage.

Because multiple users could be updating the point of interest, I would check for any changes before I add, delete, or update a point of interest.

Chapter 17

Ten Ways to Be a Happy Developer

In This Chapter

- Finding out how not to paint yourself into a corner
- Keeping it simple
- Having fun
- Avoiding, "There's no way to get there from here"

Think of all the things you know you're supposed to do but don't because you think they'll never catch up with you. Not that many people enjoy balancing the checkbook or cleaning out gutters, and after all, not flossing won't cause you problems until your teeth fall out years from now (right?).

But in iOS application development, those gotchas will catch up with you early and often, so I want to tell you what I've learned to pay attention to from the very start in app development, as well as a few tips and tricks that lead to happy and healthy users.

Keep Things Loosely Coupled

A *loosely coupled* system is one in which each component has little or no knowledge (or makes no use of any knowledge it may have) of other components. And because loose coupling refers to the degree of direct knowledge that one class has of another, it's not about *encapsulation* — one class's knowledge of another class's attributes or implementation — but rather just knowledge of that other class itself.

I explain loose coupling in more detail in Chapter 11.

Remember Memory

The iOS does not store changeable memory (such as object data) on disk and then read it back in later when needed as a way to free up some space. This means that running out of memory is easy; you should therefore definitely use automatic reference counting (ARC) to make the most of the memory available to you. All you have to do is follow the rules:

- **Rule 1:** Do not send `retain`, `release`, or `autorelease` messages.
- **Rule 2:** Do not store object pointers in C structures.
- **Rule 3:** Inform the compiler about ownership when using Core Foundation–style objects.
- **Rule 4:** Use the `@autoreleasepool` keyword to mark the start of an `autorelease` block.
- **Rule 5:** Follow the naming conventions.

If you follow the rules, all you have to worry about is the `retain` cycle. This cycle occurs when one object has a back pointer to the object that creates it, either directly or through a chain of other objects, each with a strong reference to the next leading back to the first. Use the `weak` lifetime qualifiers for objects and the `weak` property attribute.

The fact of the matter is, though, that even if you do everything correctly, in a large application you may simply run out of memory and need to implement the methods that `UIKit` provides to respond to low-memory conditions. Such methods include the following:

- Overriding the `viewDidUnload` and `didReceiveMemoryWarning` methods in your custom `UIViewController` subclass
- Implementing the `applicationDidReceiveMemoryWarning:` method of your application delegate
- Registering to receive the `UIApplicationDidReceiveMemoryWarningNotification:` notification

Don't Reinvent the Wheel

iOS devices are cutting-edge enough that opportunities to expand its capabilities are plentiful, and many of them are (relatively) easy to implement. You're also working with a very mature framework, so if you think that something you want your app to do is going to be really difficult, check the framework; somewhere there you may find an easy way to do what you have in mind.

For example, I once needed to compute the distance between two points on a map. So I got out my trusty trig books, only to find out later that the `distanceFromLocation:` method did exactly what I needed.

Understand State Transitions

The `UIApplication` object provides the application-wide control and coordination for an iOS application. It is responsible for handling the initial routing of incoming user events (touches, for example) as well as dispatching action messages from control objects (such as buttons) to the appropriate target objects. The application object sends messages to its `application` delegate to allow you to respond — in an application-unique way, when your application is executing — to things such as application launch, low-memory warnings, and state transitions (moving into background and back into foreground, for example).

You should implement the `UIAppDelegate` methods shown in Table 17-1 in your application:

Table 17-1 UIAppDelegate methods

Method	*What You Do with It*
`application:didFinishLaunchingWithOptions:`	In this method, do what you need to do to initialize your application after it's launched.
`applicationWillResignActive:`	This message is sent when the application is about to move from an active state to an inactive state. Use this method to do things such as pause ongoing tasks and anything based on a timer (such as a game). Using this method doesn't mean that the app will be entering the background, but it does mean that your app won't be executing.

(continued)

Table 17-1 *(continued)*

Method	*What You Do with It*
`applicationDidEnterBackground:`	This message is sent when your application is going to be entering the background. At this point, you need to assume that your application may eventually be terminated without warning, so save user data, invalidate timers, and store enough application state information.
`applicationWillEnterForeground:`	This message is sent when your application has been rescued from the background. In this method, reverse what you did in `applicationDidEnterBackground:`.
`applicationDidBecomeActive:`	Your application is now active. You should reverse whatever you did in `applicationWillResignActive:`. You also may want to refresh the user interface.

Do the Right Thing at the Right Time

While there are many places where timing is critical, it pays for you to pay attention to the way view controllers work. When it comes to the view controller, you need to be aware of two methods, and you need to know what to do in each method.

The `viewDidLoad` message is sent to a view controller when the view has been loaded and initialized by the system. It is sent only when the view is created — and not, for example, when your app returns from the background or when a view controller is returned to after another view controller has been dismissed.

The `viewWillAppear:` message, on the other hand, is sent whenever the view appears, including when the view reappears after another view controller is dismissed.

Do view initialization in `viewDidLoad`, but make sure that anything you do to refresh a view whenever it appears is done in `viewWillAppear:`.

Avoid Mistakes in Error Handling

Opportunities for errors abound. Use common sense in figuring out which ones you should spend time on. For example, don't panic over handling a missing bundle resource in your code. If you included it in your project, it's supposed to be there; if it's not, look for a bug in your program. If it's *really* not there, the user has big problems, and you probably won't be able to do anything to avert the oncoming catastrophe.

Having said that, here are two big potential pitfalls you do have to pay attention to:

- Your app goes out to load something off the Internet, and (for a variety of reasons) the item isn't there, or the app can't get to it. You especially need to pay attention to Internet availability and what you're going to do when the Internet isn't available.
- A geocoder may fail for any number of reasons. For example, the service may be down, there may not be a street address at a certain GPS coordinate, or the user may access the data before the geocoder has returned.

Use Storyboards

Storyboards are a great way to examine the flow of the application as a whole. In addition, they require you to use less code. They are one of my favorite parts of Xcode 4.3 and iOS 5.0, and I use them in all my apps.

In this book, storyboards make creating a universal app as easy as possible.

Remember the User

I've been singing this song since Chapter 1, and I'm still singing it now: Keep your app simple and easy to use. Don't build long pages that take lots of scrolling to get through, and don't create really deep hierarchies. Focus on what the user wants to accomplish and be mindful of the device limitations, especially battery life. And don't forget international roaming charges.

In other words, try to follow the Apple iOS Human Interface Guidelines, found with all the other documentation in the iOS Dev Center website at `http://developer.apple.com/iOS` in the iOS Developer Library section. Don't even *think* about bending those rules until you really, *really* understand them.

Keep in Mind that the Software Isn't Finished Until the Last User Is Dead

One thing that I can guarantee about app development is that nobody gets it right the first time. The design for RoadTrip (the example app in this book) evolved over time as I learned the capabilities and intricacies of the platform and the impact of my design changes. Object orientation makes extending your application (not to mention fixing bugs) easier, so pay attention to the principles.

Keep It Fun

When I started programming for the iPhone, it was the most fun I'd had in years. Keep things in perspective: Except for a few tedious tasks (such as provisioning and getting your application into the Apple Store), expect that developing iOS apps will be fun for you, too. So don't take it *too* seriously.

Especially remember the *fun* part at 4 a.m., when you've spent the last five hours looking for a bug.

Index

• Symbols •

• A •

• D •

• E •

• F •

• G •

• H •

• I •

• M •

• N •

• O •

• P •

• T •

• U •

• W •

ple & Mac

ad 2 For Dummies,
d Edition
8-1-118-17679-5

hone 4S For Dummies,
n Edition
8-1-118-03671-6

od touch For Dummies,
d Edition
8-1-118-12960-9

ac OS X Lion
r Dummies
8-1-118-02205-4

ogging & Social Media

tyVille For Dummies
8-1-118-08337-6

cebook For Dummies,
h Edition
8-1-118-09562-1

om Blogging
r Dummies
8-1-118-03843-7

vitter For Dummies,
nd Edition
78-0-470-76879-2

ordPress For Dummies,
h Edition
78-1-118-07342-1

usiness

ash Flow For Dummies
78-1-118-01850-7

vesting For Dummies,
h Edition
78-0-470-90545-6

Job Searching with Social Media For Dummies
978-0-470-93072-4

QuickBooks 2012 For Dummies
978-1-118-09120-3

Resumes For Dummies, 6th Edition
978-0-470-87361-8

Starting an Etsy Business For Dummies
978-0-470-93067-0

Cooking & Entertaining

Cooking Basics For Dummies, 4th Edition
978-0-470-91388-8

Wine For Dummies, 4th Edition
978-0-470-04579-4

Diet & Nutrition

Kettlebells For Dummies
978-0-470-59929-7

Nutrition For Dummies, 5th Edition
978-0-470-93231-5

Restaurant Calorie Counter For Dummies, 2nd Edition
978-0-470-64405-8

Digital Photography

Digital SLR Cameras & Photography For Dummies, 4th Edition
978-1-118-14489-3

Digital SLR Settings & Shortcuts For Dummies
978-0-470-91763-3

Photoshop Elements 10 For Dummies
978-1-118-10742-3

Gardening

Gardening Basics For Dummies
978-0-470-03749-2

Vegetable Gardening For Dummies, 2nd Edition
978-0-470-49870-5

Green/Sustainable

Raising Chickens For Dummies
978-0-470-46544-8

Green Cleaning For Dummies
978-0-470-39106-8

Health

Diabetes For Dummies, 3rd Edition
978-0-470-27086-8

Food Allergies For Dummies
978-0-470-09584-3

Living Gluten-Free For Dummies, 2nd Edition
978-0-470-58589-4

Hobbies

Beekeeping For Dummies, 2nd Edition
978-0-470-43065-1

Chess For Dummies, 3rd Edition
978-1-118-01695-4

Drawing For Dummies, 2nd Edition
978-0-470-61842-4

eBay For Dummies, 7th Edition
978-1-118-09806-6

Knitting For Dummies, 2nd Edition
978-0-470-28747-7

Language & Foreign Language

English Grammar For Dummies, 2nd Edition
978-0-470-54664-2

French For Dummies, 2nd Edition
978-1-118-00464-7

German For Dummies, 2nd Edition
978-0-470-90101-4

Spanish Essentials For Dummies
978-0-470-63751-7

Spanish For Dummies, 2nd Edition
978-0-470-87855-2

vailable wherever books are sold. For more information or to order direct: U.S. customers visit www.dummies.com or call 1-877-762-2974. U.K. customers visit www.wileyeurope.com or call (0) 1243 843291. Canadian customers visit www.wiley.ca or call 1-800-567-4797.

Connect with us online at www.facebook.com/fordummies or @fordummies

Math & Science

Algebra I For Dummies, 2nd Edition
978-0-470-55964-2

Biology For Dummies, 2nd Edition
978-0-470-59875-7

Chemistry For Dummies, 2nd Edition
978-1-1180-0730-3

Geometry For Dummies, 2nd Edition
978-0-470-08946-0

Pre-Algebra Essentials For Dummies
978-0-470-61838-7

Microsoft Office

Excel 2010 For Dummies
978-0-470-48953-6

Office 2010 All-in-One For Dummies
978-0-470-49748-7

Office 2011 for Mac For Dummies
978-0-470-87869-9

Word 2010 For Dummies
978-0-470-48772-3

Music

Guitar For Dummies, 2nd Edition
978-0-7645-9904-0

Clarinet For Dummies
978-0-470-58477-4

iPod & iTunes For Dummies, 9th Edition
978-1-118-13060-5

Pets

Cats For Dummies, 2nd Edition
978-0-7645-5275-5

Dogs All-in One For Dummies
978-0470-52978-2

Saltwater Aquariums For Dummies
978-0-470-06805-2

Religion & Inspiration

The Bible For Dummies
978-0-7645-5296-0

Catholicism For Dummies, 2nd Edition
978-1-118-07778-8

Spirituality For Dummies, 2nd Edition
978-0-470-19142-2

Self-Help & Relationships

Happiness For Dummies
978-0-470-28171-0

Overcoming Anxiety For Dummies, 2nd Edition
978-0-470-57441-6

Seniors

Crosswords For Seniors For Dummies
978-0-470-49157-7

iPad 2 For Seniors For Dummies, 3rd Edition
978-1-118-17678-8

Laptops & Tablets For Seniors For Dummies, 2nd Edition
978-1-118-09596-6

Smartphones & Tablets

BlackBerry For Dummies, 5th Edition
978-1-118-10035-6

Droid X2 For Dummies
978-1-118-14864-8

HTC ThunderBolt For Dummies
978-1-118-07601-9

MOTOROLA XOOM For Dummies
978-1-118-08835-7

Sports

Basketball For Dummies, 3rd Edition
978-1-118-07374-2

Football For Dummies, 2nd Edition
978-1-118-01261-1

Golf For Dummies, 4th Edition
978-0-470-88279-5

Test Prep

ACT For Dummies, 5th Edition
978-1-118-01259-8

ASVAB For Dummies, 3rd Edition
978-0-470-63760-9

The GRE Test For Dummies, 7th Edition
978-0-470-00919-2

Police Officer Exam For Dummies
978-0-470-88724-0

Series 7 Exam For Dummies
978-0-470-09932-2

Web Development

HTML, CSS, & XHTML For Dummies, 7th Edition
978-0-470-91659-9

Drupal For Dummies, 2nd Edition
978-1-118-08348-2

Windows 7

Windows 7 For Dummies
978-0-470-49743-2

Windows 7 For Dummies, Book + DVD Bundle
978-0-470-52398-8

Windows 7 All-in-One For Dummies
978-0-470-48763-1

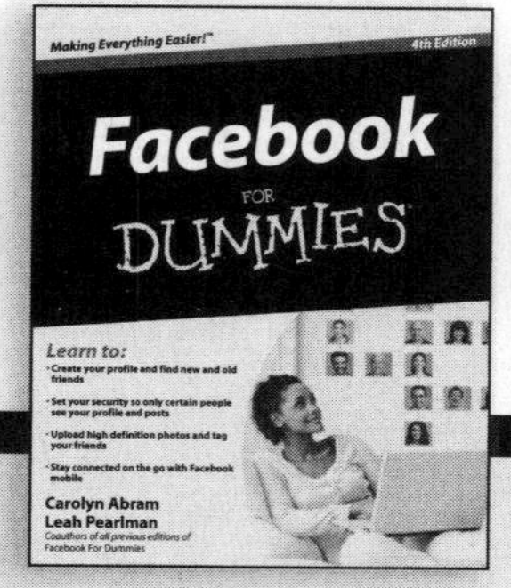

Available wherever books are sold. For more information or to order direct: U.S. customers visit www.dummies.com or call 1-877-762-2974. U.K. customers visit www.wileyeurope.com or call (0) 1243 843291. Canadian customers visit www.wiley.ca or call 1-800-567-4797.

Connect with us online at www.facebook.com/fordummies or @fordummies